Librarians, Poets and Scholars

AP   The Chair he sat in,   Lalor
      like a burnished Throne   2005

'The Chair he sat in, like a burnished throne'; copperplate etching by Brian Lalor, 2005.

Librarians, Poets and Scholars

A *Festschrift* for Dónall Ó Luanaigh

Felix M. Larkin

EDITOR

FOUR COURTS PRESS

in association with

THE NATIONAL LIBRARY OF IRELAND SOCIETY

Set in 10.5 pt on 13.5 pt Bembo for
FOUR COURTS PRESS LTD
7 Malpas Street, Dublin 8, Ireland
e-mail: info@fourcourtspress.ie
http://www.fourcourtspress.ie
and in North America for
FOUR COURTS PRESS
c/o ISBS, 920 N.E. 58th Avenue, Suite 300, Portland, OR 97213.

A catalogue record for this title
is available from the British Library.

ISBN 978–1–84682–017–5

Printed in England
MPG Books, Bodmin, Cornwall.

Contents

Illustrations and tables

Foreword

Aongus Ó hAonghusa
Director, The National Library of Ireland

THERE CAN BE NO more fitting tribute to one's life and career than to have a book published in one's honour. That so many distinguished persons have contributed to this *Festschrift* in honour of Dónall Ó Luanaigh is eloquent testimony to the esteem in which he is held by the staff of the National Library, its community of users and indeed the many people who have been fortunate to know him.

To dedicate all of one's working life and virtually all of one's adult life to a single public institution is a remarkable achievement in this day and age: that is what Dónall Ó Luanaigh has done. On reaching retirement age in June 2006, he had given forty-three years of dedicated service to the National Library and its users. In that time he worked tirelessly to develop the Library's collections and to make them accessible to the public. Through his encyclopaedic knowledge of the collections and of Irish history, politics and society, he assisted an enormous number of users to access material relevant to their particular research projects.

In all of Dónall's work in the Library, three key traits stand out: his absolute commitment to the Library and its ethos, his unfailing personal generosity and good nature, and his commitment to serving the Library's users. The number of acknowledgements to Dónall in scholarly publications is a testament to his helpfulness, a trait that he has passed on to many other Library staff.

Dónall's forte was working with collections and with people. His remarkable talents for sourcing material in private hands and acquiring it for the Library deserve special mention. He was at his best in working with books, manuscripts and other collections – discussing them, negotiating for their acquisition and so on. The Library's collections have been considerably enhanced by Dónall's work.

Many remarkable people have worked in the National Library in its 130-year existence. From a previous generation of staff, some of whom were historical figures in their own right, Dónall gained an understanding of the Library and its traditions. The official neglect of the institution that hindered it so much in the past saddened him greatly, and he constantly reminded younger colleagues of the 'bad old days'. Dónall's legacy is the new generation of staff now serving with distinction in the Library whom he has supported and encouraged.

On behalf of all of Dónall's colleagues and friends in the National Library, I join with the distinguished contributors to the *Festschrift* in honouring a remarkable public servant.

Editor's preface

For in that wide spacious world of the record of mankind which we call a Great Library all things, good and evil, fall into their true place, are seen in their true proportion. Thus keepers of libraries may with truth inscribe above their doors the words of the Governor of the city in the *New Atlantis*: 'We maintain a trade, not for gold, silver, or jewels, nor for silks, nor for spices, nor for any other commodity of matter, but only for God's first creature, which was Light.' With this thought − that our trade is in *Light* − we librarians may be content for the moment to close our consideration of the subject.

T.W. Lyster, *The Idea of a Great Public Library* (Aberdeen, 1903), p. 22.[1]

THE NOTION THAT a librarian's trade is in Light is an appealing one, and a corollary of it is that volumes like this are products of a special photosynthesis. For they would not be possible without the research materials − books, newspapers, manuscripts, photographs, prints and drawings − so carefully and often lovingly preserved in libraries. Nor would they be possible without the librarians' knowledge of the materials in their care and their skill in facilitating access to them. That is why it is appropriate to honour Dónall Ó Luanaigh with a *Festschrift* of essays and poems written by people who have all used the National Library of Ireland and are happy to acknowledge their debt to it.

Dónall was a member of the Library's professional staff for over four decades until his retirement on 2 June 2006, and he served the Library and its readers with exemplary dedication, great learning and old-fashioned courtesy. In a note to me in connection with this *Festschrift*, he described his role − with characteristic modesty − as that of a 'service provider', assisting the scholarly endeavours of others. This he undoubtedly did, and much more besides. He also said in that note that he was not a scholar − a ridiculous assertion, as those who know him can attest, though his commitment to his profession has naturally limited his scholarly output to date.[2] It was precisely in the depth of his scholarship and his generosity in putting his scholarship at the disposal of the Library's readers that his genius as a librarian lay.

One way in which Dónall served the Library was through his active participation in the National Library of Ireland Society, an association of friends of

---

1 Quoted in G. Long, *A twinge of recollection: the National Library in 1904 and thereabouts* (Dublin, 2004), pp 20−1. **2** But see C. McDonnell, 'The writings of Dónall Ó Luanaigh' in this volume.

the Library established in 1969 to increase public awareness of the Library, to promote its interests and to support its staff and readers. He was a founding member of the Society, and its honorary secretary from 1983 to 1991. The Society took the initiative in arranging this *Festschrift* for Dónall, and it is being published under the Society's auspices. Most of the contributors are members of the Society or are otherwise associated with it or with the Library. Many of the essays are revised versions of papers delivered to the Society, and some of the poets included have given readings to the Society. Accordingly, the *Festschrift* reflects the work that the Society has helped to foster in recent years by providing a forum in which scholars and other writers can present their latest efforts.

Since no single idea links the contents of this volume, its title denotes the range of the contributors rather than their contributions. There are, however, three broad themes, and each essay can be identified with one or more of them. This largely determines the order in which the essays appear. The first theme, predictably, is the National Library of Ireland, its history and collections. The opening essay is an account of Dónall Ó Luanaigh's career and his contribution to the Library by his long-time friend and colleague, Gerard Lyne. It is supplemented by Ciara McDonnell's bibliography of Dónall's writings. Adrian Frazier then reveals how two earlier members of the Library staff, W.K. Magee (better known under his pen name 'John Eglinton') and Richard Irvine Best, assisted the writer George Moore. Frazier's essay shows how writers and librarians collaborate – how, in fact, the latter trade in Light. Gerard Long also takes writers and librarians as his subject: his essay reviews what has been written about the Library in newspaper articles, memoirs and imaginative literature, and this provides an interesting new perspective on its history.

Five essays relating to the Library's collections follow next. In the first, Dermot Whelan and Ellen Murphy survey the important Sheehy Skeffington papers which they catalogued while holding temporary studentships in the Library, and they profile the three extraordinary people – Frank, Hanna and Owen Sheehy Skeffington – whose lives these papers document. The Library had particular significance for the Sheehy Skeffingtons, since – as Whelan and Murphy tell us – the young Frank and Hanna carried on much of their courtship there and so Owen might never have been born but for the Library. The second essay in this sequence, written by Ciarán Ó hÓgartaigh and Margaret Ó hÓgartaigh, is about hedge schools and early business education in Ireland, and the authors make good use of some little-known eighteenth-century textbooks held in the Library. Owen Dudley Edwards then discusses George Bernard Shaw and Christianity: the manuscript copies of Shaw's early novels are among the Library's treasures, having been secured – as Edwards points out in his essay –

in somewhat unusual circumstances. The fourth of these essays is my own, on Caroline Agnes Gray and the *Freeman's Journal*, which draws attention to the Library's very extensive holding of Irish newspapers. Moreover, the Library has recently acquired an album of letters and newspaper cuttings about Edmund Dwyer Gray MP, Caroline's husband – and in my essay I refer to this acquisition. The fifth essay is by L.P. Curtis Jr, the distinguished American historian: he illustrates his case study of an eviction in Co. Louth in 1888 with two press cartoons from the Library's huge archive of prints and drawings.

The last two essays mentioned above also introduce the *Festschrift*'s second theme, which is the impact of change. My essay is partly about the changes in the Dublin daily newspaper market brought about by the Parnell split of 1890–1, and the consequences for the *Freeman* and for the family – the Grays – who owned it for over fifty years. Curtis, on the other hand, places the events recounted in his essay in the wider context of the Plan of Campaign of 1886–90 and the economic changes that precipitated both that crisis and the previous phase of the Land War in the early 1880s.

Change is the dominant theme in the essays by Finola Kennedy, Brendan O Donoghue, Monica Henchy and Ian d'Alton. Finola Kennedy outlines recent changes in family life in Ireland, and brings her study up to date by commenting on the report on the family by the All-Party Oireachtas Committee on the Constitution published in 2006. Brendan O Donoghue writes about the changes in the system of local government effected by the Local Government (Ireland) Act 1898, and draws on his vast knowledge and experience of administrative practice in government bodies to enhance the results of his research. He notes – with, I think, some surprise – that the structures put in place in 1898 have largely survived to this day despite the initial lack of enthusiasm for them in most quarters and despite the more fundamental changes in the Irish political system that occurred later as a result of independence. In contrast, Monica Henchy's study is of an institution – the Irish College at Salamanca – that did not survive, and she interprets its history in the light of the changing fortunes of the Catholic church both at home in Ireland and in Spain. Her essay brings the Library's collections back into focus – for Fr Alexander McCabe, the last rector of the Irish college at Salamanca, donated his unpublished journals to the Library. Ian d'Alton examines how southern Irish Protestants responded to the threat to their culture – and even their survival – posed by the political, social and economic changes in Ireland in the nineteenth and twentieth centuries. Concentrating mainly on Cork Protestants, he rejects the view that this threat ever amounted to anything resembling 'ethnic cleansing' – *pace* Peter Hart and others.[3]

3 See, for example, P. Hart, *The IRA at war, 1916–1923* (Oxford, 2003), pp 237, 245–6.

Ian d'Alton's essay is, however, also concerned with how we view the past – as its title suggests. That is the last of the three broad themes of this volume, and it is addressed most obviously in complementary essays by Síghle Bhreathnach-Lynch and Wesley Hutchinson. Both essays are about public monuments, and each is set against a background of political change – so they pick up our second theme too. The former gives an overview of public monuments of a nationalist character erected in Ireland from the 1840s to 1950, and analyzes the political preoccupations they indicate and the agenda – political and religious – that they were sometimes intended to advance. The latter homes in on what is probably the most significant public monument for those of the Ulster unionist tradition – located not in Ireland, but at Thiepval in northern France. This is the memorial – a replica of Helen's Tower at Clandeboye, Co. Down – to those of Ulster origin who were killed in the First World War, particularly those in the 36th (Ulster) Division who died on the first day of the battle of the Somme on 1 July 1916. Hutchinson explains its iconography, and emphasizes the importance of the memorial in legitimizing the new political dispensation of Northern Ireland in the early 1920s.

The next three essays – by Fergus Gillespie, Adrian Hardiman and Maurice Harmon – and the memoir by the poet Dennis O'Driscoll explore in very different ways the theme of how we view the past. Fergus Gillespie recalls the legend of the Spanish origins of the Irish race – according to which the Irish are descended from Míl or Milesius of Spain whose sons supposedly conquered Ireland long before the birth of Christ – and he traces the persistence of that legend and the uses made of it at various times. Adrian Hardiman considers how, and why, James Joyce in *Ulysses* represented – or, more accurately, misrepresented – the trial of Samuel Childs for the murder of his brother Thomas. Hardiman's account of the trial relies heavily on contemporary press reports, as also do the essays by L.P. Curtis Jr and Wesley Hutchinson; those three essays – by Hardiman, Curtis and Hutchinson – demonstrate the inestimable value to scholars of the National Library's newspaper collection. Maurice Harmon's essay is a study of the elegy in Anglo-Irish literature, and he compares five poems – by Yeats, Clarke, Kavanagh, Montague and Harmon himself – which, while written within the strict conventions of the elegy form, adapt that form in order to look back and reflect on the lives of certain individuals and groups, their social significance or insignificance, and the plight of subcultures doomed to extinction. For example, Harmon's own elegy tells the story of the virtual destruction of Native American civilizations by white settlers – a process of colonization for which he sees Irish precedents.[4] Dennis O'Driscoll's memoir has

4 For another interesting treatment of the colonizing impulse of the United States, see

itself a distinctly elegiac quality: he shares with us his memories of childhood in Co. Tipperary some forty years ago, and specifically his memories of the books that he read and loved when he was a boy – and he shows that these memories resonate in his poetry today.[5]

'Poetry', Maurice Harmon has written elsewhere, 'refreshes, purifies and strengthens the language … Almost every day we see language abused by politicians, spin doctors and others. Poets counter that abuse in the precision and clarity with which they write.'[6] This volume is thus enriched by the eight poems that are interspersed among the essays. Only two have previously appeared in print.[7] Three of the poets – Gerard Lyne, Michael Comyns and Éilís Ní Dhuibhne – are former colleagues of Dónall Ó Luanaigh in the Library, and Gerard Lyne's poem is his first ever published. Michael Comyns' poem is inspired by lines from the Annals of Connacht (in reference to the year 1388),[8] while Éilís Ní Dhuibhne's contribution echoes Yeats' 'The Hosting of the Sidhe'. The other poems are by Theo Dorgan, Gabriel Fitzmaurice, Brendan Kennelly, Seamus Heaney and Brian Lalor. Theo Dorgan's poem is a personal meditation on Dónall Ó Luanaigh's commitment to his profession, while both Gabriel Fitzmaurice and Brendan Kennelly deal with matters familiar to the Library's readers – respectively, the imponderables of a family's history and the nature of one's interaction with a book. Seamus Heaney's 'Five Quatrains' are translated from the Irish: one of the originals can be found in *Thesaurus Palaeohibernicus*, another in Kuno Meyer's *A Primer of Irish Metrics* and the remainder in Gerard Murphy's *Early Irish Lyrics*.[9] Brian Lalor's poem, which won the

N. Ferguson, *Colossus: the rise and fall of the American empire* (paperback ed., London, 2005), especially pp 35–6 in regard to the displacement of the Native Americans. **5** Dennis O'Driscoll's memoir is based on a talk he gave in November 2004 at the 'Reading Lives, Writing Lives' conference, Church of Ireland College of Education, Rathmines, Dublin. It was previously published in *New Hibernia Review*, 9:1 (St Paul, MN, Spring 2005), 9–23. **6** From an editorial in *Poetry Ireland Review*, 70 (Summer 2001); repr. Maurice Harmon, *Selected essays*, ed. Barbara Brown (Dublin, 2006), p. 201. **7** Brendan Kennelly's poem 'Book' appears in his *Familiar strangers: new and selected poems, 1960–2004* (Tarset, Northumberland, 2004), p. 431, and was previously published in his collections *The voices* (Dublin, 1973) and *A time for voices: selected poems, 1960–1990* (Newcastle-upon-Tyne, 1990). Brian Lalor's poem 'On publishing: a rhapsody' was first published in *THE SHOp: a magazine of poetry*, 18 (Summer 2005), 8–14. **8** Both the Irish text and the English translation at the head of Comyns' poem are as in the edition of *Annála Connacht: the Annals of Connacht*, ed. by A.M. Freeman (Dublin, 1944: Dublin Institute of Advanced Studies). **9** 'East coast' is from W. Stokes and J. Strachan (eds), *Thesaurus palaeohibernicus: a collection of glosses, scholia, prose and verse*, 2 vols (Cambridge, 1903), ii, p. 290; 'The monk's tryst' is from K. Meyer, *A primer of Irish metrics* (Dublin, 1909), p. 21; 'Whet-beak', 'Colmcille's Derry' and 'Gráinne's words about Díarmait' are from G. Murphy, *Early Irish lyrics* (Oxford, 1956), pp 6, 68, 160.

2004 Kilkenny International Swift Society award for Juvenalian satire, is a play on Jonathan Swift's *On Poetry: A Rapsody (sic)*.

Lalor is better known as a graphic artist than as a poet, and the beautiful frontispiece is based on a copperplate etching he executed in 2005 specially for this volume. This image of a reader's desk and chair in the Library's main reading room will evoke happy memories for anyone who, whether as a member of the Library's staff or as a reader, has had occasion to work in that 'sacred space'.[10] Its title — 'The Chair he sat in, like a burnished throne' — is a variation of a line in T.S. Eliot's *The Waste Land*, 'The Chair she sat in, like a burnished throne, / Glowed on the marble', which is itself derived from Shakespeare's *Antony and Cleopatra*: 'The barge she sat in, like a burnished throne, / Burned on the water; the poop was beaten gold ...'[11]

The penultimate essay of this *Festschrift* is Mary Beard's study of the Roman triumph, and she returns to the theme of how we view the past: her essay begins with a cartoon from the British *Independent on Sunday* that exploits our residual understanding of this feature of Roman life for a current political purpose. Her essay is, as she says herself, a 'lightly edited and footnoted version' of the John O'Meara memorial lecture delivered to the National Library of Ireland Society on 14 September 2005.[12] This was the first in a series of annual lectures which the Society will host in memory of the late Professor John O'Meara, professor of Latin at University College, Dublin from 1948 to 1984. It is intended that all of these lectures should be on topics relating to O'Meara's academic or other interests.[13] The lectures have been made possible by an endowment from Professor O'Meara's family, for which the Society is most grateful.

In *The Singing-Masters*, his elegant account of his early years and his intellectual formation, John O'Meara defined his *credo* as a scholar as follows:

> Yet one goes on, partly perhaps for reasons of *history*: to make known the truth, however little more, about some important figure in the past; to remove from him the imputations, favourable or unfavourable, which successful groups in bolstering their power, in good faith or confusedly

---

10 So described by Colm Toibín in RTE Radio 1's *Tonight with Vincent Browne* programme broadcast live from the National Library on 12 Jan. 2006.   **11** *The waste land* (London, 1922), pt 2; *Antony and Cleopatra* (1606–7), 2. 2.   **12** For an account of Dr Beard's lecture, see F.M. Larkin, 'Inaugural John O'Meara memorial lecture', *Classics Association of Ireland Newsletter*, 16 (Oct. 2005), 13. Another article about the lecture series appeared in *NLI News*, 21 (Autumn 2005), and contains a short biographical sketch of John O'Meara.   **13** The second O'Meara lecture was given on 31 January 2007 by Professor Denis Donoghue, Henry James Professor of English and American Letters, New York University, on 'The Latin factor: a chapter of autobiography'.

or in simple bad faith, attribute to him. This, however small an achievement in itself, participates in the transcending importance of the discovery of truth, which is ultimately one.[14]

An admirable manifesto – but, since it sets an exacting standard, I trust that I do not tempt fate by quoting it. My reason for doing so is that it allows us to extend T.W. Lyster's appealing notion that a librarian's trade is in Light, for O'Meara's manifesto reminds us that the objective of that trade – the profit to be derived from it – is 'the discovery of truth, which is ultimately one'.

It is with this objective in mind that the National Library of Ireland Society offers the tribute of these essays and poems to Dónall Ó Luanaigh on the occasion of his retirement from the Library's staff – as a mark of our affection and respect, and of our gratitude for his service to the Library and its readers, and to the Society. We look forward to his continued participation in the affairs of the Society for many more years, though now not as one of the Library's staff, but simply as what every member of the Society is proud to be: a friend of the Library. And the National Library of Ireland has had no truer friend than Dónall Ó Luanaigh.

It remains for me to express my thanks to Noel Kissane, formerly keeper of manuscripts in the National Library of Ireland and a colleague of Dónall for over thirty years, for undertaking much of the copy-editing of this volume. In addition, I should like to record the financial and other assistance which the National Library of Ireland Society and some of its members have given the project. Sandra McDermott, until recently honorary secretary of the Society, has been particularly helpful. Fr J. Anthony Gaughan, chairman of the Society, has kindly compiled the index and has also contributed the short, final essay on the Irish embassy in Paris. This is a fitting subject for inclusion in the *Festschrift*, for embassies have much in common with great libraries – imposing buldings, enquiring minds, diligent and courteous staff. Financial assistance was also received from the National Library of Ireland and from the American Conference of Irish Studies, and I am grateful to both. Finally, I am much indebted to Michael Adams and his team at Four Courts Press for their patience and constant support.

FELIX M. LARKIN

---

14 J. O'Meara, *The singing-masters* (Dublin, 1990), p. 64.

Dónall Ó Luanaigh: a personal appreciation

Gerard Lyne

DÓNALL Ó LUANAIGH BELONGS to a generation which, as the Chinese would say, has lived in interesting times. The Ireland into which he was born was dominated by Eamon de Valera, John Charles McQuaid, strict censorship, monolithic Catholicism, 'the Emergency', wartime rationing, mass emigration, frugal living and, more often than not, grinding poverty. In Dublin there were still electric trams and slum tenements, while rural Ireland was a place of paraffin lamps, muddy boreens and bicycles. Only a tiny minority of people, in city or country, owned motor cars. Holidays, for those fortunate enough to afford them, consisted of a week in Ballybunion, Bray or Kilkee. Few people had ever flown. Shannon and Dublin airports – or Rineanna and Collinstown, as they were then called – were places rarely visited by the plain people of Ireland. If they went there at all, they did so merely to gawp from a balcony at the wondrous flying machines and their exotic human cargoes. Hitler was rampaging towards Moscow, and it seemed that Fascism was destined to rule the world.

Dónall was born in 1941 at Salthill in Galway, the only child of William Looney (Liam Ó Luanaigh) and Bridget Helen (known as Evelyn) Coyne. He was baptized Daniel Gerard Looney, but has always been known as Dónall. The place of his nativity, Seamount nursing home, was also that of Proinsias Mac Aonghusa and Breandán Ó hEithir. His father was from Ballymacelligott, Co. Kerry, while his mother was a member of a west of Ireland family, with roots in Creggs and Moycullen, Co. Galway. William Looney, a local government official, served in Cos. Cavan and Galway, retiring in 1971 as assistant manager of the latter county. Dónall began his education in 1946 at Farnham national school, near Cavan town. Rather unusually for the time, the school was interdenominational. Later, when the family moved to the town of Cavan, he was sent to a private school there, operated by a 'gentle lady' named Mrs Daly. Early in 1947 his father was appointed county secretary for Galway and Dónall was obliged to move again, this time to the Presentation primary school in that city. One of his teachers was a sister of Siobhán Ní Fhualáin (Julia Folen), a close family friend who became county librarian successively of Cos. Cavan and Louth. A dedicated professional at a time when libraries attracted little in the way of public funding, Siobhán was one of the influences on his future choice of career. She and her sister were also fluent Irish speakers.

Dónall received part of his early formation from the Jesuits. In 1948 he entered Coláiste Iognaid (St Ignatius' College), Galway. This he describes as 'an Irish Jesuit school with a difference'. Founded in 1863, it had encountered a very lean period just after the establishment of the Irish state, and even had to close its doors for a year or two. The *deus ex machina* which saved it, however, was its decision to become a *scoil lán Gaelach*, teaching all subjects save English and religious knowledge through the medium of Irish. During his time in both the primary and secondary schools, the staff was composed mainly of Jesuit priests, along with one or two seminarians, while there were only two or three lay teachers. Although the Galway Jesuits took their commission to teach Irish seriously, they displayed little in the way of strident nationalism. The students were given rather a romantic view of Ireland, centred on figures from olden days, such as Art Mac Murrough Kavanagh, Aodh Ruadh Ó Domhnall and Eoghan Rua Ó Néill, rather than Pearse, Collins or de Valera. No doubt this emphasis was designed – in part, at least – to circumvent the still-bitter Civil War divisions of the time. Above all, Dónall believes, the Jesuits sought to cut through the Anglo-Saxon 'paper wall' so much deplored by Arthur Griffith; at a time when the EU was still in the future, they made the students look to Europe in general and France and Spain in particular. Here, no doubt, lie the seeds of Dónall's abiding interest in all things French, enhanced in recent years by the marriage of one of his daughters to a Frenchman. The couple and their two children (the eldest named Dónall, after his grandfather) reside in France.

Dónall having secured a good Intermediate Certificate, his parents decided that, as an only child, he would benefit from consorting with boys of his own age in boarding school. His education was again placed in the hands of one of the great orders of the Catholic church, this time the Cistercians of Mount St Joseph's, Roscrea, where a cousin of his was already boarding. Rather like the present writer, who was also a boarder there a little after Dónall's time, his new environment occasioned, in his own words, a rude awakening. Food, while wholesome – it was produced on the monastery farm – was sparse. Extras, however, could be procured from the college shop and in addition the students were all furnished with stout 'tuck boxes', stored securely in the 'tuck room' and topped up by regular food parcels from home. The college was situated only a few miles from Birr, where some of the lowest temperatures in Ireland have been recorded. In winter the classrooms and living quarters were cold and draughty. The students rose shortly after 6.30 a.m., performing their obligatory ablutions with cold water which, if standing since the night before, was often in winter covered by a scum of ice. As in all boarding schools of the period, active participation in sport was *de rigueur*. While Dónall enjoyed watching football and other sports, regular participation went somewhat against the grain. Anyone with direct experience of the Roscrea playing fields on a cold, damp evening in the depths – both physical and psychological – of a midlands' winter, will readily sympathize with his point of view. Nevertheless, he made many friends in the college and in 1958 achieved a good Leaving Certificate.

It will come as no surprise to anyone who has heard Dónall speak in public that he was not only an active member of the college debating society but had the distinction on one occasion of representing it victoriously in a debate with Glenstal Abbey school. He still recalls that he and his fellows were somewhat awe-struck by the genteel atmosphere of the rival institution, in particular its refectory, which he describes as more like a tea-shop in the English home counties, frequented by Miss Marple, than its noisy, rough-and-ready Roscrea equivalent. In the latter institution the majority of the teachers were laymen. The English and history teachers, in particular, gave him an enduring interest in their subjects. Fr Austin maintained a museum devoted mainly to memorabilia of the War of Independence. Dónall and a friend would often engage Fr Austin in conversation and heard from him many stories of the national movement.

His interest in another side of the Irish historical spectrum was also being fostered by his father, with whom from an early age he was able to visit many surviving Anglo-Irish 'big houses'. His first such visit occurred when he was about 10 years old. His parents had a friend from Kerry who was a district nurse in Clonbur, on the Galway-Mayo border, between Lough Corrib and Lough Mask. One day, when the family were visiting her socially, she announced that she was going to pay a call on a patient, wife of the caretaker of Peterborough, then a semi-derelict house of the Catholic Lynch family. She invited them along to see it. Dónall recalls being impressed by the beautiful situation of the residence and saddened by its ruinous state. He remembers, in particular, the forlorn atmosphere of its private chapel. During his childhood and adolescence, he and his father visited many other old houses and Dónall traversed their plundered woodlands, parks and demesnes. Among them were Castle Ellen, home of Edward Carson's mother's family, the Lamberts; Castledaly and Dunsandle, residences of the ancient Galway family of Daly; Monivea, seat of another old Galway family, the ffrenches; and Kilcornan, home of the Redingtons. It can scarcely have occurred to Dónall that he would one day be visiting such houses in a professional capacity, in pursuit of family and estate papers.

From his father also he received intimations of a darker aspect of Irish history. When cycling to school in Tralee on 7 March 1923, during the Civil War,

1 Dónall Ó Luanaigh, on the occasion of his retirement from the National Library of Ireland in June 2006; this photograph first appeared in *NLI News*, 25 (Autumn 2006).

the latter came on the scene of the infamous Ballyseedy massacre in which – by way of reprisal – members of the Free State army took nine Republican prisoners from Ballymullen barracks in Tralee and tied them to a landmine concealed beneath a heap of stones at Ballyseedy Cross. The mine was then detonated and those who remained alive were shot. However, one of the victims, Stephen Fuller, was blown clear and lived to tell the tale. Whether or not Dónall's father was exposed to the full horror of the scene – it was said that for days afterwards 'the birds were eating the flesh off the trees'[1] – or merely saw it from a distance, the effect on him, a youth of about 16, can only be imagined.

1 D. Macardle, *Tragedies of Kerry, 1922–1923* (Dublin, 1924), p. 14.

This, however, was all in the past; for Dónall, a bright future beckoned. On 8 October 1958 – the day, he recalls, of Pope Pius XII's death – he registered as a student in the faculties of arts and commerce in University College, Galway (UCG). The five years that he spent there were among the happiest of his life. The college at that time had only 1,200 students. A former director of the National Library, Patrick Henchy, who was a student there in the mid-1930s, told him that the atmosphere at this earlier period was very similar to that which prevailed during the 1950s and early 1960s. In contrast, the much larger college attended by Dónall's daughter in the 1990s was very different. Student life in Dónall's days was surprisingly free and easy. Though never lacking in intellectual challenge, there was none of the grinding examination pressure of the present day. Much stimulating and inexpensive entertainment was to be found in college debates and society meetings, where distinguished guests included the young Fianna Fáil minister Charles Haughey – who was heckled – and the veteran socialist Jack McQuillan TD – who was cheered. Among other guest speakers, he recalls, was the poet Pádraic Colum.

In Ireland no less than the world at large, Dónall remembers, this was a time of hope. The aged de Valera had 'gone to the Park' as president of Ireland, making way for the pragmatic Lemass. In Northern Ireland, the grim-faced Brookeborough was succeeded by a smiling Terence O'Neill, who seemed to be reaching out to the Republic. De Gaulle seemed to be regenerating France. Former old enemies were working together for a united Europe. Pope John XXIII was bringing a message of renewal to the Catholic church, while in the United States the drab White House of Ike and Mamie Eisenhower had given way to the Camelot of John F. Kennedy and his glamorous young wife Jackie. Elvis, the Beatles, Bob Dylan, Muhammad Ali and Marilyn Monroe were symbols of a new era. All these people and developments, Dónall remembers, were eagerly discussed by him and his fellow students at lectures, on their way home from college, or over coffee at Lydon's restaurant. In marked contrast to the students of today, alcohol featured little, if at all, in their lives, while the drug culture was completely unknown. Among his fellow students were Pádraic McKernan, afterwards Irish ambassador to France; Thomas Mitchell, later provost of Trinity College, Dublin; Christopher Murray, distinguished academic and biographer of Sean O'Casey; Brian Joyce, who was to head up several state enterprises; and Mícheál Ó Seighin, recently in the headlines as one of the 'Rossport Five' protesting against the establishment of an on-shore oil terminal in Co. Mayo.

After graduating with an honours degree in commerce in 1961, a year later Dónall took an honours BA in English and French. In 1963 he acquired an honours MA in French, specialising in Molière and Balzac. His lifelong enthusiasm for France and all things French was further strengthened by two summer courses which he attended in Paris in 1960 and 1963. He fell in love with the French capital which, he says, was then far less commercial than now, resembling still the city of the great nineteenth-century authors and artists. Later, he was to develop his interest in Franco-Irish connections, publishing several articles on the period from the fall of Napoléon Bonaparte to the outbreak of the Great War. In this he was encouraged by the teacher and historian Dom Mark Tierney, of Glenstal Abbey.

In the early summer of 1963 his professor, Proinsias Mac Giollarnáth (Frank Ford), drew his attention to an advertisement for three posts of assistant librarian (now called assistant keeper) in the National Library of Ireland. Professor Mac Giollarnáth had himself worked there briefly in that capacity before going on to take up a lectureship in French at University College, Dublin (UCD). He observed that the Library was a fairly pleasant place in which to work, but counselled Dónall against remaining there. The latter had visited the Library as a child. In 1955, when he and his parents were in Dublin for a family funeral, his father took him to the great, domed reading room which he himself had frequented many years earlier as an accountancy student. It may be of interest to observe, somewhat ironically, that accountancy students were barred from the reading room in Dónall's own day. Given that they relied on their private texts, they were deemed to be occupying the seats of more deserving readers who were using the Library's books and other resources. Weeding out the accountancy students, with attendant public stand-offs and dramatic games of cat-and-mouse, was one of the more diverting activities for fledgling assistant keepers, even in the present writer's day. For Dónall, however, all this was far in the future. Still very much an innocent abroad, he remembers only being captivated on his first visit to the Library by the green lampshades on the readers' desks.

The interviews were held in September 1963. The board consisted of the then director, Dr Richard Hayes, John O'Meara, professor of Latin in UCD, and two civil servants. Dónall remembers that in the course of the interview Professor O'Meara broke briefly into French. One suspects that he was impressed by Dónall's fluency in the language. Be this as it may, he got the job and took up duty in the Library on the following 9 December. A former college friend of his used to joke that Dónall in the Library was rather like the dramatist Racine who, as a young man, lodged with the elderly and solemn Jansenist divines of Port-Royal, all the professional staff being much older than him. They included Patrick Henchy, keeper of printed books; Gerard Slevin, chief herald and keeper of manuscripts; Alf Mac Lochlainn, assistant keeper of manuscripts; and assistant keepers Desmond Kennedy, Michael Hewson and Gearóid Mac Niocaill (later professor of early Irish in UCG). Another assistant keeper, Thomas P. O'Neill – who was to become professor of modern Irish history, also in UCG – was on leave of absence, being engaged on his bio-graphy of Eamon de Valera. From this, it will be seen that there was a distinctly academic caste to the professional staff of the day. Other notable staff included Mary McCarthy (cataloguer and director's secretary), and senior library assistant Francis A. (Frank) Ward. The members of the science and art staff – then only two in number – were John Butler and Thomas Watson. With the exception of Alf Mac Lochlainn and Mary McCarthy, all of the foregoing are now *imithe ar Shlí na Fírinne*.

Fortunately, Dónall's isolation in this somewhat senatorial setting was not destined to endure. Two other assistant keepers were appointed from the same panel. Margaret (Maura) Deignan, who was to marry Dr Hayes, took up her post in January 1964; she later became co-editor of *Sources for the History of Irish Civilisation: Articles in Irish Periodicals*. Donal Begley, afterwards chief herald, arrived the following June.

The preoccupations – and, indeed, expectations – of the professional staff of the day, and the social circles in which they moved, were reflected in their conversations over morning coffee. These took place in the inner section of the librarian's office, in what is now the room housing the guard book catalogue. The morning pleasantries included speculation concerning appointments to uni-versity chairs and diplomatic posts. Some of Dónall's immediate predecessors had left the Library for careers not just in the universities but also in the depart-ment of foreign affairs. The turnover may in part have been due to the fact that, like the National Museum and the Public Record Office, the Library was suf-fering from government neglect, and even able and diligent staff were not immune from demoralisation.

Despite the demoralisation, perhaps the greatest work published by the National Library, *Manuscript Sources for the History of Irish Civilisation*, dates from this time. Devised and edited by Richard Hayes and published in its entirety by G.K. Hall of Boston, this massive compendium appeared in 1965. It consists of an eleven-volume guide to the location of manuscripts of Irish interest both at home and abroad. A supplement was published in 1979. A complementary work, *Sources for the History of Irish Civilisation: Articles in Irish Periodicals*, was also published in 1979. Even in our present age of electronic technology, the com-pilation of works of such magnitude would represent formidable undertakings. In a pre-electronic age, the task of bringing them to completion was nothing less than heroic. Production involved reliance on typewritten entries and masses of index cards, which had to be manually sorted and filed before being filmed by the publishers. On his arrival in 1963, Dónall remembers his colleagues being all agog with the initial phase of the project. Later, he himself served at the cutting edge of the supplement to *Manuscript Sources*, in which his name appears as co-editor. The supplement stands as a permanent monument to his diligence and industry.

From 1963 to 1968 Dónall served his apprenticeship as a cataloguer and as duty librarian in the reading room. One day, he remembers, he answered a telephone query in Irish concerning an article in a mathematical journal from President de Valera in person. A regular reader at the time was Dr Eileen McCarville, lecturer in English at UCD – who, as a member of Cumann na mBan, had worked for Michael Collins and had been arrested by the British authorities. Another frequent reader was General Richard Mulcahy. The chairman of the council of trustees was Professor Felix Hackett and one of the members was Dr Constantine (Con) Curran. Both had been fellow students of James Joyce. One of his first major cataloguing assignments involved a huge collection of books donated to the Library by Lady Powerscourt. He also listed copyright donations, which at that time were published in *An Leabharlann*, and in 1968 spent six months working in the old Genealogical Office, then situated beneath the Bedford clock tower in Dublin Castle.

His library duties were not, however, so onerous as to impinge unduly on his social life. In October 1969 he was married in Galway to Mary Walsh, a secondary teacher. They had first met as students in UCG. As anyone who knows them will readily attest, Mary has been the light and mainstay of Dónall's life for close on forty years. They have five children – four daughters and a son, who himself now works in the Library – and two grandsons.

Also in 1969, Dónall remembers, two long-term future colleagues, Brian McKenna and Noel Kissane, joined the Library staff as assistant keepers. Dónall sees both as having had a considerable impact on the institution. Brian, by his pioneering work in introducing modern technology, has ensured that details of the National Library's holdings are now available worldwide. Noel, by his ambitious programme of travelling exhibitions, lectures and publications, gave the Library a high public profile at a time when, due to circumstances beyond its control, it could otherwise achieve little in the public domain. Three years later, in 1972, the foregoing were joined by another assistant keeper, Fergus Gillespie, a graduate in Celtic studies from UCD and future chief herald.

While working as periodicals librarian from 1969 to 1973, Dónall compiled the first computerized edition of the *Union List of Periodicals and Serials in Irish*

Libraries. The project involved liaison with other libraries in Dublin and else-where, a form of collaboration which Dónall has always enjoyed and for which he has a remarkable aptitude. On transferring to the department of manuscripts in 1973 he got a year's sabbatical to take the diploma course in archival studies in UCD. A fellow student on the course was the eminent Celtic studies scholar, Dr Pádraig de Brún.

From 1976 to 1982 Dónall acted as honorary secretary of the Business Records Committee of the Irish Manuscripts Commission. The chairman of the committee was the formidable and colourful Professor R. Dudley Edwards. Dónall had first encountered him when taking the archival studies diploma. Not surprisingly, they got on well together. During the period of Dónall's incum-bency, the committee appointed a number of manuscript surveyors who were to achieve distinction in the world of Irish archives, including Sarah Ward-Perkins, Patricia Kerneghan, Ken Hannigan and Brian Donnelly. Since 1997 he represented the National Library on An Chomhairle Leabharlanna.

In 1982, when Alf Mac Lochlainn resigned the post of director of the National Library to become librarian of UCG, Dónall moved from being keeper of manuscripts to keeper of printed books. This post in turn changed during the early 1990s to keeper of collections, involving overall responsibility for col-lection development throughout the Library. It is from this post that he retired in June 2006.

From 1989 onwards Dónall was associated with NEWSPLAN, a co-operative project involving libraries throughout Britain and Ireland designed to preserve rare or fragile newspapers. In this connection, Dónall established a fruitful working relationship with senior officials in the British Library – including, in particular, Geoffrey Hamilton and Andrew Phillips. This is in keeping with the good *rapport* which he has also maintained down the years with the antiquarian book trade, not only throughout Ireland, but in the United Kingdom and further afield. To cite but one example of the value of such *rapport*, he first encountered Stephen Griffin of Massachussetts when the latter was a bookseller. Later, he was instrumental in persuading him to donate to the National Library his splendid collection of books on Irish-American topics.

From 1983 to 1991 he served as honorary secretary of the National Library of Ireland Society, founded in 1969 by his good friend Patrick Henchy – then direc-tor of the Library – as a public pressure group to promote the interests of the Library and its staff. Among notable persons who addressed the Society under his stewardship were the radical political thinker and novelist Peadar O'Donnell and the Nobel laureate Seamus Heaney. His abiding memory of O'Donnell was the latter's absolute refusal, even though old and frail, to avail of the Library's lift! He also recalls Seamus Heaney's graciousness in fielding numerous questions from the very large number of young people attending his lecture.[2]

A great supporter of the Society at that time was its treasurer, the late Nóra Ní Shúilleabháin, best known as collaborator with her friend Eoin ('The Pope') O'Mahony in his weekly genealogical programme on Radio Éireann called *Meet the Clans*. The programme had a huge Sunday lunchtime audience and confirmed – if confirmation were needed – the universal belief among Irish people of the day that they were all descendants of kings and princes. A native of Valentia Island in Kerry, as a young girl she had witnessed the shooting dead of her two cousins, young Free State officers, in their home in Kenmare by Republicans from north Kerry. She often said that she never fully recovered from the trauma of that episode. Be this as it may, she was a most gracious and hospitable lady, maintaining at her apartment in Pembroke Road a salon frequented by poets, scholars and other *literati*. She loved above all to discourse *ar na maithe agus na mór uaisle* of times gone by. Another great contemporary supporter of the Society was Nóra's long-time friend, Peter Tynan O'Mahony, *Irish Times* journalist and founder of the O'Mahony Records Society. His younger brother, David, a brilliant television comedian, achieved household notoriety in both Ireland and Britain under the stage name Dave Allen. With Nóra and Peter, the present writer, no less than Dónall, enjoyed many a convivial glass. She was eventually succeeded as honorary treasurer by Dermot Blunden, a highly dedicated and efficient incumbent of the post, whose untimely death in 1997 saddened us greatly.

Dónall believes that the most important occurrence in the history of the Library since its foundation was the government decision in 1986 to move responsibility for the institution from the *main morte* of the over-burdened department of education, first to the department of the Taoiseach and later to the department of arts and culture, under its various titles. Thanks to this new dispensation, the Library has progressed dramatically. Some directors of the past, such as Hayes and Henchy, had ambitious plans for the institution, but their eloquent pleading fell on deaf ears. Indeed, soon after his appointment as director in 1967, Patrick Henchy persuaded the trustees to commission a report on the Library by a world authority on libraries, K.W. Humphreys. Sadly, this report, which contained many useful recommendations, was never even published. The *laissez-faire* attitude of the department of education, coupled with national economic recession, left the Library in a parlous state. Michael Hewson had the misfortune to be director at probably the lowest point in the Library's

2 Heaney's graciousness is again evident in his generosity in contributing a poem to this *Festschrift*.

history, from 1982 to 1988. Dónall thinks it particularly sad that Michael did
not live long enough to enjoy his retirement. By contrast, more recent directors, such as Pat Donlon and Brendan O Donoghue, have generally enjoyed
good access to controllers of the official purse strings.

Dónall regarded Patrick Henchy not only as a close personal friend and mentor, but a great librarian.[3] Although appointed by the celebrated Richard Hayes,
he did not know him on a personal level. He is keenly aware, however, of
Hayes' achievements, including his compendious *Clár Litridheacht na Nua-
Ghaeilge*,[4] as well as his monumental catalogues of Irish manuscripts and periodical articles, to which reference has already been made. In addition, Hayes
commissioned the filming of over 6,000 reels of microfilm of manuscripts and
archives of Irish interest in many parts of the world, comprising the historical
record of successive Irish diasporas, from the early medieval missionaries to the
Wild Geese and beyond.

In 1989 Pat Donlon became the first and – thus far – the only woman to
hold the post of director. Her principal contribution was in the modernization
of various library systems, especially through the introduction of digital technology. She also recognized that the Library had a particular duty towards the
general public. For much of Dónall's career the institution had seen itself as
catering very much for scholars and gentlefolk. Brendan O Donoghue, who
succeeded Seán Cromien as director in 1997 after the latter's all-too-brief incum-
bency, was the right director at the right time. A public servant of considerable
accomplishment and experience both at home and abroad, he had a keen sense
of history and tapped into the prevailing economic prosperity to the Library's
great advantage.

Dónall was also acquainted with figures from a more distant past. Prominent
among them was Edward MacLysaght, a larger-than-life figure – historian,
genealogist and Irish language enthusiast – who, though already several years
retired from his post of chief herald and keeper of manuscripts at the time of
Dónall's arrival, invariably went out of his way to assist new members of staff.
In his youth he had been politically active in the nationalist cause. In 1917–18
he represented Sinn Féin as an observer at the Irish Convention, which sought
to devise a constitutional agreement between the contending sides in the wake
of the 1916 Rising. He also took part in the War of Independence, and was a
member of Seanad Éireann in the period 1922–5. He was a close friend of the

3 See the obituaries of Patrick Henchy which Dónall Ó Luanaigh wrote for the *Irish Times*,
12 May 2001, and the *Library Association Record*, 103:9 (2001).   4 *Clár litridheacht na Nua-
Ghaeilge, 1850–1936*, compiled by R. de Hae [R.J. Hayes] and B. Ní Dhonnchadha, 3 vols
(Baile Átha Cliath, 1938–40).

writer, poet and mystic, George Russell (Æ), who had also been a member of the Irish Convention. He remained mentally and physically active even in advanced old age and continued to frequent the Library almost until his death in his hundredth year in 1986.

Dónall recalls that Alf Mac Lochlainn – director, 1976–82 – imparted to him a great fund of knowledge concerning the Library's resources. Mac Lochlainn, a brilliant but avuncular man who did not suffer either fools or slackers gladly, possessed an extraordinary run in verbal abuse, all the more devastating for being invariably devoid of a single expletive. Our verbally challenged younger generation of today might learn a thing or two from his technique. Be this as it may, he had a genuine love for the Library's collections. Another of Dónall's early mentors was the inspector of manuscripts, Sir John Ainsworth, Bart. An old Etonian and erudite classical scholar, Ainsworth – albeit rather eccentric – was a very effective member of the professional staff, who used his social *entré* to procure a great mass of priceless estate papers as gifts for the nation. Never the most natty of dressers, during the week of the annual Dublin Horse Show he was wont to blossom briefly, sporting a blazer, canary waistcoat and floral buttonhole and greeting old friends from the hunting and horsy set in a resonant but beautifully modulated public school accent. Sadly, he received only a pittance for his work on behalf of the Library, having accepted a fixed stipend on appointment in the 1940s, and spent much of his life in near penury. MacLysaght, Mac Lochlainn and Ainsworth were the founders of the modern department of manuscripts. It is only in recent years that increases in staff have allowed access to the hugely valuable materials secured for posterity by these founding fathers.

Another of Dónall's mentors, the Irish scholar, Nessa Ní Shéaghdha, who worked on compiling an analytical catalogue of the Library's Gaelic manuscripts, was similarly always on hand with help and advice. In her day she had been a great beauty. One of those who fell under her spell was the distinguished Scots-Gaelic poet, Sorley Maclean (Somhairle Mac Gill-Eain) who composed in her honour a collection called *Dàin do Eimhir,* which first established his reputation as a major poet.

Among the library assistants of the time were Gerard (Gerry) Nash, a quiet but extremely knowledgeable presence in manuscripts; Liam Byrne, who had an immense knowledge of the photographic archive – his untimely death deprived the Library of a great asset; James (Jim) Scully, who had a profound knowledge of Irish newspapers – as Dónall discovered when they worked together on a major movement of stock in 1969; Martin Ryan, who always had the welfare of his colleagues at heart; Richard (Dick) Mooney, who was a pillar of the photographic section, ably assisted by the brothers Philip and Séamus McCann and Patrick (Paddy) McGee. Present-day pillars of the institution, Kevin Browne, Tom Desmond and Jim O'Shea, were at that time still 'babes in arms' in Library terms. Elsewhere on the staff, Máire Ní Churraidhín, besides being a most efficient secretary, had fluent Connemara Irish. Edward (Ned) Keane, armed only with a pencil and jotter and the services of another great secretary, Peggy O'Hara, not only indexed *Griffith's Valuation*, but went on to list the records of the Irish Land Commission – a task for which he literally gave his life, catching a fatal pleurisy while working in an unheated repository during the severe winter of 1980–1. Among the science and art attendants, Dónall recalls in particular Philip (Gerry) Conran, aviation historian, much of whose valuable collection on aviation history was acquired by the Library before his death.

Dónall has very positive memories of the old council of trustees which, after enduring for a period of some 130 years from the foundation of the Library, finally became defunct in 2005. A member whom he particularly recalls is the Revd Professor F.X. Martin. A champion of Viking Dublin, Martin was a fount of energy – witty, urbane and helpful to boot. Another, Eric Lambert, he recalls as a most charming man who, on one occasion, engaged a dramatic Garda escort to convey the Headfort estate papers – which he had been instrumental in acquiring – from their home in Co. Meath to Kildare Street. Lambert knew a thing or two about such operations. During the Second World War he had served as chief of police in British India. He subsequently worked, under cover of a diplomatic posting, for British intelligence in the Far East. Later still, he was active in preventing the spread of left-wing ideologies in South America – becoming intimate, in the process, with various military regimes. Beneath the satin and velvet of his demeanour there lurked, apparently, pure steel. Dónall also recalls two amiable scientific trustees, Professor Denis Crowley of UCD, a faithful supporter of the National Library Society, and Professor Stanley McElhinney. The latter was part of a Trinity College team which made a most valuable contribution to cancer research, before sadly succumbing to the disease himself. He had a particular love for the history and topography of his native Donegal. Another trustee, the distinguished architect, historian, poet and man of letters, Maurice Craig, was also a most valuable member of the council.

In 1989 Maurice Line – then considered a leading authority on library administration in these islands – was engaged to help devise a strategic plan for the Library. In the company of Brian McKenna, Dónall travelled to York in April 1990 to attend a seminar organized by Line. It was, he remembers, a truly international gathering, attracting librarians from such diverse countries as Slovenia, Chile, Singapore, Venezuela and Malta. In keeping with his experience of other such gatherings, the delegates got on very well together, venting their spleen on their respective niggardly governments rather than each other. In the evenings Line liked to treat his charges to a guided tour of the historic city of York. Being an extraordinarily tall, fit and rangy man, however, he tended to set a pace which led to large sectors of his entourage – including Dónall, if not also Brian – deserting to seek consolation in various hostelries and coffee shops along the way.

The Library has always had its share of extraordinarily generous donors. Among those whom Dónall got to know personally was Andrée Sheehy Skeffington, widow of Owen Sheehy Skeffington and French by birth, who donated the extensive and very valuable papers of her husband and his family to the Library. He recalls visiting her often in a 'wonderfully rural setting' situated just off the busy Terenure Road, where a cup of coffee and a friendly chat were the invariable prelude to the handing over of yet another tranche of fascinating correspondence and other materials relating to women's suffrage, trade unions and the Irish national movement. At his prompting she agreed to give a lecture to the Library Society. Dónall had the lecture published as a pamphlet, along with another on a related topic by Alf Mac Lochlainn.[5] In July 1994 the pamphlet was presented by the committee of the Society to President Mary Robinson at Áras an Uachtaráin.

He also recalls Linda Kernoff, sister of the artist Harry Kernoff, who told him that her brother liked to frame his own paintings. Unfortunately, being an indifferent carpenter, he did his canvasses no justice. Dónall also remembers visiting the veteran Republican, Máire Comerford, who in her youth, along with other female companions, tore down the Union Jack from the Kildare Street Club – which now houses the Library's department of manuscripts and office of the chief herald. Fortunately for them, in the process of making a hasty exit from the scene of their misdemeanour, they ran into Brigadier General Sir William Hickey, a friend of the Comerford family, who spirited them out a rear door in double-quick time. Yet another notable donor was Kathleen McKenna Napoli, who had been secretary to both Arthur Griffith and Kevin O'Higgins. Griffith, she recalled, was a perfect gentleman. She was less enamoured of Michael Collins, because of his volatile disposition. Having married an Italian, she resided for many years in Italy and developed a beautiful accent, which Dónall describes as rural Irish replete with Italian intonations.

On occasion, also, he was actively involved in surveying manuscript collections. In the process he travelled mainly round the area of the historic Pale, extend-

5 A. Sheehy Skeffington, 'A coterie of lively suffragists' in *Writers, raconteurs and notable feminists: two monographs*, with a foreword by D. Ó Luanaigh (Dublin, 1993).

ing within a radius of fifty or so miles from Dublin. Sometimes, however, he went further afield. He recalls, for instance, driving to Castle Leslie in Glaslough, Co. Monaghan, on a bitter winter's morning, On arrival he found the rentals he wished to inspect stored in a vast freezing ballroom. He was saved from imminent hypothermia by his host, the author Desmond Leslie, who tendered him a generous bumper of spirituous liquor before commencement of operations which, no doubt, were thereby rendered all the more effective. One of his more exotic venues was Huntington Castle, Clonegal, Co. Wexford, where he met with the novelist Olivia Robertson and her brother, Lawrence Durdin Robertson, both appropriately attired as devotees of the cult of Isis and Osiris. A note of anti-climax entered the proceedings, however, when, towards nightfall, Mr Robinson changed into rustic attire and sallied forth to gather in his flocks and herds.

Auctions were particular highlights of the National Library routine. Although careful to stay within pre-arranged financial limits, professional staff often had disposal of substantial sums on such occasions. Sometimes this would take on the semblance of a duel, the bids becoming interspersed with increasingly pregnant pauses and the tension rising steadily in proportion, until the supreme moment of triumph, when an opponent would be driven from the field and the manuscript or other material successfully secured by the Library. There were also, of course, occasions when the institution failed gloriously, but somehow these were never as clearly remembered!

And so, a veteran of close on forty-three years in the Library's service, Dónall has finally come to the end of a long career – often arduous, occasionally tumultuous, but always challenging, enriching and rewarding, no less for Dónall himself than for the numerous people of diverse origins, preoccupations and stations who had the good fortune to encounter him along the way. My own first face-to-face meeting with him took place around the year 1965 when, as an undergraduate of UCD, I applied for a reader's ticket. He received me with characteristic courtesy and helpfulness. Later, during my years as an MA student, and while working in the Library as assistant editor of the correspondence of Daniel O'Connell, I came to know him better – though our relationship remained formal. It was only on joining the staff of the Library in the autumn of 1973 that I really came to know him. Over the years he has become not just a colleague, but a most valued friend.

He is a man of enormous kindness and courtesy, of unfailing tact and astute diplomacy, cosmopolitan, cultured and civilized, unostentatious in his wide knowledge, unassuming in matters of precedence, rank and hierarchy, invariably fair-minded, exercising his authority by example, seeking never to coerce but always to achieve consensus, conscientious, dedicated and industrious in the

2 A group photograph of National Library of Ireland staff, *c.*1950. From left to right:
Alf Mac Lochlainn, later director of the Library; Desmond Kennedy, later keeper of
manuscripts; Proinsias Mac Giollarnáth (Frank Ford), later professor in University
College, Galway; Patrick Henchy, later director of the Library; T.P. O'Neill, later
professor in University College, Galway; Michael Hewson, later director of the
Library; and John Barry, later professor in University College, Cork
(by courtesy of Monica Henchy).

performance of his duties, endlessly helpful and considerate to colleagues and
public alike and maintaining under every circumstance not only an innate dignity but a keen wit, laced with a lively sense of the absurd. In another era he
would be classified as a true Christian gentleman. Perhaps the best measure of
his stature, in both human and professional capacities, is to be found in his relations with successive directors, to all of whom he extended impeccable courtesy and his unstinted support. In so doing – as I have no doubt they themselves
would graciously admit – he greatly facilitated the smooth transition from one
regime to another and rendered the tenure of each successive director as comfortable and as productive as it could possibly be.

His kindness, I would add, is never of the intrusive or patronising variety.
Early in our acquaintance I myself encountered a typical example. In 1978 I was
transferred from the periodicals department, for which I had hitherto held
responsibility, to the department of manuscripts which was then under Dónall's

stewardship. At the time – astonishing as it may seem – the present genealogical consultancy room just off the public stairs of the main Library building doubled both as a manuscripts store and manuscripts staff workplace. Early on a Monday morning I quit the rather fraught environment of periodicals and took the short walk across the stairs to my new work area. Although absent on business, Dónall had not forgotten me. On my desk lay a tiny antique greeting card, depicting what could be the mountains of my native Kerry. Beside it was a copy of Tolstoy's *Resurrection* – a choice of reading incisively tailored to fit, in certain respects, the circumstances of my life at that particular juncture. It was a gesture of understanding which I have never forgotten.

Working with Dónall was both an educational experience and a pleasure. In allocating cataloguing projects he was always at pains to wed, insofar as possible, a particular collection to the cataloguer's academic or personal interests. He consulted with his staff at all levels and on occasion would defer to their judgment. This was at a time when rigid hierarchical structures were still very much the rule throughout the public service – a culture in which, inevitably, some of those dressed in a little brief authority sought actively to impress subordinates with a due sense of their consequence. Dónall, let be it said, had a markedly different management style. More than anything else he liked, when opportunity offered, to take an active place at the coalface. I have seen him begin sorting a small manuscript collection in the morning and go on through the day, tirelessly inscribing catalogue slips – this was long before the days of electronically generated lists – and have all in readiness for boxing and typing by close of business. The whole exercise would be accompanied by a running commentary, often witty and always informative, illustrating the depth of his interest in the material and his pleasure at bringing it into the public domain.

Towards the same public he was endlessly helpful and would often put himself to quite extraordinary trouble to deal with their inquiries. For this he has received many acknowledgements in learned books and journals. I remember him noting once, with wry humour, that sometimes it was those who had received least who gave most in the way of public recognition. He possessed, in addition, the advantage of an elephantine memory, which enabled him not only to recall names of both readers and donors wherever encountered – an important attribute for an officer of the Library in the area of public relations – but also helped him develop a knowledge of the Library's collections seldom equalled by any other member of staff, before or since. In this, as in so many other respects, he will be sadly missed.

His aptitude for public relations was also unsurpassed. He has the capacity to communicate easily with persons of every age and social background. His accomplishments in this regard emerge, in particular, in the realm of public speaking. I have heard him deliver many public tributes to staff members at all levels on their retirement. Sometimes it happens that such occasions coincide closely one with another. Even under such circumstances he managed, through his ability to capture the unique qualities of each personality, to bring a freshness and immediacy to every such occasion. This he did for persons who spent only a few years in the institution no less eloquently than for those who had given a lifetime's service. Only someone endowed with an unusual degree of human understanding and insight could be capable of so doing. Indeed, I have often wondered whether Dónall's gifts in the foregoing areas might not have found greater scope in a diplomatic career rather than within the confines of a library. Be this as it may, our institution has reaped untold benefit from his long and selfless career within its precincts.

It is our earnest hope that in retirement Dónall will find the time, long denied him by the demands of a busy daily schedule in Kildare Street, to devote to the subjects closest to his heart. In his main area of interest, Franco-Irish relations, he has, no doubt, much to contribute. He may rest assured that in his new *persona* as reader – or consumer, as the current jargon would have it – we will endeavour to make him some small return for the assistance, courtesy and consideration which he himself has extended to untold thousands in the course of his long and estimable career.

The writings of Dónall Ó Luanaigh

Ciara McDonnell

'Irishmen and the Franco-German war, 1870–1871', *Capuchin Annual*, 1971, 155–63.

With Sean Cooney, *Union list of current periodicals and serials in Irish libraries, 1972*, 2 vols (Dublin, [1972]).

'Ireland and the Paris commune, 1871', *Capuchin Annual*, 1972, 233–46.

'David B. Warden – fear nár thuill go ndearmadfaí é', *Inniu*, 7 Meán Fomhair 1973.

'Father Keller of Youghal – a patriot of the Land War', *St Vincent's Hospital Annual*, 1973, 18–22.

'Ireland and the Franco-Prussian war', *Éire-Ireland*, 9:1 (Spring 1974), 3–13.

'The dean of Kildare and a revolution in France: Thomas Trench's account of events in Paris towards the end of July 1830', *Irish Sword*, 14:55 (Winter 1980), 129–34.

'"J'ai débarqué à Calais, et l'aventure a commencé": voyageurs Irlandais en France, du 17ème au 19ème siècle', *Contacts*, 20 (Automne 1981), 28–30.

'Roger Casement, senior, and the siege of Paris (1870)', *Irish Sword*, 15:58 (Summer 1982), 33–5.

'Suspected importation of Fenian guns through the port of Waterford', *Decies: Journal of the Waterford Archaeological and Historical Society*, 22 (January 1983), 29–32.

'The French connection: some French visitors to Galway in olden times', *Connacht Tribune, 1909–1984: 75th anniversary supplement*, 29 June 1984.

'Contemporary Irish comments concerning the revolution of July 1830 in France', *Éire-Ireland*, 22:2 (Summer 1987), 96–115.

'Tawin's adopted English son who was an unsung defender of Irish culture', *Connacht Tribune*, 14 August 1987.

'Eighty years after Eugénie', *Cara: the inflight magazine of Aer Lingus*, 22:6 (November/December 1989), 6.

'Fenianism and France in March 1867: some comments on the Irish insurrection', *Études Irlandaises*, 15:2 (December 1990), 105–12.

'Marie Antoinette painting in Dublin', *Dublin Historical Record*, 46:1 (Spring 1993), 67.

Foreword to Alf Mac Lochlainn and Andrée Sheehy Skeffington, *Writers, raconteurs and notable feminists: two monographs* (Dublin, 1993), p. 3.

With Noel Kissane, 'Printed books', in Noel Kissane (ed.), *Treasures from the National Library of Ireland* ([Drogheda], 1994), pp 11–33.

'A gentleman of the press: William J.H. Brayden OBE (1865–1933)', *Dublin Historical Record*, 47:1 (Spring 1994), 103–4.

'Glimpses of the 1916 Rising in Co. Galway', *Galway Roots*, 2 (1994), 30–1.

'A railway pioneer looks at Galway', *Galway Roots*, 2 (1994), 1–5.

'Inter-church appeal for relief of distress in Galway, 1831', *Galway Roots*, 2 (1994), 20–3.

'Popular outbreaks in Galway, September–October 1846', *Galway Roots*, 3 (1995), 44–6.

'A UCG professor and the Easter Rising, 1916', *Galway Roots*, 3 (1995), 61–3.

Introduction to Maurice Semple, *Around and about Galway* (Galway, 1995), pp 5–6.

'Great and awful earthquake in Ireland: account of an "earthquake" in Connemara in 1821', *Galway Roots*, 4 (1996), 67.

'The Rev. J. Duncan Craig: an Irish chaplain in the Franco-Prussian war', *Dublin Historical Record*, 50:1 (Spring 1997), 76–8.

'Glimpses of Drumcondra in the time of the young James Joyce', *Dublin Historical Record*, 50:2 (Autumn 1997), 189–95.

'Prince Napoléon's visit to Dublin and Kerry in August 1865', *Dublin Historical Record*, 53:1 (Spring 2000), 71–6.

Obituary, 'Dr Patrick (Paddy) Henchy: promoted major development of National Library', *Irish Times*, 12 May 2001.

Obituary, 'Patrick Henchy', *Library Association Record*, 103:9 (2001), 562.

'Nóra Ní Shúilleabháin (RIP): some personal recollections', *The Kerry Magazine*, 13 (2002), 20–1.

'Richard J. Hayes', in the Royal Irish Academy's *Dictionary of Irish biography* (Cambridge, forthcoming).

The keeper of collections

for Dónall Ó Luanaigh

The empty reading room, blue light of the moon
Through the ribbed frosted skylight overhead.

An echoing footstep on the floor, nobody there,
A slight sway in the air between bare tables.

A green shaded lamp in the far corner, a sigh
Turns the pages of a thick bound book.

Someone smoothing the paper, squaring the edges:
The Keeper at night, keeping his hand in.

THEO DORGAN

How librarians and writers collaborate: George Moore, W.K. Magee and Richard Best

Adrian Frazier[1]

IN THE 1890s, early in its history, the National Library of Ireland was espe-cially hospitable to young men of a literary bent. The Trinity College scholar Edward Dowden was then a trustee of the Library and served more than one turn as the chairman of its council. In the 1890s, he rewarded favourite pupils – those who had won prizes for poetry or composition, or who had come first in the examinations – with posts at the Library. W.K. Magee won four prizes at Trinity from 1889 to 1893, then became sub-librarian. Richard Best did well in his exams in 1895 (a 'senior bachelor'), spent some years in Paris rooming with J.M. Synge, then returned to find a job awaiting him in the Library. T.W. Lyster, the head librarian until 1920, was another protégé of Dowden. All three men were literary, scholarly and Protestant – and, strangely, all of Ulster ances-try. They shared Dowden's sense that Ireland was and should remain part of a modernizing, English-speaking strand in European civilization; that is what the Union meant to them. While Magee and Best were closely involved with lead-ers of the literary revival, they were followers not of Yeats but of Dowden.

It goes with being a librarian that one often assists in projects which one does not wholly approve of. From a few sidelights in the letters of Yeats and Joyce, one can see how the Library itself and its staff were at the centre of the literary revival, even when they did not approve the narrowness of its nation-alism or the occasionally Roman Catholic thrust of its politics. In 1898, to adver-tise the Irish Literary Theatre, Yeats and Lady Gregory cooked up a contro-versy in the *Daily Express* about the proper objects of great literature. Yeats thought ancient legends, national customs, and symbolism were the pathway to modern literature, and he drew W.K. Magee into argument on this score. Magee thought Yeats wrong right down the line. Modern literature, he thought, should be about modern European life; it should not narrow its character to fit one tribe, especially in a way that exalted one's own people, but should broaden its scope to include universal humanity;[2] and finally, he considered Wordsworth

1 Based on a lecture given to the National Library of Ireland Society, Dublin, 12 Dec. 2002.
2 J. Eglinton, *Bards and saints* (Dublin, 1906), pp 39–40.

to be a better model for a young poet than a symbolist like Mallarmé. These
views were not simply written in private and then posted in to the editorial
office of the *Daily Express*. In early November and December of 1898, Yeats
was going to the National Library to seek authorities for his opinions. He sat
in a private passage outside the Reading Room – evidently behind the gate and
to the side of the office – to be in solitude and away from the draughts. Every
once in a while, W.K. Magee (pen name 'John Eglinton') would come out of
the office and argue with him in the corridor; then each would go back to writing out his latest contentions.³ A few weeks later, Lady Gregory came to Dublin
and had Magee over to dinner with Æ. He was, she noted, 'a nice quiet young
fellow, but he was quickly dragged away from his tea by the rushing Yeats'.⁴
The next time Lady Gregory met Magee, she found him openly discouraged.
He could not keep pace with Yeats – his old schoolmate – and was thinking of
giving up writing altogether.⁵

Four years later, when the young James Joyce returned from his first brief
sojourn in Paris, he met up with his friend Oliver St John Gogarty at the Library
early in 1903. Gogarty introduced Joyce to Richard Best and W.K. Magee. The
latter were a bit suspicious of the new University College, Dublin graduates –
people like Francis Sheehy Skeffington, Joyce, Gogarty and Tom Kettle – with
their bawdy jokes, 'seedy hauteur' (Magee's phrase) and flash intellectual style.
Every reader of *Ulysses* remembers the scene in the Library in which the
Shakespeare/Bacon controversy is batted around by Magee, Best, Buck Mulligan,
Stephen Dedalus and others. Dedalus calls Magee 'uglington', an allusion at once
to Magee's pen name, 'John Eglinton', and to his appearance, 'dwarfish, brown-
clad, with red-brown eyes like a ferret' and scruffy red hair, in the description of
Stanislaus Joyce. In 1904, when Magee started a magazine called *Dana*, he asked
Joyce for a contribution, and paid him for it. Yet subsequently Magee turned
down an early essay version of *A Portrait of the Artist*, saying: 'I can't print what I
can't understand.'⁶ Magee's father was Belfast-born Revd Hamilton Magee, head
of the Presbyterian Mission in Dublin devoted to the conversion of Roman
Catholics. Joyce's loyal brother Stanislaus thought the *Dana* editor simply did not
like Catholics, especially James Joyce, no stranger to Nighttown (Joyce called
Magee 'the horrible virgin').⁷ But the rejection of his manuscript did not stop the

3 W.B. Yeats to Lady Gregory, 6 December 1898: W. Gould, J. Kelly and D. Toomey (eds),
The collected letters of W.B. Yeats, ii: *1896–1900* (Oxford, 1996), p. 313.   4 J. Pethica (ed.), *Lady
Gregory's diaries, 1892–1902* (Gerrards Cross, Bucks., 1996), p. 198.   5 Ibid., p. 246.   6 J.
Eglinton, *Irish literary portraits* (London, 1935), p. 136.   7 A. Mac Lochlainn, '"Those young
men …": the National Library of Ireland and the cultural revolution', in *Writers, raconteurs and
notable feminists: two monographs*, with a foreword by D. Ó Luanaigh (Dublin, 1993), p. 14.

novelist: 'Jim is now beginning his novel', Stanislaus noted in his diary, 'as he usually begins things, half in anger.'[8] Thus, paradoxically, fury with the assistant librarian may have spurred the novelist to turn an essay into one of the classic fictions of the twentieth century, *A Portrait of the Artist as a Young Man.*

As a controversialist, editor and essayist, Magee contributed – and not always indirectly – to the Irish literary revival, but as librarian he was perhaps an even greater influence. Certainly he was upon one writer, George Moore. Their relationship was all that that between a librarian and patron might be, as well as being much more than that – being, ultimately, a relationship between friends. At a lending library, the desk person is often asked by a reader to recommend a book. The good librarian does not suggest a book he or she thinks personally most interesting, but a book that that particular reader will enjoy or benefit by. In that capacity, Magee was from the start of their relationship a good librarian for Moore. Often the novelist would appear just as the Library was closing in order to go for a walk through the streets with Magee or Best. At other times, he would meet the librarians in a little café in the building, until that pleasant institution was closed by the head librarian, causing Moore to begin a rhyme on the pattern of 'Who killed Cock Robin', a rhyme he hoped Gogarty would complete: 'Who killed the café? / I did, said Cock Lyster, with my little blister …'

When Moore would inveigle the librarians into conversation, they would talk together of Ireland: not of Ireland as a subject of political controversy, but as a subject for literature. From what angle of approach might it best be addressed? Magee suggested that Moore read – which he had not yet done – *Don Quixote*. Indeed, one hears John Eglinton repeat the suggestion in Joyce's *Ulysses*. The hint bore fruit. From Cervantes' novel, Moore derived a major theme in his trilogy *Hail and Farewell*: the hero's quixotic mission to save Ireland from Roman Catholicism. He also borrowed the relationship between its two major characters: Moore and Edward Martyn stand to one another like Quixote and Sancho Panza. Another inspired suggestion from Magee was Rousseau's *Confessions,* in a certain English translation. From his reading years earlier of volume one in French, Moore had been converted to Rousseau's gospel of shamelessness; the rereading led him further to the unbuttoned disclosures of *Memoirs of My Dead Life*, published in 1906. The most fruitful suggestion of all, however, was made on the amble home after a dinner party with Professor Dowden at the Provost's House. Moore had just remarked that he was thinking of writing a book of interlinked stories about Irish life. 'And the face that would be ugly if unlighted

---

8 S. Joyce, *Dublin diary* (Ithaca, NY, 1971), pp 147–8.

by intelligence lit up', Moore says, as Magee inquired: 'Like Turgenev's *Tales of a Sportsman*?'[9] Moore 'caught the suggestion', reread the book and, on subsequent strolls around Merrion Square or St Stephen's Green, would explain to Magee how one or another scene in the great Russian's book *should* have been constructed – and would be, he might have added, in his own *The Untilled Field*, published in 1903, those highly personal and lordly, affectionate stories of life in the provinces, far from that Paris beloved of both Turgenev and Moore.[10] A decade later, Moore handsomely thanked his librarian friends, saying: 'I didn't know how to write until I went over to Ireland – it was you fellows that taught me; and in *The Untilled Field*, my first book written in Ireland, you had only just put me in the right road. It was a book of transition, in style, and I hope you will think that I did well to shove it over the frontier.'[11]

To judge from his correspondence, when Moore left Dublin for residence in London in 1910, one of the things he missed most was its great National Library, and two of the people he missed most were Best and Magee. Distance, however, did not prevent the novelist from attempting to avail himself of their services. Moore had a number of common assumptions about librarians. First, he believed that they were there to serve others – himself above all – whenever he had need of service. Secondly, he believed that librarians were generally highly educated people with a strict sense of what is correct, both in spelling, grammar, diction and all other forms; they were professors of perfect formality and therefore ideal fact-checkers and proof-readers. Thirdly, he believed librarians had all information at their command and the leisure to search through it for the answer to whatever question landed on their desk. These assumptions, however common, made Moore an unusually trying friend for the two librarians. He was surely as much work as a coachful of Americans seeking assistance in the search for their Irish ancestors.

In 1911, just a year after he left Dublin, Moore was begging Magee to supervise the passage through Maunsel Press of the proofs of his play, *The Apostle*: 'It won't take you an hour to glance through the revise', he wheedled, and 'it would be better to do it in [George] Roberts' shop' than to have it sent over to the Library. 'O, if you will only take the tram, the dear tram I shall never see again, and go down … I shall be very grateful. Yours, George Moore.'[12] Once Magee went through the proofs and reported back to Moore solely on the subject of typesetting mistakes, not of the theme or upon infelicities of phrase, Moore stubbed his toe on what he took to be yet another attribute of librarians: their

9 G. Moore, *Salve* (London, 1937), p. 121. **10** Eglinton, *Irish literary portraits*, p. 4. **11** J. Eglinton (ed.), *Letters of George Moore* (Bournemouth, 1942), pp 22–3. **12** George Moore to W.K. Magee, 6 Apr. 1911, Harry Ransom Humanities Research Center, University of Texas, Austin, TX; hereafter cited as HRHRC.

reluctance to advance any direct expression of opinion. Librarians, he concluded, are averse to offering anything other than technical assistance; they do not express an opinion on the value of a project. Moore needled Magee that he would like to know if the action of the play was being carried in the right direction, but he understood that it would be a 'violation of [Magee's] instinctive nature' to let his own view of these questions be known.[13] Could not Magee at least go as far as letting the writer know if the language of the play ought to be a little more archaic, or a little less? Evidently, in addition to the librarians' customary professional discretion, Magee was not eager to participate in concocting a scenario along the lines of *The Apostle*, in which Jesus does not die on the cross and therefore was *not* resurrected, but remains alive to meet St. Paul in the flesh, who is shown to be preaching a religion with an entirely false basis in fact.

Moore's next task for Magee was an imposition perhaps unparalleled elsewhere in the experience of librarians. The novelist was trying to finish *Salve*, volume two of his autobiographical trilogy about the ten years he spent in Dublin. For one scene, he wished to describe a house in which he planned to install for the purposes of his story – entirely fictitiously – his mistress, the original of whom, Clara Christian, had died in 1906. Moore told Magee he had seen the model for such a house just once, when looking for a residence for himself. He gave Magee the following information: the house was in Clondalkin; Moore had bicycled there in 1901; it had a moat; there was water in that moat. Then came the request: 'I shall feel obliged if you will cycle out there and write me a few particulars about the house, the moat and the situation. Is there a view of the Dublin mountains from the windows?' The letter concludes with self-contradictory impatience: 'I don't want to hurry you, but the first part of my manuscript is due at the printers.'[14] So pushy and coaxing was Moore in a second letter making the same request that Magee actually did get on his bicycle and headed off for Clondalkin. It happened to be a cold day, with a biting wind, and there is a hill between Kildare Street and Clondalkin; the little man – by then 44 years old – became very tired. Once he had arrived in Clondalkin and made extensive inquiries, he found that there were in the area not one, but two houses with moats. Magee described them both, but not in the way Moore wished – so he asked Magee to do it over again. Evidently, Magee did so; and he also suggested a mock-scriptural title for an episode at the climax of the book, 'Jubiliation in the garden'.[15] For such service, there ought to have been an award – some ceremonial plaque for services to readers above and beyond the call of duty – for the year 1912 and presented at a banquet for the sub-librarian of the National Library.

13 George Moore to W.K. Magee, 11 Apr. 1911, HRHRC. **14** George Moore to W.K Magee, 1 Feb. 1912, HRHRC. **15** Eglinton, *Letters of George Moore*, p. 19.

Moore's next big project was based on the scenario for *The Apostle*, nothing less than a novel that incorporated and supplanted the gospels. It would have three major characters: Jesus, Paul and Joseph of Arimathea, the last being developed as a kind of stand-in for the young George Moore. This particular author was not especially well positioned, one might think, to take on such a subject. Moore had no natural feeling for religion, and no scholarly knowledge of it. He had no Latin at all, and no Greek. He had never been to the Holy Land. But that was no real obstacle, Moore concluded, because his librarian friend had what he did not: the travel experience,[16] some of the relevant languages and the knowledge of history and religion. Indeed, it was Magee who got the whole thing off the ground by mentioning, apparently in the room behind the library desk, beside a fire still lit in those days, that he had come across an article by a German scholar which made a case that it was entirely possible that crucifixion was not always a death penalty and that Jesus in particular may well have been survived it.

Once Moore got started on his epic novel, he did repair some of his deficits. He read the Bible, for instance – which was an excellent beginning – then commentaries upon it, the works of Josephus and some of Suetonius and Pliny, and he travelled to Palestine. But primarily his stock of knowledge was Magee and the National Library. From the desk of composition, he would dash off importunate letters that posed questions like the following:[17]

- I must know something about the towns in Galilee and Judea at that time. Travels in Asia Minor, in Palestine, books of that kind would be of great use to me (19 January 1914).
- In my story I shall have to make a good deal of Joseph of Arimathea. Where is Arimathea? (2 May 1914)
- How did the Jews get rich in those times? (2 May 1914).
- And now I have to ask you where is Calvary? (2 May 1914).
- I believe the [cross] to have been a sort of pillory – I don't believe very firmly in the nails. Am I right? (2 May 1914).

Magee answered such questions, and put questions of his own:

- What could Moore possibly mean by saying that Paul never looked upon Jesus as God, and that Jesus himself only believed in his godhead at times? (11 July 1914).

16 In 1907 Magee travelled to the Mediterranean, stopping for a time in Nazareth; see W.K. Magee to James Starkey, 25 Mar. 1907, Trinity College, Dublin, O'Sullivan correspondence, MSS 4,630–49. 17 Magee's correspondence with Moore, paraphrased and quoted below, is at the HRHRC.

- How could he call Jesus 'one of the most terrifying fanatics that ever lived in the world', and say that 'he out-Nietzsched Nietzsche in the awful things he says in the gospel of Luke'? (27 July 1914).
- What did Jesus say that caused Moore to accuse him of 'blasphemy against life'? (30 July 1914)
- How could Moore believe Judas was right to betray his master? What could Moore possibly mean by his phrase in which God is called 'the last uncleanliness of the mind' by Jesus himself? (15 November 1915).
- Was it a sufficient basis for Moore's development of Paul as the past lover of Eunice and father of Timothy that 'in literary composition it would be impossible to have three men and each of them a virgin'? (21 March 1916).

To Magee's puritanical objections to his stories, Moore rejoined: 'You write very stiffly. But are you sure your prejudices are not those of a discredited little sect whose importance in Europe is infinitesimal … Your intellectual calm, though it has freed you from the fable of the Virgin birth … has not been sufficient to free you from the [fable of sexual morality].'[18] So much for Presbyternianism. Joyce could not have been more condescending as an ex-Catholic to a current Protestant. The novelist was unshaken in his intuitions and fancies. Amazingly enough, *The Brook Kerith*, upon its publication in 1916, struck many scholars and clergy as not just shocking but remarkably honest and well-informed.[19]

Moore appreciated Magee's assistance profoundly; indeed, he appreciated Magee's whole sensibility, but was also bewildered by it. No one's letters, he confessed, did he receive with more excitement than those of Magee. In one of many stirring tributes from one man to the other, Moore wrote: 'Behind your simplest sentences there is a mind, or quality of mind, that charms me.' Why wouldn't Magee put that mind on display more frequently in works of literature? Why was he content, as he said, with conservation?[20] 'Of what use is it to write?', Magee forlornly asked in reply: 'A sufficient amount that is great has already been written.' 'Of course there is no use', Moore answered: 'The planet is burning up and will one day be as sterile as the moon, with traces of Hellenic civilization lying about and a stray volume of Shakespeare; but meantime, if you were to write, you would pass your own time away pleasantly and give a good deal of pleasure to your friends.'[21] In supplement to this excellent answer, Moore continued to chaff, beg and plead with his friend to write − not just to help another to write.

18 George Moore to W.K. Magee, 16 Apr. 1918, HRHRC.   **19** See A. Frazier, *George Moore, 1852–1933* (New Haven and London, 2000), p. 403, for a summary of the favourable reviews.   **20** George Moore to W.K. Magee, 28 Mar. 1916, HRHRC.

By means of a cluster of letters to Kildare Street in July 1915, Moore proposed a collaboration on a topic he thought might please them both. The result would be inserted within *The Brook Kerith*. First, he asked Magee to look up an article in *La Revue de Paris* that appeared when Moore was living in Dublin, a period of ten full years for a monthly – in other words, 120 issues of double-column pages. Magee declined to carry out the search, but Moore was unrelenting. The subject 'could not but interest' the librarian. It was an article about a newly discovered fragment of Menander. Moore considered that he had himself subsequently found another quotation from Menander in the writings of St Paul. What if one of the characters in Moore's novel of gospel times goes to a play by Menander? The play could be the missing one from which the fragment was recently discovered. Moore would write a seemingly suitable scene in English that Magee could put into Menander-ish Greek. This fabrication would then be passed off as a major, inexplicable recovery of the classical world occurring in the midst of a contemporary English novel[22] – that, Moore concluded, would surely 'have a smack of the National Library and Magee upon it'.[23]

Yet this was not a game Magee would play. It seemed a pity to Moore that Magee would never follow a thing up, whether it was his own idea or Moore's. Magee used the English language, the novelist admitted, just as he should himself like to be able to use it.[24] It was, of course, pleasant to be able to avail himself of Magee's unequalled sense of the unusual but right turn of phrase. This was especially useful in the course of revision of his own proofs, but why not employ that talent on works to be signed by Magee himself – or rather by his *nom de plume* 'John Eglinton'? His 'gnarled style' and 'kindly heart' were qualities that deserved preservation in print. Certain sentences crafted by the librarian remained cherished possessions of the novelist – such as this one, which might otherwise have come from Walter Pater or Walter Savage Landor: 'Walking in the woods, or by the seashore, or among men, it often happens that a man experiences a rising of the tide of perception, life inundates consciousness and, as it recedes, casts up in his brain a melody, a gospel, an idea.'[25]

But Magee was usually proof against Moore's anger and cozening. Something in him wished to remain unknown; and something also made him believe himself better than all writers then writing. It was a case of a man paradoxically blocked by both extreme pride and extreme humility. Moore was able, if very painfully, to accept that he would never be bigger than he, in fact, was – or, as

21 Eglinton, *Letters of George Moore*, pp 22–3.   22 George Moore to W.K. Magee, 30 July [1915], HRHRC.   23 George Moore to W.K. Magee, 31 July 1915, HRHRC.   24 George Moore to W.K. Magee, 18 Dec. 1915, HRHRC.   25 George Moore to W.K. Magee, 9 Nov. 1916, HRHRC.

he more vulgarly phrased it once, 'you can't fart higher than your arse'. Magee seems to have felt that to be less great than Yeats was to be of no value at all. Often enough, he employed as an excuse for not undertaking an extensive literary project that his duties at the Library, seven hours a day, 'squelched all the literary life' out of him.[26]

Moore did praise Magee's occasional articles for the *Irish Statesman* in the late 'teens; furthermore, he obtained commissions from J.L. Garvin for articles to appear in the *Observer*. Subsequently, Magee was given a post with the American *Dial*, providing its 'Irish letter'. The significance of this post will be evident when you consider that at the time Ezra Pound provided the 'Paris letter' and T.S. Eliot the 'London letter' for the same monthly. Magee's articles provided one of the first, and still one of the best-informed, accounts of the Irish literary revival. The actual achievements of that movement have often been exaggerated because of its affiliation with the movement toward national independence, but Magee was undeceived. 'The bulk of Anglo-Irish literature', he informed American readers, was 'uncanonical' – both unreflective of Catholic Ireland and unworthy of a place with the best that had been thought and said.[27] These well-paid articles combined with other circumstances to launch John Eglinton on a late-starting career as a serious critic.

What were those other circumstances? First of all, Magee formed a relationship with a young female employee of the Library, a Catholic, named Mary Louise O'Leary. She converted to Protestantism, and they were married on 6 April 1920. Secondly, the events of the War of Independence and the Civil War, especially the conflagration of the ancient archives of Ireland in the Public Record Office at the Four Courts in 1922, caused him to come to the conclusion that Ireland was no longer hospitable to northern Protestants like himself. Thirdly, the political situation in Ireland brought about cutbacks in the budget for the Library, so there was a shortage of staff and the workload became heavier. Finally, the Anglo-Irish Treaty of 1921 offered early pensions to civil servants who did not care to continue their employment under the Irish Free State. Exhausted, Magee remarked, with lamely answering inquiries from patrons such as 'where shall I find some material for the history of the press gang?', he accepted retirement in 1921 and moved to Wales in 1923.[28]

Thereafter, Moore resorted to the services of his remaining friend at the Library, Richard Best. He had already benefited from Best's scholarly habit of ticking the mistakes he noticed in books he was reading. On the first occasion

26 Eglinton, *Letters of George Moore*, pp 26–7. **27** J. Eglinton, 'Dublin letter', *Dial*, May 1921, 332. **28** W.K. Magee, *Confidential: or, Take it or leave it* (London, 1951), p. 9; National Library of Ireland, *Report of the Council of Trustees for 1922–1923* (Dublin, 1923).

when Moore saw one of his books in Best's possession, he was staggered by the great number of ticks in the margins. Subsequently, he applied to Best to read his page proofs. As he had done with Magee, Moore tried to get Best started on a literary project of his own – particularly, in 1914, a memoir of Best's time in Paris with Synge. 'But I can't write', Best shyly responded: 'It would be all so trivial. I told [the French scholar Maurice] Bougeois most that was of interest.'[29] Best had a temperament not entirely common to librarians, but was perhaps more at home in a library than elsewhere. He cared for the scholarly record rather than for the pleasure or glory of scholarship, much less independent authorship. Yet while he had a passion for custodianship of knowledge of the past, he held teaching in contempt. University College, Dublin was nothing, he snorted, but 'an examination-ridden shop', one that was becoming increasingly clerical in its administration – 'ultimately', he concluded, 'a sort of Maynooth'.[30] His greatest passion was for the 'think-tank' atmosphere of the School of Irish Learning founded by Kuno Meyer in 1903; Best was its honorary secretary throughout the school's existence.[31] Best's belief in the European centrality of early Irish culture was profound, and his knowledge of its manuscripts was extensive. It was on this score that the novelist sought him out. Magee was not ignorant of Ireland's ancient literature, but he was more of an amateur classicist and scholar of modern European literatures. Moore himself knew no Irish, and no Greek, Latin or German; his French was confident, but not correct.

In 1917 Moore decided to take up a hint dropped in a book by Kuno Meyer, a collection of his translations of ancient Irish poetry. Moore himself would compose a cycle of stories set in medieval Ireland. There would be two main threads: Catholic celibates and woodland sex. Each would intensify the other. For the verisimilitude of his reconstruction of medieval Ireland, the novelist relied almost entirely on Best. For a story about a Frenchman coming to Ireland on a mission – bringing a wolfhound from the Pyrenees – who lodges at a convent and makes love to all the nuns, Moore asked Best to supply:[32]

1. A description of a medieval Irish nunnery.
2. An account of routes across Ireland.
3. A list of ports active in the period.

29 R.I. Best to Kuno Meyer, 2 June [1914], National Library of Ireland, NLI MS 11,002 (61).   **30** R.I. Best to Kuno Meyer, 6 Apr. 1914, ibid.   **31** *Ériu* 9 (1921–3), 181; *Fiftieth anniversary report, School of Celtic Studies* (Dublin, 1990), pp 3–4. As it was not supported by public funds in the new Irish state, the School of Irish Learning was eventually absorbed into the Royal Irish Academy.   **32** George Moore to R.I. Best, 21 Mar., 3, 5, 9 Apr. 1917, HRHRC.

4. A contemporary account of a journey across the country to Mayo.

5. A name for the Frenchman.

6. Names for the nuns.

7. Verification of the tale he had heard of Irishmen sitting around a fire naked and talking Latin.

8. The facts about the forests of Ireland – how extensive they were, of what species etc.

9. A spelling for the Irish word for storyteller, *seanchaí*.

That was just for the first of his cycle of tales. Later, he requested the best translation available of the Sweeney story. He offered to pay Best – 'price no object', he added – for translations of ancient texts that might be useful to him. Best did the translations, but refused payment. He liked to indulge Moore; it was a way of indulging himself. As he explained to his friend Kuno Meyer: 'It is a sort of spiritual refresher … to emerge from your shell into the outer world of artists.' 'A periodical airing of this kind' did him a lot of good.[33] Moore enjoyed his side of the collaboration as well, but was outraged – 'Fie for shame on the truly national', he cried – when the Library refused to buy *The Story-teller's Holiday* because there was too much sex in it.[34]

In 1923 Moore applied once again to Best for help with an Irish tale, the novel *Ulick and Soracha*. What would one call an Irish Don Juan of the twelfth century?[35] What would be served at a feast in Castle Carra, Co. Mayo, in medieval times –'venison, wild swine, kid, lamb, sirloin'? Did they eat cakes? Sweetened with what? Honey? There was no sugar. And what did they drink, mead and beer?[36] Ten days later, the librarian sent pages and pages of detailed replies to these historical questions, so much that Moore felt ashamed of himself – and he almost never felt that way whatever the provocation.[37] Best continued to supply reader services to the novelist up to within months of his death. In 1932 his list of corrections on the page proofs of Moore's last novel, *Aphrodite at Aulis*, was so long and precise that it infuriated the old man. It would spoil the book, Moore complained, to speak of the bronzes of Phidias, rather than his marble statues; the whole conception was of a sculptor. Anyway, beauty was Moore's aim – not erudition. Erudition was simply a means, however essential it was to his methods of composition.

When Moore died, after years of obstreperous youth and crabby old age, he had few enough friends left to observe his passing with regret. However, among

33 R.I. Best to Kuno Meyer, 17 Apr. 1914, National Library of Ireland, NLI MS 11,002 (61). **34** George Moore to W.K. Magee, [June? 1919], HRHRC. **35** George Moore to R.I. Best, 17 Oct. 1923, HRHRC. **36** George Moore to R.I. Best, 2 Oct. 1924, HRHRC. **37** George Moore to R.I. Best, 14 Oct. 1924, HRHRC.

those present at the Golders Green chapel in London prior to his cremation was W.K. Magee. He came up from his home in Bournemouth for the purpose; Magee, his wife and their young son had moved to Bournemouth from Prestatyn, in Wales, in 1928. The ashes were then taken to Mayo for burial on an island in Lough Carra and Richard Best was among the half-dozen present for the internment. Indeed, it was Best who read out the memorial address written by Æ.

Not many people at the time knew how much influence the two librarians had had on the works of George Moore. The whole turn in his work after 1900 to a more perfect English depended on the more perfect sense of grammar and diction supplied at the proof-reading stage by Magee and Best. His historical fiction – *The Brook Kerith, A Story-Teller's Holiday, Heloise and Abelard* and *Ulick and Soracha* – would not have been possible without their aid, and the change from modern realistic fiction to historical romance is the chief transition in Moore's career as a prose writer. The irony is that Moore's exploitation of the reliques of ancient Irish literature, which time and again undermined the pieties of cultural nationalism, was fed by the sceptical and somewhat unionist learned friends he had in Kildare Street.

One should not, however, confine one's sense of the National Library's importance to its effect on one writer. The construction and endowment of a great national library in the heart of Dublin significantly shaped the Irish literary revival as a whole. That revival, as its name partly suggests, was founded on seeking inspiration from Ireland's history, ancient beliefs and native language. Many of those participating in the revival – through the composition of plays, poems, and stories – did not themselves know much of the history or language of Ireland. Not knowing, they did just what anyone now would do: they went to the National Library and asked for help. The National Library was, just as it is represented in *Ulysses*, a central gathering place for writers – writers who engaged in learned conversation over the counter with librarians. The librarians were, as their profession required them to be, modest, helpful and reticent of opinion. But at heart, they knew much of the revival's ideology was founded on passion, not research – and on sectarianism, not high culture. So when they did permit themselves to make a remark, it was often to express scepticism about the new Ireland. This attitude had an overall influence on the vague mysticism of the early revival; it encouraged that emerging belief-system to be more controversialist, more intellectual, more pedantic. The fact that the works of Yeats, Joyce and Moore are all remarkably scholarly and allusive pieces of literature may partly be the reflection of international modernism, but it is also a result of the presence in Dublin at the turn of the century of the National Library of Ireland, staffed by learned and very literary librarians.

The National Library of Ireland, 1890–1983: informal perspectives

Gerard Long

OFFICIAL SOURCES ARE invaluable for the history of the National Library of Ireland, as they are for any government institution. The most important single source for the National Library is the annual reports of the council of trustees, the first of which covers 1877, the year in which the Library was established by the Dublin Science and Art Museum Act. There are, however, other sources, such as newspaper interviews, articles, memoirs and imaginative literature, which may lack the authority of official publications, are sometimes tendentious and not necessarily concerned with strict accuracy, but which compensate by having a greater liberty of expression and frequently a more personal or anecdotal approach. This essay uses a number of such sources to give an informal portrait of the Library, its readers and staff, and of the public perception of the institution between 1890 and 1983, focusing as much on individuals as on events. It is, of necessity, a very selective approach; several important events in the Library's history are entirely ignored.[1]

Most famous of the readers is, of course, James Joyce. The Library appears in *A Portrait of the Artist as a Young Man*, *Stephen Hero*, and the 'Scylla and Charybdis' episode of *Ulysses*.[2] He is not the only novelist to use the Library as a setting. Lennox Robinson's only novel *A Young Man from the South* is the story of Willie Powell: from a Protestant and unionist background, he becomes involved in the cultural life of Dublin and turns into a nationalist and a playwright. As a social and intellectual centre where people from different backgrounds meet and interact, the Library plays a part in this process. The narrator recalls:

---

1 For a brief history of the Library, see G. Long, 'The National Library of Ireland', in A. Black and P. Hoare (eds), *The Cambridge history of libraries in Britain and Ireland*, iii: *1850–2000* (Cambridge, 2006), pp 266–75. 2 Joyce's connections with the National Library are described in A. MacLochlainn, '"Those young men …": the National Library of Ireland and the cultural revolution' in *Writers, raconteurs and notable feminists: two monographs*, with a foreword by D. Ó Luanaigh (Dublin, 1993). See also G. Long, *A twinge of recollection: the National Library of Ireland in 1904 and thereabouts* (Dublin, 2005).

I suggested that he should read at the National Library, and as my road home lay past it he walked there with us. We brought him even up the stairs and looked in on the reading room. I remember now that by a strange chance Isabel Moore [a character based to a degree on Countess Markievicz] and Gerald Twomey were sitting at a table near the door … It was a little curious (I continued) that his reading at the National Library should have led, on the occasion of his second visit, to an acquaintanceship with Gerald Twomey … He and Willie had chanced to sit side by side two nights running in the Library, had left the building together, and had found themselves turning in the same direction … I believe they met often after that at the Library.[3]

The popularity of the Library as a meeting place is described by 'K.K.K.', writing in the *Irish Independent* (2 October 1908):

Outside on the steps is the habitat of the students' parliament, the site of election, where they foregather to discuss the news of their world, and where their joys and sorrows are related and known … I have said that the Dublin student is not totally a creature of blood and iron. Even if he were, there is that in the Library that may convert him. For truth and exactness compel me to state that all its habitués do not belong to one stern sex … There are little journeys homewards, not alone, where the conversation may or may not be confined to subjects in the university calendar.

Several decades later Mary Lavin, a trustee of the Library for many years, observed this phenomenon and set a short story 'A Lucky Pair', which appears in the 1967 collection *In the Middle of the Fields*, in the Library and its environs. A notable user of the Library from *c*.1940 to 1980, she gave an account of her reminiscences of the Library in the film *Portrait of a Library* made in 1976 – in which she said that she had tried to repay her debt to the Library by featuring it in one of her stories.

A most interesting portrait of the Library is to be found in a novel entitled *The Irishman*, by John Weldon (better known as Brinsley MacNamara), published in 1920 under the pseudonym 'Oliver Blyth'. The protagonist Martin Duignan befriends one of the library assistants; the descriptions of the Library indicate the extent to which poets and writers frequented the reading room:

3 L. Robinson, *A young man from the south* (Dublin and London, 1917), pp 39, 40–2.

> He was fond of sitting down by the side of those whose names he soon learned – by Thomas MacDonagh and Pádraic Colum, and Sheehy Skeffington and Pádraic Pearse. It was here he entered into the friendship of Seán O'Hanlon. It began one evening that he had asked at the counter for a copy of Mr Yeats's poems. O'Hanlon immediately sprang into spiritual friendship with him … At the instigation of O'Hanlon, he had read the poems of Pádraig Pearse, Thomas MacDonagh, and Alice Milligan, whom he saw so often writing in the Library … Now and then he turned around to observe those who came in through the turnstiles, strangers to him for the most part, new students at University College, young men and women eager for jobs and knowledge … Then there were the famous, old frequenters, whose tastes were on histories and statistics and encyclopaedias, a dismal crowd.[4]

The character of O'Hanlon is based on the library assistant James Crawford Neil, who joined the Library staff in 1902 to replace John (Seán) T. O'Kelly, later president of Ireland, who had resigned. Among the regular readers was Arthur Griffith, journalist and politician, and Neil became a contributor to Griffith's *United Irishman* – in which, in September 1913, he published an article, 'Kildare Street', containing this description or interpretation of the Library:

> Though the reading room bears a share of journalists, literary hacks and lexicographers, the most of its habitués are young university students. Thither in the spring of its youth pours the young blood of the nation, poor and crude, but being still amenable to the ministration of the erythrocytes and scavenger phagocytes of culture, it becomes fine and enriched and then throbs back into the old veins – hearth, school, farm, dispensary or presbytery – with a heightened vigour.

Like his fictional counterpart O'Hanlon, Neil died in the 1916 Rising. He was engaged to the actress Gypsy Walker, sister of Máire Nic Shiubhlaigh. On the night of Easter Tuesday, returning from her home in Glasthule to Drumcondra where he lived, he was shot in the back on Liffey Street while attempting to prevent looting, and died a fortnight later.[5] His fellow assistant Paddy O'Connor was suspended from the Library because of his involvement in the Rising, but was later reinstated. The esteem in which the library assistants were held is indicated by this extract from *T.C.D.: A College Miscellany*:

4 J. Weldon (pseud. O. Blyth), *The Irishman* (London, 1920), pp 99, 126, 225; an American edition was published as *In clay and bronze* by B. MacNamara. **5** See G. Long, *A writer of great promise* (Bethesda, MD, 2006).

The system we would like to see adopted is that which prevails in the National Library in Kildare Street. There the seeker after knowledge finds at his service many clerks, young in years, but surpassing the angels for wisdom and helpfulness. It is only necessary to murmur a vague desire for light upon any subject and immediately they can name all the books dealing with it however remotely, and not only that, but find them on the spot without needing minute directions to aid their research. It is like being served by genii out of the Arabian Nights, and the extravagant language of those admirable fictions would be a fitting medium in which to convey a grateful appreciation.[6]

A more irreverent note – though not at the expense of the Library's staff – is to be found in the following article, 'The unemployed', by 'Gee'. It is from *St Stephen's*, the University College, Dublin (UCD) student magazine:

Driven by a sudden shower of hail to seek shelter for some time in the reading room of the National Library, Kildare Street, I was amazed to notice the number of unemployed in this seemingly prosperous part of the city. At first I thought, that, like myself, the majority of the idle people in the reading room were only waiting for the shower to pass over, but on making enquiries from the gentleman presiding at the counter, I was informed that such was not the case – that these unfortunate people were in the reading room every day. My informant added that, in the summertime, they change from the reading room to the front steps. For the most part, they are extremely well dressed, in fact, some might say, that the better they were dressed, the more idle they looked; and instead of the dejected look one would naturally expect to see on the faces of people out of work they simply beamed contentment and enjoyment of life. Nor can I describe them as thin and starved-looking, for, on the contrary, they appeared well cared for and fat. Surely, thought I, some efforts have been made to give these people work. Efforts, I learn, have been made with indifferent success by various public bodies – principally, the Royal University of Ireland, the College of Surgeons and Physicians, and the executive committees of race meetings – perhaps, I should also mention the benchers of the King's Inns, Ireland; though some say that the amount of work they provide is infinitesimal.[7]

6 *T.C.D.: A College Miscellany* 18:329 (12 Feb. 1913), 2.   7 *St Stephen's: A Record of University Life*, 2:12 (May 1906), 271.

As this passage indicates despite its ironic tone, the Library was much used by students of all ages at this time – and particularly UCD students. One such, Constantine P. Curran – friend and contemporary of Joyce, and later a trustee of the Library – recalled his first visit to the building:

> Now, rising fifteen, I ventured into the National Library and, without the usual formality of introduction and reader's ticket, became a regular reader ... I ventured in, mounted the shining staircase to the rotunda where garlanded cherubs circled in a frieze over the bowed heads of attentive readers. The assistant librarian, then, I think, that fine naturalist Robert Lloyd Praeger, was at his post at the counter, a stalwart Nordic, sturdy as an oak tree. I timidly enquired if he had Donnelly's *The Great Cryptogram* and the files of Mitchel's *United Irishman*. He looked dubiously at me, but with humorous eyes. He asked me my age and had I a reader's ticket. Presently, T.W. Lyster was quietly beside me and I found myself conducted to a chair at a table, and the two big red and gold volumes of *The Great Cryptogram* planted carefully in front of me.[8]

Desmond Ryan likewise recalled the Library, and one of its best known and most loyal readers, Fr Patrick Dinneen, in his memoir *Remembering Sion*:

> Father Dinneen always sat at a table preparing his Irish dictionary in its future fullness and completeness of definitiveness or resurrecting the poets of Munster with suitable veils to their erratic strayings into taverns and wildness and heresy *en route* to fame in his editions and an edifying deathbed. Sometimes he turned earthwards, his lost blue eyes and wan face quickening, to read a light novel to refresh his mind before he passed through the turnstile for a breath of air or bent over the counter to talk amiably to the assistants.
>
> In their way these assistants struck me as being as learned as Father Dinneen or any one else in the commonwealth of letters and lore. They always warned you not to bother about the catalogue near the turnstile, but to ask them first since their memories were so good that they knew every book on every shelf ...
>
> At that time under the roof of the National Library fermented many minds which would stir Ireland in a few short years. Even as the students swallowed and digested all the knowledge necessary to pass from the Fairy City via examinations' halls, Arthur Griffith had learned much there

8 C.P. Curran, *Under the receding wave* (Dublin, 1970), pp 63–4.

and Connolly's pencil had scribbled many a note from the classics of socialism or perhaps from the musty files in the newspaper room below where he had gone to live and learn with Mitchel and Lalor in the red, hungry and futile year of Forty-Eight. Sheehy Skeffington had bustled in with shining eyes glowing in his vital and bearded face, all mirth and challenge from knickerbockers to whatever badge of defiance he wore on the lapel of his coat. James Joyce and Pádraic Colum and James Stephens and Thomas MacDonagh dipped and argued and brooded over the tables, and Father Dinneen went on with improvements to his dictionary and tracked down more and more melodious and repentant poets, and year and year after year the students passed out to strange cities and places ere tragedy should halt on the very steps outside.[9]

Fr Dinneen died on 29 September 1934. The *Irish Press* (2 October 1934) noted: 'Readers in the National Library will long remember the gentle-mannered and venerable old priest who was the most assiduous of all the many readers in the Library. Father Dinneen was actually reading in the Library on the day when he took ill.'

In *Life and the Dream*, Mary Colum has described how, as a student at UCD, she saw the Library.[10] From a slightly later generation, Kate O'Brien has recorded her memories:

When I sit in that reading room now in age, as often it is my pleasure to, I look up sometimes to the silly encirclement of naked amoretti or whatever they are, a décor surely eccentric, devised in the 1870s for our good and gravely intentioned library – I look up at them and at the dictionaries and biographies just below them – and try to remember forcedly, against the Proustian instruction, what this silent place used to mean when it was new to me, a gate and a revelation. And I cannot remember. All I can do is apprehend that indeed I was young, under this round roof – and at peace, restlessly and in confusion at peace. I remember of course, in the ordinary sense, a few unimportant things: as, being shown de Valera where he stood – when can that have been? – by the Irish dictionaries. He wore some terribly ugly black gaiters – an anti-hero who said nothing to immediate curiosity. With generations I remember Father Dinneen's messy bags of food. And there was a seminarist who used to hand me love letters at the turnstile. But of the real-

9 D. Ryan, *Remembering Sion: a chronicle of storm and quiet* (London, 1934), pp 71–3.   **10** M. Colum, *Life and the dream* (revised ed., Dublin, 1966), pp 86–7.

ity of long hours in that room, of reading Taine and Renan and Santayana, of being alarmed and enchanted, of silence and isolation and the catalogues leading on into mazes of questions, of cheeky librarians, of poets and friends and first readings of Joyce; of the weather beyond that window, of the love I had for the green lamps and the clacking book rests – of drifting out and down the street with the amusing, great friends of that time – to the Café Cairo, to the Grafton Picture House – through the Green, in the rain or over noisy leaves – all of that I do not well remember, but only apprehend it – in a kind of desolation.[11]

Piaras Béaslaí, journalist and prolific Irish language writer, moved to Dublin in 1904; nearly sixty years later, he recalled the Library in Joyce's time:

I have always had a great admiration for the National Library of Ireland in Kildare Street, Dublin, and its splendid staff. Before I came to live in Dublin I had experience of public libraries in London and other English cities, but none of them appeared to have assistants of the high standard of reading, education and intelligence of those I met in the Kildare Street building. It was hard to find any subject, however recondite, of which at least one member of the staff had not expert knowledge. When I came to Dublin, working as a freelance journalist, I spent a large amount of my time there ... At that time the reading room was always crowded with interesting characters, some already famous and some yet to be so. There was Father Dinneen, who spent all his days between that place and the reading room of the close-by Irish Academy; working steadily, and startling the other readers by spoken phrases and ejaculations, apparently addressed to himself. There were Frank Sheehy Skeffington, Cruise O'Brien, Hugh Kennedy, later to be the first chief justice of a self-governing Ireland, Tomás Ó Máille of Galway, still a student, later a professor; W.J. Lawrence, the writer on old drama – and many others.

I liked the chief librarian of those old days, the courteous Lyster, and his scholarly assistant chief, Dr Best, a fine Gaelic scholar. Joyce has brought them both into *Ulysses*, in a dialogue, or rather trialogue, in the Library, in which he himself, as Stephen Dedalus, lays down the law as to Hamlet to the much-impressed Lyster and Best, and makes stupid puns on the latter's name. I fancy I knew the National Library better than

11 K. O'Brien, 'UCD as I forget it (1916–19)', *University Review*, 3:2 (1962), 6–11 (7–8); repr. in A. Macdona (ed.), *From Newman to new woman: UCD women remember* (Dublin, 2001), pp 2–9.

Joyce – not to mention the *Evening Telegraph* office – though he may
have excelled me in his knowledge of Barney Kiernan's, which, none
the less, I knew fairly well.[12]

Not everyone was happy with the Library, however. 'Wanted, a National
Library' was the title of an article in the June 1902 issue of the *Irish Protestant
and Church of Ireland Review*: it quotes a letter from 'A Dublin priest' published
in the *Leader* which, noting the 'very respectable list of Catholic authors in the
Library', contrasts this with the Library's apparent reluctance to acquire a copy
of *Five Years in Ireland* by M.J.F. McCarthy – a Catholic author critical of the
Irish Catholic church – and states that 'as a state-funded institution, we do not
intend to allow the authorities at the National Library to pursue their work of
bigotry without a public protest'. [13] In a somewhat similar vein, the *Irish Nation*
(December 1916) combines praise of the staff with an unpleasant diatribe:

> The assistants are always polite, indefatigable, obliging. They *always* know
> the book you want and where to get it.
>
> THE MEN BEHIND
> They are a mixed band of Catholics and Protestants. They are, in view
> of their education and their heavy responsibilities, and in fact from every
> point of view, miserably, wretchedly paid. They are men of refinement,
> and many of them men of great literary ability. One of them, the late
> Mr Crawford Neil, who unhappily perished in the Rebellion, was a poet
> of the rarest ability. Yet the superior gentry who have charge of the
> museum, the officers, the men behind, look down upon these gentle-
> men as mortals of an inferior mould, and uniformly treat them as such.
>
> THE QUEER FACT
> Now, the very queer fact about the conditions of employment in this
> National Library of ours is that no position worth over £100 *per annum*
> is open to anyone who is so unutterably unfortunate to be a papist. The
> staff consists of the librarian, three assistant librarians, two cataloguers,
> and then (you here jump the uncrossable abyss) the unfortunate assistants
> – who, of course, do all the real work of the Library.[14]

12 P. Béaslaí, 'Pleasant hours in the National Library', *Irish Independent*, 25 Sept. 1963.   **13**
Irish Protestant and Church of Ireland Review (June 1902), 104.   **14** *Irish Nation*, 1:24 (2 Dec.
1916).

T.W. Lyster, librarian from 1895 to 1920, died on 12 December 1922. Francis Cruise O'Brien wrote of Lyster for the *Irish Independent* as follows:

> I do not think you will find a library which bears so much the impress of a single personality as does the National Library of Ireland. It is not a great library in its collection, for it has no manuscripts, in its endowment for it is very poor, or in its material equipment. But it is a great library in its service. That was Lyster's gift to the nation. That is for the people, he would say, for the generation that is coming. We are their servants. And if he insisted on those who served with him giving of their best, he was always unsparing of himself. Not the humblest reader was denied access to him, nor was any suggestion for improvement, however small, passed by.

HIS OUTLOOK

> He looked to an Ireland cultured and European. He was impatient of many things in the Ireland of his day, but he was never intolerant, never bitter, never cynical. He believed in the people. Give them their opportunity, he often said, give them access to noble and beautiful things, to books above all, and the country of the coming time will be a fine and worthy thing. He looked out upon the reading room of his library as a workshop of the future. He was right. The younger generation of students knew him not, but his presence made many things possible for them. We who knew and loved him mourn a friend, but all of us can mourn the passing of one who strove finely and with single-minded endeavour for country, for letters, for humanity.[15]

Lyster's colleague and eventual successor, Richard Irvine Best, wrote an appreciation of him published in the *Irish Times*:

> His delight was to look out on the crowded reading room, the sea of youthful faces intent on study, and reflect that the future lay there. He always maintained that his Library was the real University of Ireland, and nothing gave him so much pleasure as a remark of George Moore's – that there, at any rate, people seemed to be happy. When an over-zealous Metropolitan [policeman] once tried to prevent the students from sitting about on the Library steps – their favourite summer meeting ground – he broke into a fierce denunciation of officialdom in general

15 *Irish Independent*, 15 Dec. 1922.

and Castle government in particular. 'Why, the Library is theirs!' he exclaimed; and that was in great measure the secret of his success as a librarian …

Lyster had a delightful sense of humour, and also – what few outside his intimate circle would suspect – an astonishing power of mimicry. Nothing seemed to escape his keen observation; peculiarities of accent or gait or manner he could take off to perfection. But there was no tinge of malice in these little turns, which usually ended in a peal of laughter. He was a good-humoured spectator of life's comedy.[16]

Robert Lloyd Praeger, who succeeded Lyster as librarian in 1920, has recorded his memories of the Library in *A Populous Solitude*. His interest was in natural history, particularly botany, rather than literature:

> With George Moore, brilliant writer and fascinating talker, my acquaintance was slight. He came often to the National Library, but my literary colleagues were the men he came to see: for science he had little use. He stopped me in the hall one day: 'Oh! Praeger, I'm sure you can tell me the name of a little brown bird…' and he attempted to describe it. 'I am not an ornithologist,' I said, 'and there are a lot of little brown birds; but I fancy it was a meadow pipit.' Six months later I met him in the street; he stopped me. 'Oh! Praeger, can you tell me the name of a little brown bird …' and he ran over its points again. 'I believe it was a meadow pipit', I answered. He wrote the name on his cuff and thanked me. Later on I met him again. 'Oh, Praeger …' 'I know,' I said, 'it's about that little brown bird. I'm *sure* it was a meadow pipit.' And as a meadow pipit, I believe, it appeared in one of his books. Episodes concerning famous men are usually held to be of interest; I think this one is hard to beat – for mere inanity![17]

The advent of the new Irish Free State marked the end of an era during which the Library had been a remarkably accessible institution. The Library was, in fact, closed to the public from 28 June 1922 until 13 February 1924.[18] When it reopened, it had shorter opening hours – the main difference being that the Library no longer remained open until 10.00 p.m. on Saturday, but closed at 1.00 p.m. instead – and there were new restrictions on the admission

---

16 *Irish Times*, 16 Dec. 1922.   **17** R.L. Praeger, *A populous solitude* (Dublin and London, 1941), p. 211.   **18** The Office of Public Works erected the railings between the Library and Leinster House, the new seat of parliament, in Dec. 1922.

of undergraduates and other junior students. The former library assistant, J.J. O'Neill, by then librarian of UCD, told the *Irish Independent*:

> The National Library authorities had transferred to University College library, roughly, about 400 text-books, for the use of students, as the former institution had been used mainly by students of the college. A good reading room was provided at University College, and it remained open until 9 p.m. each night.
>
> The main fact is that the National Library, under the new régime, becomes to Ireland what the British Museum library is to England. It will be fostered by a national government. Hitherto, of course, it was a starved institution. In the future, I take it, the Library will be for the benefit of [graduate] students alone, but I am emphatically of opinion that the ordinary college students should find the book they require in their own college libraries ... The money saved by retrenchment in the matter of these students' textbooks could be spent for the benefit of the public by filling gaps in the already depleted staff and buying expensive new books dealing with subjects such as the higher branches of education. It should be remembered that the National Library is the property of the whole nation.[19]

Predictably, the shorter opening hours and restrictions on undergraduate access led to criticism. The following is from the *Catholic Bulletin*:

> Down to 1921 the National Library of Ireland was really a public library. Anyone could go in and use its collections, all provided at public expense, and it is an obvious public fact that the very poor, here in Ireland, always bear far more than their fair share of that expense. Now all this is changed. Formalities and tickets are set up. The public reading room was always well filled many hours of the day. Now it is practically a desert; we doubt if, even two months after its re-opening, a dozen readers are ever seen there together; and, as a rule, there are less than half a dozen. There is more in this, however, than is seen on the surface. An utterly illegal discrimination is being practised in the issue of reading tickets. The full use that, with great advantage to university and professional studies, was formerly made of the National Library has now been most arbitrarily cut off, and they are excluded from the Library. To be an undergraduate is, it appears, an unpardonable offence in this respect, or very

19 *Irish Independent*, 11 Jan. 1924.

nearly so; and, of course, the carefully packed board of trustees is sub-
limely ignorant of the fact that nine-tenths of those who are so shut out
as a body are mere Irish Catholics, students of the National University
of Ireland.[20]

It is perhaps an indirect compliment to the institution that it should be accused
of bigotry by both the *Irish Protestant* and the *Catholic Bulletin*.

Coinciding with the re-opening of the Library in February 1924, Richard
Irvine Best became librarian following Praeger's retirement. Like his colleague
John Eglinton, Best appears in Joyce's *Ulysses* and in George Moore's *Hail and
Farewell*. The Library, now with its more scholarly focus, prospered in the years
immediately following. The east wing of the building was completed, the book
grant was increased, staff were promoted – notably Dorothea Ferguson and
Rosalind Elmes, who, having worked as cataloguers from 1897 and 1900
respectively, were promoted to become assistant librarians in 1924 – and new staff
were recruited. During the celebration of the Tailteann Games (August 1924),
the Library presented an exhibition of books, manuscripts and illustrative material
relating to Irish history, evidence of a greater emphasis on Irish studies.

The division of the printed books collection into two separate sequences,
Irish and general, took place in 1928. This collection is described in 'A treas-
ure-house of literature', an article by M. Lyster in the *Sunday Independent* (16
September 1928) which contains the following reference to Best and his assistant (and later successor), Dr Richard Hayes:

> The Library is very fortunate in its staff. Mr Hayes, who works under
> the able supervision of Dr Best, is acquainted with almost all the
> European languages from Russian to modern Irish, and to see Dr Best
> among his books, moving among those newly arranged on the main
> floor, is to see a man conversing with old friends who have been raised
> to new and more fortunate positions.[21]

The distinguished French Celtic scholar Dom Louis Gougaud recalled the
Library of this period with admiration and a degree of nostalgia, remarking: 'I
spent most of my time, while in Dublin, at the National Library, which is really

20 *Catholic Bulletin*, 14:5 (May 1924), 361–3. **21** M. Lyster is presumably Margaret Lyster,
the pseudonym of Geraldine Lia Cummins (writer on spiritualism, and first wife of the poet
Austin Clarke) who had briefly worked in the National Library in 1918 'in place of a man
who had gone to the war', as she mentions in her autobiography, *Unseen adventures* (London,
1951), p. 28.

a wonderful institution. The accommodation there is splendid, and the arrangements very efficient. It is also very up-to-date. I can get at the National Library books which I failed to secure even in the British Museum.'[22]

The composition of the Library staff – particularly the assistant librarians – gradually changed after the establishment of the Free State. While the Library continued to act as a general reference library in the sciences as well as the humanities, there was an increasing emphasis on Irish studies. A number of eminent scholars worked as assistant librarians during the following decades, and then went on to distinguished careers elsewhere, usually in the academic world. Very few went on to work in other libraries – an interesting phenomenon in itself – though several of the assistant grade did so, usually in libraries in government departments.

Gerard Murphy, later founder of the journal *Éigse* in 1939, author of *Early Irish lyrics* (1956) and professor of the history of Celtic literature at UCD, worked as an assistant librarian in the period 1922–9. Louis P. Roche, later a distinguished lecturer in French at UCD, served as an assistant librarian from 1930 to 1935. He had published his doctoral thesis on the French renaissance poet Claude Chappuys in 1929 and translated Jean Plattard's biography of Rabelais into English (1930). James Carty, who was appointed assistant librarian in 1933, had already at this stage published his four-volume *Class-book of Irish History*. His textbooks were in use in Irish schools for several decades. Carty had served in the foreign affairs department of Dáil Éireann during the war of independence, and had also worked as a journalist. He is remembered for his *Bibliography of Irish History, 1912–1921* (1936) and its companion volume *Bibliography of Irish History, 1870–1911* (1940). Tomás Ó Cléirigh, author of *Aodh Mac Aingil agus an Scoil Nua-Ghaeilge i Lobháin* (1935), also spent some years in the late 1930s as an assistant librarian, and the Irish scholar David Greene (Daithí Ó hUaithne) worked as an assistant librarian from 1941 to 1948. Gearóid Mac Niocaill, later professor of history at University College, Galway (UCG), and Proinsias Mac Giollarnáth (Frank Ford), subsequently professor of French in the same university, also worked as assistant librarians.

Richard James Hayes, whose contribution to Irish bibliography is unequalled, joined the staff of the Library in 1924, having graduated from Trinity College, Dublin with degrees in Celtic studies, modern languages and philosophy. Along with his colleague Brighid Ní Dhonnchadha, he compiled the three-volume *Clár Litridheachta na nua-Ghaeilge, 1850–1936* (1938–40). Shortly after the outbreak of

22 *Standard* (Dublin), 4 May 1929. **23** See E. O'Halpin, *Defending Ireland: the Irish Free State and its enemies since 1922* (Oxford, 1999), p. 187; also E. O'Halpin (ed.), *MI5 and Ireland, 1939–1945: the official history* (Dublin, 2003), p. 76.

the Second World War, he was seconded to the department of defence to work on cracking German codes.[23] He was appointed director of the Library in 1940 – the title having been changed from that of librarian in the mid-1930s – and many of the developments from which readers benefit to this day are due to his foresight and energy. A report of an interview with Hayes in the (Dublin) *Times Pictorial* in 1943 indicates his remarkable energy and interest in new developments:

> Given the proper staff facilities, he would even encourage the notion of answering enquiries on the telephone, as they do in the US ... After the war, Dr Hayes hopes to install a number of microfilm readers in the reading room. The microfilming of manuscripts, old newspapers and records would help to solve the Library's ever-increasing space problem.[24]

Newspaper reports suggest a great interest in the Library's project of locating and microfilming manuscript material of Irish interest abroad. Hayes attended a conference of cultural experts at the Council of Europe in 1950, at which, according to the *Irish Press*, 'with a nice sense of humour, he told the Scandinavian delegates that that he expected their support, "because you have destroyed all the manuscripts in Ireland from the year 900 to 1,000"; he told the English that he expected theirs because "you took on the destruction of our manuscripts where the Danes left off".'[25]

The cataloguing of the microfilm material and the manuscripts in the Library formed the basis for the monumental work in eleven volumes with which Hayes' name will always be identified, *Manuscript Sources for the History of Irish Civilization* (Boston, 1965). The Library's first ever press conference took place on 13 May 1966 to announce the publication of this *magnum opus*, an event which generated a commendable amount of press coverage. 'In the sombre and suitably bookish surroundings of the board room of the National Library of Ireland in Dublin', the *Irish Times* (14 May) informed its readers, 'the Library's trustees yesterday unveiled what undoubtedly is the most ambitious work of reference ever to have been undertaken by Irish scholars.' Upon his retirement in 1967, Hayes became the first director of the Chester Beatty Library, having served as honorary librarian there since 1957. Following his death on 21 January 1976, Alf Mac Lochlainn wrote in the *Irish Times* (23 January) that 'far into the future, scholars in any field of enquiry relating to Ireland will remain deeply in his debt'.[26]

In 1943 the office of the Ulster King of Arms was transferred to the control of the Library, and renamed the Genealogical Office. The first genealogical

24 *Times Pictorial* (Dublin), 23 Oct. 1943.   **25** *Irish Press*, 19 July 1950.   **26** *Irish Times*, 23 Jan.1976.

officer and chief herald was Edward MacLysaght. In 1949, he became the Library's first keeper of manuscripts. He gives an interesting account of his years in the Library in his memoir *Changing Times*, where he has written: 'Of all the various jobs – or, if that is too colloquial a word, let me say professional and business activities – in which I have ever been engaged that of keeper of manuscripts in the National Library is the one I liked best.'[27] His memoir contains fascinating recollections of his travels throughout Ireland inspecting manuscripts.

Thomas P. O'Neill was appointed assistant librarian in 1946. He was seconded to the All-Party Anti-Partition Conference in 1949, and was subsequently the biographer of Eamon de Valera. He is remembered with gratitude by many young assistant librarians for his willingness and ability to answer the most challenging of enquiries. John Brophy, author of the novel *Sarah* (about Sarah Curran), provides a vignette from 1948: 'At the National Library I had a few words with another young man named O'Neill, who last winter came to a lecture I gave, on Sarah Curran, to the London Irish Literary Society. My high opinion of his taste is confirmed by the way he phrases his appreciation of *Sarah*.'[28]

One of the best known of the assistants – along with F.J. Poulter, one of two assistants promoted to assistant librarian during 'the Emergency' – was Joseph J. Bouch, remembered to this day for his pioneering research on the printing of the 1916 Proclamation of the Irish Republic. The *Irish Press* published an appreciation when he died in 1945:

> Men and women all over the country who are now holding down the jobs for which they once studied in the National Library, will be sorry to hear of the death of Joe Bouch, one of its assistant librarians. His tall and portly figure was for years a feature of the reading room, that place of lofty beauty with its simple lines, its silent ranks of books, its preserved and cherished wisdom. In his thirty-seven years as a librarian Mr Bouch must have seen many generations of students come and go – either to pass their exams, and be seen no more, or to come back, year after year, chronic cases of delayed action.
>
> But Mr Bouch's most valuable contribution was his study of the Proclamation of Easter Week. The origin of its printing was wrapped in mystery or legend, the people connected with it being either scattered or dead. With infinite pains, Mr Bouch carried out his research …
>
> Students who knew Mr Bouch solely as a bookworm in the National Library would have been surprised to hear that he was a better athlete

27 E. MacLysaght, *Changing times: Ireland since 1898* (Gerrards Cross, Bucks., 1978), p. 201.
28 J. Brophy, *The mind's eye: a twelve-month journal* (London, 1949), p. 260.

than many of them. He was an expert handballer, a great player at one time at the Boot Inn; a good swimmer and a golfer at Woodbrook. He loved Dublin and was a member of the Old Dublin Society. His musical career was a profession in itself. For not only was he deputy conductor of Rathmines and Rathgar Musical Society, he also found time to conduct church choirs as well, especially those of Catholic University, Haddington Road and Monkstown. These varied activities Joe Bouch fitted into a life that was all too short.[29]

Another library assistant known to generations of readers has left some memories, recorded in the *Irish Times* of 9 October 1968:

A man who has dealt with almost everybody who is anybody in Ireland retires today after nearly fifty years' service in the National Library. Mr Leo A. Cleary, a Dubliner, joined the Library staff in 1919, at the age of 15 years 10 months. Nobody else is known to have worked so long in the establishment. Judges, politicians, professors, diplomats – they all passed through his helpful hands as students. He also dealt with many writers. 'Hilaire Belloc and Oliver St John Gogarty were among the most pleasant and entertaining', Mr Cleary recalls. 'I didn't like W.B. Yeats very much. He was a bit awkward. But his brother, Jack, the painter, was a very pleasant man.'

Mr Cleary, a first class assistant in the Library, has also had an interesting sporting career. He has been a soccer legislator since 1935 and has been on the Football Association of Ireland Council since 1945. He was chairman of the Association in 1964–66, and for the past fifteen years he has been hon. treasurer of the Leinster Football Association. Over the past few years he has travelled abroad with the Irish international teams and has visited nearly every country in Europe from Iceland to Yugoslavia.

The Library's serious space shortage is an issue that concerned William Archer, the first librarian, and has preoccupied each of his successors. Though a number of alternative sites had been proposed at various stages, nothing actually happened to alleviate the problem until the late 1960s. The initiative came from Patrick Henchy, a native of Corofin, Co. Clare, who was appointed assistant librarian in 1941, became the first keeper of printed books in 1949 and succeeded Hayes as director in 1967. In his informative memoir, *The National Library*

29 *Irish Press*, 27 Apr. 1945.

of Ireland, 1941–1976: A Look Back, Dr Henchy stated: 'There was serious over-crowding of material – even the entrance hall was packed with maps and hundreds of boxes of deeds.'[30] He was responsible for having Dr Kenneth Humphreys (1916–1964), then librarian of the University of Birmingham, appointed as a consultant. Humphreys's report, never formally published, was submitted to the minister for education. Eventually, this led to the Library acquiring additional premises, though this was to take some time. The *Irish Independent* (15 October 1971) featured an article by Bruce Arnold headed 'College of Art to become part of National Library: possession expected in 1974'. In his memoir Dr Henchy outlined the new policy: 'With the promise of the College of Art premises and site, and with the acquisition of the other premises in Kildare Street and Leinster Lane, it was accepted that there would be no need to build a new National Library in another site; but rather to expand from the existing one.'[31] Decades were to pass before this came to completion, but the groundwork had been done by Dr Henchy.

At Dr Henchy's instigation, the National Library of Ireland Society was founded in 1969. The *Irish Times* (17 October 1969) reported the occasion:

> The official motion, calling for the establishment of the new society, was proposed by Senator Michael Yeats, who described it as one of the most important and encouraging developments in the cultural life of the country. The Library had been for a long time the victim of shameful neglect. However, the deterioration had been so gradual, he said, that the public had never really been enlightened as to what was going on. 'The formation of this new society will enable us all to make sure that a new start is made.'

Dr Henchy reflected on his career in an interview with the *Irish Times* on the occasion of his retirement as director in 1976:

> Of what has been achieved during his directorship, Dr Henchy is most proud of the Humphreys report which was presented to the minister for education in 1971 and which made a series of recommendations for the future of the Library. It advocated the training of members of the staff, the dividing of the Library into departments, and 'it was partly due to its suggestions that the extensions were found to be essential'. He is also proud of the National Library Society, which was formed in 1969.

30 P. Henchy, *The National Library of Ireland, 1941–1976: a look back* (Dublin, 1986), p. 21.
31 Ibid., p. 26.

And if, when he leaves his office next Thursday evening, he were allowed to take one book with him, what would he choose? 'Well, I think I would walk up the stairs and take the earliest edition that we have of Izaak Walton's book, *The Compleat Angler*, first published in 1653. It's a poetic sort of book and it's one that I can open at any paragraph and get something new from it each time. You see, there are some books that you are never, never finished with.'[32]

Alf Mac Lochlainn served as director after Dr Henchy. In 1982, he left to become librarian of UCG, having described his situation in a refreshingly frank interview published in the *Sunday Press* (21 February 1982):

> I'm a bureaucrat, and I'm in no way ashamed of it, but here I'm just one of many minor bureaucrats. I'm paid as a principal officer in the department of education ... there are maybe thirty guys with the same rank as me all over there in the department. I'm here a couple of miles away, my voice is no stronger than theirs, and it's hard to get yourself heard.

A reader who has seen much change since he first visited the Library in 1958 is the distinguished American historian, L. Perry Curtis Jr., who recalls 'the "good old days" of dark and draughty rooms, peeling paint, and all those well-worn giant folio volumes that comprised the guard book catalogue'. He writes:

> What draws me to the 'old' or pre-computerised library is not the musty and dusty aura but rather the people ... who could ever replace the likes of (Lady) Christine Longford or Terence de Vere White? As someone who has lived through seven directorships (R.J. Hayes, Patrick Henchy, Alf MacLochlainn, Michael Hewson, Pat Donlon, Seán Cromien, and now Brendan O Donoghue) and who can remember working in four different manuscript rooms, I feel qualified to bestow on the NLI the encomium of Dublin's liveliest, most inter-denominational, and least pretentious centre of learning and good conversation.
> —Of course, I miss the cosy, almost intimate, character of the NLI before the exponential growth of both Irish studies and the Library staff

32 'Caroline Walsh talks to Dr Patrick Henchy', *Irish Times*, 25 Sept. 1976. On his retirement in 1976, Dr Henchy's friend Ciaran McAnally gave him a gift of a fine nineteenth-century facsimile of the 1653 edition of Walton's *The Compleat Angler*. His widow, Mrs Monica Henchy, presented this book to the Library in December 2002 in memory of her husband who died on 6 May 2001; it now has an honoured place in the rare books collection.

since 1980. In those years, made golden by the sunset of selective memory, the non-undergraduate readers and the Library staff comprised a loose and informal loyal community whose members depended on one another in many ways. And if we readers sometimes imposed undue stress and strain on the men (almost all men in those days) behind the counter owing to our endless requests for books and periodicals, the basic goodwill of the institution survived any upset over undue delays or curtailed opening hours.[33]

The friendly relationship of staff and readers is also emphasized by Fr J. Anthony Gaughan, who has recorded his memories of the Library in his *Recollections of a Writer by Accident*:

> The staff of the National Library reminded me of an extended family and I became a friend of quite a number of them. I enjoyed occasionally meeting a few of the junior members – staunch 'Dubs' supporters – at Croke Park. Another friend was Edward MacLysaght. He was the outstanding 'character' associated with the National Library and the Genealogical Office. Even after he retired, he continued to haunt the premises, while researching his books on Irish families ... The reading room was a great leveller and imbued a spirit of camaraderie. It gave me the opportunity to become acquainted with some of the country's leading writers and historians, including Tim Pat Coogan, Peter Costello, David Fitzpatrick, Peter Harbison, Charles Lysaght, D.R. O'Connor Lysaght, Leon Ó Broin, Maurice R. O'Connell, Seán Ó Lúing, Pádraig Ó Snodaigh, Fintan O'Toole and Christopher J. Woods ... It was also pleasant to renew the acquaintance of American academics who arrived each summer. Among these were L. Perry Curtis, James Donnelly, Robert Hogan and Arthur Mitchell, each a recognised specialist in his own field of Irish studies.[34]

This roll-call of notable readers includes many who were happy to help the staff with enquiries and who frequently brought the attention of the staff to an item or collection which subsequently made its way to the Library. Fr Gaughan recalls that in 1980 he was invited to become a member of the executive committee

33 L.P. Curtis Jr, 'Forty years on: confessions of an NLI addict', *National Library of Ireland Trustees' Report, 2001*, pp 66–8. Brendan O Donoghue retired as director in September 2003 and was succeeded by Aongus Ó hAonghusa.   **34** J.A. Gaughan, *Recollections of a writer by accident* (Blackrock, Co. Dublin, 2002), pp 98–9.

of the National Library of Ireland Society – he is the present chairman of the Society – and he notes correctly that 'much of the credit for the success of the Society must go to Dónall Ó Luanaigh and Gerry Lyne'.[35]

Dónall Ó Luanaigh was appointed assistant librarian in 1963. Until 1968, he worked in the department of printed books, and – after a period of six months in the Genealogical Office – from 1969 to 1973 as periodicals librarian and then in the department of manuscripts. Appointed keeper of manuscripts in 1976, he became keeper of printed books in 1982 and was appointed keeper of collections in 1993. For over forty years, the Library has benefited from his scholarship, diplomacy and perception. Dónall makes an anonymous but recognizable appearance in the following anecdote related by Conor Kenny, of the well-known and much-missed Galway bookshop:

> When I was a young man I used to go to Dublin regularly to visit the bookshops. You could buy interesting pamphlets for as little as 10p a time. I would take them back to Galway, catalogue them, and sell them to the National Library of Ireland. One day I was walking past a demonstration outside the Irish parliament with the keeper of rare books from the National Library. One of the protesters handed him a leaflet which he carefully put in his pocket, saying to me, 'That's so Kennys won't charge me a fiver for it in a few years' time.'[36]

My colleague Gerard Lyne has, in his essay in this volume, given a remarkable account of the Library over the last four decades and Dónall's outstanding contribution to it during his forty-three years' service. His essay is an important addition to the informal sources for the history of the Library. But I will leave the last word to another of Dónall's former colleagues. One lunchtime, a few weeks after I joined the staff of the Library in June 1983, by chance I met Kevin Whelan who had started work in the Library a few months before. As we walked along Nassau Street, we began to discuss our new colleagues. 'Dónall …', I began. 'Dónall', said Kevin with the incisive perception which is characteristic of one of our most eminent historians, 'is a gentleman.'

---

35 Ibid., p. 100. 36 Conor Kenny, 'From bricklaying to the Great Wall of China' in Sheila Markham, *A book of booksellers: conversations with the antiquarian book trade, 1991–2003* (London, 2004), p. 291.

Lines from the Annals of Connacht, 1388

Seaan Ruad h. Tuathail ri h. Muiredaig, fegi enig agus engnama Erenn ina amsir fein, do marbad do-sam iarom.

Seaan Ruad O Tuathail, king of Ui Muiredaig, ridgepole of the bounty and valour of Ireland in his time, was killed in his own house by a clown. He killed the clown afterwards.

He killed the clown *afterwards*?

Well slap me
with a fool's bladder.
Hell's bells are stitched to his cap!

Some ages, this, before the rubber dagger
but Sean Roe's ribs
were tickled
anyway.

Lament bards.
Annalists commemorate
O'Toole,
pit-prop of a goldmine
to poets, harpists
and concert-party artists.

O'Toole ruled, then
catching an infectious jest
he lived just long enough
to harpoon the buffoon and so,
we suppose, died laughing.

But who wrote *a line*
for the clown?

Well actually, my mother.

Or hers, or hers
– however many generations make
six hundred years –

'I'm warning you, stop clowning,
it'll end in tears.'

MICHAEL COMYNS

A conscience shared:
the Sheehy Skeffington papers

Diarmuid Whelan & Ellen Murphy[1]

IT IS CUSTOMARY in volumes such as this to acknowledge the unseen
mediators between history as it happens and history as it is written or discovered. In the case of the Sheehy Skeffington papers, the gentle, trusting, evolving
and personality-shaped method by which these papers have been brought into
the public domain is a little special. And so it is entirely fitting that an essay on
this remarkable family should appear in a *Festschrift* honouring Dónall Ó Luanaigh.
Dónall's imprint is all over the process of transferring these papers to the National
Library of Ireland. Over a period of twenty-five years – between 1974 and 1997
– Dónall was the conscientious intermediary between the National Library and
Andrée Sheehy Skeffington, the engaging donor of this collection. Throughout
those years, Dónall carefully fostered a relationship of trust between Andrée and
the Library. That he appears frequently in the catalogue of these papers is a tribute
not just to Dónall's centrality to the National Library, but also to the entirely
organic way in which he and the Library staff secured this fascinating collection.

While the relationship between the National Library and the Sheehy
Skeffingtons may have ended with Andrée's death in 1997, it began much earlier. In fact, it is no exaggeration to say that the name Sheehy Skeffington – in
itself a unique and principled mix of love and politics – was born in the reading room and on the steps of the National Library. For it was under the Library's
vaulted ceiling that the courtship of two of the three protagonists of this collection came to pass. In the words of Andrée, it was the 'steps of the National
Library' that led Hanna Sheehy and Francis (Frank) Skeffington up the path to
marriage. In the collection itself there are some of the tokens of their fledgling
relationship in the form of 'slip notes' which, because of the mores of the day
as well as Hanna's own instinctive reserve, were dropped silently as they each
walked past their lover in the reading room.[2] Of course, without the Library to

---

1 The authors arranged and listed the Sheehy Skeffington papers while holding temporary
studentships at the National Library. They would like to thank their erstwhile colleagues in
the Library, especially all in the manuscripts department. 2 A. Sheehy Skeffington, 'A coterie
of lively suffragists' in *Writers, raconteurs and notable feminists: two monographs*, with a foreword

bring them together, the third person featured in this essay, their son Owen, would never have been brought into this world.

The novelist and social activist Rosamund Jacob, a lifelong friend of Hanna Sheehy Skeffington, observed in a letter to her cousin Deborah in 1914: 'From what I have seen of 11 Grosvenor Place [the home of Frank and Hanna], I should say there is no limit to the amount of papers and books that might be temporarily or permanently lost there. It is one mass of books and papers all over the ground floor, and I believe there is another room full upstairs.'[3] She need not have worried. Although the scene might have resembled Francis Bacon's studio more than an Edwardian library, the Sheehy Skeffington papers eventually came to be accommodated in the National Library of Ireland.

That the collection eventually became so extensive was largely due to the rigorous application of a simple family precept: 'Keep everything.' These papers document the professional and personal lives of Frank, Hanna and Owen and the plethora of activities and causes in which they engaged. The papers include scribbled notes and jottings; drafts of articles, radio broadcasts and speeches; committee minutes and diaries; printed material such as books, pamphlets, programs, posters; and ephemeral material including menus, birthday cards and Christmas cards. An assortment of rare newspapers and newspaper cuttings reflects their interest in local, national and international issues. The voluminous collection of magazines, leaflets, flyers, handbills, notices and catalogues provide glimpses into the detail of their obsessively busy lives on a day-to-day basis. Their frequent travels can be retraced through the cache of tourist ephemera consisting of schedules, guides, maps, and tickets for journeys by bus, boat and train. Their enthusiastic support for cricket and rugby is attested by programmes, fixture lists, photographs, membership cards and admission tickets. Carefully filed financial receipts, invoices, bills, and itemized accounts suggest a meticulous and thrifty household. Their work as writers and publishers generated its own particular forms of documentation: notes, notes towards drafts, the drafts themselves, fair copies, finished typescripts and, in most cases, the actual publication. From their public engagements there are the scribbled minutes of meetings, drafts of speeches, attendant votes of thanks and the occasional hastily formulated rebuttal. Their political convictions are attested by receipts for donations and subscriptions to a wide range of organizations and causes, backed up by sundry political literature emanating from many countries and representing many diverse philosophies, generally of a left-wing radical hue.

by D. Ó Luanaigh (Dublin, 1993). **3** Rosamund Jacob to 'Cousin Deborah', 27 May 1914, National Library of Ireland, Sheehy Skeffington papers (hereafter cited as SSP), NLI MS 41,177/27.

And then there are the letters, of which there is an extraordinary variety and range. We have those early 'slip notes' and love letters after the modest fashion of the day, many with pressed flowers enclosed, which it was thought fitting to retain just as the sender intended. There are forget-me-nots, earnest poems of endearment and cards for the anniversaries of their wedding – all testifying to their shared and undying commitment. On the opposite side of the spectrum, there are quite a few examples of hate mail – both anonymous and signed – with vitriolic sketches and portrayals, and filled with intemperate and frequently unfounded accusations. Such invective is easily outweighed by letters of support and encouragement from friends and colleagues and a host of unknown well-wishers. These echoes of battles long ago are testament to the fact that Hanna, Frank and Owen were hitting home in their challenge to the entrenched views and injustices of the Ireland of their day. Who then were these characters who inspired such extremes of love and hate in so many people across the political spectrum?

Hanna Sheehy Skeffington was one of the key figures in the suffrage movement in Ireland. She was born in Kanturk, Co. Cork, in 1877, the eldest daughter of David Sheehy, Irish Parliamentary Party MP, and Elizabeth (Bessie) McCoy. She was a member of an emerging generation of middle-class women who benefited from the general change of attitude to higher education for women in the later half of the nineteenth century.[4] She attended St Mary's University College, 48 Merrion Square, Dublin, which had been founded in 1893 by the Dominicans to provide third level education for Roman Catholic girls who wished to obtain degrees from the Royal University of Ireland. In 1899 she was awarded a BA in French and German; in 1902 she gained an MA in German with first class honours. The following year she married Frank Skeffington and joined the Women's Suffrage and Local Government Association established by Anna and Thomas Haslam. This organization tried to raise awareness and attract support for the cause of women's suffrage by employing techniques of a traditionally 'genteel' nature, such as writing letters to politicians and newspapers and circulating petitions among the general public. Frustrated with the lack of success of these methods, in 1908 Hanna helped to establish the Irish Women's Franchise League (IWFL). When the women's suffrage bill was defeated in Westminster and the Irish Parliamentary Party continued to ignore resolutions in support of female suffrage, the IWFL felt that it had exhausted constitutional methods and committed its first acts of militancy

---

4 Eileen Breathnach, 'Charting new waters: women's experience in higher education, 1879–1908' in Mary Cullen (ed.), *Girls don't do honours: Irishwomen in education in the nineteenth and twentieth centuries* (Dublin, 1987), pp 55–76.

in June 1912. Eight members of the IWFL, including Hanna, resorted to breaking windows in public buildings, including the General Post Office, the Custom House, the Land Commission office and Ship Street barracks. Between 1912 and 1914 there were thirty-six convictions against women for symbolic acts of destruction against government property.[5] Hanna was imprisoned twice during this period, going on hunger strike on both occasions.

The suffrage campaign faced a number of 'uniquely Irish' obstacles. For example, many Irish politicians were not just ideologically opposed to female suffrage but also felt that the activities of the IWFL were endangering the passage of a home rule bill. Hanna's papers document various aspects of these obstacles and the difficulties they presented: the IWFL's unsuccessful lobbying of John Redmond, leader of the Irish Parliamentary Party; the disparaging of the IWFL by nationalists who believed they were colluding with English suffragettes; and the criticism and antipathy directed at IWFL members for engaging in distinctly unfeminine activities such as heckling politicians, destroying government property and willingly accepting prison sentences. The various phases of the campaigns are recalled by posters, pamphlets and handbills issued by the IWFL; by notes copied from IWFL committee minutes; by remarkable scraps of paper containing Hanna's prison diaries; and by prison letters from Margaret (Gretta) Cousins and others. Hanna's papers also include many letters from key figures in the women's movement in Ireland, England, India, the United States and elsewhere. Prominent individuals such as Mary Hayden, Maud Joynt, Margaret and James Cousins, the Haslams, Kathleen Emerson, Louie Bennett, the American feminist Alice Park, the Pankhursts, and Emeline Pethwick Lawrence are all represented in the collection. Hanna's papers will enable historians to interpret her role and that of her associates in the suffrage movement, particularly in the events leading up to the Representation of the People Act 1918 (which gave the vote to women over the age of 30) and the Irish Free State constitution of 1922 (which gave the vote to women over 21).

While one section of the collection documents the passions and interests of Hanna, another major component deals with Frank's life, which was abruptly cut short at what seems the incongruously young age of 38. Though the time between his birth in 1877 and death in 1916 was brief, this is not reflected in his output and achievement. He was brought up in Downpatrick, Co. Down, where his father, Dr Joseph B. Skeffington, a schools inspector and a forceful character, chose to educate his son at home. The results were obviously successful. While still a teenager, the young Frank engaged his father in a newspaper controversy – more than holding his own – concerning the Irish language revival question which was gathering pace at that time. He went to University College, Dublin where he was highly successful. He quickly made a name for himself by virtue of his appearance, his outspokenness and the general whirligig of intellectual energy that he seemed to embody. He was clearly unconventional, as evidenced by his woollen knickerbockers and his refusal to shave. James Joyce rated him the second most intelligent student in the college after himself, and the pair privately published their first works together in a now-rare pamphlet, *Two Essays*.[6] Skeffington's essay dealt with the unfair status – in effect, the non-status – accorded to women in the university. He is the McCann figure in *Stephen Hero*, where he is most memorably described by Joyce as 'hairy Jaysus', an epithet that conjures up Skeffington's appearance and enthusiasms. In 1902 he was appointed registrar of the university, but resigned the post within a year when the college authorities protested at his advocacy of the equal rights of women. For the remainder of his life he was essentially a journalist, either freelance or as editor of the *Irish Citizen*, which he set up in 1912 with James Cousins. As a result, money was always tight and his father frequently had to support him.

The great 'find' of the collection was the discovery of hundreds of 'love letters' between Hanna and Frank. They mainly run from 1900 to 1916, though they fall off dramatically after the couple were married in 1903. These letters are fascinating in their own right, if only as an almost daily account of life at the turn of the century. The correspondence begins in earnest in October 1900 and continues on an almost daily basis thereafter. Each of the letters is quite formulaic in its own charming way: after beginning with an endearment, it depicts the writer's situation before bringing the correspondent up to date on various people; it then generally delivers 'journal' – an account of the newspapers and of social and political events since the last letter. The less political parts of the letters are full of penetrating assessments and intelligent gossip. There is also a good deal of hypochondria which, especially in the case of Frank, takes up a sizeable portion of the letters. On one occasion, after another benign 'affliction', Hanna was moved to write: 'Frank, I wish I could nurse you, sweetheart. You must be sure to be sick an odd day when we're married just to give me the treat.'[7]

It is no exaggeration to say that he gave her plenty of opportunity to make good on her wish. Contrary to the general impression of Frank – industrious

---

6 F.J.C. Skeffington, 'A forgotten aspect of the university question' and James A. Joyce, 'The day of the rabblement' in *Two essays* (Dublin, 1901).   **7** Hanna to Frank, 12 May 1901, SSP, NLI MS 40,464/6.

and possessed of iron discipline – it comes as a pleasant surprise to discover that he was rarely either. In his case, it seems that the traditional Northern work ethic was the utopia for which he always hankered but never quite attained. He was far more familiar with the slough of despond, the pitfalls of late starts and the many maddening distractions which he bemoaned at length. Good journalist that he was, however, there was nothing better than a deadline to snap him into action and bring out his talents to best effect.

Another refreshing side to the collection is that it reveals that these committed pacifists had a good number of arguments and fights. Generally, the disagreements were not very serious. One or two, however, quite clearly were and, according to Hanna, left a shadow over their relationship. Again, contrary to the general public perception of their relationship – a fusion of hearts and minds and an idyll of two *intellectuels engagés* – we discover that, with such principled and politically committed people, compromise did not come easily. However, to be fair, if there were clouds, they were few and not such as to obscure their mutual love and respect. Just as the stock portrait of Frank as indefatigable and iron-willed is largely a misconception, so too is the sketch of Hanna as singularly high-minded and self-assured. An extract from her diary, which she entitled 'A glimpse of myself', reveals an all-too-human outlook:

> From my earliest years I have been a sensitive – even morbid – being, fond of weighing the slightest words and giving undue importance to the most trifling accidents. Pride, obstinacy and ambition are my characteristics. Later on, I got a tinge of sarcasm. Under different circumstances I may have been affectionate, for I have a kind heart enough, but a crust of coldness has hidden all that and only 'once in the moon' does it appear.[8]

If the collection challenges some of the widely held perceptions of the personal side of this couple, the commonplace observation that Frank and Hanna were both dedicated political animals is spot on. In the case of Frank, his interests were broad and ranged across many spheres: in the rapidly changing Ireland of the time, many issues attracted his attention. He brought an admirable cosmopolitan blend of attitude and outlook to everyday Irish affairs as a result of his contacts in India and Egypt and his journalism for French and German newspapers. His fund of knowledge was deep as well as wide; it was typical of him that his admiration and interest in Michael Davitt led to a fully-fledged biography (1908) that has seen publication in three separate generations. It is of inter-

8 SSP, MS 41,183.

est that this work was conceived in the National Library some days after Davitt's death, when he had spent a full day absorbed in his writings. No less than the conception, the entire research and writing were also carried out in the Library. Perhaps in part inspired by Davitt, he threw himself into the Young Ireland branch of the United Irish League (the grassroots organization of the Irish Parliamentary Party), which regarded itself as an intellectual force in the struggle for home rule. At the same time he apparently saw no conflict in being a fully paid up member of the Socialist Party of Ireland – later the Independent Labour Party of Ireland – and mingling with such people as James Connolly, William O'Brien and Fred Ryan[9] who had little time for the Irish Parliamentary Party. He became increasingly sympathetic to the labour movement, especially at the time when Dublin was polarized by the 1913 lockout, an attitude reflected in his work for the Citizen's League and his role as Connolly's literary executor.

But the concern to which he devoted most of his attention was the suffragist cause. It was the shared passion in his relationship with Hanna: from his earliest college days to his last lectures and editorials, it informed his entire political outlook. With the outbreak of war in 1914, he sought to link the two causes of universal suffrage and pacifism, and with increasing fervour he addressed antirecruitment rallies on a weekly basis. As a result, he was imprisoned in 1915. Despite a splendid speech from the dock – or because of it – he was sentenced to six months' hard labour. His final lines from this speech vindicate his assessment of just how undemocratic and brutal the régime in Ireland had become:

> This prosecution would be intelligible in a country run by an autocrat, in a country under the iron heel of military despotism; in a country ruled by a narrow oligarchy fearing the smallest breath of criticism. It would be intelligible above all in a country held by force by another country, the rulers of which would fear to allow any expression of opposition amongst the subject people. If you condemn me, you condemn the system you represent as being some or all of these things. Any sentence you pass on me is a sentence upon British rule in Ireland.[10]

Perceptive though he may have been, his six-month sentence of hard labour was much more severe than the sentence he envisaged when he began his speech from the dock with the observation: 'You may think it necessary to add to the eleven days I have spent in prison by a few days more.' After his release he went

9 Journalist and a leading member of the Socialist Party of Ireland. **10** SSP, NLI MS 40,475/4.

to the United States and remained there until Christmas 1915. Back in Ireland, his letters show an increasing apprehension that the authorities might force 'another 1798'. When the Rising did come at Easter 1916, he attempted to form a citizens' militia to prevent looting. While walking home from the city centre, however, he was arrested and taken to Portobello barracks. Next day he was shot, illegally and without trial. The officer who ordered the execution, Captain J.C. Bowen-Colthurst, was discharged from the British Army having been found guilty but insane.

The collection supports the view of Hanna Sheehy Skeffington's biographer that her life falls into two distinct units, with Frank's murder the dividing line.[11] After intensive lobbying and the rejection of a compensation offer from the prime minister, H.H. Asquith – reputedly £10,000 – Hanna secured an official inquiry into the murder in August 1916. Chaired by Sir John Simon, the commission of enquiry established that Frank was completely innocent of any involvement in the Rising. Hanna's papers include correspondence with military authorities, letters from her solicitors, letters from influential individuals such as MPs Joseph King[12] and John Dillon, statements of witnesses, newspaper clippings and other material documenting her efforts to secure justice for her husband. The personal tragedy of Frank's death is reflected in a multitude of letters from friends and members of her family. Bowen-Colthurst, meanwhile, spent less than a year in a mental asylum. On his release, he emigrated to Canada, where he lived until his death in 1965. He was at one time a member of the Alberta legislature. While travelling in Canada in 1939, Hanna's friend Katherine Gillett Gatty tracked down Bowen-Colthurst; she wrote to Hanna of her encounter with 'that miserable felon and lunatic', who was known locally as the 'Crazy Colonel' and as a fascist supporter. She noted that she told as many of her Canadian acquaintances as possible about the Sheehy Skeffington murder, concluding: 'It will "help" you, perhaps, to know he is mad.'[13]

The murder of her husband had set Hanna on a path of unyielding republicanism. In December 1916, she toured the United States lecturing on British rule in Ireland and raising funds for Sinn Féin. In September 1918, she joined the MacDonagh branch of Sinn Féin in Ranelagh, and by November she was a member of the Sinn Féin executive. She served as a judge in the Sinn Féin courts and worked alongside Áine Ceannt, widow of the 1916 leader Éamonn Ceannt, as a director of organization for Sinn Féin. In the 1920s Hanna was a republican member of Dublin Corporation and played a key role in organizing the Irish Republican Prisoners' Dependents' Fund. In 1926 she joined Fianna

11 Maria Luddy, *Hanna Sheehy Skeffington* (Dublin, 1995), p. 6.   12 King was Liberal MP for North Somerset.   13 K. Gillet Gatty to Hanna, 14 June 1939, SSP, NLI MS 41,177/17.

Fáil and was briefly a member of the executive. She resigned from the party in the following year when de Valera and other members of Fianna Fáil took the oath of allegiance prescribed in the 1921 Anglo-Irish treaty in order to be allowed take their seats in Dáil Éireann.

Hanna's involvement with republican politics is well documented in the collection. The papers include, for example, a biographical account of her work as a judge in the Sinn Féin courts. Each court consisted of a panel of men, women and 'public-spirited priests' elected from within the Sinn Féin organization. Hanna was a member of a panel that included Maud Gonne MacBride, Erskine Childers and Darrell Figgis. The court sat in secret locations in Dublin, including a labour hall in York Street and a laundry in Hatch Street. Hanna recalled that 'often we heard Tan lorries tearing up the streets oblivious of our whereabouts'. The cases with which she dealt ranged from trading disputes between Dublin business firms to squabbles relating to rent, repairs and liabilities arising from the desperate housing conditions of the Dublin tenements. As the level of fees was low and the rulings were based on common sense rather than legal precedent, the Sinn Féin courts were more accessible to the lower classes than the official court system. By acting as a judge in the Sinn Féin courts, Hanna directly challenged the authority of British rule in Ireland.[14]

A particular strength of Hanna's papers is the diversity of subjects and themes for which they provide evidence. In addition to her involvement in the republican and feminist movements, Hanna also supported many liberal causes including socialism, anti-fascism, anti-vaccination and anti-vivisection. She attended the conference of the Women's International League for Peace and Freedom held in Dublin in 1926 and in Prague in 1929. She was secretary of the Friends of Soviet Russia, and visited Russia as part of a delegation in August 1930. She had occasion to meet various eminent statesmen including President Woodrow Wilson of the United States and President Tomáš Masaryk of Czechoslovakia. She earned her living through teaching, setting state exams, journalism and lecturing extensively in Ireland, Britain and the United States. She died in 1946.

Her papers include many intriguing items such as the draft of an article relating to the Irish Hospitals' Trust sweepstakes which she wrote in 1934. She wrote to a number of personalities and activists from the worlds of politics, art, literature and the theatre to ask how they might spend the £30,000 prize if they won it. The respondents include the painter Harry Kernoff who declared that 'it would never make me give up my painting but only help it as I was never a worshipper of the bitch-goddess money'.[15] Maud Gonne MacBride claimed

14 'Sinn Féin courts', SSP, NLI MS 41,189/6.   15 Harry A. Kernoff to Hanna, 3 May 1934, SSP, NLI MS 41,178/86.

that £30,000 was an insufficient sum to carry out her wish of establishing a national newspaper free from advertisements,[16] and Professor Mary Hayden expressed a wish to 'establish a cottage home in the mountains for poor Dublin babies where they might spend a year or thereabouts in pure air and so lay a foundation of health for their future'.[17]

Owen Sheehy Skeffington, born in 1909, was the only child of Frank and Hanna. Family life seems to have been happy, money being the only recurring source of worry. As a very young boy, Owen imbibed the atmosphere of a household resolutely dedicated to politics – he was just three years old when his mother was first imprisoned for her militant activities. Many of the crucial events of the period had taken place before Owen was through his fifth year – the Wexford and Dublin lockouts, the third home rule bill, the outbreak of the Great War and the founding of such pivotal organizations as the IWFL, the Irish Volunteers and the Labour Party. Hanna and Frank were either intimately acquainted with many of the main players of the day or were themselves actively involved in these events; one or both of them were frequently away, generally at political meetings. Owen was present when the British army raided their home in Grosvenor Place in a futile search for evidence to justify his father's murder.

In subsequent years he travelled with Hanna to the United States where he witnessed her denunciation of Britain's rulers with her trademark clear-minded passion. In America, he attended various 'advanced' schools – the experience may well have imprinted in him an appreciation of the benefits of non-denom-inational education. Back in Ireland, he received his secondary education in the multi-denominational Sandford Park school in Ranelagh in Dublin. For uni-versity, he chose Trinity College, where he excelled in French. Throughout his school and college years he was notably successful at sport – be it rugby, cricket or athletics. The papers include an extensive archive of his sporting cor-respondence, and also exam papers, essays and juvenilia. For many years his life interweaved with that of Trinity College, and the collection contains volu-minous correspondence, papers and ephemera generated during his time as a member of staff there.

A recurrent theme is Owen's lifelong love of France and all things French. Indeed, the teaching of the French language and literature provided his liveli-hood from the time he succeeded to Samuel Beckett's post in Trinity College in 1934, having previously spent two years teaching in the École Normale in Paris. That same year he married Andrée Denis, whom he had known from holidays and exchanges in Amiens and who was later to become the dedicated

16 Maud Gonne MacBride to Hanna, *c.*1934, SSP, NLI MS 41,178/86. **17** Mary Hayden to Hanna, *c.*1934, SSP, NLI MS 41,178/86.

custodian of the Sheehy Skeffington papers. In 1936, however, he was diag-
nosed with tuberculosis and went to Schatzalp in Switzerland to recuperate.
While there, and later in France, he observed the irreversible drift towards war.
He witnessed at first hand the refugees from the civil war in Spain, a conflict in
which both he and Hanna were firmly committed to the Republican side. Back
in Ireland before the outbreak of the Second World War, Owen became a
notable activist on behalf of socialism, writing articles, lecturing and making
speeches. He joined the Labour Party and served for a time on its administrative council. In 1943, however, the Labour Party expelled him in highly con-
tentious circumstances.[18] Nonetheless, his three years on the administrative
council, his deep involvement in the municipal elections in 1942, and his jour-
nalistic and propaganda contributions to the journal *Torch* and to *Workers' Action*
have generated considerable source material for the study of the working class
politics of the period. The documentation arising from his involvement with
the Pearse Street Council of Action provides a unique view of the living conditions of the Dublin working class. The Council of Action was a voluntary
effort to improve the conditions of people living in slum tenements. It provided
advice for tenants and offered free legal aid years before it was introduced by
the state in an attempt to prevent the worst excesses of rack-renting landlords.

In 1950 Owen became involved in a public duel with the Revd Felim Ó
Briain, of University College, Galway, in the letters page of the *Irish Times* – a
controversy that became known as 'the liberal ethic'. Apart from challenging
the increasingly clerical ethos of the Irish state, in which he was to some extent
successful, the exchange crystallized the image of Sheehy Skeffington in the
public mind as a controversial figure. Subsequent conflicts with institutional,
generally clerical, intolerance earned him a national profile. The family tendency to take issue with such forces led him to seek a seat in Seanad Éireann,
to which he was elected as a representative of the University of Dublin – i.e.
Trinity College – in 1954 at his second attempt. He held this seat, with one
interruption (1961–5), until his death in 1970.

It was in the forum of the Seanad – a 'sounding board', as he put it – that
he was most successful. From this time onwards, the level of correspondence,
always voluminous, increases substantially. He appears to have been extremely
effective in raising and highlighting issues, most notably in the sphere of education and specifically on the issue of corporal punishment. He crossed swords

---

18 Owen chose the wrong side in the Labour Party's long-running battle with Jim Larkin;
he was accused of conducting an anonymous campaign against the party in the newspapers,
an accusation which he heatedly denied. See A. Sheehy Skeffington, *Skeff: a life of Owen
Sheehy Skeffington, 1909–1970* (Dublin, 1991), pp 110–13; also *Irish Times*, 24 Apr. 1943.

with various government ministers, most notably Richard Mulcahy in the 1950s and George Colley in the 1960s. He used his position to sound out people who had personally experienced corporal punishment and in some cases more extreme forms of abuse. Many people wrote to him of their experiences. These voices of protest began the process – not yet of uncovering clerical abuse, but rather of quickening public opinion – which resulted in inquiries into industrial schools and, in some instances, their closure as recommended in the Kennedy report of 1970.[19] Such abuse was an ugly manifestation of a general and pervasive authoritarian culture in mid-twentieth-century Ireland. Perhaps the primary symptom of that era of endemic authoritarianism was censorship. And in all the campaigns against censorship of any kind – whether of books, film or the theatre – the name of Owen Sheehy Skeffington can be found.

While there are parallels, the Ireland of the Sheehy Skeffington papers is not the Ireland of the present day. The collection transports us back to the world of the three Sheehy Skeffingtons, all variously involved with the political issues and *dramatis personae* of their day – not least the 'dismal poltroons' of the Labour Party,[20] with their viciously contested fiefdoms and attendant hypocrisies. A particular aspect of their world is recalled through a dispiriting little mountain of acknowledgement letters from civil servants kicking to touch on behalf of ministers who went to ground time and again in the face of Owen's harrying swoops from the Seanad. Such minutiae attest the deep commitment of all three to their country and to the welfare and moral opinion of its people. They may have had 'a conscience shared' (to quote the title of this essay), but it was one that was unique and singular to that family. The Sheehy Skeffington papers present many facets of Ireland's failures and successes on the road to independence as evidenced through the lives of its premier radical family.

Before she died Hanna had begun writing her autobiography, which unfortunately was never completed. In her draft 'Foreword' she summed up her life of constant campaigning: she explained that she had not written her autobiography earlier because 'I am more keen on doing things than writing about them'.[21] She also expressed a fear that 'much of the toil and passion of the years

---

19 The 1970 report by Justice Eileen Kennedy into the running of industrial and remand schools recommended that such institutions should be a last resort for the care of children. The report resulted in the closure of a number of the schools, including Daingean, Marlborough House and Letterfrack. Peter Tyrrell, one of those who wrote to Sheehy Skeffington, described his experiences in Letterfrack in a 70,000-word memoir, the text of which is published in D. Whelan (ed.), *Founded on fear: Letterfrack, war and exile* (Dublin, 2006).   **20** So characterized by Conor Cruise O'Brien in 'The embers of Easter, 1916–1966', *New Left Review*, 1:37 (May/June 1966), 11; repr. in O. Dudley Edwards and F. Pyle (eds), *1916: the Easter Rising* (London, 1968), p. 235.   **21** 'Foreword: Dublin memories', SSP, NLI

will never be told, or will be lost in old newspaper files or dusty museums'.[22] It is a tribute to the work of Dónall Ó Lunaigh and the staff of the manuscripts department of the National Library of Ireland that these papers have been so carefully preserved and are now available to the public at large.[23] Simply because the Sheehy Skeffingtons were 'more keen on doing things', it is certain that their papers will not languish undisturbed in the Library's vaults.

MS 41,190/2. **22** Ibid. **23** While it is unfair to single out individuals, Noel Kissane, Gerry Lyne and Tom Desmond have greatly contributed to making the Sheehy Skeffington papers available to the public.

Hedge schools, books and business education in eighteenth-century Ireland

Ciarán Ó hÓgartaigh & Margaret Ó hÓgartaigh[1]

HEDGE SCHOOLS have been described by Chambers as 'pay schools run by independent schoolmasters'[2] and by Coolahan as 'a wide-ranging, if rather haphazard, system of unofficial schools'.[3] This study examines the nature and extent of accounting and business education in hedge schools and explores the reasons why business constituted such an important part of the curriculum in such schools a century before the formation of professional accounting associations, in what was a pre-professional period in business and education history – a period before professional regulation and 'credentialism'. The study utilizes primary sources including contemporary textbooks, newspapers and diary entries incorporating observations on the educational context. A further extension of this study places these findings in the accounting literature, suggesting that 'the Irish underclass in eighteenth-century Ireland was finding the measure of empire through an imperial instrument such as bookkeeping'.[4]

The study is in three parts. The first outlines the educational context of eighteenth-century Ireland and introduces the hedge school as a feature of educational provision. The second draws on a range of sources which suggest that bookkeeping and business education were important elements of the curriculum of some hedge schools. The third outlines the reasons why the study of business methods constituted such an important feature of the hedge school curriculum: essentially, hedge schools were responding to market needs. The study concludes with a brief discussion of the wider implications of the research findings.

* * *

1 We are very grateful to Professor Louis Cullen for his advice and encouragement in the development of this study. It is a slightly revised version of a lecture given by us to the National Library of Ireland Society on 31 May 2006. 2 L. Chambers, 'The Irish hedge school and its books, 1695–1831', *Eighteenth-century Ireland: iris an dá chultúr*, 19 (2004), 231 (a review of A. McManus, *The Irish hedge school and its books, 1695–1831*, Dublin, 2002). 3 J. Coolahan, *Irish education: history and structure* (Dublin, 1981), p. 9. 4 C. Ó hÓgartaigh and M. Ó hÓgartaigh, '"Sophisters, economists and calculators": bookkeeping education in eighteenth-century Ireland', *Irish Accounting Review*, 13:2 (2006), 73

Eighteenth-century Irish society was profoundly hierarchical, with the middle classes, both Protestant and Catholic, constituting a relatively small but expanding segment.[5] Land signified political and economic power, most land being held by Protestants following the calamitous defeat of Catholic interests in the early 1690s and the subsequent imposition of a system of penal laws. Catholics were further marginalized by their exclusion from the professions, with the exception of medicine. Historians have, however, identified a rise in Catholic confidence in the course of the eighteenth century. This can be largely attributed to a marginal increase in prosperity and greater economic independence, despite the political and economic restrictions maintained by the penal laws.[6]

Many members of the Catholic middle classes became extremely adept at improving their position within the restrictive and hostile environment. For example, a number of notable merchant families succeeded in expanding their trade by developing commercial links with Catholic families in continental Europe. Other middle-class Catholics opted for careers in continental armies. An example, typical in some respects, of the middle-class Catholic *émigrés* of the period was Patrick Hennessy who left Co. Cork around 1740 for service in Dillon's regiment in France and went on to establish the renowned brandy business. A couple of generations later, a member of the Hennessy family writing from France in the early-nineteenth century lamented that he had forgotten the bookkeeping he had learned in a Co. Cork hedge school, incidentally that attended by Edmund Burke for a period.[7]

Hedge schools were common in Ireland from the seventeenth century onwards. Dowling claims that the number of hedge schools 'increased very rapidly during the latter half of the eighteenth century … and it was to these that the education of the great bulk of the population was entrusted'.[8] McManus suggests that the hedge schools provided 'a fine education … in reading, writing and bookkeeping, even to the poorest child'.[9] In his brief death notice in a Limerick newspaper, Brian Merriman, author of *The Midnight Court*, was not remembered as a poet but as a 'teacher of mathematics'.[10] In his recent translation of Merriman's

5 For an assessment of the vertical social structures in eighteenth-century Irish society, see S.J. Connolly, *Religion, law and power: the making of Protestant Ireland, 1660–1760* (Oxford, 1992).   6 M. Wall, 'Catholics in economic life' in G. O'Brien (ed.), *Catholic Ireland in the eighteenth century: collected essays of Maureen Wall* (Dublin, 1989), pp 85–92; M. Whelan, 'Edward Hay, styled "Mr Secretary Hay": Catholic politics in Ireland, 1792–1822' (MA, University College, Galway, 1991), pp 19–22.   7 We are grateful to Professor Louis Cullen for drawing our attention to this information.   8 P.J. Dowling, *The hedge schools in Ireland* (Cork, 1968), pp 141–2.   9 McManus, *The Irish hedge school and its books*, pp 133–4.   10 *General Advertiser and Limerick Gazette*, 29 July 1805.

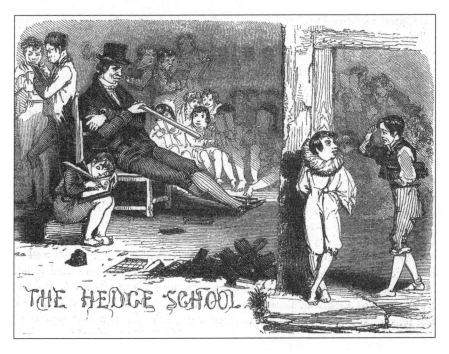

3 'The hedge school'; illustration from William Carleton,
Traits and stories of the Irish peasantry (Dublin, 1830).

epic on late eighteenth-century gender relations, Ciaran Carson claims that
Merriman was a 'resident tutor with one or other of the local gentry.'[11]

Penal laws in the seventeenth and early eighteenth centuries forbade Catholic
schoolmasters from teaching; consequently, they were forced into a peripatetic
existence, secretly teaching out of doors and sometimes out of sight behind
hedges. Enforcement of such laws was relaxed in the late eighteenth century.
Following the passage of the 1782 relief act, a Catholic could establish a school
provided he held a licence. Indeed, St Kieran's College, Kilkenny, was established in that very year.[12] Yet traditional hedge schools were still carried on in
barns, huts or similar casual locations. They remained an important feature of
educational provision in the Irish countryside until the formation of the national
school system in 1831.[13]

11 C. Carson (ed.), *The midnight court* (Oldcastle, 2005), p. 9. **12** Our thanks to John Kirwan
for facilitating access to the voluminous archives in St Kieran's College, Kilkenny.
Significantly, the school educated future members of the British army, such as Philip and
James Hay, brothers of the partisan historian of 1798, Edward Hay. **13** The second report
(1826–7) of the Commissioners of Irish Education Inquiry revealed that a total of 560,549
children attended 11,823 places of education. This represented approximately 40% of

Hedge schoolmasters varied in age, ability and erudition: 'anyone from the highest attainments to the lowest could open a school and hope to attract pupils.'[14] Dowling, Adams and McManus all argue that some hedge schools were relatively sophisticated and provided a curriculum that was wide-ranging and included arithmetic, Greek and Latin and, in some cases, bookkeeping.[15] There was undoubtedly great variety in the quality and context of hedge schools. Daly, however, suggests that the accounts of Dowling and others 'seem excessively eulogistic' as 'many contemporary observers described [hedge schools] as places of squalor and educational anarchy. The truth, no doubt, lies somewhere in between.'[16]

The emergence of a merchant class in Ireland at this time raises the issue of business education in general – and bookkeeping in particular – in the educational provision of the period. Allied to an increased 'monetization',[17] there was an expanding bookkeeping tradition in eighteenth-century Ireland. In addition, many Irishmen were exposed to continental bookkeeping practices in Spain, France or Italy. 'Apprenticeship abroad in an Irish counting house' was a source of training and employment for the sons of many Catholic families.[18] Wall mentions that in 1789 Patrick Bellew, a member of a Co. Louth gentry family, 'sent a son to Rouen to learn French and figures to prepare him for that calling [merchant]'.[19] But what was the extent of business and bookkeeping education in Ireland, and specifically in hedge schools?

The content and the context of such education are relevant considerations in attempting to answer this question. Evidence of the business and bookkeeping curriculum in hedge schools may be found in a range of sources, including books and publications of the period, school advertisements and accounts written by visitors to Ireland. The next section of this paper draws on each of these in turn to trace the patterns of business and bookkeeping education in eighteenth-century Ireland.

* * *

children of school-going age. The overwhelming majority of these (394,732, or about 70% of children at school) attended 9,352 hedge schools. See M.E. Daly, 'The development of the national school system, 1831–40' in A. Cosgrove and D. McCartney, *Studies in Irish history presented to R. Dudley Edwards* (Dublin, 1979), p. 151. **14** J.R.R. Adams, 'Swine-tax and eat-him-all-Magee: the hedge schools and popular education in Ireland' in K. Miller and J.S. Donnelly (eds), *Irish popular culture* (Dublin, 1998), p. 78. **15** Dowling, *Hedge schools in Ireland*; Adams, 'Swine-tax and eat-him-all-Magee'; McManus, *The Irish hedge school and its books.* **16** Daly, 'The development of the national school system', p. 151. **17** C. Ó Gráda, *Ireland: a new economic history 1780–1939* (Oxford, 1994), p. 41. **18** L.M. Cullen, 'Catholic social classes under the penal laws' in T.P. Power and K. Whelan (eds), *Endurance and emergence: Catholics in eighteenth-century Ireland* (Dublin, 1990), p. 78. **19** M. Wall, 'The rise of the Catholic middle class in eighteenth-century Ireland' in O'Brien (ed.), *Catholic Ireland in the eighteenth century*, p. 80.

McManus's work, *The Hedge School and its Books*, explores the curriculum of hedge schools by studying the textbooks generally in use and suggests that bookkeeping featured prominently. It presents evidence that hedge schools offered instruction in 'bookkeeping, surveying and land measuring'.[20] As the focus of the work was not on bookkeeping in particular, this study complements it by using the textbooks as primary evidence for bookkeeping in the curriculum.

The curriculum in hedge schools also featured a considerable element of instruction in mathematics. Dowling suggests that mathematics textbooks of 'great merit were in the hands of a great many [hedge] schoolmasters'.[21] Books stocked by contemporary booksellers[22] included titles on arithmetic by Edward Cocker,[23] George Fisher,[24] John Gough,[25] and Elias Voster.[26] The books by Gough and Cocker, in particular, appear to have been extensively used. While first published in the 1700s, all these books were still being used up to the 1830s. According to the records of the Christian Brothers' school in Carrrick-on-Suir, Co. Tipperary, Gough's *Practical Arithmetick*, Voster's *Arithmetic* and Jackson's *Book-keeping* were part of the curriculum in 1836.[27] McManus suggests that the most commonly used text was Gough's *Practical Arithmetick*. John Gough was a Quaker and seems to have written a number of texts in that subject area. His *Treatise of Arithmetic* went to at least five editions.[28]

Gough's *Practical Arithmetick* was indeed 'practical' and is replete with business and bookkeeping calculations as set out in Table 1. The content is not only practical but also sophisticated, with a whole section dedicated to international trade (pp 235–61), including specifically trade between Dublin and London (p. 235), England, Holland and Flanders (p. 239) and England and France (p. 246). A set of definitions (p. 207) deals with factoring.

Edward Cocker's *Arithmetick* also appears to have been a popular text, having gone to fifty-two editions. In the introduction, the author claims 'as mer-

20 McManus, *The Irish hedge school and its books*, p. 118. **21** Dowling, *Hedge schools in Ireland*, p. 63. **22** See Adams, 'Swine-tax and eat-him-all-Magee'. **23** *Cocker's arithmetick: being a plain and familiar method* (8th ed., Dublin, 1714; the earliest edition in the National Library of Ireland). **24** G. Fisher (possibly a pseudonym for a Mrs Stack), *Arithmetic in the plainest and most concise methods* (9th ed., Dublin, 1754; the earlier of two editions in the National Library of Ireland). **25** J. Gough, *Practical arithmetick both in theory and practice adapted to the commerce of Ireland as well as Great Britain* (Dublin, revised ed., 1793, the earliest edition in the National Library of Ireland). **26** E. Voster, *Arithmetic in whole and broken numbers … adapted to the trade of Ireland* (Dublin, 1772; the earliest edition in the National Library of Ireland). **27** Correspondence with Christian Brothers schools, University College, Dublin, Eamon de Valera papers, P150/2862. Only the surnames of the textbook authors are cited in the Christian Brothers records. **28** J. Gough, *A treatise of arithmetic in theory and practice* (2nd ed., Belfast, 1770; the earliest edition in the National Library of Ireland).

Table 1: Business applications in Gough's Practical Arithmetick

p. 195:	Calculations based on goods bought and sold
	Estimating imports and exports
p. 207:	Estimating allowances per cent
	Definitions including commission as a 'premium allowed by the employer to his factor for transacting business abroad'.
p. 212:	Interest calculations
p. 226:	Annuities and pensions
p. 228:	Rebate and discount calculations
p. 234:	Equation of payments
p. 235:	Exchange
p. 239:	Exchange between England, Holland and France, including a discussion of rates of exchange
p. 252:	Arbitrations of exchange
p. 258:	Invoice for exercise
p. 261:	Barter
p. 264:	Profit and loss
p. 267:	Calculations of 'profit per cent per annum' at a specific rate
p. 270:	Fellowship [partnership] and the division of gain or loss

chandise is the life of the wealthy publick, so practical arithmetick is the soul of merchandise'.[29] Like Gough, Cocker has a significant focus on business and bookkeeping, including barter (ch. 27), the calculation of gains and losses (ch. 28) and the equation of payments (ch. 29). Voster's *Arithmetic* includes the by-line 'to which is added (never before printed) instructions for bookkeeping'. Both Gough and Voster were of Quaker background.

A study of Irish accountants in Australia examines the claims of two brothers from Ireland that they could teach 'bookkeeping according to the Italian mode'.[30] Craig, Ó hÓgartaigh and Ó hÓgartaigh claim that accounting education featured in the formation of several convicts deported from Ireland to colonial New South Wales in the late eighteenth and early nineteenth centuries.[31]

A notice in *Finn's Leinster Journal* (2 January 1793) for a Carrick-on-Suir school run by a Mr O'Brien, states that 'an excellent mathematician *lives in the house*, who instructs the young gentlemen in writing, arithmetic, bookkeeping and the branches requisite for those who may be intended for the revenue, the army, the

29 *Cocker's arithmetic*, p. 12.   **30** *Sydney Gazette*, 6 Oct. 1805   **31** R. Craig, C. Ó hÓgartaigh and M. Ó hÓgartaigh, '"Clowns of no account": reflections on the involvement of four Irishmen in the commercial life of the colony of New South Wales, 1788–1818', *Accounting History: Journal of the Accounting History Special Interest Group of the Accounting and Finance Association of Australia and New Zealand*, 9:2 (2004), 63–85.

navy or the university'.[32] There is also mention by Dowling of 'a town teacher', Philip Fitzgibbon, who taught 'classics, English grammar, geography, the use of the globes, bookkeeping, and he is said to have been a good mathematician'.[33]

Advertising by schoolmasters took various forms in this period. Daniel Corkery reproduces a letter from the poet Eoghan Ruadh Ó Súilleabháin (1748–84) to the parish priest of Knocknagree, Co. Cork, asking him to announce from the altar Ó Súilleabháin's intention of opening a school:

> Reverend Sir–
> Please to publish from the altar of your holy mass
> That I will open school at Knocknagree Cross,
> Where the tender babes will be well off,
> For it's there I'll teach them their criss-cross;
> Reverend Sir, you will by experience find
> All my endeavours to please mankind,
> For it's there I will teach them how to read and write;
> The catechism I will explain
> To each young nymph and noble swain,
> With all young ladies I'll engage
> To forward them to with speed and care,
> With book-keeping and mensuration,
> Euclid's elements and navigation,
> With trigonometry and sound gauging,
> And English grammar with rhyme and reason.
>
> With the grown-up youths I'll first agree
> To instruct them well in the rule of three;
> Such of them as are well able,
> The cube root of me will learn,
> Such as are of a tractable genius,
> With compass and rule I will teach them,
> Bills, bonds and informations,
> Summons, warrants, supersedes,
> Judgment tickets good,
> Leases, receipts in full,
> And releases, short accounts,
> With rhyme and reason,
> And sweet love letters for the ladies.[34]

---

32 Dowling, *Hedge schools in Ireland*, p. 79; emphasis in the original. **33** Ibid., p. 114. **34** D.

The content is of interest, suggesting as it does that bookkeeping and men-suration were to be taught to 'young ladies' and that more detailed aspects of business at a more advanced stage would be taught to 'grown-up youths ... such as are of a tractable genius'. Corkery recounts that 'the school did not last long'; he speculates that Eoghan Ruadh, an ex-soldier, 'had lost the power of work-ing steadily day-by-day'.[35] Lyons suggests that 'the list of subjects offered by Eoghan Ruadh was quite typical of those offered throughout Ireland at the time. This was what was being offered by the general body of hedge schoolmasters, many of whom could claim to be polymaths of renowned erudition, at the end of the eighteenth century and at the beginning of the nineteenth century.'[36]

Rather similar to Corkery's account of the poet Eoghan Ruadh is a con-temporary poem by George Dugail – which is quoted by Adams – referring to instruction in a nineteenth-century hedge school and conjuring up images of mathematics with a practical, business bent: 'By loxodromics or dynamics deep, / I measure land or else I sail [sell] a sheep.'[37] A contemporary account, by William Carleton, comments on a Mr O'Brien: 'A most excellent teacher, and probably the best bookkeeper of the day of the month.[38] Several respectable young fellows used to come from long distances to be instructed by him in the art of keeping accounts.'[39] These observations of individual schoolmasters are also reflected in contemporary recordings of the population at large. In 1824, the Commissioners of Irish Education Inquiry were established to undertake a survey of education throughout the country. On the basis of their report, Clifton estimates that in Co. Carlow alone there were up to one hundred hedge schools at the time. The report recorded that several of them – for example, those of James Tallon at Rathoe and James Lyons of Ballontraine – taught 'reading, writ-ing, arithmetic, bookkeeping, mensuration, surveying, dealing, geometry, trigonometry and English grammar'.[40]

Corkery, *The hidden Ireland: a study of Gaelic Munster in the eighteenth century* (Dublin, 1924), pp 201–2. **35** Corkery, *The hidden Ireland,* p. 202; while Eoghan Ruadh may not have learned all his 'bookkeeping and mensuration' in the army, the teaching and practice of business methods had an important role within its economy, one of the texts most widely used being B. Cuthbertson, *System for the compleat interior management and economy of a battalion of infantry* (1768); see J.A. Houlding, *Fit for service: the training of the British army, 1715–1795* (Oxford, 1981), p. 216. We are very grateful to Dr Neal Garnham for these references. **36** T. Lyons, 'Hedge schools of Kerry', *Journal of the Kerry Archaeological and Historical Society,* 4 (2004), 37. We are very grate-ful to Dr Lyons for this reference. **37** G. Dugail, *The northern cottage, book I, and other poems* (Londonderry, 1824), p. 50. **38** The meaning of 'day of the month' here is unclear. It may be a translation of the Irish phrase 'lá den mhí' or a reference to the preparation of monthly accounts, a common bookkeeping practice since Roman times, as outlined by, for example, G. Abs et al., 'Historical dates in accounting', *Accounting Review,* 29:3 (1954), 486. **39** 'The hedge school' in W. Carleton, *Traits and stories of the Irish peasantry* (Dublin, 1830). **40** H. Clifton, 'The hedge

* * *

James Glassford, an English visitor to Ireland at the time, states that 'arithmetic is a favourite branch of instruction of the Irish people generally' and that arithmetic is 'the Irishman's hobby'.[41] In 1808, Richard Lowell Edgeworth wrote to Lord Selkirk: 'The higher parts of arithmetic are better understood and more expertly practised by boys without shoes and stockings than by young gentlemen riding home on horseback or in coaches.'[42] In 1850, Sir Thomas Wyse, in a letter to the Catholic bishop of Kildare and Leighlin, enthusiastically asserted that 'the lower class (in Ireland), proportionally to their position, are better educated than middle and upper'.[43] An account by James Bicheno published in 1830 indicates that 'in the common catholic schools [hedge schools], arithmetic and geometry were carried to some length ... the inducement to study these seems to be the practical application of them in measuring land'.[44]

It was in this 'practical application' that the study of bookkeeping and business had its rationale and explanation: hedge schoolmasters were responding to the needs of the age, with a market operating in an unregulated context. Brennan claims: 'The livelihood of a hedge schoolmaster was largely dependent on his mathematical expertise as "the ordinary people of Ireland would set no store by a school in which arithmetic did not figure prominently".'[45] Hedge schoolmasters who depended on demand for their services responded to the requirements of the growing Catholic mercantile classes. McManus claims that 'Irish parents had three main ambitions which they held in prospect for their sons, and these were that they would become either a "priest, a clerk, or a schoolmaster"'.[46] Wall attributes the rise of the 'Catholic class which we find established in many of the towns and cities of Ireland by the middle of the eighteenth century' to 'two sources – from the landed gentry on the one hand, and on the other from the usual, gradual rise of persons from the lower to the middle class'.[47]

As mentioned earlier, hedge schoolmasters were often peripatetic and travelled the countryside selling their services to a population that knew the value of education but rarely had the means of paying for it. Fees were often paid in kind, such as through the provision of accommodation or food. While on the

schools of Carlow', *Carloviana: Journal of the Old Carlow Society*, 12 (1963), 18.   **41** J. Glassford, *Notes of three tours in Ireland* (Bristol, 1832), pp 2, 66. **42** Dowling, *Hedge schools in Ireland*, p. 60.   **43** W.M. Wyse, *Notes on education reform in Ireland from the unpublished memoirs of Sir Thomas Wyse* (Waterford, 1901), p. 16.   **44** J.E. Bicheno, *Ireland and its economy, being the result of observations made in a tour through the country in the Autumn of 1829* (London, 1830), p. 75.   **45** M. Brennan, *Schools of Kildare and Leighlin, AD 1775–1835* (Dublin, 1935), p. 81.   **46** McManus, *The Irish hedge schools and its books*, p. 127.   **47** Wall, 'Catholic middle class', pp 78–9.

supply side of the market there was no curriculum until the advent of the
national school system in 1831, on the demand side the needs of the Catholic
classes were relatively pragmatic. While they generally did not own land, they
rented land which they worked as tenant farmers; skill in measuring land and
the fruits of the land was extremely useful.

The restrictive land system and the changing economic environment led to
the growth of a Catholic merchant class; as a result, commercial savvy and business
skills became increasingly valuable. The success of the hedge schoolmasters
depended on their ability to respond to market needs. In the case of students
aspiring to the priesthood, market needs were institutionally shaped by the
Catholic church (and included, for example, the study of Latin, the catechism
and the classics). In the case of many others, however, the curriculum had to
address the aspiration to be clerk rather than cleric. This meant that, in the absence
of a curriculum, a practical approach to the provision of education required the
inclusion of bookkeeping as an important element of hedge school instruction.

* * *

Dickson evocatively suggests that

> Once upon a time eighteenth-century Ireland seemed simple: it was the
> story of a new landowning class that had inherited the earth in the wake
> of Catholic defeat in 1691 and proceeded to grind down the dispossessed
> and to persecute the old church for more than half a century ... Most
> historians since the 1960s have rejected this 'penal' paradigm, with its
> subtext of a heroic but silenced Catholic nation, and have concentrated
> on such themes as ... the transformation of the material world.[48]

The evidence of bookkeeping education in eighteenth-century Ireland outlined
in this study sheds new light on the origins – and implications – of such trans-
formations in the material world. The eighteenth century in Ireland was an era
where the calculations of commerce, and the need for numeracy, were increasingly woven into the fabric of ordinary life.[49] The evidence suggests that some
hedge schools at least were places of pragmatic pedagogy, with a curriculum of
calculation as well as the classics.

48 D. Dickson, 'Jacobitism in eighteenth-century Ireland: a Munster perspective', *Éire–Ireland*,
39:3 & 4 (2004), 38.   **49** Ibid.; Wall, 'Catholic middle class'.

Shaw and Christianity: towards 1916

Owen Dudley Edwards[1]

WHY NOT GIVE CHRISTIANITY A TRIAL?

The question seems a hopeless one after 2000 years of resolute adherence to the old cry of 'Not this man but Barabbas'. Yet it is beginning to look as if Barabbas was a failure, in spite of his strong right hand, his victories, his empires, his millions of money, and his moralities and churches and political constitutions. 'This man' has not been a failure yet; for nobody has ever been sane enough to try his way. But he has had one quaint triumph. Barabbas has stolen his name and taken his cross as a standard. There is a sort of compliment in that. There is even a sort of loyalty in it, like that of the brigand who breaks every law and yet claims to be a patriotic subject of the king who makes them. We have always had a curious feeling that, though we crucified Christ on a stick, he somehow managed to get hold of the right end of it, and that if we were better men we might try his plan.

THUS BEGINS SHAW'S PREFACE to his *Androcles and the Lion* (play written 2–6 February 1912, performed 1913, preface dated December 1915).[2]

---

1 Shaw's place in this *Festschrift* proclaims its right above all in the letter from Dr Richard Hayes (1902–76), director of the National Library of Ireland from 1940 to 1967, who wrote in April 1945: 'Dear Bernard Shaw, I can think of no more appropriate place than the National Library of Ireland for the permanent preservation for posterity of your manuscripts, correspondence, and first editions. Can you?' His letter, with salutation and signature, ended there. Shaw replied from Ayot St Lawrence, Welwyn, on 6 December 1945, 'Your invitation as National Librarian is in the nature of a command', and he would send the only literary manuscripts he had, his novels, having written his plays in shorthand, subsequently destroyed. See N. Kissane (ed.), *Treasures from the National Library of Ireland* (London, 1995 [1994]), p. 151; also Shaw, *Collected letters*, ed. D.H. Laurence, 4 vols (London, 1965–88), iv, 761 and Shaw to Hayes, 23 Apr. 1946, ibid., pp 766–7 – all Laurence's editions of Shaw are masterly. In adding my small, inadequate tribute here to the scholarly aid, courtesy and kindness of Dónall Ó Luanaigh over many years, I must also express gratitude to and admiration for his mentors Patrick Henchy and Alf Mac Lochlainn, successors of Dr Hayes as director of the Library, and the staffs of the Library over the past half-century, as well as to the Library's historian, Gerard Long, my fellow contributor. The present article has been made possible by the patience and (I trust bloodless) self-sacrifice of Felix Larkin, and by the staff of the only other library fostering a scholarly climate with the warm hearts as well as wise heads to be found in such abundance as in the National Library of Ireland, viz. the National Library of Scotland. 2 'Preface on the prospects of Christianity' in

Would you mind reading it out loud? Thank you. Are your eyes a trifle damp? Or is your throat slightly constricted? If so, you acknowledge (said A.E. Housman, who should have known) that you have been speaking poetry.[3] Why you should register these effects I have no idea; or else I have several ideas, all in mutual conflict. It seems to sound a harmony – which Shaw might have denied – with the last lines of Wilde's *The Sphinx* (published twenty-one years earlier, first drafted ten to twenty years before that): '... leave me to my cruci- fix, / Whose pallid burden, sick with pain, watches the world with wearied eyes, / And weeps for every soul that dies, and weeps for every soul in vain.'[4] So I open by arguing that for all of Shaw's giant logic, in relation to Christianity his most accessible impact can be profoundly aesthetic.

This Christ – isolated, bereft of followers, usurped by Pauline Christianity and its sectarian progeny – arises in much of the Protestant Irish Renaissance: Yeats, in the plays *Calvary* (1920) and *The Resurrection* (1931); George Moore, Catholic-born but Protestant fellow-traveller, in *The Brook Kerith* (1916), whose idea he seems to have pinched from a story told by Wilde; Frank Harris, in 'The Miracle of the Stigmata' (1910), likewise stolen from the same story; J.M. Synge, in *The Playboy of the Western World* (1907), at least by somewhat questionable

---

The Bodley Head Bernard Shaw collected plays, with their prefaces, ed. D.H. Laurence, 7 vols (London, 1970–4), iv, 458. Both play and prefaces may stand independently of one another and of anything else (though the preface really requires Sunday-school perfection in the gospels from its readers – and not by the methods of Mark Twain's Tom Sawyer). The idea of a play on Christian martyrdom arose from Shaw's reviewing the most famous such attempt twenty years earlier, Wilson Barrett's *The sign of the cross* (review in the *Saturday Review*, 11 Jan. 1896; repr. in Shaw, *Our theatre in the nineties,* 3 vols (London, 1932), ii, 7, 12–14). Shaw insisted Barrett made no use of the Bible and was profoundly influenced by Ibsen; but this fun on his part was allowed a touch of indictment thus: 'On the intellectual side, Christianity hardly receives justice from Mr Wilson Barrett. "Christianity is not in itself a crime", says Marcus to Nero. "Marcus argues strongly, Caesar", is Poppea's comment. I must say I think Poppea is rather too easily satisfied' (ibid., p. 13). Hence Shaw's insistence on making *Androcles* a play of ideas in conflict, chiefly among the Christians. Desmond McCarthy, reviewing it for the *New Statesman*, 6 Sept. 1913 (repr. in his *Shaw* (London, 1951), p. 102 and in T.F. Evans (ed.), *George Bernard Shaw: the critical heritage* (London and Boston, 1976), pp 211–15) concluded by quoting two of the audience departing after curtain-fall: '"But what's the point to the whole thing?" "Oh", said his friend, "it's a skit on plays like *The sign of the cross* and *Quo vadis*. That's what it comes to." I was jammed up close against them and I could not help saying, "I think it would be nearer the mark to say that *The sign of the cross* is a skit upon it."'   **3** Housman, 'The name and nature of poetry', the Leslie Stephen lecture for 1933 (delivered at Cambridge, 9 May); repr. in Housman*, Selected prose,* ed. J. Carter (Cambridge, 1960), p. 193.   **4** First ed. 1894. Wilde seems to have written an initial version (at least in part) when at Oxford 1874–8, and certainly worked on it in Paris 1883–4; see R.H. Sherard [Kennedy], *Oscar Wilde: the story of an unhappy friendship* (London, 1908 [1902]), pp 31–2.

inference.⁵ Some of this certainly derives from early nineteenth-century Protestant evangelicals whence Shaw, like Wilde and Yeats and Harris, descended – to say nothing of more orthodox Church of Ireland placemen so prominent in Synge genealogy. The Renaissance leaders were their own evangels, none more so than Shaw, their mission to enlighten their archipelago culturally pursued with the same zeal originally making unsuccessful proselytizers of their grandparents. Their forsaken Christ was in some respects their apotheosis of the old Protestant zealots who wore themselves into early deaths while fruitlessly seeking the seduction of the masses from Catholicism. There is an element of personal identification with Christ in all cases – Wilde's particularly in 'Poems in Prose' and *De Profundis,* as opposed to works in which Christ redeems a Wildean figure directly ('The Selfish Giant', *The Ballad of Reading Gaol*) or indirectly ('The Canterville Ghost', 'The Young King', 'The Star-Child'). Shaw as playwright was virtually Wilde's designated heir, Yeats Wilde's protégé. This did not make their Christs any less Shavian or Yeatsian, but it was unavoidable that their Christs were shaded by Wilde, the greatest cultural martyr either of them ever knew.

Execution is a different matter. Shaw as a teacher sought to be explicit, Wilde and Yeats variously pursued implicities. All three worked for effect, and each of them wanted to excite and irritate their audiences into thought, whether obstinate or pliable. Shaw perhaps brings off the most emotive effect by unexpected tenderness in the midst of hard-bitten hectorials: his initial 'I am no more Christian than Pilate was, or you, gentle reader' co-exists with 'It is Luke's Jesus who has won our hearts', while his preceding description of the stable birth in Bethlehem is introduced as 'the most charming idyll in the Bible' and the reader

---

5 For Wilde as origin of the story of Jesus' survival and secret life after crucifixion, see H. Pearson, *The life of Oscar Wilde* (London, 1946), pp 217–18. Pearson describes it as 'the foundation of several later romances by men who heard him tell it or heard others report it'. However, he charitably refrains from mentioning Harris, 'The miracle of the stigmata', *English Review* (April 1910), repr. in his *Unpath'd waters* (London, 1913), or Moore – perhaps because Pearson's friend Shaw, with his usual good nature, wrote Harris that 'it is rather significant that you and I and George Moore should be on the same tack', although Shaw's play and preface assumed Christ's crucifixion fatal (and the preface denied both his divinity and resurrection). Shaw continued: 'The main thing that I have tried to bring out, and indeed the only thing that made the job worth doing for me, is that modern sociology and biology are bearing Jesus out in his peculiar economics and theology.' (Shaw to Harris, 11 Nov. 1915; quoted in S. Weintraub (ed.), *The playwright and the pirate* (Gerrards Cross, Bucks., 1982), pp 20–2). Harris, by now a permanent exile from the UK and supporter of Germany in the war, wrote Shaw on 29 September 1916: 'As I predicted, George Moore's book is negligible – nothing in it worth reading' (ibid., p. 48). Lord Alfred Douglas attempted – unsuccessfully – to have Moore and his publisher, T. Werner Laurie, prosecuted for blasphemy.

is deliberately reconquered by the aesthetics of the birth of Christ despite its
annual commercialization. In such moments the archbishop's affirmation to Joan
that she is in love with religion might seems applicable to her dramatist.[6] Even
Shaw's denial of Christianity becomes akin to the publican's self-portrait as a
sinner, or St Peter's similar cry when professionally confronted by the impossible draught of fishes. Like Wilde, Shaw genuinely – and gently – loves Jesus.
And in the best traditions of love, he will accept no substitutes: Christianity for
Shaw is a usurpation of Christ. Like the other Protestant Irish creative writers
of his time, he was in deep rebellion against both its Roman Catholic and its
Protestant varieties. Their anti-Catholic rebellion was instinctive and tribal; their
anti-Protestant rebellion took many forms, including migrant sympathies with
Catholicism. In Shaw, as in Wilde, Yeats, O'Casey and others, all of this flour-
ished on deep knowledge and aesthetically creative use of the Bible.

In the period from the writing of *Androcles* until after its publication alongside its very belated preface, Shaw took up the theme of Christ versus
Christianity at various points – more correctly, Christ versus 'Christianity'. For
example:

> I do not profess to be a Christian ... I have no religion whatever in the
> sectarian sense. In this my position is curiously like that of Jesus himself,
> who seems to have no religion ... Christianity was a growing thing
> which was finally suppressed by the crucifixion ... Our police and sol-
> diers ... profess to prevent murder and theft, but they do not. They do
> not profess to prevent Christianity, but they do.[7]

Inevitably he was accused of creating a Jesus in his preface 'in my own image':

> Of course, Jesus was as like me as any one man is like another ... I may
> go further and claim that, as we were both led to become preachers of
> the same doctrine in spite of different ways, I may reasonably be con-
> sidered a little more like Jesus than, say – well, perhaps I had better name
> no names. At all events, whether Jesus be placed in a sub species or in a
> super species, it is a species to which I apparently belong philosophically.
> But beyond this I cannot see that I have gone. I am not a faith healer.
> I am a teetotaller and vegetarian ... If any attempt is made to crucify me

6 Shaw, Preface to *Androcles*, in *Collected plays and prefaces*, iv, 459, 495–7; *Saint Joan*, sc. 2,
ibid., vi, 109.   7 Shaw, speaking under the auspices of the Revd Reginald Campbell on
'Christianity and equality', City Temple, quoted by the invaluable Michael Holroyd, *Bernard
Shaw: the pursuit of power, 1898–1918* (London, 1989), pp 286–7.

(and my dislike to blatant pseudo-patriotic nonsense may yet get me into trouble), I shall most certainly not submit as to a fatal ordeal and undertake to rise after three days ... Still, I shall not affect to regard the comparison as uncomplimentary. It is not in modest depreciation that I insist that 'my Jesus' is not mine at all, and not one and indivisible, but the three Jesuses of the gospels: the harsh, bigoted, vituperative, haughty Jesus of Matthew, the charming, affable, woman-beloved Jesus of Luke, and the restlessly intellectual debater, poet and philosophic genius described by John.[8]

This does less than justice to the preface to *Androcles*, which clearly shows Shaw fulfilling his iconoclastic duty and distinguishing himself from the Sunday school prizewinner no doubt often held up as an example in Protestant Dublin when – beginning with Matthew (he takes the four in their order in the Bible) – he takes a dislike to Matthew and blames him for at least some apparent blemishes in Matthew's Jesus: 'Matthew, like most biographers, strives to identify the opinions and prejudices of his hero with his own.'[9] But even here, as the ex-Calvinist Ulsterman, St John Ervine, saw so well (in a largely blind six hundred page book): 'If anything is clear in the preface of *Androcles and the Lion*, it is the respect and reverence GBS feels for Jesus Christ.'[10] Love would have been a better word – it always is where discussions of Jesus are concerned – but Ervine was very uneasy about ascribing sentiments of love in one man about another. Shaw comes into his own on Luke (he makes very little of Mark): has anyone exhaled the breath of its charm so well? He is less at ease with John, and for an obvious reason: in John, Shaw recognized an intellect comparable to his own. But, while allowing for all their divergences, Shaw – child of a folklore-dominated Ireland – saw the unity of the figure whose contrasts in the telling he enjoyed so much. In fact, he mocked the then fashionable preoccupation with attempted demo-

---

8 Shaw to editor, *New Statesman*, 17 June 1916, replying to Desmond MacCarthy, 'Mr Shaw on Christianity' [notice of the preface to *Androcles and the lion*, published now with its play, *Overruled* and *Pygmalion*], *New Statesman*, 3 June 1916 (repr. in his *Shaw*, p. 117), which declared: 'No array of terms can express my contempt for this portrait [of Jesus]. Mr. Shaw, in painting it, has neither as artist nor as philosopher tried to get out of himself. He has not paid his subject the respect which would have been due even had his subject been one of the meanest of mankind instead of one of the greatest – namely, that of treating him as someone different from himself. There is egotistical delusion latent in this picture: all great men are really like me.' Shaw's reply was reprinted in Shaw, *Agitations: letters to the press, 1875–1950*, ed. D.H. Laurence and James Rambeau (New York, 1985), pp 204–7.   9 Shaw, Preface to *Androcles*, in *Collected plays and prefaces*, iv, 487.   10 St John Ervine [J.G. Irvine], *Bernard Shaw: his life, work and friends* (New York, 1956), p. 440.

lition of the gospels from their discrepancies, stressing instead the value of the variety. We might amuse ourselves by seeing Shaw's self-portraiture initially in his ideas of the evangelists: Luke as his childhood innocence, Matthew as his awkward immaturity or nonage as he would call it, while John

> was obviously more of a man of the world than the others, and knew, as mere chroniclers and romancers never know, what actually happens away from books and desks … John's claim to give evidence as an eye-witness whilst the others are only compiling history is supported by a certain verisimilitude which appeals to me as one who has preached a new doctrine and argued about it, as well as written stories. This verisimilitude may be dramatic art backed by knowledge of public life; but even at that we must not forget that the best dramatic art is the oper-ation of a divinatory instinct for truth.[11]

But however much Shaw might feel common ground with John, (more occasionally) with Luke or (more surreptitiously) with Matthew, he now had all too good reason for comparison with Jesus, as his mirthless mockery over his own possible crucifixion bore testimony. His pamphlet, *Common Sense about the War*, issued shortly after the outbreak of European hostilities in August 1914 as a supplement to the *New Statesman* (14 Dec. 1914), resulted in ostracism, witch-hunting, attempted press-inspired boycotts of his plays, the premier's son's assertion in the Royal Naval Division mess that he ought to be shot, his illegal expulsion from the Dramatists' Club from which he then obligingly resigned, the *New Statesman* literary editor J.C. Squire's demand that he be tarred and feathered, H.G. Wells' description of him as an idiot child laughing in a hospital, and the *New Statesman*'s own reluctance to publish him further on war issues. The pamphlet was not pacifist, but its cold realism made it unpopular in a war whose thin justification was being sustained by demagogic official and officially-inspired propaganda.[12] Shaw, like his beloved antagonist, G.K.

---

11 Shaw, Preface to *Androcles*, in *Collected plays and prefaces*, iv, 504–5.   **12** Shaw's account of this is given in H. Pearson, *Bernard Shaw* (London, 1975 [1942 & 1951]), pp 341–54, largely accepted by S. Weintraub, *Bernard Shaw, 1914–1918: journey to 'Heartbreak'* (London, 1973), pp 60–1, the leading study of these years, and also in Michael Holroyd's excellent multi-volume biography. It may need some closer scrutiny for individual cases, not necessarily all errors being due to Shaw (e.g. Weintraub assumes the Herbert Asquith asserting that Shaw should be shot was the prime minister but it is clear from Shaw's narrative that the speaker was a serving officer and therefore the son). The loss of friends serving at the front brought Squire closer to *Common sense about the war* (which in any case he had to help distribute as part of his assistant editorial duties, especially since it proved a money-spinner for the *New*

Chesterton, would end the war campaigning in Ireland to boost Irish recruits to the colours – for which he had written *O'Flaherty, VC* in September 1915, only to find its production impossible in the UK. It was first staged by the officers of Squadron 40, Royal Flying Corps, on the Western Front in Belgium on 17 February 1917.[13] But his fate analogized him to fellow-Irishmen also self-identifying with Jesus, headed by Patrick Pearse.

The idea of Jesus as exemplar is old, and its roots precede the historical Jesus. The bardic tradition depended for its own survival on hero-chieftains learning in youth to emulate the precursors of whom the bard sang that they were first in peace, first in war, first in the patronage of bards. Bards of more cosmopolitan range invited youthful identification with glorious bellicose heroes whose courage would fulfil prophesies at their infancy that their lives would be short: Achilles and Cú Chulainn, for instance. A subordinate but subtler theme was the receptive pupil as future hero: Telemachus or Fionn Mac Cumhail. Ethics change over time and instruction by example with them: Achilles' insubordination to Agamemnon, deplorable to modern war-lords, is largely praiseworthy to the Homeric tutor being a question of honour, Cú Chulain's combat with his beloved Ferdia ultimately a matter of honour also. How far pupils read the lesson that bards and masters intend is another matter: Xenophon, the pupil of Socrates, supposedly desired youthful audiences to learn from the character of Cyrus the younger in his *Anabasis*, notably that Persia could be penetrated by a Greek army under resolute leadership; but students of its first book might well draw the moral to avoid a young leader so obsessed by hatred of his elder brother and king that in a furious personal attack he threw away his life, the safety of his generals and the prospects of his army. Werner Jaeger with amusing anachronism drew Greek and Christian traditions together in saying that Plato 'began by a concentration on the pure intellect which looks quite Protestant; and now [in the *Laws*] he discusses the importance of those visible

---

Statesman). Within a few months Squire had written 'The dilemma': 'God heard the embattled nations sing and shout / "Gott strafe England!" and "God Save the King!" / God this, God that, and God the other thing – / "Good God!" said God, "I've got my work cut out."' 'The dilemma' was published in J.C. Squire, *The survival of the fittest and other poems* (London, 1916), for which he in his turn was duly censured in a largely favourable review by G.K. Chesterton's brother Cecil (by now a convert to Roman Catholicism, which Gilbert would not be until 1923) in *New Witness*, 8 June 1916: 'Here and there in these excellent verses a false note is struck ... savouring of the unclean thing called pacifism. For instance, I am not impressed by poems like "The dilemma" ... The same criticism applies to ... "The higher life for clergymen" in which one discovers the fantastic idea – extraordinary in a man of Mr Squire's education – that there is something historically inconsistent in men who claim to be representatives of Jesus Christ applauding the prosecution of war. Why on earth not?' **13** For the problems arising from *O'Flaherty, VC*, see Weintraub, *Shaw: 1914–1918*, pp 126–30.

expressions of the spirit which Catholic education always tries to mould as early as possible'.[14]

This may offer itself as a pleasing contrast between Shaw and Pearse as teachers (and before we go further, let us salute them as remarkable educational theorists, whatever their other demerits).[15] But Jesus Christ is one convergence. Surprisingly, little use had been made of Jesus as hero-exemplar down the centuries. No doubt many bad teachers sought to repair their own deficiencies by impairing the religious faith of their charges through caricaturing Jesus as a sort of child toady on the teacher's side. Cecil Alexander, whose husband would later become archbishop of Armagh, was an unfortunate instance of this in what is in many other respects a beautiful carol, 'Once in Royal David's City': 'Christian children all must be / Mild, obedient, good as he.' The popularity of Thomas à Kempis' early fifteenth-century *Imitation of Christ* among Catholics and Protestants, notably in the pre-war years of the twentieth century, may seem to support the notion of Jesus as exemplar, but in fact à Kempis' cult of humility would naturally reject as impious and immodest any self-likening to Jesus. His readers are being told how to make themselves fit for salvation by Christ Jesus, who becomes a speaker in the text but with no implication that His hearer – or pupil – is being moulded to resemble Him. The dialogue is bold enough in itself, and valuable in deepening a sense of prayer, and perhaps in putting words in Jesus' mouth; à Kempis was as reckless as any would-be imitator, but like many another great writer, including Shaw and Pearse, he knew his reader's place.[16]

---

14 Jaeger, *Paideia: the ideals of Greek culture*, trans. G. Highet, 3 vols (London, 1945), iii, 228; see also i, 8–11, 18–33, 38–9 and iii, 160–1, 226–9, 252–3, 349 (n. 302). My thanks to Roger Savage for this most interesting reference. B.M. Coldrey, *Faith and fatherland: the Christian Brothers and the development of Irish nationalism, 1838–1921* (Dublin, 1988), p. 204, notes Pearse's staging Standish James O'Grady's 'The coming of Fionn' and 'Boy-deeds of Cuchulain' in 1909 (O'Grady wrote 'Finn'). **15** On Pearse, I follow R. Dudley Edwards, *Patrick Pearse: the triumph of failure* (London, 1977), to which all subsequent scholarship is profoundly indebted, but see also J.J. Lee, *The modernization of Irish society, 1848–1918* (Dublin, 1973), pp 141–3, on Pearse's value as an educationalist. His admirable reply to the father who complained his son only wanted to play a tin whistle – 'buy him a tin whistle' – seems so Shavian as to affirm a direct influence, such as he covertly drew from Wilde and more openly from Ibsen. C. Cruise O'Brien, *Ancestral voices: religion and nationalism in Ireland* (Baldoyle, Co. Dublin, 1994), p. 98, points to Pearse's embrace of Irish nationalist pieties and rejections being at the expense of his father's British assumption (and where he cites me as disagreeing with that thesis, he is right and I was wrong): 'The subsequent fervour of Pearse's commitment … was proportionate, I believe, to the pain of that conversion.' **16** The National Library of Scotland catalogue records thirty-three translations of the *Imitation* published between 1901 and 1914, one in Scots and five in selections: this seems relevant to the sacrificial yearnings of that generation up to 1916, despite my *caveat* about à Kempis' intentions. Works inviting identification with Jesus were appearing just before and during the First

Shaw's first mature engagement with Christianity on stage was written in the last third of 1896: *The Devil's Disciple*. The play turns on a profound but not invariable circumstance, that revolutions above all else make human beings discover themselves anew: in the American Revolution the Revd Anthony Anderson discovers himself to be a soldier and Dick Dudgeon, devil's disciple, discovers himself to be a Christian pastor. It recoils in bitter irony from the attempted revolution in Dublin in 1916, when Pearse the schoolmaster tried to discover himself as a soldier and found he was no such thing, and General Sir John Maxwell the soldier tried to discover himself as a statesman and proved not to be one, whether or not he realized it. Dudgeon proves a true follower of Christ when he deliberately allows himself to be arrested by British soldiers who take him for Anderson and then accepts death, first to protect Anderson and, when his identity is known, for 'the world's future' – a fair description of what Christ died for, if 'the world' includes the world dead before the crucifixion. But at the gallows the Christian pastor tearing himself into existence within Dudgeon will not tolerate what he regards as violation of Christ's message by a supposedly Christian chaplain:

> REV. MR BRUDENELL [*gently reproving Richard*]. Try to control yourself, and submit to the divine will. [*He lifts his book to proceed with the service.*]
>
> RICHARD. Answer for your own will, sir, and those of your accomplices there ... I see little divinity about them or you. You talk to me of Christianity when you are in the act of hanging your enemies. Was there ever such blasphemous nonsense! [*To Major Swindon, more rudely*] You've got up the solemnity of the occasion, as you call it, to impress the people with your own dignity – Handel's music and a clergyman to make murder look like piety! ...
>
> REV. MR BRUDENELL [*beginning to read*]. Man that is born of woman hath –

World War (e.g. F.B. Reynolds, *Jesus the hero* (London, [NLS stamp, 25 Mar.] 1914), as detailed in studying the historical socio-economic context as Pearse was in his teaching on Ireland in Jesus' time (Pearse, *In first-century Ireland*, Dublin, 1936, repr. from *An Claidheamh Soluis*, 21 Dec. 1907). G.C. Leader, *Follow the Christ: a series of talks to boys on the life of Jesus* (London, [NLS stamp, 4 July] 1916), p. 211, equated calls of God and country more crudely than Pearse: 'You boys who read this can help Jesus. You have what He can use. Have you seen that picture of Lord Kitchener on our hoardings, with keen gaze and pointed finger and the message underneath, "Your king and country need you"? Millions have responded to that call. Do not be less loyal to the greater King. Jesus needs you, your strength of body, your keenness of mind, your eagerness, your enthusiasm, your energy, your all.' There is a hint of faint anxiety lest patriotism outweigh religion in Leader: no such doubts seem present in Pearse.

> RICHARD [*fixing his eyes on him*]. 'Thou shalt not kill.' [*The book drops in Brudenell's hands.*][17]

Religion to Shaw was a matter of generations. The evangelical identity had existed among his grandparents. His parents' generation reacted sharply against religious belief, having been steeped in it. Shaw wrote of his mother's brother Walter, 'Being full of the Bible, he quoted the sayings of Jesus as models of facetious repartee', and that his humour,

> though barbarous in its blasphemous indecency, was Scriptural and Shakespearean in the elaboration and fantasy of its literary expression ... The raising of Lazarus ... he said ... was what would be called in these days a put-up job, by which he meant that Jesus had made a confederate of Lazarus – had made it worth his while, or had asked him for friendship's sake, to pretend he was dead and at the proper moment to pretend to come to life.

He remembered a discussion of the religion of a visitor who was a Unitarian:

> I asked my father what a Unitarian was; and he, being the victim of a sense of humor [*sic*] and a taste for anticlimax ... thoughtlessly replied that the Unitarians are people who believe that our Lord was not really crucified at all, but was seen 'running away down the other side of the Hill of Calvary'. Childlike, I accepted this statement *au pied de la lettre*, and believed it devoutly until I was thirty-five or thereabouts ...[18]

It is a little unclear whether he simply believed this to be a summation of Unitarian non-theology (not to be confused with atheology) or believed in it himself. Certainly he never seems to have believed Jesus was God subsequent to his eleventh year, and what he believed before this was left to the mood in which he chose to recollect it. But he identified with his vision of youth, rejecting the anti-socialist secularism of the previous generation which he handles with instructive frivolity in *You Never Can Tell* (written 1895–6, first published 1898 and performed 1899) and with harder cutting edges in the first act of *Man and Superman* (written 1901–2, with first publication 1903 and performance 1905). The dethronement of secularism for spirituality may not have been as clear in those plays as was its supersession by socialism, but it was made almost

17 Shaw, *The devil's disciple*, in *Collected plays and prefaces*, ii, 134.   **18** S. Weintraub (ed.), *Shaw: an autobiography, 1856–1898* (New York, 1970), pp 26, 36, 38.

brutally frank to everyone, including himself, in *John Bull's Other Island* (written and first performed 1904, first published 1907). It rejected several secularisms: that of the English Liberal capitalist Broadbent, that of his acclimatized Irish-born economic partner Larry Doyle, that of the Catholic parish priest Father Dempsey, that of the newly enriched Irish agrarian small capitalists. Shaw wrote it with the extraordinary credential of twenty years primarily in Dublin followed by immersion in London for twenty-eight years without return to Ireland – let alone to the play's rural Ireland. The play's phenomenal accuracy about Irish society seems to have been achieved by ruthless vacuum-cleaning of every possible Irish detail from his Irish acquaintances. But its hilarious iconoclasm was all the stronger by his use of Keegan, the unfrocked priest, authentic in detail (including the local Catholic belief in neo-druidic powers of such priests) and at the same time a towering rebuke to us all, himself included, for our compromises with Mammon. Shaw may have often put himself into a play flashing various facets – to date, at the very least, he had been Marchbanks in *Candida*, Valentine in *You Never Can Tell*, Tanner in *Man and Superman* and, presumably, Caesar in *Caesar and Cleopatra* – but to his play dissecting his native land he gave two Shaws, Larry Doyle and Peter Keegan, the Shaw remade in England and the Shaw that might have evolved in Ireland. But the Shaw who stayed in Ireland stands for a modern Jesus as well as for a better Shaw. Shaw had played with Christ-like goodness before – Morell in *Candida*, 'William' in *You Never Can Tell* – but Keegan is his first mature portrait based on Christ (with a strong dash of St Francis). Appropriately he is an outcast, feared, scorned, patronized.

Peter Keegan in many ways is consistent with the post-crucifixion Jesus of the story Wilde told whence Frank Harris would later spin 'The Miracle of the Stigmata' and George Moore *The Brook Kerith*: a figure at odds with the clergy from whom he has been expelled, highly spiritual in contrast to their materialism and – more pointedly – their success in acquiring, ruling and disciplining followers. Keegan is even more consistent with the Jesus on whom Shaw would sum up his preface to *Androcles and the Lion* eleven years later: 'For priests he had not a civil word; and they shewed their sense of his hostility by getting him killed as soon as possible. He was, in short, a thoroughgoing anti-Clerical.'[19] Keegan does not make war on Dempsey, although Dempsey clearly both abominates and fears Keegan, but Keegan is implacably opposed to the greed, ruthlessness, ambition and treachery into which Doyle and Broadbent are rapidly lowering themselves and the townland of Roscullen on which they will prey with Dempsey's blessing. Keegan usually keeps himself apart and silent, but cruelty to animals – Shaw's chief reason for vegetarianism – brings him into a rage

19 Shaw, Preface to *Androcles*, in *Collected plays and prefaces*, iv, 579.

blindingly reminiscent of Jesus' expulsion of the moneylenders from the temple, as when the men are laughing at Broadbent's adventures with the pig in the motorcar ending in the pig's destruction:

> NORA. I don't know how you can laugh. Do you, Mr. Keegan?
>
> KEEGAN [*grimly*]. Why not? There is danger, destruction, torment! What more do we want to make us merry? Go on, Barney: the last drops of joy are not squeezed from the story yet. Tell us again how our brother was torn asunder.
>
> DORAN [*puzzled*]. Whose bruddher?
>
> KEEGAN. Mine.
>
> NORA. He means the pig, Mr Doran. You know his way.
>
> DORAN [*rising gallantly to the occasion*]. Bedad I'm sorry for your poor bruddher, Misther Keegan; but I recommend you to thry him wid a couple o fried eggs for your breakfast tomorrow. It was a case of Excelsior wi dhat ambitious baste; for not content wid jumpin from the back seat into the front wan, he jumped from the front wan into the road in front of the car. And –
>
> KEEGAN. And everybody laughed!
>
> …
>
> DORAN [*reflectively*] … Oh, you never heard such a hullaballoo as there was. There was Molly cryin Me chaney, me beautyful chaney! n oul Matt shoutin Me pig, me pig! n the polis takin the number o the car, n not a man in the town able to speak for laughin –
>
> KEEGAN [*with intense emphasis*]. It is hell: it is hell. Nowhere else could such a scene be a burst of happiness for the people.

It is classic Shavian use of the last laugh: a just revenge for endless English ridicule of the Irishman and his pig – with the Englishman now the ludicrous butt of a pig joke, explosive beyond anything the original form and its excruciating variations could offer – ends in Keegan showing the Irish countryfolk, and their audience in the English theatre, what hell they have found so funny. And Shaw has lifted it beyond the usual standoff between Irish Protestants and Catholics, the former apparently indifferent to lower-class Catholic sufferings but solicitous for their own animals, the latter the converse, as Somerville and Ross so eloquently brought to life in *The Silver Fox* (1898). Keegan is emphatically Irish Catholic in ancestry as well as in person, just as is the other Shaw, Larry Doyle. If this seems alien to Shaw (for all of his infant acquaintance with Catholic nurses and, briefly, schoolmates), what of Keegan's final speech, where Shaw, denier of divinity to Jesus or anything else, articulates an ideal of the Trinity with which Roman Catholic doctrine – now if not then – might find little to quarrel:

> KEEGAN. In my dreams it is a country where the State is the Church and the Church the people: three in one and one in three. It is a commonwealth in which work is play and play is life: three in one and one in three. It is a temple in which the priest is the worshipper and the worshipper the worshipped: three in one and one in three. It is a godhead in which all life is human and all humanity divine: three in one and one in three. It is, in short, the dream of a madman. [*He goes away across the hill.*][20]

The next identification of Shaw with Jesus was made in 1909 by G.K. Chesterton, of all people, in his *George Bernard Shaw*'s first chapter, 'The Irishman':

> There exists by accident an early and beardless portrait of him which really suggests in the severity and purity of its lines some of the early ascetic pictures of the beardless Christ. However he may shout profanities or seek to shatter the shrines, there is always something about him which suggests that in a sweeter and more solid civilisation he would have been a great saint. He would have been a saint of a sternly ascetic, perhaps of a sternly negative, type. But he has this strange note of the saint in him: that he is literally unworldly. Worldliness has no human magic for him; he is not bewitched by rank nor drawn on by conviviality at all. He could not understand the intellectual surrender of the snob.[21]

Shaw was duly quoted in most, if not all, subsequent editions saying that Chesterton's was 'the best work of literary art I have yet provoked'.[22] Neither he nor Chesterton seem to have followed up the point and Chesterton, on the verge of creating Father Brown, kept well away from formal analysis of Father

---

20 Shaw, *John Bull's other island*, in *Collected plays and prefaces*, ii, 981–3, 1021. C.B. Purdom (ed.), *Bernard Shaw's letters to Granville Barker* (London, 1956), although now superseded by Dan Lawrence's four-volume edition of the *Collected letters*, contains convenient textual and editorial data on the first production of *John Bull's other island*, in which Shaw lured Granville Barker into playing Keegan, partly by hinting that it could be well played by J.L. Shine who, in fact, played Larry Doyle. Shaw, *The matter with Ireland*, ed. D.H. Lawrence and D.H. Greene (2nd ed. with new material, Gainesville, 2001 [Gainesville, 1962]) is the basis of all study of Shaw and Ireland.   **21** G.K. Chesterton, *George Bernard Shaw* (London, 1961 [London, 1909]), pp 11–12.   **22** Ibid., jacket.

Keegan. Chesterton and Shaw were once to take part in a film, in which they
were got up as cowboys: it may be no more than coincidence that Shaw's next
confrontation with Jesus was set in a cowboy context, *The Shewing-up of Blanco
Posnet* (written and first performed – in the Abbey Theatre – 1909, first published 1911). 'This little play is really a religious tract in dramatic form', begins
Shaw's preface,[23] and it was doubly conceived as such, firstly in order to confront theatre censorship under the English lord chamberlain – and any possible
alternative – with the folly of its situation, and secondly to fulfil the artistic intent
of its creator for the result described by his friend (and original of Cusins in
Major Barbara), the classical scholar Gilbert Murray:

> The actual theme of the play is both grand and tragic, in spite of its ugly
> and grotesque setting … This is the play in which Shaw has quite directly
> and without any subterfuge or nervous laughter expressed his religious
> faith – or a fragment of it … As a matter of fact Shaw is entirely in earnest
> about his religious preaching though it is possible that all he has done is
> to discover the Ten Commandments over again.[24]

Lady Gregory told the under-secretary for Ireland, Sir James Dougherty, that
it was 'a deeply religious play, and one that could hurt no man, woman or child'
when Dougherty threatened to withdraw the Abbey's performance patent should
it stage *Posnet*, now banned in England by the lord chamberlain. Dublin's
exemption from English censorship invited Shaw's resort to his birthplace – as
well as the conviction of the king (Edward VII, an interesting choice of moral
judicature), the chamberlain, the lord lieutenant and his court that Dublin ought
to know its duty to follow London's decisions.

Lady Gregory predicted to Shaw that, while herself liking *Blanco Posnet* better and better, 'you will have the jealousy against you of priest and preacher,
who think the pulpit has a monopoly of sermons'.[25] When it was staged, the

23 Shaw, Preface to *The shewing-up of Blanco Posnet*, in *Collected plays and prefaces*, iii, 763. 24
Gilbert Murray to Robert, first earl of Crewe, 17 Aug. 1909, quoted in D.H. Laurence and
N. Grene (eds), *Shaw, Lady Gregory and the Abbey: a correspondence and a record* (Gerrards Cross,
Bucks., 1993), p. xvi. Crewe was then lord privy seal and colonial secretary and had been
lord lieutenant of Ireland 1892–5, and hence was believed to carry weight in the cabinet on
Irish questions. 25 Augusta Lady Gregory, Journal, 12 Aug. 1909; Gregory to Shaw, 24
Aug. 1909: Laurence and Grene (eds), *Shaw, Gregory*, pp 16, 46. Shaw was convinced that
the lord lieutenant, the earl of Aberdeen, capitulated to the Abbey under the impact of Shaw's
telegrams to Gregory – e.g. 'It is an insult to the lord lieutenant to ignore him and refer me
to … a subordinate English official. I will be no party to any such indelicacy' (14 Aug. 1909,
ibid., pp 21–2) – being convinced, as he wrote Gregory on 17 Aug (ibid., p. 28), that the

reviewer for the Trieste *Il Piccolo della Sera* (published 5 September 1909) acidly agreed, he being James Joyce:

> It is a sermon. Shaw is a born preacher. His lively and talkative spirit can-
> not stand to be subjected to the noble and bare style appropriate to mod-
> ern playwriting ... He has dug up the central incident of *The Devil's*
> *Disciple* and transformed it into a sermon. The transformation is too
> abrupt to be convincing as a sermon, and the art too poor to make it
> convincing as a drama.[26]

This was a little snobbish of Joyce. Shaw, invading the world of Bret Harte, had to conjure up sermons of a coarse crudity alien to those which Joyce (and the present writer) received from the Jesuits of Belvedere College, immortalized in the then gestating *A Portrait of the Artist as a Young Man*. From Harte, too, Shaw had taken the central idea of the redeeming child:[27] the Belvedere Jesuits, all

Dublin Castle officials 'made an appalling technical blunder in acting as agents of the lord chamberlain in Ireland; and I worded my telegram in such a way as to make it clear that I knew the value of that indiscretion. I daresay the telegram reached the Castle before it reached you.' Shaw gleefully capitalized by telegram on the news that the king wanted his Dublin viceroy to conform to his London censorship and 'instructed' Gregory to abandon the pro- duction after implicating the king. Aberdeen's Dublin Castle staff realized that any such ges- ture would unite warring nationalist factions in solidarity against Edward VII. The Castle had coyly hinted that the play might cause trouble for the Abbey with the Roman Catholic Archbishop William Walsh of Dublin, but Shaw – remembering Walsh's nationalism in Parnell's time – instructed Yeats to make public Shaw's assurance to 'the lord lieutenant that there is nothing in the other passages objected to by the English censorship that might not have been written by the Catholic archbishop of Dublin and in point of consideration for the religious beliefs of the Irish people the play compares very favorably with the Coronation Oath' which Edward VII had taken despite the violence of its anti-Catholicism (ibid., p. 44) – the subsequent outcry making him the last king to use that form of it. As a result most anti- Abbey Catholic nationalists rallied against Dublin Castle censorship. **26** Evans (ed.), *Shaw: the critical heritage*, pp 197–9. The dignity of Joyce's critical reproof is somewhat lessened by its having been printed over the signature 'James Yoyce'. **27** The Harte source was promptly identified by the diarist Joseph Holloway whose journal is such a mine of information on Dublin theatre history: 'Lords and ladies were present a [*sic*] galore [Holloway seems unac- quainted with the Irish *go leor* – enough – which fed the fashionable UK slang of his day "galore"] and many "nice people with nasty ideas" had come on the off chance of hearing and seeing something strongly unpleasant. They were doomed to disappointment as Shaw's play proved a sort of sermon set in vivid melodramatic frame and all the audience at its con- clusion wondered only why the censor vetoed it and put a bad name on it ... The stirring events leading up to the conversion of Posnet were like a page torn out of Bret Harte and brought to life on the stage.' He also saw the link with Bizet's *Carmen* (Shaw had thoroughly dissected the title-role in a savage review of Henry Hamilton's dramatization of Prosper

too aware of the more earthly character of their child charges, made less of that particular cult. But the romantic Pearse would use it in his stories and plays of these years, and if he preserved the innocence of his educational theories in the face of schoolboy realities, we may envy him. He had derived it, after all, from Wilde – whose 'The Selfish Giant' is the parent of Pearse's 'Iosagán', but whose 'The Birthday of the Infanta' and 'The Star-Child' (not to speak of 'Salomé') showed a firm hand in the creation of selfish children. The conceit draws on the Victorian obsession – in literature and, less frequently, in legislation – with *kindertötenlieder*, in which Dickens' Little Nell and Paul Dombey and Harriet Beecher Stowe's Little Eva breathe their beautiful last *pour encourager les autres*, but the ruthless social critic of self-gratifying, self-destructive English aristocracy, Frances Hodgson Burnett, made her eponymous hero of *Little Lord Fauntleroy* (1886) the American child-saviour of his repulsive earl-grandfather while staying vigorously alive. The story of Jesus challenges the artist: on the one hand, as Shaw said, Luke's account of the nativity 'has won our hearts'; on the other, the redemptive Jesus is an adult and a most articulate one, be Shaw once again our witness. The Nicene Creed ably links God the Son's choice of incarnation to crucifixion, for us and for our safety, but greater narrative length loses the force of the redemptive child. Wilde circumnavigated the problem magnificently by the last epiphany: 'on the palms of the child's hands were the prints of two nails, and the prints of two nails were on the little feet'. When the Giant seeks to 'take my big sword and slay him' who 'hath dared to wound thee', the child tells him they are the wounds of love and takes him to paradise.[28] This probably shows familiarity with T.D. Sullivan's 'The death of Conor MacNessa', as might be expected from Wilde's mother's son: Conor dies in rage when a druid tells him of Christ's crucifixion.[29] But the Christ for whom Conor died is adult: it was from Bret Harte's 'The Luck of Roaring Camp' (*Overland Monthly*, 1868; eponymous-titled book, 1870) that Shaw drew his child-saviour, apart from yet another of his many debts to Wilde. Wilde prob-

Mérimée's novel, *Saturday Review*, 13 Jun. 1896, repr. in *Our theatre in the nineties*, ii, 152–6): 'Sara Allgood's Carmenesque 'study' of Feemy Evans, the loose woman who tries to get Posnet hanged, was picturesque' (quoted in Laurence and Grene (eds), *Shaw, Gregory*, pp 47–8). The novelist George Birmingham, pen-name of the Church of Ireland rector of Westport, Co. Mayo, the Revd James Owen Hannay, gave what amounts to a professional opinion as divine as well as theatre critic (*Manchester Guardian*, 26 Aug. 1909, quoted ibid., p. 50): 'The play is not a blasphemy, and it is not indecent. It is a sermon on the working of the spirit of God in the heart of a man.' **28** Wilde's 'The selfish giant' originally appeared in his collection of fairy-tales *The happy prince and other tales* (London, 1888): it was one of the stories he told his infant sons. **29** Apart from appearing in T.D. Sullivan's poems, it was also included in his brother Alexander's *The story of Ireland* (Dublin, 1870).

ably also owed inspiration to Harte's story of the newborn child whose presence reforms the California gold-diggers' camp of 1850–1, and whose presence saves the souls of at least two of its hardboiled denizens.

Shaw, like Harte, makes the saviour another doomed infant who embraces the supposed horse-thief Blanco. Harte has the baby 'Luck' hold its tiny fist fast around Kentuck's finger shortly after its birth and Kentuck later dies in a vain attempt to save the child. Wilde's infant 'stretched out his two arms and flung them round the Giant's neck, and kissed him' when he led the Giant to abandon selfishness. Blanco Posnet gives the horse on which he is trying to escape to the Woman trying to get her croup-struck baby to a doctor – too late, as it proves. As she tells it,

> WOMAN ... The man looked like a bad man. He cursed me; and he cursed the child: God forgive him! But something came over him. I was desperate. I put the child in his arms; and it got its little fingers down his neck and called him Daddy and tried to kiss him; for it was not right in its head with the fever. He said it was a little Judas kid, and that it was betraying him with a kiss, and that he'd swing for it. And then he gave me the horse, and went away crying and laughing and singing dreadful dirty wicked words to hymn tunes like as if he had seven devils in him.

The sheriff trying Blanco and expecting to convict and hang him assumes that the Woman will not testify against him, but Blanco's bitter enemy, the township's leading whore, will:

> THE SHERIFF ... You tell the truth, Feemy Evans, and let us have no more of your lip. Was the prisoner the man or was he not? On your oath?
> FEEMY. On my oath and as I'm a living woman – [*flinching*] Oh God! He felt the little child's hands on his neck – I can't [*bursting into a flood of tears and scolding at the other woman*]. It's you with your snivelling face has put me off it. [*Desperately*] No: it wasn't him. I only said it out of spite because he insulted me. May I be struck dead if I ever saw him with the horse![30]

It must have been a terrific moment in the Abbey, Feemy being played by Sara Allgood and the Woman by Máire O'Neill, the great sisters who had created

30 Shaw, *The shewing-up of Blanco Posnet*, in *Collected plays and prefaces*, iii, 791, 793.

Synge's *Playboy* on the Abbey stage and would bring O'Casey's *Juno* to the Hollywood screen, a comparable moment to Maud Gonne's appearance on the first night of *Cathleen Ni Houlihan*. It was a more patriotic challenge than *Cathleen* in actual performance since nobody tried to close down *Cathleen* – even if members of the audience taking their own pulse on departure felt that perhaps somebody should. By attending *The Shewing-up of Blanco Posnet* you showed up the British government which had banned it in England and had tried to close its theatre down in Ireland.[31] Even the Abbey's bitter enemies on the nationalist front – apart from D.P. Moran's *Leader* – rallied to its support over *Blanco*, and Pearse could hardly have avoided it.[32]

Pearse's own *Passion Play* was performed eighteen months later at the Abbey, in Irish-Gaelic, by his own schoolboys. It is doubtful if Pearse had witnessed any theatrical antecedent more appropriate than Blanco: his play also had its redeemed whore, in Mary Magdalene (though Pearse would have died rather than use such a term); its mob screaming for execution; its corrupt judge with his moments of integrity, in Pilate; its mother trying hopelessly to rescue her doomed child, in the Virgin Mary; its repentant villain, in Judas – whom Pearse, with remarkable artistry, made repent immediately after his betrayal of Christ at Gethsemane. Pearse already had the four gospels and the Irish-Gaelic poem 'The three Marys' lament' on which to draw for his script, and sensibly he drew buckets from them. What *Blanco Posnet* would have given him was the way to conceive his work for staging. And with every allowance for posthumous canonization, the evidence is strong that Pearse's production put Irish-Gaelic drama for the first time on a par with the aspirations of modern Europe. But it also looked forward to the Easter Rising, which would prevent any further production. As Pearse's pupil and secretary, Desmond Ryan, who would be with him in the Rising, wrote in its aftermath:

> Some of us, too, thought, though to many it may seem an irreverence, that our national and individual struggle was in ways a faint reflection of the Great One just enacted. Is it not so? The Man is crucified as the Nation and the Soul moves slowly, falteringly, towards the Redemption.[33]

---

31 Another treatment of the *Blanco Posnet* controversy is entitled 'The shewing-up of Dublin Castle', published as chap. 3 of L. McDiarmid, *The Irish art of controversy* (Dublin, 2005), pp 87–122. **32** Pearse was still the editor of the Gaelic League paper *An Claidheamh Soluis* which had, somewhat self-protectively, stated its lack of interest in 'the literary fate of Mr George Bernard Shaw', but 'we are bound to stand by the Theatre in its fight against the importation of a British censorship' (quoted in Laurence and Grene (eds), *Shaw, Gregory*, p. 27). **33** D. Ryan, *The story of a success* (Dublin, 1917), pp 101–8, has the fullest account of the play

Pearse's next stage (in all senses) was to mingle the nativity and crucifixion as best he could in *The King* (*An Rí*) in 1912, culminating in a child's martyrdom to save his country, although as leader of an army, not as a doomed prisoner. Shaw cannot have seen it – though he just might have read it – but the effect is eerily similar to army, nobles and clergy rallying behind the generalship of the near-child Joan in his *Saint Joan*, whose composition in Ireland in 1923 certainly inhaled an atmosphere of high symbolic national sacrifice.[34]

But in 1912 Pearse had yet to work out his evolution of 'redeemer sacrifice' into its ultimate form, in which the people of Ireland were to play Jesus Christ's part. More specifically, this would mean that the leaders of the 1916 Easter Rising would be martyred as guardians of the popular will – regardless of the people's inability to express that will, still less to dissent from Pearse's interpretation. Somebody else got in first with the idea of Jesus as sacrifice being replayed in an early twentieth-century Ireland, and ironically that writer also loved Ireland in as fervent and as unreal a form as Pearse: he had shown it in a novel about an Irish boy – *Kim*, whose eponymous hero is Kimball O'Hara. Rudyard Kipling, although ready to commit treason rather than let Ireland be sundered from Kipling himself and his English people, accepted the use of Ulster as the means to thwart the devolution he identified with separation. His poem 'Ulster' made the Ulster Protestants into Jesus as emotively as that biblically-tuned people could ask:

> Before an Empire's eyes
> The traitor claims his price.
> What need of further lies?
> We are the sacrifice.

The economy of the identification was matchless. Pilate, Judas, the false witnesses when Jesus faced the high priest, the inevitability of Jesus' own doom – the four lines captured them all, leaving the rest of the poem to maximize the mythologies to mobilize less scripturally adept Ulster Unionists.[35] Pearse's messianic writhings included nothing as neatly inflammatory as that.

(unpublished and apparently lost). Ryan's comment is from p. 108. See also Edwards, *Pearse*, pp 140–3. I have ignored Shaw's 'Passion play', written 1878 when he was 21, as too remote from his post-atheist writing twenty to forty-five years later: its considerable interest needs separate analysis. The surviving fragment appears in *Collected plays and prefaces*, vii, 487–527 (in blank verse, sometimes very blank). **34** For *Saint Joan*, see N. Grene, *Bernard Shaw* (London, 1984), pp 132–50; also Shaw, *The matter with Ireland*, ed. Laurence and Greene (1st ed.), pp 185–273. **35** The poem, although apparently written in 1913, is 'Ulster 1912', and is fundamentally anti-English in its furious unionism. The most incendiary of Fenian bards

Yet as the poets' warfare heightened religious tension in the Ireland of 1912–13, Shaw was reconsidering the idea of martyrdom for stage purposes in *Androcles and the Lion*. His choice of form – fable, becoming pantomime – drew strength and integrity from its child-conceived basis, much as had Kipling in his outstanding recent writing, or Pearse with his occupational dependence on schoolchild actors. Pearse neatly fixed his imagery into the *Zeitgeist*, writing in his magazine *An Macaomh* for May 1913:

> I dreamt [four years ago] that I saw a pupil of mine, one of our boys at St. Enda's, standing alone upon a platform above a mighty sea of people; and I understood that he was about to die there for some august cause, Ireland's or another. He looked extraordinarily proud and joyous, lifting his head with a smile almost of amusement; I remember noticing his bare white throat and the hair on his forehead stirred by the wind, just as I had often noticed them on the football field. I felt an inexplicable exhilaration as I looked upon him, and this exhilaration was heightened rather than diminished by my consciousness that the great silent crowd regarded the boy with pity and wonder rather than with approval – as a fool who was throwing away his life rather than as a martyr that was doing his duty ... I dreamt then that another of my pupils stepped upon the scaffold and embraced his comrade ... Mr J.M. Barrie makes his Peter Pan say (and it is finely said) 'To die will be a very big adventure', but I think that in making my little boy in *An Rí* offer himself with the words 'Let me do this little thing', I am nearer to the spirit of the heroes.[36]

By then Shaw had written *Androcles*, but Pearse cannot have known that text when writing. The climax of the play turns on Androcles, not a child but usually presenting himself as a childlike fool, being told that there is to be one martyr – him – and walking to meet his death with the beautiful line: 'Well, it was to be, after all.' Androcles differs from Pearse's dream-boy in not wanting to die, any more than the recorded cases of Jesus, Joan, Thomas More and Thomas

---

could hardly equal the fury of 'Rebellion, rapine, hate, / Oppression, wrong and greed / Are loosed to rule our fate, / By England's act and deed'. Kipling subsequently committed treason at Tunbridge Wells where he publicly pledged resistance to the third home rule act (if enacted) by force if necessary. The poem employs inflammatory anti-Catholic propaganda, but Kipling was not anti-Catholic and his only supporter among major British creative artists, Elgar, was a Roman Catholic. **36** Quoted in Edwards, *Pearse*, p. 143. Kipling might have had that dream, boys and all, but the Ulster Protestant crowd – unlike the majority of Irish nationalists – would have expressed approval: that contrasted the two Irelands at that time.

Cranmer did – or their Shavian counterparts Dick Dudgeon, Blanco Posnet and Joan again. Even better, Androcles anachronistically anticipates and mocks the deathbed instructions of Joseph Addison (to see how a Christian could die) and David Hume (to see how a sceptic could die): 'Caesar, go to your box and see how a tailor can die.' As in Pearse's dream, Androcles is strengthened in facing his death before a derisive crowd by a comrade's loving gesture, in this case the offer of Lavinia (gloriously based on the Fabian, Beatrice Webb): 'I'll go in his place, Caesar. Ask the Captain whether they do not like best to see a woman torn to pieces. He told me so yesterday.' The Captain's horror at her ruthless commandeering of his words for self-destruction would have needed fine facial expression, as he is now in love with her. Androcles declines her offer and goes to the arena 'on the faith of a Christian and the honor [*sic*] of a tailor'. Shaw was enough of a Marxist to relish the little bourgeois craftsman shining in a nobility that utterly blights the venal, cruel aristocrats and emperor. But, unlike his fellow-Christians, Androcles really has a faith more than the 'humanitarian naturalist' as Shaw identified him and certainly more than the play's other 'articulate Christians' whose

> different enthusiasms ... they accept as the same religion only because it involves them in a common opposition to the official religion and consequently in a common doom ... Lavinia, a clever and fearless freethinker, shocks the Pauline Ferrovius, who is comparatively stupid and conscience ridden. Spintho, the blackguardly debauchee, is presented as one of the typical Christians of that period on the authority of St Augustine ...[37]

Androcles' love of animals and conscious self-mockery make him a wholly justifiable reworking of Father Keegan and hence of Shaw's view of Jesus – appropriately in both cases a reassertion of the vulnerability of Jesus.

Androcles as holy fool is clearly also akin to Pearse as self-depicted in his 'The Fool', a poem written in the months before the Rising. Pearse now substituted himself for the imaginary and dream-boy warriors and willing martyrs, and directly assumed the role of Christ or of his deputy:

> The lawyers have sat in council, the men with the keen, long faces,
> And said, 'This man is a fool', and others have said, 'He blasphemeth'
> ...
> And so I speak

37 Shaw, *Androcles and the lion*, in *Collected plays and prefaces*, iv, 629, 636.

> Yea, ere my hot youth pass, I speak to my people and say ...
> Ye shall call for a miracle, taking Christ at his word.
> And for this I will answer, O people, answer here and hereafter,
> O people that I have loved, shall we not answer together?[38]

The 'sovereign people', in Pearse's phrase, are still invited to co-martyrdom before their resurrection, a process now a long way from the dreams of solitary sacrifice initially envisaged by Pearse (and by Thomas MacDonagh). Shaw's heroes retained heroic solitude, even if, like Pearse's dream-boy of 1909, they left a field for useful speculation as to why they were ready to die.[39] Necessarily their fates vary: Dick Dudgeon, devil's disciple, actually ends his solitude by his near-sacrifice; Father Keegan is in one sense already dead (and in hell, as he

38 D. Ryan (ed.), *The 1916 poets* (Dublin, 1963), pp 25–7. Ryan (who deeply honoured me by his friendship) claimed common ground for the ideal of self-sacrifice among Pearse, his colleague Thomas MacDonagh, and MacDonagh's friend Joseph Plunkett, yet the other two seem to me to have more a Keatsian embrace of death for its own sake in their mature work. MacDonagh had, I think, outlived his imagery of patriotic self-sacrifice; and while Plunkett's best poem 'I see his blood upon the rose' is a rich pantheizing of Jesus' self-sacrifice, it (unusually) omits poet from poem.   **39** So, in the end, did MacDonagh. Aindreas Ó Gallchóir, compiler and producer for RTE of *On behalf of the provisional government* (1966), portraits of the seven signatories of the 1916 proclamation from the memories of contemporaries, saw the best finale in James Stephens' preface to MacDonagh, *Poetical works* (Dublin, [1916]), pp x–xi: 'There was a certain reserve behind his talkativeness. Often, staring away at the hills or at the sky, he would say, "Ah me!" – an interjection that never expressed itself further in words. Yet that interjection, always half humorous, always half tragic, remains with me as more than a memory. I think that when he faced the guns which ended life and poetry and all else for him, he said in his half humorous, half tragic way, "Ah me!" and left the whole business at that.' Donagh MacDonagh, an infant when his father died, put his spirit instructively among European counterparts in his essay on Plunkett and MacDonagh in F.X. Martin (ed.), *Leaders and men of the Easter Rising* (Dublin, 1968). On the other hand, whatever the level or the duration of Christ-identification in the leaders of the Easter Rising, it was quickly made when they were dead, even for those who showed least sign of such complexes. In 'On behalf of the provisional government', the indefatigable IRB conspirator Seán MacDermott was described by his octogenarian sister Rose as having lived a most holy life like 'Our Blessed Lord', full of poverty and suffering (he had been a polio victim, and was a migrant worker in Belfast and Glasgow). The one who really ensured posthumous popular support was Patrick Pearse's brother William, who alone of the insurgent martyrs pleaded guilty at his court martial, thereby ensuring his own execution on 4 May 1916 (the day after his brother) and the subsequent Irish revulsion against the British authorities: to have killed Patrick might seem like justice, if harsh justice; to have killed the apparently harmless Willie seemed sheer vindictiveness. Willie even more than his brother was (in the words of Desmond Ryan and Ruth Dudley Edwards) the triumph of failure (B. Barton, *From behind a closed door: secret court martial records of the 1916 Easter Rising*, Belfast, 2002, pp 36, 159–67, 326–7).

stresses), having been sacrificed in the killing of his priestly identity by the ecclesiastical authorities, and – for what the action of the play is worth – in his phan-
tom existence, he is more isolated than ever at its end; the sheriff, having acquitted Blanco Posnet, tells him to get out of town fast; Androcles delights his child
audience by walking off stage with his new friend, evidently his forever, but
however gratifying to lion, children and himself, his farewell isolates him from
his fellow humans – a fate much desired by many early Christians. As for Saint
Joan, she may seem the loneliest of all – and here the identification with Jesus
is at its height, being with Jesus as God. At the play's ending, Joan discovers she
is still cut off from her fellow-humans.

Shaw's great preface to *Androcles*, proclaiming the wisdom of Jesus as economist and sociologist, won him execration from Christians and anti-Christians
alike. But time had deepened the message of the play, being published as it was
amidst wartime hysteria. What must have been saddest for Shaw was not the
inevitable outcry from enemies and rivals, but the defection of former friends.
In particular, the clergyman whose view of Jesus had done so much to win Shaw
over from anti-Christianity, the Revd Reginald Campbell, had become one of
the leading exponents of the war as 'holy war'.[40] The high tragic moment of

---

40 Shaw, lecturing from the pulpit in the City Temple under the auspices of Campbell, then
a Congregationalist, on 14 Oct. 1908, stated: 'Mr Campbell has made me believe in Christ
... Mr Campbell put before me a credible Christ; he recreated Christ for me, he reconstructed the environment, he made me see the Jesus of history in a way that I had not done
before ... he placed before me something which I desired to believe in, which on the whole
I was quite content to believe in. I said, Here at last is really something which an educated
man living in the twentieth century can believe, and here also is a Person whose ideas are
worth examining; here is a person, by the way, a great many of whose ideas are coming to
the front after having been completely submerged for centuries in a great flood of something
that called itself Christianity, but which was frank irreligion, frank commercialism ... It is
my belief, to which nobody else is committed, that because Mr Campbell among you has
thrown off the priest and become the inspired artist, that that is the reason he has come to
share the privileges of the artist, to inspire love, and to escape the odium of the priest' (Shaw,
Platform and pulpit, ed. D.H. Laurence, London, 1962, pp 48–9). Characteristic of Campbell
were such utterances as: 'The Christ Spirit in man is that which does what Jesus did, accepts
anything and everything in the service of love. The man who is possessed by that Spirit does
not pause to inquire, "Who deserves what?" He just goes on working as though all the dis-
abilities of the [human] race were his very own.' Shaw might have found it difficult to see
how that could have been regarded as consistent with support of war against other humans.
But Campbell was consistent with humans becoming saviours: 'All men are capable of showing the Christ-Spirit at times, but it is only as they begin to see and to enter into the full
meaning of the Christ-Life that they can properly be said to be saviours. Jesus has made more
saviours than all the masters of mankind put together, but even He knew that He stood in
a grand historic succession'. That could inspire *Androcles and the lion*; it could also inspire volunteers for war, including the Easter Rising. Campbell's turn to war which also led him into

Androcles and the Lion is when the Christian Ferrovius kills the soldiers in the arena instead of being martyred, and so well did Shaw judge his audience that he knew it would elicit cheering.[41] But it is Androcles who realizes that, if Ferrovius has survived, it is as fully at the cost of his faith as if he had simply conformed to the demands of his pagan persecutors:

> ANDROCLES [*running in through the passage, screaming with horror and hiding his eyes*] !!!
> LAVINIA. Androcles, Androcles, what's the matter?
> ANDROCLES. Oh, don't ask me, don't ask me. Something too dreadful. Oh! [*He crouches by her and hides his face in her robe, sobbing.*]

And initially Ferrovius, hot from the slaughter, is as horrified: 'Lost! Lost for ever! I have betrayed my Master. Cut off this right hand: it has offended. Ye have swords, my brethren: strike.' But he ends in realistic terms:

> FERROVIUS. In my youth I worshipped Mars, the God of War. I turned from him to serve the Christian god; but today the Christian god forsook me; and Mars overcame me and took back his own. The Christian god is not yet. He will come when Mars and I are dust; but meanwhile I must serve the gods that are, not the God that will be.

But when war came, Shaw found that Ferrovius, whom he seems until then to have gently despised, was a monument of honour and integrity. He declared in an afterword to the play:

> Great numbers of our clergy have found themselves of late in the position of Ferrovius and Anthony Anderson. They have discovered that they hate not only their enemies but everyone who does not share their

---

the Church of England is expounded in his *The war and the soul* (London, 1916), e.g. 'Is it so certain that Jesus would not have sanctioned the taking of human life?' (p. 62). It quotes Captain La Hire in the Hundred Years War on going into battle: 'So do with me this day, God, as I would do with thee if I were God and thou wert La Hire.' Shaw would make instructive fun of La Hire in *Saint Joan*, sc. 2. The earlier quotations from Campbell are taken from E. Esdaile et al., *A rosary from the City Temple: from the writings and sermons of the Rev. R.J. Campbell* (London, 1912), p. 42. **41** Gabriel Pascal's 1952 film is better than Shavians will allow, but the tension as to what Ferrovius has done in the arena is lost, and the impressive ferocity of Robert Newton going berserk throws the audience thoroughly into the applauders of violence. Not knowing what has happened at least gives a sporting chance for the ideals of non-violence to rally.

hatred, and that they want to fight and to force other people to fight. They have turned their churches into recruiting stations and their vestries into munition workshops. But it has never occurred to them to take off their black coats and say quite simply, 'I find in the hour of trial that the Sermon on the Mount is tosh, and that I am not a Christian. I apologise for all the unpatriotic nonsense I have been preaching all these years. Have the goodness to give me a revolver and a commission in a regiment which has, for its chaplain, a priest of the god Mars: *my* God.' Not a bit of it. They have stuck to their livings and served Mars in the name of Christ, to the scandal of all religious mankind.[42]

Back in Ireland, the aspirants for Jesus-like martyrdom likewise saw no necessity to acknowledge Mars as their real God, when the chosen martyrdom proved to take the lives of many others, combatant or civilian. Perhaps Shaw in a sense followed them, for Mars versus Jesus is nowhere evident as a theme in the nationalist-martyr play *Saint Joan* – although, in the person of Chaplain de Stogumber, the incendiary cleric is made to discover into what torture he had condemned his country's enemy and, like Ferrovius, to see himself as a traitor to his divine Master. Shaw himself never embraced pacifism, but he had a point in seeing it as the attribute of the God who was not yet. And he formally disagreed with innumerable tenets of Christianity. Yet it is hard to deny him his place, if not as a Christian doctrinaire, at least as an evangelist for the Christianity of the future, as we think of that opening salvo about the success of Barabbas in stealing Jesus' name and ask ourselves how much of what has been professed as religion is, in fact, that old Barabbas with his strong right hand. And we may not find it perfectly easy to shrug off Shaw's reply to the clergyman who asked him if he was a Christian: 'Yes, but I often feel very lonely.'

42 Shaw, *Androcles and the lion*, in *Collected plays and prefaces*, iv, pp 626–7, 637.

Yeats exhibition

after driving a Swedish poet around Sligo

I drove until my hands swelled
along the roads of Sligo
marvelling at the precise mating
of Yeats's writing
with rock and hill,
with wave and wind and water.

For the first time –
so it seemed – I saw
how the old tales
of long-haired fairy girls
and fiery heroes
grew from the contours of the land
and from the ocean's heaving.

Under bulky Knocknarea
Caoilte's hair burns
like a summer storm
or the long grass bending
in the small fields that run all the way to the
edge of the sea. And Niamh becomes again
the waves in their long gallop
up the shining sand,
her voice their constant whispering:
'Away,
Come away,
Come away with me.'

ÉILÍS NÍ DHUIBHNE

Mrs Jellyby's daughter: Caroline Agnes Gray (1848–1927) and the *Freeman's Journal*

Felix M. Larkin[1]

> There are women enough in the world, Mr Tulkinghorn thinks – too many;
> they are at the bottom of all that goes wrong with it.
>
> Charles Dickens, *Bleak House* (London, 1853), ch. XVI.

LORD FITZALAN, FORMERLY Lord Edmund Talbot, was the last British viceroy in Ireland and the only Catholic to hold that office. When his appointment was announced in April 1921, Sir Mark Sturgis, joint assistant under secretary at Dublin Castle, recorded in his diary: '[Talbot's appointment] is badly received ... That he is a Catholic is outweighed ... by the fact that he is an Englishman and a Tory politician, and *Irish RCs dislike English RCs anyway* [my italics].'[2] A possible explanation for this dislike lies in Conor Cruise O'Brien's observation that 'the Catholicism of the English is not felt to be the same as the religion of the same name practised in Ireland'.[3] English Catholics would doubtless draw comfort from that, thereby reinforcing the dislike.

1 One of the treasures of the National Library of Ireland is its newspapers and periodicals collection, an extremely valuable source of information for historians and others. However, there are dangers in relying on any newspaper or periodical as a source without some background knowledge of the publication in question, in particular its political bias. In relation to Irish newspapers and periodicals, such knowledge is often difficult to come by. Very little has been written about the history of the press in Ireland. It seems to me, therefore, that this essay – a small contribution to Irish press history – is an apposite tribute to Dónall Ó Luanaigh who for many years had overall responsibility for, *inter alia*, newspapers and periodicals in the National Library. The essay is a slightly revised version of a lecture I delivered to the National Library of Ireland Society on 23 March 2005. On that occasion, Colette O'Daly, newspapers and periodicals librarian at the National Library, responded to my lecture on behalf of the Society and I have taken account of her response in revising the lecture. I am grateful to Ms O'Daly and to her colleagues in the National Library, especially Sandra McDermott, Ciara McDonnell and Katherine McSharry, for their help and support. My thanks are due also to Dr Ian d'Alton, Philip Hamell, Dr Carole Walker, Dr Roger Willoughby, Professor Kevin B. Nowlan, Dr Noel Kissane, Fr J. Anthony Gaughan, Irene O'Daly and my niece Beatrice Larkin, who each assisted in various ways in the preparation of the essay.   **2** M. Hopkinson (ed.), *The last days of Dublin Castle: the Mark Sturgis diaries* (Dublin, 1999), p. 152.   **3** C. Cruise O'Brien, *Herod: reflections on political violence* (London,

The subject of this essay is another English Catholic who played a significant role in Irish politics and who, in addition to being an English Catholic,
had the distinction of being a woman. She was Caroline Agnes Gray, wife of
Edmund Dwyer Gray, the prominent Irish home rule MP and proprietor of
Dublin's *Freeman's Journal* newspaper. After his death at the early age of 42 in
1888, Mrs Gray effectively controlled the *Freeman* for the next four years. The
Parnell split occurred during that period, ushering in a time of unprecedented
volatility in Irish politics which had huge implications for the *Freeman*. The
paper's decline, which led ultimately to its closure in 1924, had its origins in the
split and its turbulent aftermath. Mrs Gray's response to the challenge of steer-
ing the *Freeman* through the crisis was ham-fisted. Neither her bizarre family
background, nor her marriage to an ambitious politician forced to play second
fiddle to the great Charles Stewart Parnell, had equipped her for the problems
she had to face. Her difficulties were exacerbated by the antagonism which she
seemed effortlessly to arouse and for which there is no obvious explanation
other than the unpropitious combination of her nationality, her religion and
her gender.

Mrs Gray was the daughter and namesake of the Victorian philanthropist
Caroline Chisholm, celebrated as 'the emigrants' friend' but caricatured by
Charles Dickens as Mrs Jellyby in *Bleak House*: hence the title of this essay. Who
was Caroline Chisholm? She is better known today in Australia than in Britain
or Ireland, not least because she was depicted on the Australian $5 banknote in
issue between 1968 and 1991. Born Caroline Jones in 1808 in Northampton –
where her father was a prosperous pig dealer – she married Archibald Chisholm,
a Scot who was a captain in the East India Company army, in 1830. Shortly
after her marriage, Mrs Chisholm converted to Catholicism, her husband's religion. Her philanthropic work was deeply rooted in her religious convictions.[4]

Her first philanthropic venture was in Madras, India, where her husband
was posted. Horrified at the vices of Madras, she opened a school to provide
basic education for the daughters of poor soldiers. This established the main

1978), p. 92. **4** Biographical data on Mrs Chisholm in this and succeeding paragraphs have
been gleaned mainly from the following biographies: M. Kiddle, *Caroline Chisholm* (abr. ed.
Melbourne, 1969 [1950]); M. Hoban, *Fifty-one pieces of wedding cake: a biography of Caroline
Chisholm* (Kilmore, Victoria, Australia, 1973); and J. Bogle, *Caroline Chisholm: the emigrant's
friend* (Leominster, 1997 [1993]). I have also consulted biographical essays on Mrs Chisholm
in the *Australian encyclopaedia* (Sidney, 1958), the *Australian dictionary of biography*, i (Melbourne,
1966) and the *Oxford DNB* (Oxford, 2004). In addition, Dr Carole Walker (of Walton-on-
the-Wolds, Leics.) has very generously allowed me to use some of her recent research on
Caroline Chisholm; see her unpublished doctoral thesis 'Caroline Chisholm, 1808–77: ordinary woman, extraordinary life, impossible category' (Loughborough University, 2002).

theme of her life's work: the moral and physical welfare of people of European origin in the colonies, especially women. In 1838 her husband was granted leave from the army on health grounds and the couple, now with two young sons, went to Australia and settled in Sydney. Before long, Mrs Chisholm became aware of the pitiful plight of young girls newly arrived from England in search of a better life – many of whom, stranded and penniless, quickly became prostitutes. She began helping such girls find shelter and jobs, and went on to set up an employment registry and temporary home for them in an old barracks in Sydney. She secured the use of these premises by a personal appeal to the governor of New South Wales, Sir George Gipps, who was astonished to find that she was 'a handsome, stately young woman who … thought her reason, and experience too, to be worth as much as mine'.[5]

By her efforts, thousands of girls were settled in New South Wales. In order to see them safely placed with families on far-flung farms, she accompanied parties of girls in wagons out across the bush – often riding on her white horse Captain, so named after her husband. He had been recalled to army service in 1840, leaving his wife behind in Australia to pursue her mission. One aspect of this mission which particularly pleased her was that the dispersal of her girls provided opportunities for lonely settlers to find wives and start families.[6]

Captain Chisholm retired from the army in 1845 and the family returned to England soon afterwards. Their house in Islington, north London,[7] was the base for the next phase of Mrs Chisholm's work. She travelled throughout Britain tracing the relatives of former convicts and other settlers in Australia, and helping to reunite them by arranging for the relatives to go out to Australia. She became an enthusiastic advocate of Australian emigration as the best way of coping with over-population at home, and in 1849 launched the Family Colonisation Loan Society, which provided savings facilities for intending emigrants and would eventually lend them the balance of the money required to pay for their passage. When the emigrants arrived in Australia, the society's agents would find them employment and arrange for them to repay the loans by instalments. Her work also extended to Ireland: she visited Cork and Dublin in 1852 to encourage Irish emigration to Australia.[8]

5 *Sidney's emigrants' journal* (Sydney, 1850), p. 271; quoted in Kiddle, *Caroline Chisholm*, p. 15. **6** Mrs Chisholm's efforts have been described as 'one of the most remarkable matchmaking campaigns in history' (M. Durack, *Kings in grass castles* (London, 1959), p. 13); my thanks to the late Barbara Durack for this reference. **7** Their house, at Charlton Crescent (now Charlton Place), Islington, is marked with a blue plaque. **8** *Cork Examiner*, 9, 12, 14, 19 May, *Freeman's Journal*, 24 May, *Observer*, 19 Sept. 1852; my thanks to Dr Carole Walker for these references. See also P. Connole, 'Caroline Chisholm: the Irish chapter' in C. Kiernan (ed.), *Australia and Ireland, 1788–1988: bicentenary essays* (Dublin, 1986), pp 241–51. Mrs

Captain Chisholm left England for Australia in 1851 to look after the affairs of the Family Colonisation Loan Society there. His wife and by now six children joined him in 1854. They settled in Victoria, and Mrs Chisholm's last campaign was for the improvement of conditions in the Victoria goldfields. Her health began to fail in 1857 and she gradually withdrew from public life. In 1865 her husband and younger children returned again to England. She came back to England in 1866. Granted a civil list pension of £100 per annum,[9] she lived first in Liverpool and later in London. Her final years were spent in poverty, as a bedridden invalid, and she died on 25 March 1877. The French historian, Michelet, wrote of Mrs Chisholm: 'The fifth part of the world, Australia, has up to now but one saint, one legend. This saint is an Englishwoman.'[10] The Catholic church in Australia is currently (2007) pursuing the cause for her canonization.

This extraordinary woman was the inspiration for Mrs Jellyby in *Bleak House*, probably Dickens' most critically acclaimed novel and a powerful indictment of the legal system.[11] Mrs Jellyby is introduced into the novel apparently for the sole purpose of caricaturing Mrs Chisholm. Before we encounter her in person, she is described as:

> a lady of very remarkable strength of character who ... is at present (until something else attracts her) devoted to the subject of Africa, with a view to the general cultivation of the coffee berry – *and* the natives – and the happy settlement, on the banks of African rivers, of our superabundant home population.[12]

She is obsessed by good causes in far-away places – characterized by Dickens as 'telescopic philanthropy'[13] – and, as a result, shamefully neglects her person, her family and her household. At one point, she proclaims that 'my public duties ... [are] a favourite child to me'.[14] This does not accord with the author's values – as is evident when he has his narrator, Esther Summerson, write that 'if Mrs Jellyby had discharged her own natural duties and obligations before she

Chisholm's work for Irish female emigrants is noted in the permanent exhibition 'Cobh, the Queenstown story' at Cobh Heritage Centre, Cobh, Co. Cork; my thanks to my father, Terence Larkin, for telling me about this.   **9** Equivalent to some £6,000 sterling today (for the relevant price indices, see R. Twigger, *Inflation: the value of the pound, 1750–1998*, House of Commons Library Research Paper 99/20, 1999; my thanks to Dr James F. Golden for directing me to this paper).   **10** J. Michelet, *Oeuvres complètes*, xviii: 1858–60 (Paris, 1985), p. 565; quoted in the essay on Mrs Chisholm in the *Australian encyclopaedia*.   **11** *Bleak House* was first published in one volume in 1853. It had previously appeared in monthly parts, 1852–3.   **12** *Bleak House*, ch. IV.   **13** Ibid., ch. IV; 'telescopic philanthropy' is, in fact, the title of this chapter.   **14** Ibid., ch. XXIII.

swept the horizon with a telescope in search of others, she would have taken the best precautions against becoming absurd'.[15]

Dickens' indignation at what he sees as Mrs Jellyby's misplaced philanthropy – and, by implication, that of Mrs Chisholm – fuels some sharp satire. Thus, Esther Summerson gives the following account of her first visit to Mrs Jellyby:

> [Mrs Jellyby] was a pretty, very diminutive, plump woman of from forty to fifty, with handsome eyes, though they had a curious habit of seeming to look a long way off. As if ... they could see nothing nearer than Africa! ... [She] had very good hair, but was too much occupied with her African duties to brush it. The shawl in which she had been loosely muffled, dropped on to her chair when she advanced to us; and as she turned to resume her seat, we could not help noticing that her dress didn't nearly meet up the back, and that the open space was railed across with a lattice-work of stay-lace – like a summer-house. The room, which was strewn with papers and nearly filled by a great writing-table covered with similar litter, was, I must say, not only very untidy but very dirty ... But what principally struck us was a jaded and unhealthy-looking, though by no means plain girl, at the writing-table, who sat biting the feather of her pen, and staring at us. I suppose nobody ever was in such a state of ink ... She really seemed to have no article of dress upon her, from a pin upwards, that was in its proper condition or its right place.[16]

This is an amazingly hostile portrait – and a surprising one in view of Dickens' positive treatment of emigration in *David Copperfield*,[17] published only three years earlier: the departure of the emigrant ship for Australia in *David Copperfield* is an event full of promise for those on board,[18] and the promise is fulfilled in Mr Micawber's eventual success in Australia.[19] Was it really fair to suggest that Mrs Chisholm ignored, or was oblivious to, personal and domestic responsibilities? Her biographers record that, in the years 1848 to 1854 when she lived in Islington, she entrusted the care of her children and the running of her household to her mother. That should have been a satisfactory arrangement. Nevertheless, her ménage made a most unfavourable impression on Dickens when he called on her in 1850. He subsequently wrote to Angela Burdett-Coutts: 'I dream of Mrs Chisholm, and her housekeeping. The dirty faces of

15 Ibid., ch. XXXVIII.   **16** Ibid., ch. IV.   **17** *David Copperfield* was first published in one volume in 1850. It had previously appeared in monthly parts, 1849–50.   **18** *David Copperfield*, ch. LVII.   **19** Ibid., ch. lxiii.

her children are my constant companions.'[20] Moreover, in 1853 Elizabeth
Herbert – who had arranged Dickens' meeting with Mrs Chisholm – told
Florence Nightingale that 'Mrs Chisholm is living on nine pence a day, having
parted with her one maid ... [and she] is starving.'[21] Accordingly, maybe her
family did – like the Jellybys – live in squalor. On the other hand, having suc-
cumbed to the temptation of poking fun at Mrs Chisholm, Dickens was probably so carried away by the exuberance of his writing that, to quote Margaret
Kiddle, Mrs Chisholm's most notable biographer, 'his pen made a characteristic magnification'.[22] In any event, he returns to the Jellybys at intervals throughout *Bleak House*, and in the end we learn that Mrs Jellyby's project for settling
families in Africa has failed 'in consequence of the king of Borioboola wanting
to sell everybody – who survived the climate – for rum'.[23]

The girl whom Esther Summerson depicts 'in such a state of ink' is Mrs
Jellyby's eldest daughter, Caddy. She has been forced to act – much against her
will – as her mother's amanuensis. Her full name is Caroline, and it is surely no
coincidence that she shares that name with the subject of this paper, Caroline
Agnes Gray – Mrs Chisholm's elder surviving daughter – and that Mrs Gray
was known from birth by a similar diminutive, 'Carry' or 'Carrie'.[24] Caddy
Jellyby, however, is not based on Mrs Gray as a young woman. Mrs Gray was
born in London on 13 May 1848 and was therefore less than 4 years old when
the first part of *Bleak House* appeared in March 1852. Unlike Caddy Jellyby, she
was not her mother's eldest child: Mrs Chisholm had four older sons.

Of the early life of Mrs Gray, we know that in 1854 – when just six years
old – she travelled with her mother to Australia and lived there with her family until 1865. She later attended convent schools in England and Belgium.[25]

---

20 Letter dated 4 Mar. 1850, quoted in Anne Lohrli, *Household words: a weekly journal, 1850–59*
(Toronto, 1973), p. 227; my thanks to Dr Carole Walker for this reference.   21 Florence
Nightingale to her mother, 2 June 1853, Wellcome Institute, London, Florence Nightingale
papers, MS 8992/26; my thanks to Dr Carole Walker for this reference.   22 Kiddle, *Caroline
Chisholm*, p. 133.   23 *Bleak House*, ch. LXVII.   24 'Carry' was the name entered in her bap-
tism record (see Bogle, *Caroline Chisholm*, p. 114). After her second marriage – to Captain
Maurice O'Conor (see p. 138, below) – she would usually sign her name as 'Carrie O'Conor'.
As the wife of Edmund Dwyer Gray, her usual signature was 'C.A. Gray'.   25 Kiddle, *Caroline
Chisholm* (1969), p. 181. The photograph reproduced on p. 127 dates from this period; it is
in the Rathbone papers in the University of Liverpool Library (RP XXI.9.13 (1)), and was
drawn to my attention by Dr Carole Walker. Both Dr Walker and myself are satisfied that
it is a portrait of Caroline Agnes Gray, though we have not been able to establish this definitively. Her maiden name 'Caroline Chisholm' is written on the reverse side, in her mother's
handwriting – and it is clearly not a photograph of her mother. Moreover, the photographer
was P.P. Skeolan of Cheltenham – his trade stamp is also on the back of the photograph –
and the Chisholms had family connections there: two of Captain Chisholm's brothers lived

4 Caroline Agnes Chisholm, before her marriage to Edmund Dwyer Gray;
carte-de-visite photograph, *c.*1866 (by courtesy of the University of Liverpool Library).

Then, while visiting Ireland in 1868, she met Edmund Dwyer Gray. They married in the following year.[26] The circumstances of their meeting were highly unusual. A schooner was wrecked during a storm in Killiney Bay in September 1868 and Gray swam out with a rope to the doomed craft, saving five lives. His future wife, by chance, witnessed this heroic deed and was afterwards introduced to him. Gray was awarded the *Tayleur* Fund gold medal and the Royal National Lifeboat Institution's silver medal for his bravery.[27] In the entry on Gray in the old *Dictionary of National Biography*, the wrong year is given for this exploit – 1866, instead of 1868 – and it is stated incorrectly that his *Tayleur* medal was conferred by the Royal Humane Society. Both errors are repeated in the new *Oxford DNB*.[28] *Tayleur* medals were, in fact, awarded for gallantry in the

in Cheltenham. The precise address in Skeolan's stamp is correct for the date suggested for the photograph (see *Slater's directory*, 1868). Finally, the diaries of Elizabeth Rathbone (1790–1882) attest much contact between the Rathbone and Chisholm families in the mid-1860s (RP VI.2.24–29), with many references to both Caroline Chisholms *mère et fille* – so it is not implausible that the younger Caroline's photograph should be in the Rathbone papers. As late as 1875, Mrs Gray's Dublin postal address is in Elizabeth Rathbone's diary (RP VI.2.29A). **26** See marriage notice in the *Morning Post*, 15 July 1869, and a report in the *Freeman's Journal*, 17 July 1869. Mrs Chisholm wrote a touching account of their courtship and Gray's proposal of marriage in an undated letter to her son Sydney, then living in Australia, which is quoted in full in Hoban, *Fifty-one pieces of wedding cake*, pp 413–14. **27** The *Freeman's Journal* carried a report of the wreck on 26 Sept. 1868. For accounts of the ceremony at which the *Tayleur* medal was awarded to Gray, see the *Freeman's Journal* and the London *Times*, 4 Jan. 1869. A copy of the certificate accompanying the award of the Royal National Lifeboat Institution's medal to Gray is included in the Edmund Dwyer Gray album (National Library of Ireland, Acc. 6256; see fn. 49, below). That his future wife witnessed the rescue is recorded in an obituary of Gray in the *Universe* (the English Catholic newspaper) which was reproduced in the *Freeman's Journal*, 29 Mar. 1888; the author was the well-known Irish journalist John Augustus O'Shea (1839–1905), and the fact that it was reproduced in the *Freeman*, Gray's own paper, confirms its veracity. O'Shea wrote, with wonderful flourish: 'On the 25th of September, twenty years ago, the schooner *Blue Vein* was wrecked in Killiney Bay, and Gray swam through the hiss and surge of waters to the doomed craft with a rope, and was the means under God of rescuing five fellow creatures. For this he was rewarded with the *Tayleur* gold medal ... but he also gained the affections of a daughter of Caroline Chisholm, the Emigrants' Friend, who was a witness of his intrepidity.' For a maritime historian's perspective on Gray's exploit, see C.F. Lowth, 'Dublin's heroic lord mayor', *SubSea: Ireland's Diving Magazine*, 121 (Autumn 2005), 34–7; Mr Lowth has the distinction of having dived upon the remains of the *Blue Vein* in Killiney Bay. **28** See my letter, entitled 'Oxford DNB errors', *History Ireland*, 13:4 (July/Aug. 2005), 15. There is a further error in the entry on Edmund Dwyer Gray in the new *Oxford DNB*: his mother-in-law, Mrs Chisholm, is therein described as the 'author of *The Emigrant's Friend*' – whereas she was, of course, *known* as 'the emigrants' friend' and, though the author of a number of books (see app. 1 of Hoban, *Fifty-one pieces of wedding cake*, p. 420), none had that title: see C.F. Lowth's letter, entitled 'The emigrant's friend?', *History Ireland*, 13:6 (Nov./Dec. 2005), 16.

Irish Sea and its environs by the committee which administered a fund set up to assist survivors of a vessel, called the *Tayleur*, lost in 1854 at Lambay Island, off the north Co. Dublin coast. The *Tayleur* was an emigrant ship bound for Australia from Liverpool,[29] so it is apt that Caroline Chisholm's future son-in-law should be the recipient of a *Tayleur* medal.

Edmund Dwyer Gray was born in Dublin on 29 December 1845, the son of Sir John Gray, whose statue stands in O'Connell Street, Dublin commemorating his work as a member of Dublin corporation in bringing the Vartry water supply to the city. In 1841 John Gray had purchased the *Freeman's Journal* with some associates, one of whom was his brother, Moses Wilson Gray. John Gray became sole proprietor of the newspaper in 1850. A Protestant, he supported repeal of the Act of Union, and later the Irish Tenant League movement and Church of Ireland disestablishment. He was MP for Kilkenny city from 1865 until his death in 1875, and he had begun to ally himself with Isaac Butt's home rule movement in the last year of his life.[30]

The Gray family had strong links with Australasia long before Edmund Dwyer Gray married a daughter of Caroline Chisholm. In 1855 Moses Wilson Gray, having relinquished his interest in the *Freeman*, emigrated to Australia – on the same ship that brought Charles Gavan Duffy into exile.[31] Like Duffy, Wilson Gray became a diligent servant of the crown in Australia. He was a member of the legislative assembly of Victoria from 1860 to 1862. He then moved to New Zealand, and was a district judge there from 1864 until his death – also in 1875.[32]

Edmund Dwyer Gray was raised in the Church of Ireland, but converted to Catholicism in 1877, presumably through the influence of his wife.[33] He succeeded his father as proprietor of the *Freeman* and followed him into politics, becoming – from 1877 onwards – MP successively for Tipperary county, Carlow

29 My thanks to Dr Roger Willoughby for information about the *Tayleur* medals. Regarding the loss of the *Tayleur*, see E.J. Bourke, *Bound for Australia: the loss of the emigrant ship* Tayleur *at Lambay on the coast of Ireland* (Dublin, 2003); my thanks to Philip Hamell, a friend of Dr Bourke, for bringing this privately published book to my attention.   **30** T.O. Ruttledge, 'The Gray family of Claremorris, Co. Mayo', *Irish Genealogist*, 7:4 (1989), 551–62 (at 556–8); see also the biographical essays on Sir John Gray and Edmund Dwyer Gray in the *Oxford DNB*. I have written a joint entry on Edmund Dwyer Gray and his wife, Caroline Agnes Gray, for the Royal Irish Academy's *Dictionary of Irish biography* (Cambridge, forthcoming). For information on Sir John Gray's statue, see *From O'Connell to Parnell: the conservation of O'Connell Street's monuments* (Dublin, 2006), p. 24.   **31** The name of the ship was the *Ocean Chief*.   **32** See the biographical essay on Moses Wilson Gray in the *Australian dictionary of biography*, iv (Melbourne, 1972); also Ruttledge, 'The Gray family', 555–6.   **33** Papers relating to Edmund Dwyer Gray's reception into the Catholic church, 10 Sept. 1877, Archives Office of Tasmania, Hobart, NS 575/7.

county and the St Stephen's Green division of Dublin. But for the advent of
Parnell, he might have led the Irish Parliamentary Party at Westminster. A moderate, he opposed Parnell's rise within the party. He threw the weight of the
Freeman unsuccessfully against Parnell's candidate in the decisive Ennis by-
election of 1879, and then, probably wrongly, accused Parnell of having called
certain colleagues in the Irish Party 'papist rats'.[34] When, after the 1880 general
election, Parnell was elected chairman of the party, Gray was one of eighteen
MPs who voted against him.[35] Thereafter, however, he largely supported
Parnell's leadership – partly because he accepted that Parnell was now invin-
cible, but also because Parnell established in 1881 his own newspaper, the weekly
United Ireland, with the *Freeman*'s former star reporter and later MP, William
O'Brien, as editor. The threat that *United Ireland* might be turned into a daily
publication to rival the *Freeman* copper-fastened Gray's loyalty.

O'Brien wrote of Gray that he was 'the most enterprising newspaperman
Ireland ever produced'.[36] Under his management, the *Freeman*'s production
capacity was greatly expanded, its circulation increased threefold – to over 30,000
copies per day, a market share of about forty per cent[37] – and it became highly
profitable. So successful was it that in 1887 – the year before he died – Gray
converted it into a public company, while retaining control for himself. In addition, in 1882 he acquired the *Belfast Morning News*. His business endeavours,
which also included the nascent Telephone Company of Ireland, were at least
as important to Gray as politics. This is reflected in a harsh assessment by the
then viceroy, Earl Spencer, in a letter to Gladstone dated 25 August 1882:

> Gray is a man who plays a game and that a false game for he does not at
> heart believe in the policy of the extreme men in Irish politics [by which
> Spencer meant Parnell and his followers] and yet he is always pandering
> and flattering their policy and themselves. His sole object is to make his
> paper pay. I confess that I have the lowest possible opinion of him.[38]

34 F.S.L. Lyons, *Charles Stewart Parnell* (London, 1977), pp 93–5.   **35** *Freeman's Journal*, 18
May 1880.   **36** W. O'Brien, *Recollections* (London, 1905), pp 182–3.   **37** See L.M. Cullen,
Eason & Son: a history (Dublin, 1989), pp 76–7. I have assumed that the pattern of newspaper
sales in Ireland through W.H. Smith – the antecedent of Eason's – is representative of the
market generally at this time. I have also assumed that W.H. Smith's share accounted for
one-third of total sales of newspapers in Ireland (Cullen, *Eason*, p. 355). This would mean
that the *Freeman*'s circulation was about 30,000 per day, which is consistent with some
random circulation data preserved in the John Dillon papers (Trinity College, Dublin, MS
6804/125). All estimates of newspaper circulation in Ireland in the nineteenth century should
be regarded as extremely tentative; figures were generally neither published nor independently verified.   **38** British Library, London, Gladstone papers, Add. MS 44309, ff 115–18;

A similar judgment is suggested in James Joyce's *Dubliners*: in the story 'Grace', when one of the characters recalls Gray 'blathering away' at the unveiling of his father's statue, another comments that 'none of the Grays was any good'.[39]

By all accounts, Gray was not an effective parliamentarian. William O'Brien attributed this to 'a thin, piping voice'.[40] Also, his political concerns were urban rather than rural – which placed him firmly outside the mainstream of the Irish Party after 1880. He served as a Dublin city councillor from 1875 to 1883 and, in that role, took particular interest in public health issues. His expertise in municipal affairs was recognized when in 1884 he was appointed – with, among others, the prince of Wales and Cardinal Manning – to a royal commission on the housing of the working classes.

He was lord mayor of Dublin in 1880 and high sheriff of Dublin in 1882. His term as lord mayor was marked by an acrimonious dispute with the viceroy, the duke of Marlborough, over resolutions passed at a public meeting in Dublin's City Hall about famine conditions in the west of Ireland. The *Freeman* had reported the famine in a series of articles commissioned – according to their author, William O'Brien – in order to restore Gray's reputation after his unsubstantiated 'papist rats' charge against Parnell.[41] Gray, as lord mayor, chaired the city hall meeting and also organized the Mansion House Fund which raised £180,000[42] for relief of the famine. While holding the office of high sheriff, Gray was sentenced in August 1882 to three months' imprisonment and a fine of £500[43] for having published in the *Freeman* adverse comments on the composition and conduct of the jury in the trial of one Francis Hynes for murder. Since the high sheriff could not arrest himself, it fell to the city coroner to arrest him. In response to the widespread outcry over his imprisonment, Gray was set free after six weeks in Richmond Jail, Dublin. His fine was paid by public subscription.

Perhaps inevitably, given their initial antipathy, Gray and Parnell never developed a close relationship, either personally or professionally. Parnell did not trust his erstwhile rival. Thus, when Gray sought to exchange his Carlow constituency for a more prestigious Dublin seat in the 1885 general election, Parnell at first vetoed the move; Archbishop Walsh, the Catholic archbishop of Dublin, intervened on Gray's behalf, and Parnell relented.[44] Gray, however, was one of nine MPs who assisted Parnell in selecting candidates for the 1885 election.[45]

my thanks to Dr Richard Hawkins for this reference. **39** H. Levin (ed.), *The essential James Joyce* (London, 1963), p. 473. **40** O'Brien, *Recollections*, p. 183. **41** Ibid., p. 223. **42** Equivalent to over £11.5 million sterling today (see Twigger, *Inflation, 1750–1998*). **43** Equivalent to over £30,000 sterling today (see Twigger, *Inflation, 1750–1998*). **44** E. Larkin, *The Roman Catholic church and the creation of the modern Irish state, 1878–86* (Philadelphia & Dublin, 1975), pp 341–2. **45** C. Cruise O'Brien, *Parnell and his party, 1880–90* (Oxford, 1974

Moreover, in the months before that election, he acted as an intermediary between Parnell and Lord Carnarvon, the Conservative viceroy.[46] Likewise, because of his friendship with Sir Charles Dilke and Joseph Chamberlain, Gray was a conduit between Parnell and the radicals in the British Liberal Party.[47] This led to his involvement in the infamous 1886 by-election in which Parnell foisted Captain O'Shea, an associate of Chamberlain and husband of Parnell's mistress, on the Galway constituency. Gray was prepared to back Parnell in support of O'Shea's candidature, but he declined to propose O'Shea for election and expressed scepticism about Parnell's argument that his election would soften Chamberlain's opposition to home rule. The *Freeman*'s support was a vital factor in Parnell's success on that occasion.[48]

Often in poor health due to heavy drinking and asthma, Edmund Dwyer Gray died suddenly, aged 42, on 27 March 1888 at his home in Upper Mount Street, Dublin. The National Library of Ireland has recently acquired an album of letters and newspaper cuttings relating to Gray, consisting mainly of material occasioned by his death.[49] It appears to have been compiled by, or for, Mrs Gray and is particularly valuable because so little is otherwise available about him. The cuttings include tributes to Gray, reports of his funeral and extensive accounts of his career taken from Irish and British newspapers of the period from 28 March to 7 April 1888, together with copies of memorial cartoons published by the *Weekly Freeman* and by *United Ireland*.[50] The majority of items in the album are, however, formal letters of condolence to Mrs Gray, and among these are letters from Parnell, Justin McCarthy, William O'Brien, Timothy Harrington, Sir Charles Gavan Duffy, Lord Ripon and Lord Aberdeen. Two letters are specially poignant, and indeed it is somewhat surprising to find them preserved in the album alongside the formal ones from political and business associates of Edmund Dwyer Gray. The first is from the Grays' only surviving son – also Edmund Dwyer Gray – who, aged 18, was touring in Australia and New Zealand and learned of his father's death in Rotorua, New Zealand, through 'a small notice in a newspaper'.[51] The other is from the younger of their daughters, Sylvia, aged 15, then at boarding school in Waterford. Intensely religious, Sylvia Gray wrote to her mother that 'everything I and everyone else

---

[1957]), p. 146, n. 1. **46** E. Byrne, *Parnell, a memoir*, ed. F. Callanan (Dublin, 1991), pp 5–6, 35–6. **47** R. Jenkins, *Sir Charles Dilke: a Victorian tragedy* (London, 1958), pp 100–1. **48** T.W. Moody, 'Parnell and the Galway election of 1886', *Irish Historical Studies*, 9:35 (Mar. 1955), 319–38; O'Brien, *Parnell and his party*, pp 166–84; Lyons, *Parnell*, pp 321–6. **49** National Library of Ireland, Acc. 6256; see F.M. Larkin, 'Edmund Dwyer Gray album', *NLI News*, 19 (Spring 2005). **50** Both published on 7 Apr. 1888. **51** Edmund Dwyer Gray Jr. to his mother, 4 Apr. 1888, National Library of Ireland, Gray album, Acc. 6256; curiously, he signed his name at this time 'E. Chisholm Gray'.

Table 2: Gray & Chisholm family tree

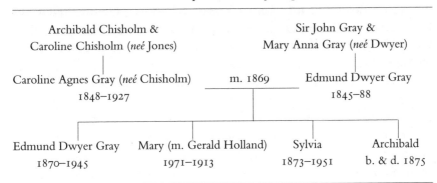

| Archibald Chisholm & | | Sir John Gray & |
| Caroline Chisholm (*neé* Jones) | | Mary Anna Gray (*neé* Dwyer) |

| Caroline Agnes Gray (*neé* Chisholm) | m. 1869 | Edmund Dwyer Gray |
| 1848–1927 | | 1845–88 |

| Edmund Dwyer Gray | Mary (m. Gerald Holland) | Sylvia | Archibald |
| 1870–1945 | 1971–1913 | 1873–1951 | b. & d. 1875 |

here can do for him by prayers, we will do'.[52] She later became an Ursuline nun, taking the name Mother Philomena. She died in 1951, the last survivor of the children of Edmund Dwyer Gray and his wife.[53]

The Grays had four children, as set out in Table 2. In birth order, they were Edmund Dwyer Gray Jr; two daughters, Mary and Sylvia; and a second son, Archibald, who died aged two months in 1875.[54] Both daughters entered convents after their father's death – reputedly placed there by their mother because, as a relatively young widow, she feared that bringing out the girls in Dublin society would prejudice her chances of securing a second husband.[55] In fairness, Sylvia seems genuinely to have had a religious vocation. However, her sister Mary, who entered the novitiate of the Irish Sisters of Charity, left shortly before her profession[56] and in 1896 married Commander Gerald Holland DSO, of the

52 Sylvia Gray to her mother, 26 Mar. 1888, ibid.; this letter may be wrongly dated, since Edmund Dwyer Gray died on 27 Mar., though it is possible that it was written in response to news of his illness and impending death.   **53** See her obituary, *Waterford News*, 2 Nov. 1951. I am grateful to the late Sr Joseph of the Ursuline Convent, Waterford, for information about Sr Philomena Gray and her sister, Mary Holland (*neé* Gray).   **54** Archibald and his father are buried in the same grave in Glasnevin cemetery, Dublin. For a photograph of the memorial stone scroll on their grave, see *Death and design in Victorian Glasnevin* (Dublin, 2000), p. 175.   **55** Ruttledge, 'The Gray family', 558.   **56** My thanks to Sr Marie Bernadette O'Leary, archivist of the Irish Sisters of Charity, for information on Mary Gray. Mary spent two years and six months in the novitiate of the Sisters of Charity, where she was known as Sr Clare Francisco. She left after her aunt, Annie Dwyer Gray, appealed to Archbishop Walsh to enquire into her case as she had been placed in the convent against her will – or so her aunt claimed (Annie Dwyer Gray to Archbishop Walsh, 11 Jan. 1892, Dublin Diocesan Archives, Walsh papers). Annie Dwyer Gray also claimed to Archbishop Walsh that Sylvia Gray – then in the novitiate of the Ursuline Sisters in Waterford – had 'expressed strongly her objections to a religious life' (ibid.); but later he learned that, when this matter was raised with Bishop Sheehan of Waterford and Lismore, the latter had said: 'not at all [and] she was

Royal Indian Marine. After he retired from the navy, Commander Holland was marine superintendent at Holyhead from 1905 to 1914. He joined the Royal Engineers on the outbreak of war in 1914, served in France, rose to the rank of brigadier general and died in 1917 while on sick leave in England.[57] Mary Holland (*née* Gray) died in 1913, aged 41.

Caroline Agnes Gray was almost 40 when her husband died, and she lived on for another thirty-nine years.[58] She had been an unusually active partner in all her husband's public endeavours and gained the reputation of being an accomplished hostess – leading one observer, well placed to form an opinion, to remark that she was 'a most ambitious and extravagant woman'.[59] William O'Brien, recalling Gray's term as lord mayor of Dublin, said that Mrs Gray 'lit up the Mansion House festivities like a Fairy Queen', and that her 'beauty and inexpressible charm enhanced tenfold her husband's popularity'.[60] After his death, she owned more than forty per cent of the shares in the *Freeman* company.[61] So, though playing no role in its day-to-day operations, she was able to exert considerable influence over it. At the outset of the Parnell split, when the *Freeman* came out in favour of the beleaguered leader, it did so with her full agreement.[62] In the first months of the split, she was one of a group of prominent Dublin women who rallied in support of Parnell.[63] She even appeared in public with him in Dublin in early 1891, dressed – according to Archbishop Walsh – in a scarlet cloak. Walsh subsequently described Mrs Gray as 'a rock of scandal'.[64] He took particular exception to her behaviour because, as a devout Catholic of high social standing, she had been granted permission to keep the Blessed Sacrament in her home; the archbishop had been unhappy about this

... likely to persevere' – which was what happened (Sr M.S. Margison to Archbishop Walsh, 28 Mar. 1892, ibid.). **57** Entry for Gerald Edward Holland (1860–1917) in *Who was who, 1916–28* (London, 1929), p. 508; see also his obituary in the London *Times*, 28 June 1917. **58** Notwithstanding that Mrs Gray married secondly Captain Maurice O'Conor in November 1891 and was known thereafter as Mrs O'Conor (and usually signed her name as 'Carrie O'Conor'), I will – in order to avoid confusion – continue to refer to her as Mrs Gray in this essay. **59** Public Record Office, London, Carnarvon papers, CAR 30/6/55 (quoted in Larkin, *The Roman Catholic church, 1878–86*, pp 341–2). The observer was chief telegraphist of the *Freeman's Journal*, and he had been induced to provide intelligence on the affairs of Parnell's party for Lord Carnarvon (viceroy, 1885–6). **60** O'Brien, *Recollections*, p. 185. **61** E.P. de Blaghd, 'I was a teenage press baron: the problems of Edmund Dwyer Gray, junior', *Dublin Historical Record*, 41:1 (Dec. 1987), 31–42; also *Freeman's Journal*, 22 Sept. 1891. **62** Archbishop Walsh wrote to Archbishop Tobias Kirby in Rome on 30 December 1890 as follows: 'All hold Mrs Gray responsible for the action of the paper. She is an avowed "Parnellite"!' (Irish College, Rome, Kirby papers; my thanks to Fr John Silke for a copy of this letter). **63** F. Callanan, *T.M. Healy* (Cork, 1996), pp 365–6, 690, n. 46. **64** Archbishop Walsh to Archbishop Kirby, 22 Feb. 1891, Irish College, Rome, Kirby papers; my thanks to Fr Mark Tierney, of Glenstal Abbey, for this reference.

arrangement even before the Parnell split, though he had not blocked it because, in his own words, 'my feeling about her seemed perhaps an unreasonable prejudice'.[65] Now he was confirmed in his misgivings.

Mrs Gray's stance was consistent with her late husband's reluctance in his latter years to oppose Parnell. It continued a policy which had served the business interests of the *Freeman* very well. However, once the anti-Parnellites launched their own daily newspaper, the *National Press*, in March 1891 and the *Freeman* began as a result to lose circulation and revenue, Mrs Gray wavered. Under the influence of her son – just returned from a second visit to Australia, now aged 21 and justifiably fearful for his inheritance – Mrs Gray resolved that the *Freeman* should abandon Parnell. This required a special general meeting of the *Freeman* company, held on 21 September 1891, at which the pro-Parnell board was replaced with one that included both Mrs Gray's son and the man soon to become her second husband, Captain Maurice O'Conor.[66]

After the *Freeman* switched sides, the Parnellites established the *Irish Daily Independent* in December 1891 to fill the vacuum caused by the *Freeman*'s defection.[67] There was not room at that time for three nationalist daily newspapers published in Dublin, and certainly it made neither commercial nor political sense to have two anti-Parnell organs. Accordingly, the *Freeman* and the *National Press* merged in March 1892. In simultaneous transactions, the *National Press* company bought Mrs Gray's *Freeman* shares for £36,000[68] and the *Freeman* company purchased the *National Press* newspaper for exactly the same sum.[69] It was a condition of any merger that Mrs Gray should sell her interest in the *Freeman's Journal*; the *National Press* had broken the Gray family's monopoly of the nationalist daily newspaper market in Dublin and the Grays would not be permitted to assume a dominant role in that market again. Mrs Gray had no option but to accept this – since, quite apart from any other consideration, her health had collapsed under the strain of the previous four years.[70] Her son and Captain O'Conor both ceased to be directors of the merged company in 1893.

---

65 Ibid. **66** E. Larkin, *The Roman Catholic church in Ireland and the fall of Parnell, 1888–91* (Liverpool, 1979), pp 236–9, 254–6, 260, 263, 269–75, 283; de Blaghd, 'I was a teenage press baron'; F. Callanan, *The Parnell split, 1890–1* (Cork, 1992), pp 110–11, 120–1, 160–1. **67** P. Maume, 'Commerce, politics and the *Irish Independent*, 1891–1919', unpublished paper read before the 24th Irish Conference of Historians held at University College Cork, 20–22 May 1999; my thanks to Dr Maume for making a copy of this paper available to me. **68** Equivalent to nearly £2.5 million sterling today (see Twigger, *Inflation, 1750–1998*). **69** T.M. Healy, *Letters and leaders of my day*, 2 vols (London, 1928), ii, 372–7; de Blaghd 'I was a teenage press baron'; Callanan, *Healy*, pp 411–12. **70** When, after Archbishop Walsh's intervention, Mary Gray was about to leave the novitiate of the Irish Sisters of Charity, her religious superior wrote to the archbishop that Mrs Gray 'is very ill (I believe mentally)' (Sr M.S.

The Grays also lost ownership of their Belfast newspaper, the *Morning News*, because of the Parnell split. Anti-Parnell during the first weeks of the split, the *Morning News* was eventually pushed into the Parnellite camp by proprietorial diktat. Later, when the Grays changed sides, it reverted to its original allegiance. However, during its pro-Parnell phase, the Belfast clergy instituted a boycott of it and the Ulster bishops put up funding for a rival paper, the *Irish News*, which first appeared on 15 August 1891 and still survives. Even after the *Morning News* abandoned Parnell, the boycott continued – presumably to ensure its rival's success. The *Morning News* was bought by the *Irish News* in July 1892 and dropped as a separate publication.[71]

With the disposal of the *Morning News* and his exit from the *Freeman's Journal*, the young Edmund Dwyer Gray *fils* was left without prospects in Ireland. He emigrated to Australia in 1894 and eventually settled in Tasmania, where he became a journalist and politician of note. He edited three newspapers in Hobart, and in 1928 was elected to the Tasmanian parliament for the Labour Party. He was treasurer and deputy premier of Tasmania from 1934 until his death in 1945, except for six months in 1939 when he served as interim premier.[72] His success – albeit in Tasmania – had been forecast by Justin McCarthy MP, who wrote of Gray in 1891: 'I see in him the future prime minister of an Irish parliament.'[73]

As regards the *Freeman's Journal*, the period after 1891 was one of relentless decline.[74] This stemmed from the divisions within Irish nationalism brought about by Parnell's fall, divisions which were replicated in the newspaper market. First, the damage inflicted by the *National Press* was huge: the *Freeman*'s circulation fell by a quarter in 1891 and by a further eleven per cent in 1892,[75] and the merger with the *National Press* cost it £36,000. Then, after the merger,

---

Margison to Archbishop Walsh, 6 Feb. 1892, Dublin Diocesan Archives, Walsh papers). I presume Mrs Gray was suffering from what we would now describe as a nervous breakdown. **71** E. Pheonix, 'The history of a newspaper: the *Irish News*, 1855–1995' in E. Pheonix (ed.), *A century of Northern life: the* Irish News *and 100 years of Ulster history, 1890s–1990s* (Belfast, 1995), pp 8–39. I have also drawn upon some unpublished research by Jamie Smyth on the nationalist press in Belfast during the Parnell split, carried out as part of his MA course in journalism at Dublin City University (DCU); my thanks to Mr Smyth, and also to Professor John Horgan of DCU who kindly facilitated my access to Mr Smyth's research. **72** See the biographical essay on Edmund Dwyer-Gray in the *Australian dictionary of biography*, viii (Melbourne, 1981). Note the spurious hyphenated version of his name: when Gray entered politics in Tasmania, he began using the hyphen so as to gain higher placement on the ballot paper. **73** J. McCarthy and Mrs Campbell Praed, *Our book of memories* (London, 1912), p. 290. **74** For a fuller account of the *Freeman*'s last years than is possible – for reasons of space – in this essay, see F.M. Larkin, '"A great daily organ": the *Freeman's Journal*, 1763–1924', *History Ireland*, 14:3 (May/June 2006), 44–9. **75** Trinity College, Dublin, John Dillon papers, MS 6804/126–8.

there was a long and bitter struggle for control of the *Freeman* between the war-ring anti-Parnell MPs Tim Healy and John Dillon, both initially directors of the merged company; this continued until 1896, when it was resolved largely in Dillon's favour.[76] Moreover, throughout this period – but especially from 1905 onwards – the *Freeman* faced strong competition from the *Independent*, the paper launched by the pro-Parnell faction when the *Freeman* defected to the other side. There was a change in the ownership of the *Independent* in 1900, fol-lowing the Irish Parliamentary Party's reunification under John Redmond MP. The *Irish Daily Independent*, now redundant as a Parnellite organ, was purchased by William Martin Murphy, an associate of Healy. Murphy transformed the paper in 1905 into the modern *Irish Independent*, at half the *Freeman*'s price – a halfpenny, instead of a penny – and in a more popular format. It was an imme-diate success. In effect, Murphy copied in Ireland what Lord Northcliffe had done in London in 1896 when he launched the *Daily Mail*, the first mass cir-culation newspaper in these islands.[77]

Thomas Sexton MP, the Irish Party's acknowledged financial expert, had been appointed chairman and business manager of the *Freeman* company in 1893. In that capacity, he proved incapable of meeting the challenge of Murphy's new *Independent*. Already weakened by its tribulations in the 1890s, the *Freeman* was thus fatally undermined and began to incur heavy trading losses. Sexton – anxious to retain the power he enjoyed as an Irish press baron – hung on as chairman until 1912, when the Irish Parliamentary Party leaders finally acted to save the paper and forced his resignation.[78] Thereafter, the *Freeman* was subsidized from Irish Party sources.[79] It continued to lose money, and its parlous condition was exacerbated by the destruction of its premises during the 1916 Easter Rising. It was, therefore, impossible for the Irish Party stalwarts who then ran the paper to keep it going once the party had been defeated in the general election of December 1918. It was sold off in October 1919.[80]

76 See F.S.L. Lyons, *The Irish Parliamentary Party, 1890–1910* (London, 1951), pp 38–45. **77** Maume, 'Commerce, politics and the *Irish Independent*, 1891–1919'; D. McCartney, 'William Martin Murphy: an Irish press baron and the rise of the popular press' in B. Farrell (ed.), *Communications and community in Ireland* (Dublin & Cork, 1984), pp 30–8; A. Bielenberg, 'Entrepreneurship, power and public opinion in Ireland: the career of William Martin Murphy', *Irish Economic and Social History*, 27 (2000), 25–43. **78** See my entry on Thomas Sexton in the *Dictionary of Irish biography*. **79** For details, see 'Note of moneys advanced to *Freeman's Journal*, 27 January 1919' in the John Dillon papers (Trinity College, Dublin, MS 6805/306). This shows that, in the period 1913–18, the Irish Party arranged funding for the *Freeman* company from various sources amounting to over £28,000 (excluding interest accrued on the funds) – of which £6,500 related to the years 1913–14. The total moneys advanced to the *Freeman* is equivalent to well over £1 million sterling today (see Twigger, *Inflation, 1750–1998*). **80** F.S.L. Lyons, *John Dillon: a biography* (London, 1968), pp 389–90,

In its final years, the *Freeman* was the property of Martin Fitzgerald, a Dublin wine-merchant of moderate nationalist sympathies who was a member of the first Senate of the Irish Free State.[81] It appeared for the last time on 19 December 1924, and was subsequently absorbed by the *Irish Independent*.

And what became of Caroline Agnes Gray when, with the sale of her shareholding in the *Freeman* in 1892, her association with the newspaper came to an end? In November 1891 she had married Maurice O'Conor, a captain (later major) in the Connaught Rangers and a scion of the Catholic gentry of Connacht. He was related to the O'Conor Don and, through his mother, to the Blakes of Ballinafad, Co. Mayo. The novelist George Moore was his first cousin.[82] Mrs Gray was over twelve years older than her new husband, and their marriage was childless.[83] They made their home in the late 1890s on Inisfale Island – also known as O'Reilly's Island – in Lough Allen, near Drumshambo, Co. Leitrim.[84] Mrs Gray passed the last thirty years of her life there in melancholy obscurity, afflicted by failing eyesight and eventually by blindness. She died on 15 April 1927 on Inisfale.[85] O'Conor died in 1941 in a hotel in Dun Laoghaire, apparently in straitened circumstances.[86]

A letter that Mrs Gray sent to William O'Brien in 1906 lifts the veil on the long twilight of what she herself called her 'troubled life'.[87] O'Brien had recently published his *Recollections*, in which he referred to Mrs Gray in the complimentary terms noted above.[88] She wrote as follows:

> Thank you, on my own behalf and for my son, for your generous remarks about my husband, Sir John [Gray] and the *Freeman*, and your all too kind remarks about myself – so delicate and graceful that I must not object … I suffered so much pain and loss in those sad events of recent years, the exile of my talented son and loss of [the] *Freeman*, that

419, 457–8.   **81** See my entry on Martin Fitzgerald in the *Dictionary of Irish biography*; also D. Ryan, *Remembering Sion: a chronicle of storm and quiet* (London, 1934), pp 256–69.   **82** *Burke's Landed gentry of Ireland* (London, 1904), pp 44, 418, 448–9, 450; A. Frazier, *George Moore, 1852–1933* (New Haven & London, 2000), pp 10–11. George Moore's mother and Maurice O'Conor's mother were daughters of Maurice Blake of Ballinafad.   **83** Ruttledge, 'The Gray family', 558.   **84** For this and other information about the latter part of Mrs Gray's life, I am most grateful to the late Josephine O'Conor, of Clonalis House, Castlerea, Co. Roscommon (a kinswoman of Captain O'Conor).   **85** See death notice in the *Irish Independent*, 21 Apr. 1927. Her grave, which has no headstone, is in the grounds of the Catholic church in Drumshambo, Co. Leitrim; Josephine O'Conor kindly located it for me.   **86** Information from Josephine O'Conor; see his obituary in the *Irish Independent*, 6 Jan. 1941. He is not buried with his wife in Drumshambo, but in the O'Conor cemetery at Clonalis House.   **87** Carrie O'Conor (formerly Mrs Gray) to William O'Brien, 24 Mar. 1906, Boole Library, University College, Cork, William O'Brien papers, box AO.   **88** See p. 134, above.

> you will understand and believe me when I say that for years I have not
> read any paper likely to remind me – so that I ceased to follow political
> events and, with failing sight, I still more recently only read books …
> and I see few visitors. I live in a few books and in a vain endeavour to
> forget![89]

Did these 'few books' include *Bleak House*? It is simply not known whether Mrs
Gray was aware of Dickens' cruel depiction of her mother and, if so, what her
reaction to it was. In any case, she was the main source of information for an
adulatory essay on Caroline Chisholm by Edith Pearson – a piece of unabashed
hagiography – published in 1914.[90]

    After Mrs Gray's death, the property on Inisfale was neglected and – to quote
the late Fr Charles O'Conor SJ, the O'Conor Don, who visited the island in
1939[91] – 'pretty well everything in it just rotted away with the damp or was
stolen by people who came across to the island at night by boat'.[92] Today the
place is a wilderness, with scant evidence of former habitation.[93] The devasta-
tion of Mrs Gray's final home is an appropriate metaphor for the sad fate of the
Gray family and its once mighty newspaper, the *Freeman's Journal*.

89 Carrie O'Conor (formerly Mrs Gray) to William O'Brien, 24 Mar. 1906, Boole Library,
University College, Cork, William O'Brien papers, box AO. **90** E. Pearson, *Ideals and realities: essays* (London, 1914), pp 71–94. **91** Information from Josephine O'Conor, sister of
Fr O'Conor. **92** M. Kiddle, *Caroline Chisholm* (Melbourne, 1950), p. 278, n. 4; this note is
not included in the abridged edition of Miss Kiddle's biography, published posthumously in
1969, which is referred to elsewhere in this essay. **93** I visited the island on 25 July 1979. I
wish to acknowledge the assistance of the late Joe Mooney, of Drumshambo, Co. Leitrim,
in arranging this expedition.

'Killed by eviction':
a case study in Co. Louth, 1888

L. Perry Curtis Jr

N O MATTER HOW MANY thousands of evictions took place during the
nineteenth century in rural Ireland, each and every one had its own
particular tale of woe to tell. It would be slighting – not to say too revisionist
by half – to assume that every execution of the dreaded notice to quit had
exactly the same constellation of causes, hardships and consequences. For this
reason it is worth taking a close look at one such incident during the second
phase of the Land War to see just how different the scenario could be. Unlike
so many other ejectments, this one turned into a *cause célèbre* that provoked political rallies, made headline news in the Irish press, caught the attention of William
Gladstone and gave rise to an inquest that set a record for longevity.

* * *

On the chilly afternoon of Thursday, 11 October 1888 a resident magistrate and
the sub-sheriff of Co. Louth, John Cornwall Bailie, led an eviction party on to
the estate of Captain Henry Sydenham Singleton at Belpatrick, several miles
from Collon. Protected by fifty policemen under the command of two RIC
officers, the evictors faced the task of ousting half a dozen tenants on orders
from the proprietor who lived at Mell on the outskirts of Drogheda.[1] Also present were the two agents who managed this property as well as the much larger
adjacent estate of Viscount Massereene and Ferrard. Athol J. Dudgeon and
Henry R. Emerson were prominent land agents and solicitors in Dublin. Ardent
defenders of landlords' rights, they had earned a reputation for putting profit
well ahead of good relations with the tenantry.[2]

---

1 Aged 69, Capt. Singleton owned 6,609 acres in Co. Cavan, 1,463 acres in Co. Louth, and
508 acres in Co. Meath, along with 24 acres in Drogheda, making a total of 8,604 acres in
Ireland, valued at £6,320; he also owned 18 acres in Hampshire valued at £141 (U.H. Hussey
de Burgh, *Landowners of Ireland*, Dublin, 1878, p. 413; J. Bateman, *Great landowners of Great
Britain and Ireland*, 4th ed. 1883, repr. New York, 1970, p. 409). The principal newspapers
spelled the sub-sheriff's name Bailey. **2** At the end of 1886, the heavily-encumbered Lord
Massereene appointed these two agents to manage his estates in Cos. Louth and Meath: 9,238

After Bailie had dealt with two tenants who had arranged with the parish priest, Fr George Taaffe, to be readmitted upon payment of a portion of the rent and arrears owed, the eviction party approached the decrepit house of James Dunne, aged 80, who suffered from chronic bronchitis. Poor health, old age, and depressed prices had resulted in arrears of over £700 since 1879; he could not come close to paying the one year's rent that would have enabled him to stay on as caretaker of his two farms, comprising in total 105 acres at an annual rent of £108.[3] The landlord had applied for and received an ejectment decree back in January, but the court granted a stay because the tenant promised to pay one year's rent. Dunne's failure to live up to this commitment resulted in the arrival of the sheriff and his party after the harvest had been gathered. If anything about the ejectment decree was surprising, it was Captain Singleton's forbearance in allowing this tenant to remain in place despite so many years of non-payment.

Among the onlookers were local and national reporters, an English MP and several priests. Because the farms had been in the family for generations, Dunne could not believe that Singleton would oust him, especially after having paid his rent faithfully for at least fifty years. However, two months previously Emerson had summoned him to Collon and warned him that eviction would ensue if he did not clear up most of his arrears. Both the landlord and his agents seemed bent on expelling a tenant who was much too old and infirm to meet his obligations.

Upon entering Dunne's abode the sub-sheriff found him seated on a stool huddled in front of a turf fire. The room was crowded with his wife Elizabeth, two sons, a daughter, a nephew, Fr Taaffe and one or two friends. Mrs Dunne implored Bailie to leave her frail husband alone, and one of Dunne's sons offered to pay £65 – to be raised by the sale of corn and hay – to gain readmission. But the agents spurned this offer and the sub-sheriff ordered the bailiffs to toss out the few pieces of furniture. At this point Dunne groaned that he would never

---

acres valued at £6,356 (L.M. Geary, *The Plan of Campaign, 1886–91* (Cork, 1986), p. 43). Dudgeon had served as hon. secretary of the emergency committee of the militant landlords' organization known as the Property Defence Association, 1881–2. **3** In 1854 Dunne was listed as holding roughly 165 acres valued at £106 10s. 0d., along with a house and outbuildings valued at £1 10s. 0d., in the townland of Belpatrick, parish of Collon and barony of Ferrard (*Griffith's Valuation,* Co. Louth, 1854, NLI fiche no. 2.A.12); Felix Larkin deserves thanks for this reference. By 1888 Dunne had shed some 50 acres of his original holding and the valuation stood at £102 10s. 0d. Since there was no mention of a judicial rent, he may not have applied for a fair rent under the 1881 Land Act. The heavy arrears had already cost him five horses that were seized by the sheriff and sold for £30 under a distraining order in 1886 (*Freeman's Journal,* 15, 19 Oct., 9, 10 Nov. 1888, 23 Jan. 1889).

survive removal; he urged the agents to arrange conveyance to the poorhouse hospital. Ignoring Fr Taaffe's plea to halt the proceedings, Bailie gave the order to remove the old man. Both sons refused his request to help move their father outside, whereupon two emergency-men picked up Dunne – stool and all – and carried him into the yard followed by the rest of the family. The door was secured with a chain and the evictors moved on to the next house. Shivering in the cold, Dunne moaned that he would not live for more than an hour outside and repeated his request to be taken to the poorhouse hospital. According to the *Drogheda Argus and Leinster Journal* (13 October), he cried out: 'Emerson, Emerson, get me the poorhouse van for God's sake. I have not a half-hour to live.'

For almost two hours Dunne sat amidst his broken furniture with only a frieze coat and a thin blanket to cover his bony body. Curiously enough, no family members bestirred themselves to find him shelter in a neighbouring house. Finally, some friendly labourers moved him into a draughty barn nearby, where they built a small fire to keep off the chill, and laid him down on a layer of straw. He consumed some warm tea and a morsel of buttered bread, and he drank a little whiskey that his son had just fetched from Collon. Up to this point the eviction had been uneventful, with no sign of resistance from any kin or friend. Dunne grew steadily weaker and told his wife that the exposure had doomed him. His condition rapidly worsened and he expired in the early hours of 12 October, surrounded by his family.[4]

The *Drogheda Argus* (13 October) minced no words in a headline article about Dunne's demise: 'Killed by eviction: a real sentence of death'. A leader-writer in the *Freeman's Journal* (13 October) deplored the callous nature of the eviction and the refusal to heed the victim's pleas to be hospitalized. 'The evicted tenant', he wrote, 'lies stark dead in the stable near his humble but happy home, where lived his wife and where his children were born to him.' Calling Dunne's demise a homicide, he declared that 'there shall be no effort to burk [*sic*] the dread reality of his death sentence'. Only a coroner's jury could, in his view, satisfy the public's need to know who was responsible for the tragedy. A reporter revealed that he had overheard Dunne predict his own death if forced to leave. Another editorial in this paper (on 15 October) heralded the opening of the inquest, warning that the jurors would be denounced by the chief secretary, Arthur Balfour, and the Dublin Castle regime if they pursued the truth and delivered 'an honest verdict' on a poor man who had been 'flung out to die like a beggar' at the whim of his landlord.

On Sunday evening, 14 October, the mayor of Drogheda and other local dignitaries took part in a large rally organized by the National League to protest

4 *Freeman's Journal, Irish Times,* 12 Oct. 1888.

not only Dunne's death, but also the evictions on the adjacent Massereene estate where many tenants had embraced the Plan of Campaign. Two prominent nationalist MPs, T.P. Gill and Pierce Mahony, addressed the large crowd after marching through the town accompanied by several brass bands.[5] Gill spoke at length about Dunne's fate and the rack-rent imposed by the hard-hearted Singleton. For three centuries, he asserted, the Dunne family had held these farms and James had paid his rent for sixty years. But when poor health and falling prices hampered his ability to pay, Singleton 'cast [him] out ruthlessly on the roadside' and left him to die. To compound the crime in Gill's view, no other tenant had dared to take Dunne in for fear of suffering eviction. So he was left to die alone in a cold stable. He applauded the Massereene tenants for their commitment to the Plan of Campaign and condemned Dudgeon and Emerson, 'the emergency agents of the modern bumbailiff style'. Dunne's martyrdom had 'riveted the attention of civilized men upon the barbarities of landlordism (cheers) and enabled every Irishman to understand that so long as landlordism existed they could not hope to regenerate the country (cheers). This curse of landlordism was a blight upon the fields, and its most potent enemy today was the Plan of Campaign.' Because Dunne's death was clearly an act of 'murder', the people of Co. Louth should join the great struggle to rebuild the country so that 'the ancient race and ancient nation would take its place in the vanguard of civilisation'.[6]

Such grandiloquence proved the ease with which nationalists could exploit eviction in the name of not only tenant right and nationhood but also racial pride. To keep the protest going, a veteran organizer for the National League and promoter of the Plan, John Kelly, whipped up indignation meetings in several other county towns. Amidst all the anger, dismay and recriminations, no one bothered to ask why Dunne's sons had not helped their father to pay the rent over the previous decade and why no one had found him shelter after his eviction.

* * *

During the preliminary autopsy on Monday, 15 October, the medical examiner from Collon, James J. Davis, found no marks of violence on Dunne's body, but noted signs of cyanosis or discoloration of the facial skin and oedema on his legs. He attributed death to chronic bronchitis and 'fatty disease of the heart', while pointing out that the shock of eviction had hastened death. A second doctor, John Wilson, assigned the cause of death to asphyxia, while confirm-

5 Gill and Mahony were the local MPs, representing the constituencies of Louth South and Meath North respectively.   6 The *Drogheda Argus* (20 Oct. 1888) devoted a full page to this rally, which drew hundreds of people from Co. Meath as well as Co. Louth.

ing Davis's conclusion about the lethal effects of shock and exposure to the cold.
Both medical examiners mentioned the filthy state of the body with vermin
swarming on his clothes and flesh. The coroner for Co. Louth, Dr Thomas J.
Moore JP, called it disgraceful that Dunne had been exposed to the cold for so
long in view of the fatal consequences. The death certificate he signed months
later attributed the cause to 'the effects of shock and exposure to cold ... ten
hours'. He then added the chilling word 'homicidal'.[7]

Before the medical examiners performed their full autopsy, the inquest into
the cause of death opened in a large barn at Belpatrick, close to Dunne's farm.
After being sworn, the jurors filed out to view the body in the barn where it
had apparently lain undisturbed for three days. To call the 'inquisition' politi-
cized would be an understatement. Most of the jurors were shopkeepers from
Ardee with nationalist sympathies. Representing the landlord was Henry William
Jackson, a well-known Dublin barrister, instructed by those two intrepid solicitors, Messrs Dudgeon and Emerson. With the National League's help, the
Dunne family retained M.C. McInerney as their legal counsel; the sub-sheriff
also had a lawyer, Richard M. Dane. After summarizing the events leading up
to the eviction, the coroner charged the jury with the duty of ascertaining the
cause of death. The inquest then adjourned and reconvened two days later (on
17 October) in Ardee courthouse, where Elizabeth Dunne testified that her late
husband suffered from bronchitis, but had never wanted a doctor. Able to walk
about the house, he had eaten breakfast on the morning of the eviction and
showed no signs of disease. She recited the events of 11 October and admitted
that the 'grippers' had not handled her husband roughly.[8]

A unique feature of this inquest was its duration: it ran on for nine sessions
– a remarkable achievement in the case of a non-violent death. By way of contrast, the inquest following the assassination of the third earl of Leitrim and his
two employees in Donegal in April 1878 had lasted for only a day and a half.[9]
At the third session (on 19 October), Nicholas Dunne explained that his father
had made no provision for shelter because he refused to believe that he would
be evicted after all the rent paid over the years. Nicholas emphatically stated
that he recalled hearing his father beg to be taken to the poorhouse, saying that
he would surely die if forced outside.

7 *Freeman's Journal*, 18 Oct. 1888. See also Dunne's death certificate dated 21 Feb. 1889,
F526/60, Office of the Registrar General, Roscommon; the registrar, J.J. Davis, noted on
this official form: 'Inquisition quashed' (many thanks to Kevin Browne, National Library of
Ireland, for tracking down this certificate). **8** *Freeman's Journal*, 16, 18 Oct., *Drogheda Argus*,
20 Oct. 1888. **9** See the articles on the Leitrim inquest in *Freeman's Journal*, 4, 5 Apr. 1878;
also L. Dolan, *The third earl of Leitrim* (Letterkenny, Co. Donegal, 1978), pp 96–8.

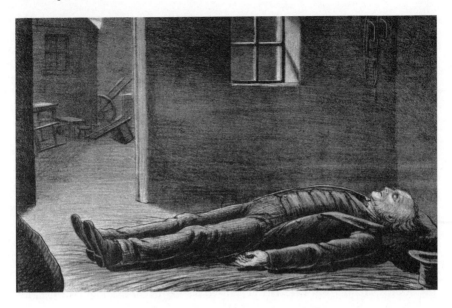

5 'The vindication of the law'; cartoon from *United Ireland*, 20 October 1888.

When the inquest resumed on Monday, 22 October, James McMahon, editor of the nationalist *Drogheda Independent,* entered the courtroom armed with a copy of John D. Reigh's cartoon published in *United Ireland* on the previous Saturday, 20 October. It is reproduced above. Entitled 'The vindication of the law', this morbid and melodramatic image featured the dead man lying all alone on some straw and bathed in the cold, bluish light of the moon. An inverted top hat rests next to his head and a bridle hangs on the wall near the window. A few bits of furniture may be seen through the door. The caption spelled out the old man's anguished plea to Emerson for the workhouse van 'or my death will be on your soul'. Seated on a stool 'under a freezing sky' and surrounded by the wreckage of his furniture, the caption continued, Dunne shivered until some 'kindly neighbours' took pity and carried him into an adjacent barn. 'Two hours later he was dead. So the law was vindicated.' Reigh's emphasis on the solitary state of Dunne's corpse inside the barn tempts one to wonder if he visited Belpatrick over the weekend before the autopsy commenced.

McMahon boldly laid this colour supplement on the table where the lawyers and agents were sitting. As the *Freeman's Journal* reported (23 October), an irate Jackson rose to denounce this act as 'a monstrous violation of every decency in a court of justice'. He pressed the coroner to charge the editor with criminal contempt. Denying any intent to show this cartoon to the jurors, McMahon declared that he would retract nothing. For his part, the coroner admitted that he had the power to cite someone for contempt, but refused to punish the editor unless he repeated his offence.

The proper business of this fourth session began with Fr Taaffe's description of the events leading up to the eviction. Boasting that he had been a nationalist 'ever since I was as high as my knee', he recounted his warning to Dunne of the impending eviction. Once he had seen the old man's condition on the fatal day, he offered to administer the last rites. But Dunne had refused his offer. Despite Singleton's refusal to accept a token payment and grant readmission, Taaffe conceded that he was a 'kind and humane man' and that the bailiffs had not mistreated Dunne. The next witness, McMahon, deposed that he had never seen anything so shocking as this eviction and that he had warned the sheriff of the risk. At this point, Jackson handed the coroner a copy of a scathing editorial in the *Drogheda Independent* praising the National League for organizing opposition to Dudgeon and Emerson who would otherwise 'have [had] a walkover'. The coroner admitted that it was a 'very ... nasty' article and asked for the author's name, but McMahon refused to identify him. The coroner, Dr Moore, then adjourned the inquest after declaring that he would not tolerate the display in court of any more inflammatory articles.[10]

* * *

The widespread sense of outrage over Dunne's death found further expression in a second cartoon – entitled 'Evicting to death', and unsigned – published in the *Weekly Freeman* on the same date as Reigh's image in *United Ireland* (that is, 20 October). It is reproduced on page 149. In this cartoon, the *Freeman*'s leading cartoonist, John Fergus O'Hea, indulged in considerable artistic licence by depicting the moribund old man sprawled on a pile of boulders next to a ridge of brush or gorse with dusk approaching. In the left-hand corner, the thuggish crowbar brigade marches past a ruined cabin escorted by the police and waving a large Union Jack. Adding insult to injury, the top-hatted sheriff waves cavalierly to his latest victim. According to the caption, Dunne was 'flung out on the side of the road by Balfour's gang of emergency-men' and left to die in a 'deserted outhouse' despite his prophetic warning of this very fate. On another page, the following verses appeared complete with a comparison to the martyrdom of Christ:

> In Law's august and righteous name
> How many crimes from day to day
> Set Erin's anguished heart aflame!

10 Almost all the files of the *Drogheda Independent* seem to be missing from both the National Library of Ireland and the British Library newspaper archive at Colindale.

O! ye who 'gainst our race inveigh
As sordid knaves gaze on the scene
Of death our artist brings to view;
Say had this victim English been,
What would his sturdy kinsmen do?

Recall the facts – for eighty years
To glut an idler's greed for gold,
And in return get scorn and sneers
In summer's heat and winter's cold,
The old man toiled, and when his hand
Had lost its power the spade to ply
And tribute wring from sterile land,
He's cast from out his home – TO DIE!

The 'Law' cannot allow him time,
So in a stable dark and cold,
Death cleanses him of legal 'crime'!
God's mercy on that peasant old!
Christ! Saviour! in a stable born,
By tyrants scourged and crucified,
Have mercy on the judgment morn
On him who in a stable died!

O! Sons of Albion, do ye deem –
Like one by whom our land's opprest [sic] –
Each deed that makes Éire's teardrops stream
A thing for mirth, a jovial jest?
Ah, surely no! tho' dastards smile,
And lightly fling their poisoned darts;
Ye are not made of clay so vile,
What'er your faults, ye still have hearts!

Say, honest Briton, long misled –
On falsehood led from early youth –
Here in the presence of the dead
Does prejudice give way to truth?
It does – then pluck these despots down –
Our country's curse – thy country's shame.
So shall your name with fresh renown
Shine brighter on the roll of fame!

O'Hea's cartoon about Dunne resembled his recent commemoration in the *Weekly Freeman* of the death of another old farmer, named Bartley Geary, who had 'crept back' into his ruined cottage near Kilkerrin in Connemara only to perish before dawn. Both victims were drawn lying alone, with no family or friends to mourn their passing.[11]

* * *

The fifth session of the inquest was held on 24 October. By then, the jurors were complaining about the protracted proceedings. When the foreman requested compensation for their loss of income, the coroner replied sarcastically that they would have to ask the chief secretary for money. According to the *Freeman's Journal* (25 October), Thomas Moonan, a local farmer, who had witnessed the eviction, recalled hearing Dunne beseech Emerson to send for the poorhouse van and then cry out that he would not survive in the cold. When the sub-sheriff's lawyer asked why no shelter had been found for the victim, Moonan replied that he could not explain it but he had placed a blanket around the old man's shoulders. Exploiting this response, the lawyer suggested that Dunne's family had deliberately left him outside in order to 'screw better terms out of the landlord'. To this insinuation Moonan replied weakly: 'I don't know.'

When the inquest resumed on 2 November, the sub-sheriff described the events leading up to the eviction and flatly denied ever having heard Dunne predict his death. When asked what kind of chair Dunne had been seated on, Bailie replied with a chuckle: 'It was a piece of stick with four legs in it.' This response prompted laughter in the courtroom, and the Dunnes' lawyer rebuked him for trying to turn this case into a laughing matter. Bailie stated that he had detected no signs of Dunne's unfitness for the ordeal and denied that Taaffe had ever warned him about the possible consequences.

At the seventh session (on 5 November), the jury heard Dudgeon insist that Dunne had never said anything about dying if evicted. Had anyone told him about the danger, he would not have gone ahead; and he made it clear that landlords were not obliged to provide a doctor at every eviction. Another medical examiner attributed the cause of Dunne's death not to shock but rather to 'congestion of the lungs, resulting from exposure to the cold'.[12] On 8

---

11 In the earlier cartoon ('How long, O Lord!!!'), the dying Geary lies on his back clutching the fatal eviction warrant while a shaft of light from a distant star illuminates his head (*Weekly Freeman*, 18 Feb. 1888). I am much indebted to Joanna Finegan, curator of prints and drawings, National Library of Ireland, for tracking down these cartoons. **12** This doctor was Professor Rawdon McNamara, MD, FRCSI (*Drogheda Argus*, 10 Nov., *Freeman's Journal*, 6 Nov. 1888).

6 'Evicting to death'; cartoon from the *Weekly Freeman*, 20 October 1888.

November, Emerson took the witness stand and flatly denied that Dunne had ever asked to be taken to the workhouse hospital. He recalled entering the house and demanding payment of £108, whereupon Fr Taaffe countered with an offer that he could not accept. He too denied any foreknowledge of Dunne's illness. The family's lawyer, McInerney, then secured the coroner's consent to read aloud a passage from a speech by Gladstone in Birmingham on 7 November denouncing evictions in Ireland that were too horrific to be tolerated in England. To cries of 'shame' from the audience, Gladstone had brought up the case of Dunne who, he said, suffered from 'a bronchial complaint' and had 'paid the debt of nature' shortly after being evicted. Such things, he repeated, would never be allowed to happen in England.[13]

The inquest finally came to an end on 9 November when the lawyers summed up the cases for and against those deemed responsible for Dunne's demise. According to McInerney, the victim was an innocent and industrious man who had led a 'blameless life' and refused to join the Plan of Campaign. Despite this unblemished record, he had been 'thrown out like a dog on the roadside to die in a cold empty barn'. He urged the jury to return a verdict of

13 *The Times*, 8 Nov., *Freeman's Journal*, 9 Nov., *Drogheda Argus*, 10 Nov. 1888. In the course of his speech to the National Liberal Federation meeting in Birmingham, Gladstone blamed this example of tenant suffering on rack-renting landlords whose abuse of power left behind 'bitter recollections' that would never be effaced until property rights were reformed (*The Times*, 8 Nov. 1888).

manslaughter against the three principals who had acted with no regard for Dunne's parlous condition. For his part, Jackson tried to vindicate his clients by blaming the family for not having procured a doctor's certificate attesting the father's unfitness for removal. After an hour's deliberation, the jurors returned with the utterly innocuous verdict that Dunne had died on the morning of 12 October. Frustrated by this finding, the coroner ordered them to complete their task and decide the cause of death. In a matter of minutes they reappeared with a verdict of manslaughter against Dudgeon and Emerson and a censure of Bailie for having failed to use 'more precaution'. As the *Drogheda Argus* (10 November 1888) reported, the jurors found that the two agents 'did feloniously and unlawfully kill and slay' Dunne by subjecting him to shock and exposure at Belpatrick. With no less than eight priests in the courtroom, this judgment was greeted with loud applause. An angry Jackson stressed the lack of incriminating evidence and requested bail, which was granted. Because Dudgeon was not present in court, the coroner promised to issue warrants for the arrest of both men. However, when Jackson pledged that 'the bails would be perfected tomorrow', Emerson was allowed to return to Dublin by train.[14] Dudgeon attended Ardee court on 13 November and provided bail of £100, along with two sureties of £50 each. Emerson followed suit on the next day. Both men were scheduled to appear for trial at the forthcoming county assizes.[15]

The *Freeman's Journal,* which devoted a total of fourteen articles and three editorials to the case, hailed the jury's verdict as the rightful response to an inhumane eviction. Dismissing the denials by the agents and Bailie that they bore any blame, its leader-writer argued that they had had ample warning of Dunne's condition and therefore his eviction was 'literally a sentence of death'. Moreover, this was not the first such fatality by the roadside. Thousands of other evicted tenants had suffered a similar fate. But times had changed, and the life of an Irish cottier peasant was no longer 'the landlord's property'. Public opinion had grown 'strong enough to avenge his death' and this case should prompt the passage of laws that would prevent such evictions.[16]

A long editorial in the *Drogheda Argus* on 17 November echoed these sentiments, pointing out that the protracted inquest highlighted the callous nature of landlordism. The time had arrived when such a 'death sentence' could no longer be carried out 'with perfect immunity' because the press and the 'awakened public conscience' would not tolerate such abuses: 'Nemesis, retributive

14 *Drogheda Argus, Freeman's Journal,* 10 Nov. 1888. The latter article, 'Evicted, and dead', appeared in the same issue as the report of Jack the Ripper's carnage in Miller's Court, Whitechapel, London. 15 *Drogheda Argus,* 17 Nov. 1888. 16 *Freeman's Journal,* 10 Nov. 1888.

justice, if slow, is sure to visit the evildoer.' No matter how ineffective the punishment imposed on the culprits, they could not escape the 'bar of public opinion' and soon 'power shall be wrested from their hands'. The very fact that the
sickly Dunne had to be carried out of his house – 'O how tenderly!' – showed
in itself 'a reckless carelessness and inhumanity'. Warming to his task, the writer
described Dunne sitting on a stool outside his bolted house on that wintry day
'dying as he was – the cold hand of death slowly tightening its hold on him –
for over two hours' before being removed to a shelter. The evictors were 'callous in the extreme – atrocious and brutal'. However vehemently these
'hirelings' might deny their guilt, they had to realize that 'the palmy old days
of high-handed landlordism' were gone. Tenants could no longer be treated as
'of considerable less value than cattle, and thrust … out wholesale, to seek refuge
in the workhouse, emigration, or die in a ditch, with perfect impunity'. Given
Dublin Castle's complicity in these cruel proceedings, it could not 'conveniently
wink at such acts'. Dunne's death, in short, should teach 'the evictors and their
understrappers', as well as the government, that 'even propped up by bayonets
the system cannot stand'. Given all the evictions pending and being carried out
on Plan of Campaign estates around the country, these defiant words fell into
the category of wishful thinking.

* * *

On 21 November the defendants' new lawyer, William McLaughlin QC,
appeared before the judges in the queen's bench division to defend the application to have the verdict quashed *a certiorari*. Dudgeon and Emerson had already
composed an affidavit charging bias because seventeen of the jurors were nationalists who had been influenced by National League rallies at which the agents
had been denounced as murderers. The affidavit also condemned the inflammatory cartoons, one of which had been shown in court, as well as the 'violent' speeches reported in the press which were bound to prejudice the jurors.
Hammering away at the 'disgraceful and scandalous' conduct of the jurors,
McLaughlin characterized the inquest as a burlesque, except for the verdict of
manslaughter. In vain did the Dunnes' lawyers protest that the jurors had acted
properly. Representing the crown, Edward Carson offered no opposition to
the appeal, and the four judges granted a conditional order of *a certiorari*.[17]

When the hearing resumed in the queen's bench division on 15 January
1889, The MacDermot QC, representing the Dunne sons, scoffed at the efforts
of the defence counsel to quash the verdict of 'wilful murder' on the grounds

---

17 *The Times, Freeman's Journal*, 22 Nov., *Drogheda Argus*, 24 Nov. 1888.

of misconduct by the jury. After all, the agents had ordered the eviction and ignored Dunne's prediction of death. At this point the lord chief justice, Sir Michael Morris, recalled that during the Famine a coroner's jury in Galway had charged the prime minister, Lord John Russell, with 'wilful murder' after a poor homeless woman had died of starvation. When The MacDermot asked about the outcome, the judge replied to a ripple of laughter: 'I don't think he ever moved' to quash the verdict.[18] In The MacDermot's view, the Ardee jurors had acted properly and their verdict should stand. Representing the attorney general, William Ryan QC stated that the government would take no action even if the judges upheld the jury's verdict.[19]

On the next day McLaughlin condemned the inquest, arguing that Dunne's fate had been 'used to make political merchandise'. Not even his widow, he maintained, had known how ill her husband was. And then there was the interference of the National League's organizer, John Kelly, who had arranged the protest meetings. Something of a hired gun, Kelly had recruited Plan of Campaign supporters around the country and taught them how to fortify their houses against the evictors; for these activities he spent six months in prison in 1889. McLaughlin also condemned the 'remarkable' McMahon for having brought cartoons into court and for displaying nationalist speeches published in his paper. Such prejudicial acts, he asserted, could not have occurred in 'any place except where people had taken leave of their senses and where the masses of the community had allowed themselves to be steeped in a deeply settled conspiracy against the law of the land'. He dismissed 'the whole business … [as] a transparent and audacious attempt to prostitute the law – to make a triumph for the National League, and … political merchandise out of the dead man's body'. For these reasons, the jury's verdict was completely unjustified. At the end of his tirade, the court reserved judgment and recessed.[20]

Finally, on 22 January the judges reached a decision to overturn the charge of manslaughter. As the lord chief justice put it in his lengthy summation, the

---

18 Morris may have embroidered this tale about the charge against Lord John Russell. Perhaps he was referring to a case in January 1847 when a coroner's jury arrived at what the *The Times* called the 'sapient' verdict of murder against the prime minister and Sir Randolph Routh, chairman of the Relief Commission, for the death by starvation of Mary Commons. The coroner's objections forced the jurors to pare their verdict down to the bland finding that she had died from want and inclement weather (*The Times*, 21 Jan. 1847). I am grateful to Professor Peter Gray for this reference. **19** *Freeman's Journal*, *The Times*, 16 Jan., *Drogheda Argus*, 19 Jan. 1889. **20** *Freeman's Journal*, *The Times*, 17 Jan., *Drogheda Argus*, 19 Jan. 1889. For further information on John Kelly, a draper from Tralee, who was tried and jailed for promoting the Plan of Campaign around the country and teaching tenants how to fortify their houses against the sheriff's party, see *The Times*, 9, 16, 28–30 Jan., 4, 13 Feb., 13 Apr. 1889.

'inquisition had been impeached' owing to the jury's 'misconduct' and because the whole inquiry was 'bad' from the outset. The eviction had been perfectly legal and Dunne had suffered no brutality. 'Perverse' and 'most peculiar', the jury's finding lacked any certainty of criminal malfeasance. Not even the family had known about the severity of the old man's illness and no one had bothered to send for a doctor. Morris pointed out that Bailie was the man who had executed the eviction, while Dudgeon and Emerson had merely stood by. The agents had done nothing illegal: they had not assaulted Dunne and they had had no reason to stop the operation. Nevertheless, they had been found guilty of manslaughter. For these reasons he made the *a certiorari* order absolute and absolved the agents of any blame.[21]

Even for nationalists accustomed to landlord justice, this decision must have provoked widespread anger and depression. As the *Freeman's Journal* (24 January) put it, the crown, acting through the queen's bench, had intervened to ensure that Dudgeon and Emerson would not be punished no matter how great their guilt. What then was the use of coroners' juries if their findings could be flouted? 'Is it not a mere farce to continue them any longer if law and justice can be so easily ignored?' Obviously, 'the interests of landlordism' had to be protected at all costs; landlords and agents could rest assured that at least one high court could be counted on to uphold their appeals.

Following the queen's bench decision, news of the Dunne affair quickly gave way to feature stories about the Parnell Commission and Richard Pigott's flight and suicide in Spain, the imprisonment of William O'Brien, and the turbulence around Gweedore stirred up by the arrest and sentencing of the militant Fr McFadden. Evictions on the Massereene estate in Co. Louth continued – with much bitterness against Dudgeon and Emerson for purging Plan of Campaign supporters and replacing them with Protestant farmers from the North.

* * *

Much of the Dunne affair turned on the absence of any medical intervention because a certificate from a dispensary doctor or army surgeon could have made the difference between life and death. A family marked for eviction in August 1886 on the estate of Mrs Hannah Lewis at Woodford, Co. Galway, won a temporary reprieve because the tenant's wife had given birth prematurely owing to her agitated state. In this instance, the dispensary doctor was present and he advised against disturbing mother and child.[22] A tenant named John Diver on

21 For the lord chief justice's summation, see *Drogheda Argus,* 26 Jan., *Freeman's Journal, The Times,* 23 Jan. 1889; also *Irish Law Times Reports,* 25, 11–13 (thanks to Robert Marshall for this reference). 22 *Freeman's Journal,* 30 Aug. 1886.

the Wybrants Olphert estate in Donegal was spared eviction after an army doctor examined him and declared him too ill to be moved. So his removal was
postponed.[23] In June 1887 Michael McNamara, 'a very old man' confined to
his bed near Bodyke, Co. Clare, refused to surrender his holding. Because an
army surgeon warned that his removal might prove fatal, the agent handed
McNamara a penny which he gratefully accepted. This symbolic act conferred
on him the status of caretaker.[24] On the other hand, doctors also pronounced
tenants in poor health fit for eviction. Thus, a young man named John Fahy
was carried out of his house on the Clanricarde estate with the guarded approval
of the dispensary doctor who knew him to be 'a confirmed epileptic'. After sitting outside for an hour and a half in mild weather, Fahy was allowed to re-
enter his house.[25]

   Doctors were not the only ones with the authority to suspend an eviction.
On Mrs Lewis's estate, the sheriff called a halt to the removal of Thomas Coen's
wife who was 80 years old and an invalid. When she saw the evictors approaching, she fainted and had to be carried outside to a shed. She seemed so close to
death that two priests gave her the last rites as she lay on the ground. Moved
by the urgent pleas of the priests and alarmed by the curses of the angry crowd,
the sheriff relented and ordered her readmission as caretaker.[26] On Captain
Arthur Hill's estate near Gweedore, Co. Donegal, several frail old women as
well as a family with sickly children were readmitted as caretakers because the
sheriff and agent used their discretionary powers without the benefit of a doctor.[27] Readmission on health grounds alone, however, was the exception that
proved the rule of little or no mercy.

   Doctors or surgeons rarely accompanied eviction parties unless violent resistance was expected. A more typical case was that of the widow Coyle, an 80-
year-old tenant on the Olphert estate at Falcarragh, Co. Donegal, whose daughter had also been sick. Unlike Dunne, this crippled woman flatly refused to go
to the workhouse and so two emergency-men lifted her up from her bed, placed
her in a chair and carried her out to the road. Fortunately, a local priest, Fr
Boyle, found her shelter in a neighbour's house.[28] Perhaps Dunne would have
lived a little longer had Fr Taaffe been as active in this regard.

---

23 *The Times*, 25 Oct. 1889.   **24** *The Times*, 16 June 1887, 3 Sept. 1888.   **25** One of Fahy's
sympathizers, an Englishman named Trow, denounced his eviction as cruel because he was
'dying of consumption'. But a letter from the Irish Office tried to set the record straight by
stating that the doctor, who had been treating Fahy for epilepsy for a long time, refused to
certify that the eviction would be life-threatening (*The Times*, 29 Sept. 1888).   **26** *Freeman's
Journal*, 30 Aug. 1886.   **27** *Freeman's Journal*, 13, 14, 16, 18 Aug. 1886.   **28** *The Times*, 15,
19 Apr., 7 May 1889.

Given the resumption of evictions on the nearby Massereene estate, one might well conclude that Dunne's death and the resulting hue and cry changed nothing. Clearly, Nemesis took its time to visit 'the evildoers, and the 'despots' were not so soon 'plucked down'. But Dunne's death did give nationalists a golden opportunity to intensify their agitation against landlordism and promote the Plan of Campaign. All those feature articles, cartoons, inquest sessions and protest meetings could hardly be ignored. And the sobering verdict against Dudgeon and Emerson at the end of the Ardee inquest may have moved a few agents and sheriffs to think twice before evicting the aged and infirm.

Five quatrains

translated from the Irish

1 *Whet-beak*

Birdsong from the willow tree.
Whet-beak, note-blurt, clear, airy.
   Yellow quill-bill, ink-blot cowl:
   Blackbird, practising his scale.

2 *East coast*

A bitter wind to-night. It tosses
The white hair of the Irish Sea. It will toss
The fierce raiders from Norway off their courses.
To-night I sleep in peace.

3 *The monk's tryst*

Sweet-striking bell
   abrangle in the small hours gale:
   better up with you for chapel
   than up late with some Jezebel.

4 *Gráinne's words about Díarmait*

There's one I want to look and look at,
   to whom I'd give the light-drenched world –
all of it, all of it, and not care.
   I'd give it all and think it worth it.

5 *Colmcille's Derry*

Why I love Derry:
   It is calm, it is clear.
Rustle of white-robed angels
   at every corner.

SEAMUS HEANEY

A social revolution within an economic revolution: changes in family life in Ireland

Finola Kennedy

FAMILY LIFE IN IRELAND conjures up a thousand images from the idyllic to the obscene – from Alice Taylor's *To School through the Fields* (1988) to the Kilkenny incest case. In Ireland, family life encompasses the beauty and the beast. It is also characterized by remarkable and continuing change. Until the mid-1960s, more people were employed in agriculture than in industry; over fifty per cent of the population lived in rural areas as recently as 1961. Today, about six per cent of the population is engaged in agriculture. As the number of jobs outside agriculture expanded in the period from the 1920s to the 1970s, priority was accorded to male employment – that is, jobs for 'breadwinners'. To further this agenda, a marriage bar was introduced for women – in the civil service, in national teaching, and in certain other services, including banking; at the same time, the employment of women in industry was restricted. Some barriers to female employment remained in place until the 1970s. But, as the workplace changed, so family life also changed. The focus in this essay is on the process of rapid change that has taken place in recent decades. The essay suggests that 1973, the year Ireland entered the European Economic Community (EEC), was a defining point on the path of family change in Ireland – the time when economic growth became the dominant national goal. Thereafter, as the economy developed and expanded, the degree of influence traditionally exercised by the Roman Catholic church over Irish society proportionately declined.

HISTORICAL BACKGROUND

In the early twentieth century, Irish society recognized a clear division of labour between the sexes. When the family based on life-long marriage was enshrined in the 1937 constitution – seventy years ago – a leader in the *Irish Times* commented: 'Some day, please heaven, the nation will be so organized that work will be available for every man, so that he may marry and assume the burdens of a home, and for every woman until she embarks upon her proper profession

– which is marriage. In that more prosperous nation there will be no question of the woman who "will not allow marriage to interfere with her career".'[1]

The sexual code of the time, which proscribed access to contraception, together with the social stigma that attached to the unmarried mother and her child, placed sexual intercourse firmly within marriage. In a poor economy with limited opportunities for marriage and founding a family, a degree of sexual frustration was inevitable. This became the stuff of legend and of literature, notwithstanding the clear economic context of oppressive rural poverty. Nowhere is the famished sexual appetite of the time more keenly expressed than in Patrick Kavanagh's character Maguire in the poem 'The Great Hunger' (1942). Monsignor Tom Stack has written of 'The Great Hunger' that it 'gives the lie to the idyllic and romantic model of life on the land, close to nature and in tune with the seasons, permanently captivated by the wonders of creation, and supported by a network of close family and communal ties'.[2]

But, as historians of the medieval period claim, in former times sexuality was dealt with in a manner unrecognizable by the standards of the 1930s and 1940s. For example, Kenneth Nicholls tells us: 'Throughout the medieval period, and down to the end of the old order in 1603, what would be called Celtic secular marriage remained the norm in Ireland, and Christian matrimony was no more than a rare exception grafted on to this system.'[3] This system of secular marriage permitted easy divorce, and upper-class men and women could have a succession of spouses. For example, a noblewoman who died in 1395, Coblaith 'Mhór', daughter of Cathal Ó Conchobhair, king of Connacht, was nicknamed 'Port-na-dtrí-námhad' (the harbour of the three enemies) because she had married three chieftains who were sworn enemies. In relation to succession, medieval Irish law did not distinguish between the legitimate and the illegitimate. A mother close to death was sometimes known to 'name the father', with an eye to securing her child's inheritance.

If we fast forward to the early eighteenth century, we find families subsisting on small plots of land at a time of rapid population growth. Large numbers of children became a source of labour from an early age. A century later, in the aftermath of the Famine, an economic Iron Curtain closed which blocked easy and early marriage. When land holdings were no longer subdivided to accommodate the needs of each new generation, the opportunity for marriage was restricted to proportionately fewer people. Enforced celibacy based on economic necessity found support in values based on church teaching, both Catholic

---

1 *Irish Times*, 22 Feb. 1937. 2 T. Stack, *No earthly estate: God and Patrick Kavanagh* (Dublin, 2002), p. 113. 3 K. Nicholls, *Gaelic and Gaelicised Ireland in the Middle Ages* (Dublin, 1972), p. 73.

and Protestant, which elevated chastity and urged sexual restraint, especially condemning unmarried mothers. In the 1830s the monumental Whately commission on the condition of the poorer classes[4] found that the unmarried mother was a social outcast, whose 'stain was never forgotten, and the memory of which lingered for generations'.

In the 1950s the Commission on Emigration was dismissive of the importance of the Catholic ethos in relation to the low marriage rate and high marital fertility. The commission maintained that no convincing evidence was put before it to support the view that 'the indissolubility of marriage and, in the absence of contraception, the fear of large families deter many from marriage altogether and others until a relatively advanced age'.[5] On the contrary, the commission pointed out that other Catholic countries had higher marriage rates, while the marriage rate in Northern Ireland, with a minority Catholic population, was also low. However, no facts were given regarding the relative economic development of the various other countries. James Meenan, a member of the Commission, dissented: he had no doubt as to the influence of the Catholic ethos, writing later that 'the low marriage rate should be recognised for what it is, the form of birth control adopted by a practising Catholic people'.[6]

This was a time when the Catholic clergy, well educated and trusted by the majority of people, had attained considerable influence. One result was a powerful combination of religious and economic forces that contributed to the family patterns of the late nineteenth and early twentieth centuries. These patterns persisted until, following the developments that took place in the economy from the 1960s onwards, a social revolution occurred within the economic revolution. Class factors can never be ignored in examining family change. Then, as now, the expression 'the rich are different' was valid. For example, the distinction between farmers who had a reasonable standard of living and landless labourers was immense. The historian Art Cosgrove has pointed out that 'the widest social gap in rural Ireland was that between the farmer and the landless labourer, and marriage rarely, if ever, bridged that gap',[7] while Caoimhín Ó Danachair has described the landless labourer as 'the untouchable of Irish rural society'.[8]

In 2004 the population in the twenty-six counties of the Republic of Ireland exceeded four million for the first time since 1871. For centuries emigration was

---

4 The Commissioners for Enquiring into the Condition of the Poorer Classes in Ireland were chaired by Richard Whately, Church of Ireland archbishop of Dublin. The reports are published as Parliamentary Papers: 1835, xxxii, Parts 1–2; 1836, xxxi–iv. **5** Commission on Emigration and other Population Problems, *Reports* (Dublin, 1954: Pr. 2541), p. 80, para. 166. **6** J. Meenan, *The Irish economy since 1922* (Liverpool, 1970), p. 337. **7** A. Cosgrove, 'Introduction' in A. Cosgrove (ed.), *Marriage in Ireland* (Dublin, 1985), p. 3. **8** C. Ó Danachair, 'Marriage in Irish folk tradition' in Cosgrove (ed.), *Marriage in Ireland*, p. 101.

a notable feature of Irish life, but in recent years the trend has been reversed. There is now a strong flow of immigration, including very many from different cultural milieux. In the 1980s, young Irish people were anxiously seeking visas to enable them to work in the United States. Now many are returning home. For much of the twentieth century concern about emigration was to the forefront of public debate in Ireland; at times the level of emigration was viewed as a barometer of the capacity for self-government. For decades, emigrants were predominantly unskilled. Referring to a halving in the number of agricultural labourers in the twenty-six counties between the censuses of 1911 and 1936, J.J. Lee has written: 'There was no room at the Irish inn for those who showed their deplorable lack of breeding by being born in a labourer's cottage.'⁹ Only high levels of emigration and high celibacy rates enabled the Irish economy to survive.

TRANSFORMATION OF THE FAMILY SINCE THE 1970S

The year 1973 was a landmark year in relation to family change in Ireland. It was the year when the highest marriage rate of the twentieth century, 7.5 per 1,000, was recorded. The absolute number of marriages peaked at 23,000 in 1974; the lowest number of marriages, just over 13,000, was recorded in 1932. The year 1973 was also the year in which the marriage bar in the public service was removed and women were no longer obliged to leave employment when they married. That same year judgement was delivered in the McGee case:¹⁰ this eventually resulted in legislation, enacted in 1979, removing the ban on contraceptives that had been in place since 1935. Another notable change in 1973 was the introduction of allowances for unmarried mothers who reared their children on their own. Finally, it was the year in which the first beneficiaries of free post-primary education left school. These developments have had a marked impact on the family during the past three decades; in particular, they provided new opportunities for women and influenced their lifestyle choices.

Before joining the EEC in 1973, Ireland was essentially an agricultural society in which family farms provided basic livelihoods for a large segment of the population, although the drift away from farming was already well under way. The agricultural policy of the EEC encouraged the development of larger farms and hastened the demise of smaller family farms. Following the lean decades of the 1930s, 1940s and 1950s, when opportunities for marriage were restricted by

9 J.J. Lee, *Ireland, 1912–1985* (Cambridge, 1989), p. 159. 10 In *McGee v. the Attorney General* (1973), the Supreme Court held that there was a right under the constitution to marital privacy and that Mrs McGee was entitled to access contraceptives.

economic factors, the national economic growth of the 1960s ushered in a 'golden age' for marriage in Ireland. This persisted until the early 1970s, but then faded steadily until the mid-1990s. In the past decade there has been a sharp revival in the number of marriages. Between 1997 and 2005 the number of marriages increased by one quarter, from 15,600 to 20,700. Some of the increase may be due to a postponement factor from earlier years, as the average age of marriage has risen. The introduction of divorce in 1997 has also contributed to the increase in marriage numbers. The number of second marriages currently averages 2,500 per year, of which over 2,000 are marriages of divorced persons. In the period since the Family Law (Divorce) Act 1996 came into effect on 27 February 1997, the number of divorces has steadily increased – reaching over 4,000 in 2005.

The number of civil marriages has increased markedly since the 1970s. In 1970 there were 121 civil marriages, accounting for a half of one per cent of total marriages. In 2003 there were 4,000 civil marriages, or one in five of all marriages. In the latter year, civil marriages accounted for more than one-third of marriages of couples resident in Dublin, compared with less than one in twenty for those resident in Co. Monaghan. The proportion of Catholic marriage ceremonies has decreased significantly from more than 90 per cent to 77 per cent between 1996 and 2002.

The incidence of cohabitation has increased rapidly. In the 1979 census – the first to record cohabitation – 417 persons, either single or widowed, stated that they were living as couples. By 2004, there were over 80,000 couples – 160,000 persons – cohabiting. A factor which may contribute to the rise in the incidence of cohabitation is the increase in life expectancy. A marriage contracted early in the last century between persons who married at the average marriage age might have been expected to last about twenty-five years. Today, such a marriage has the potential to last fifty years or more, giving a whole new dimension to the commitment 'till death us do part'. The increase in the incidence of cohabitation is an indicator that marriage has become something of an optional dessert on life's menu, rather than the main course.

Since the decriminalization of homosexuality in 1993, the issue of the recognition of gay partnerships has come onto the legal and political radar. In the 2002 census, 1,300 same-sex couples were registered as cohabiting. In 2006 a case came before the Irish courts in which a lesbian couple sought recognition for their marriage which had taken place in Canada, one of a number of countries – including Spain, Belgium and Holland – that recognize gay marriages. The case, which was lost in the high court, is currently being appealed to the supreme court. The minister for justice is committed to the introduction of a civil partnership bill which would give the same tax, pension and other rights to cohabiting couples – whether same-sex or heterosexual – as are available to married couples.

A trend comparable to the marriage trend occurred in relation to births within marriage: marital births rose to a post-war peak in 1980 and then declined rapidly until the mid-1990s. Total births declined from a peak for the twentieth century of 74,000 in 1980 to 48,000 in 1994. They have since climbed back to 60,000 in 2002. Births outside marriage have risen steadily to over 30 per cent of total births, compared with around 3 per cent in 1970. There has been a steep decline in the average size of families. Forty years ago there were 2,000 births to mothers with ten children, compared with fewer than fifty such births in recent years – in a much bigger population than forty years ago. A not insignificant number of births are to young women below the legal age of consent, which is 17 years. In 2005 there were over 200 births to women aged 16 years and under, almost all of which were non-marital births. Births at young ages are not a new phenomenon. Back in 1970, when the age of marriage for girls was 14 years and the age of consent was 17 years, a total of 134 births to girls aged 16 years and under were recorded; these were almost evenly divided between marital and non-marital births.

Over the years, the place of birth – like the place of death – has moved from home to hospital. Fifty years ago the majority of people were born at home; nowadays this is the case for just five out of every thousand. Likewise, two in three persons died in their homes fifty years ago; today the proportion is less than one in five. A striking and relatively new feature is the increase in permanent childlessness, as has also occurred in the UK and in continental countries. Of women born in 1945 who eventually married, only 10 per cent did not have a child – whereas it is estimated that 25 per cent of all women now entering their child-bearing years will remain childless. 'Childless by choice' is an expression that is gaining currency at the very same time as there is an increase in those seeking fertility treatments. The scenario of 'childless by choice' may be related to women's increasing commitment to the workforce. The participation of women in the workforce changed little between 1926 and 1986, when it was 30 per cent. A high proportion of single and widowed women remained in the workforce over a long period. While the participation rate of widows declined, especially following the introduction of the widows' contributory pension in the 1960s, the most striking feature in recent years has been the increase in the participation rate of married women in the workforce from 7.5 per cent in 1971 to over 50 per cent at present. Next to single women, the highest participation rate – nearly 60 per cent – is of women who are separated or divorced.

An increasing number of women in the workforce are mothers, including mothers of very young children. Over half of all mothers in Ireland with children aged from birth to 16 years go out to work, almost 28 per cent being in full-time employment. For mothers with very young children aged from birth to three years of age, the proportion in work is over 50 per cent, with 26 per cent in full-time employment.[11] A factor that may have implications for the participation of women in the workforce in the future, and for the increased 'opportunity cost' of childrearing, is the increased participation of women in higher education. At ages 18, 19 and 20 years, 30 per cent more young women were in education than young men of the same age in 2002–3. As more mothers continue to work following the birth of their children, the breadwinner/housewife model of family life is being replaced by a more egalitarian model of parenting in which the role of fathers is increased.[12] With more births to unmarried couples and with increased separation and divorce, solo parenting by mother or father is also increasing.

UNDERSTANDING AND INTERPRETING CHANGE

Three factors are suggested as being of special significance in understanding and interpreting the changes that have occurred in family life in recent decades. The three factors are: the increasing openness of society to modernizing influences, especially the media; the changing status of children as society moved away from an agricultural base; and changes in the roles of men and women in response to the needs of the economy. Of these three factors, our thesis is that the economic one has been the most dominant. When economic forces attained sufficient momentum they tended to overwhelm traditional values, including religious teaching. Before considering the three selected factors in some detail, it is worth considering the timing of the various changes in the family – because for at least two-thirds of the twentieth-century Irish family patterns, Northern Ireland included, differed from those in England and other developed European countries. The differential timing of the changes in Ireland was closely related to the fact that economic development did not correspond to that of more developed northern European countries. The banning of access to contracep-

11 *Babies and bosses: reconciling work and family life*, ii: *Austria, Ireland and Japan* (Paris, 2003: OECD), table 2.4, p. 48. 12 For an informative study on the changing role of fathers, see K. McKeown, H. Ferguson and D. Rooney, *Changing fathers? Fatherhood and family life in modern Ireland* (Cork, 1998); see also F. Kennedy, *Cottage to crèche: family change in Ireland* (Dublin, 2001).

tives and the removal of that ban provide an example of differential timing in the central matter of the separation of sexual intercourse from marriage.

Ireland was one of the last western countries to introduce a ban on contraceptives. In the United States contraceptives were outlawed in 1873, as a result of a 'Victorian' moral crusade. When Ireland outlawed contraceptives in 1935, a ban already operated in several countries, including France, Belgium, Italy and the UK. Just as Ireland had been tardy in introducing the ban, it was the last western European country to remove the ban: it was only in 1979 that Ireland took this step, in the wake of Spain which had removed the ban the year before. Contraception was never far from the attention of the media, at least from the time of the McGee case in 1973.[13] The advent of 'the pill' in the 1960s, followed by legal access to contraceptives with the Family Planning Act 1979 – initially for married couples, and on demand from the 1980s – has facilitated behavioural change on a major scale. It is interesting in this context to recall the words of Fr Edward Cahill SJ in a letter to his friend Eamon de Valera in 1934, prior to the passing of the Criminal Law (Amendment) Act 1935 which introduced the ban on contraceptives. Cahill expressed concern regarding the availability of contraceptives, stating: 'Civil law and government cannot indeed make, or even keep, a nation moral. They can, however, keep a check on unfair temptations or allurements to vice.'[14] While the reference to 'allurements to vice' may sound quaint in an era of 'recreational sex', some checks certainly did go in the 1980s.

Increasing openness of society to modernizing influences

A striking feature of life in Ireland in the late twentieth century was the stripping of the veil of secrecy which had shrouded various aspects of institutional and public life. The former era was brought to an abrupt end by the emergence of scandals in the church – from the Bishop Casey episode to the stories of child abuse brought to light by investigative journalists, most notably Mary Raftery in the television documentary *States of Fear*. In today's era of 'openness and transparency', it is easy to forget that for decades political and church leaders thought it preferable to keep nasty happenings under wraps and to actively 'avoid scandal'. Going back over seventy years to the Seanad debate on the Criminal Law (Amendment) Bill, the remarks of Senator Jameson are striking: 'Discussion is not to be allowed publicly on the subject with which the bill deals. I lived for

13 L. Gibbons, 'From kitchen sink to soap: drama and the serial form on Irish television' in M. McLoone and J. MacMahon (eds), *Television and Irish society: 21 years of Irish television* (Dublin, 1984), p. 41. 14 Edward Cahill SJ to Eamon de Valera, 7 July 1934, University College, Dublin, de Valera papers, P150/1095.

a long time in the Victorian age, and the greatest blot on the Victorian age was its refusal to discuss facts when people thought there was something indecent or immoral or something else about them. Surely we ought not to do that now.'[15]

Access to information on contraception, as on many other matters relating to family change, came via the media – magazines, newspapers, radio, television, film. Television programmes, especially *The Late Late Show* and the serials *Tolka Row* and *The Riordans*, introduced a view of changing lifestyles into homes all around Ireland. While Victorian values, the Catholic church and the infiltration of foreign media in the form of newspapers, magazines and films were all influences operating in countries other than Ireland, what may be regarded as peculiarly Irish was a tendency to solve awkward problems by having recourse to Britain – what might be termed the 'Pierrepoint syndrome'. When capital punishment existed in Ireland, ordinary hangings – as distinct from military executions – were carried out by the English hangman Albert Pierrepoint who travelled to Ireland for the purpose. Another example of this tendency was the dispatch of Irish emigrants to English building sites in the 1950s, and their subsequent neglect – as illustrated poignantly in Ultan Cowley's book *The Men Who Built Britain*.[16] Until the late 1990s divorce was not available in Ireland, and information and travel for the purposes of abortion were restricted. Yet over the past thirty years 120,000 women who obtained abortions in Britain gave Irish addresses. This is twice the total number of births in the year 2003.

Changing status of children as society moved away from an agricultural base

The predominant Catholic ethos may have slowed the pace of social change, but the agricultural basis of the economy was even more crucial.[17] In the context of the small farm, children were a labour resource from a young age. Later, if they emigrated, they sent remittances home. The changing economic status of children is a key to understanding aspects of change in family life. In the late Victorian era an idealised concept of childhood began to emerge among the privileged classes – and actually to exist to a certain extent. Economic condi-

---

15 *Seanad Debates*, 19, 6 Feb. 1935, col. 1224. **16** U. Cowley, *The men who built Britain* (Dublin, 2001), p. 210. Cowley – whose father, John Cowley, was a star of the TV series *The Riordans* – calls them 'The forgotten men'. **17** In Northern Ireland, where the population is more evenly divided in terms of religious affiliation, marriage and birth patterns were closer to those in the Republic at the time of the comprehensive investigations of the Commission on Emigration (1954) than in any of up to twenty countries with which comparisons were made by the Commission; see Commission on Emigration, *Reports*, pp. 64, 66 & 90 (tables 49, 51 and 67, respectively).

tions, however, dictated that a work-free childhood was the exception rather than the rule.

The changing economic position of children is linked to two factors in particular: the move away from agriculture and the extension of formal education. The latter causes children to be dependent on their parents for economic support for a longer period than was formerly the case. As late as 1964, only 36 per cent of 16-year-olds and 14 per cent of 18-year-olds were in full-time education. In the context of the small-farm economy as it existed until the First World War, children were an important economic resource. Children worked on the farm while still at school. When boys or girls were old enough to obtain employment away from home they were expected to send money home. This was done by thousands of Irish emigrants, who faithfully sent home what journalist John Healy called 'slate money'[18] or what national income accountants styled 'emigrants' remittances'. A letter from a young emigrant which did not contain money was called 'an empty letter'. To illustrate the importance of emigrants' remittances, in 1944 they were equivalent to 5.4 per cent of national income – or 25 per cent of total expenditure on food in the country. The same proportion of national income – 5.4 per cent – was equal to 4.94 billion euro in 2002, while a quarter of total expenditure on food in 2002 was 3.5 billion euro.

While the Catholic ethos may have contributed to a low marriage rate – a form of family planning – and to the incidence of big families for those who did marry, big families coincided with the requirement for family labour on small farms. Regulations governing school attendance were tailored to fit the requirements of agriculture. When examining the question of raising the school leaving age in 1951, the Commission on Youth Unemployment (chaired by Archbishop John Charles McQuaid of Dublin) considered the possible opposition of the farming community due to the lack of availability of children for work on the farm.[19] The Duggan report in 1962 claimed that economic necessity dictated that large numbers of children secure employment at ages 15+ and 16+. Tellingly, it stated: 'It appears that the vast majority of parents are prepared, even at some cost to themselves, to forego the possible earnings of their children until they reach that age.'[20] The school leaving age was not raised to 15 years until 1972, and it was only in 2000 that it was raised to 16 years.

---

18 J. Healy, *Nineteen acres* (Galway, 1978), p. 70. Sending home the money to replace the thatch with slates was a priority for the West of Ireland emigrant to the United States. **19** Commission on Youth Unemployment, *Report* (Dublin, 1951: Pr. 907), p. 9, para. 29. **20** *Tuarascáil shealadach ón choiste a cuireadh i mbun scrúdú a dhéanamh ar oideachas iarbhunscoile* (Unpublished report, Department of Education, 1962), p. 7, para 7. This report, drawn up by a committee appointed by the then minister for education, Dr Patrick Hillery, and com-

Changes in the roles of men and women in response to the needs of the economy

For decades, both the tax and social welfare codes were based on the assumption that the family unit comprised a breadwinner father and a dependent wife and children. The term 'breadwinner' first appeared in the Scottish census of 1871. Challenges to the 'breadwinner-father' model of family life during the past three decades have come in various forms. In the early 1970s, equality legislation, the removal of the ban on the employment of married women in the public sector and the changing values associated with the women's liberation movement were all-important contributory factors. In the mid-1980s, the notion of a wife's economic dependency on her husband came under scrutiny when the Irish government adopted a revised definition of economic dependency, in compliance with EC regulations governing social security provision. At more or less the same time, men's wages had become less adequate for supporting a family and the concept of the 'family wage' became less prevalent. Since the 1990s, families depend increasingly on two wage earners to achieve an acceptable standard of living. Higher rates of owner occupation and the increase in house prices have also been relevant factors, as two-earner households can afford better housing and tend to bid prices upwards.

Depending on one's value system, the male breadwinner may be seen as a symbol either of women's emancipation or of women's dependency. Trade unionists once had the objective of achieving a wage that would be adequate for a man to support himself and his wife and children – a family wage. By this means women and children would be freed from the economic necessity of engaging in the workforce: women could care for the home, and children would have a work-free childhood. Mounting unemployment in the years of the Great Depression led to an emphasis on the priority of jobs for men and resulted in restrictions on the entry of women, in particular married women, to the workforce. As freedom to work became restricted for women, the family wage came to be viewed no longer as a boon but rather as a bulwark against equality.

Sean Lemass realised that de Valera's dream of a closed society was in danger of becoming a nightmare. As Charles Haughey once put it: 'He [Lemass] had no objection to the idea of comely maidens dancing at the crossroads but he preferred to see them working in factories.'[21] The growth in the economy since the 1960s increased employment opportunities for both men and women, the growth in employment in services being particularly beneficial for women. Legislative changes governing conditions of employment were important in

prised of five senior inspectors under the chairmanship of Dr Maurice Duggan, is known as the Duggan report after its chairman. **21** M. O'Sullivan, *Seán Lemass: a biography* (Dublin, 1994), p. 139.

facilitating the participation of married women in the workforce. The earliest change was the removal in 1958 of the bar against married women teachers in national schools, a bar which had been in existence since 1933. In due course, the complete removal of the marriage bar in every sector followed in the 1970s. The first Commission on the Status of Women paved the way for the introduction of equal pay in 1972, while Ireland's entry to the EEC in 1973 ensured the implementation of the European equality agenda. The tax changes subsequent to the Murphy case in 1980[22] had, at a minimum, a facilitating impact on behavioural change. The moves towards the individualization of the tax system, introduced by finance minister Charlie McCreevy in the 2000 budget, provided further incentives for labour force – as distinct from household – work.

Nowhere is the emphasis on the economic factor more apparent at the present time than in the approach to childcare. The Commission on the Status of Women in 1972 did not hesitate to express the belief that the pre-school child was best cared for at home by his or her mother.[23] Today the needs of the market dominate, and more and more mothers of young children are employed outside the home. The introduction of individualization in the tax system in 2000 was a clear signal of the government's wish to encourage women to move out of the home and into the workplace. In facilitating such a move, childcare is essential. That childcare is an issue for employers as well as for fathers and mothers and their children is clear from a recent advertisement published by the Industrial Development Authority (IDA). The advertisement contains a request for proposals 'to design, construct, finance and operate *childcare facilities* on selected IDA business parks'. It refers to six locations throughout the state – Carrigtohill in Cork, Finisklin in Sligo, and Waterford, Dundalk, Letterkenny and Navan. In addition to relevant experience in providing childcare services, the assessment criteria include 'benefit of the proposal to the employees in the relevant business park' and 'financial resources underpinning the project'.[24]

---

22 As a result of *Murphy v. the Attorney General* (1980), section 192 of the Income Tax Act 1967, which obliged a husband and wife to pay more tax on their combined income than they would if they were single, was declared unconstitutional. **23** Commission on the Status of Women, *Report* (Dublin, 1972: Prl. 2760), p. 130, para. 310. What the *Report* actually said is interesting: 'In dealing with the question of the provision of day-care facilities for babies and young children, we wish to stress that we are unanimous in the opinion that very young children, at least up to 3 years of age, should, if at all possible, be cared for by the mother at home and that as far as re-entry to employment is concerned, the provision of day care for such childrren must be viewed as a solution to the problems of the mother who has particularly strong reasons to resume employment.' **24** *Irish Times*, 17 Dec. 2003.

LOOKING FORWARD

The extent and pace of change has led to some alarmist talk about the future of the family, but as Peter Laslett, the University of Cambridge pioneer of historical sociology in the 1960s, writes: 'Talk about the family is always alarmist.'[25] If alarmist talk is indeed a feature of commentary on the family, so too is the claim that the family is a coat of many colours, changing in style and colour, but still a source of shelter and comfort.

It may be appropriate to end by asking precisely how that 'coat of many colours' should be recognized in our laws, including our most basic law, the constitution. This issue was addressed by the Review Group on the Constitution, chaired by Dr T.K. Whitaker, which reported in 1996 – and more recently by the All-Party Oireachtas Committee on the Constitution, chaired by Denis O'Donovan TD. The basic question is how to define a family. It is a question with a wide resonance. One comprehensive formulation is offered by Barack Obama, US presidential candidate and senator for Illinois, who was the first African-American president of the *Harvard Law Review* and is someone who has himself a chequered family history. He writes as follows: 'What is a family? Is it just a genetic chain, parents and offspring, people like you or me? Or is it a social construct, an economic unit, optimal for child rearing and the division of labour? Or is it something else entirely – a store of shared memories, say? An ambit of love?'[26]

It is apparent that in practice the family is in part a legal construct. The move towards divorce is part of the shift from a 'natural' to a 'legal' family model. It can be argued that even the 'natural law' family is subject to legal constraints – for example, in regard to the legal age for marriage. The minimum legal age for marriage in Ireland today is 18 years. At the time the constitution was enacted in 1937, the minimum age was 16 years for males and 14 years for females. Initially Catholic church canon law left 'nature' free to determine the age of marriage, based on the presumed age of puberty, but canon law has been altered over time in this regard.[27]

25 P. Richards, 'The family way', *CAM* 29 (2000), 19. **26** B. Obama, *Dreams from my father, a story of race and inheritance* (New York, 1995), pp 327–8. **27** Under Catholic church canon law prior to 1918, the minimum age for marriage was 12 years for girls and 14 years for boys. The presumption that puberty had not been reached before the ages of 12 and 14 years respectively could, however, yield to contrary proof. The 1918 code of canon law retained the presumed ages for puberty but raised the ages for valid marriage to 14 and 16 years. The current code of canon law (since 1983) gives no ages for presumed puberty, but retains the 1918 minimum age for valid marriage. Canon law recognises cultural differences, however, and allows local bishops to introduce higher minimum ages for marriage.

However, an expert in English family law suggests that the argument has moved to the point where the legal construct of marriage is being replaced by networks of legal-economic relationships and that it is parenthood rather than marriage which is significant with regard to the rights and responsibilities of family members, with the focus shifting from the rights of parents to the rights of the child:

> There is now less emphasis on the exclusivity of the legal status of marriage and evidence of a move towards constructing status-like relationships around new organising concepts. The primary aim, it is argued, is to construct a set of legal-economic relationships among family members that are clearly demarcated from, and thereby reduce the financial burden on, the state. In this process, the legal concept of marriage is logically and *de facto* becoming redundant.[28]

The All-Party Oireachtas Committee on the Constitution has recently stated: 'The considerable change in demography that has occurred since then [1937], and which has seen the appearance of a growing range of families other than the traditional one, means that the constitution now serves our society less well than it formerly did.'[29] For example, for the twenty thousand children born outside marriage every year there is no right under the constitution to know the identity of their father, nor is there any automatic right in law for contact between these children and their fathers. Notwithstanding the position in Irish law, the UN Convention on the Rights of the Child, which was ratified by the Irish government in 1992, states that every child has a right to knowledge of both parents and, as far as possible, to be cared for by both parents.

Despite the considerable change in demography and ethos, the All-Party Oireachtas Committee did not reach a consensus on the need to alter or extend the definition of the family in the constitution. By contrast, the Review Group on the Constitution had argued in favour of the constitutional recognition of all family rights while preserving the special character of the family based on marriage. A majority of the Joint Oireachtas Committee did not think this was possible. The majority recommended against changing the constitutional definition of marriage-based family. It did recommend constitutional change to include children's rights and also recommended substituting the term 'parent' for the term 'woman' (in reference to the home), thus rendering that element

28 J. Dewar, *Law and the family* (London, 1992), p. 71.   29 The All-Party Oireachtas Committee on the Constitution, *Tenth progress report: the family* (Dublin, 2006: Pn A5/1784), p. 121.

of the constitution gender neutral. Otherwise, the majority favoured the legislative route. For example, the majority believed that legislation should be introduced to provide civil partnership for cohabiting heterosexual and same-sex couples. A minority recommended that an insertion should be made in the constitution to the effect that 'the state also recognises and respects family life not based on marriage' and that the Oireachtas should accordingly legislate for the benefit of such families and their individual members.

As we mark the seventieth anniversary of the passing of the constitution, the definition of the family set out in the constitution has already been changed in one critical respect. The family in the constitution is no longer based on lifelong marriage, but rather on marriage which may be terminated by divorce. The government is in possession of two mammoth reports with differing recommendations – the report of the Constitution Review Group and the report on the family by the All-Party Oireachtas Committee on the Constitution – and has already indicated that it intends to introduce a referendum regarding the rights of children. As family life continues to change, all the ingredients are present for further debate leading to possible constitutional change.

From grand juries to county councils: the effects of the Local Government (Ireland) Act 1898

Brendan O Donoghue

THE CENTENARY OF THE enactment of the Local Government (Ireland) Act 1898[1] passed without fuss on 12 August 1998. Notwithstanding the exhibition which the National Archives assembled to mark the occasion[2] and the commemorative programme announced by the minister for the environment and local government, the one hundredth anniversary of the first county council elections and of the first meetings of the new county councils in April 1899 did not have any significant public impact. There is a strange symmetry between this and the reaction in 1898 to the events which laid the foundations of the system of county government as it still exists. A contemporary writer described the 1898 act as something which had come as 'a surprise upon the country' and for which there had been no 'precedent agitation'.[3] While this may have been going a little too far, it certainly seems clear that the act could not be regarded as a concession to consistent popular demand or public pressure. And, when the act was passed, there is no evidence that bonfires were lit throughout rural Ireland or that any of the different factions of nationalist MPs rushed to claim the credit. The establishment of a democratic system of local government was, for most of them, never a major objective in its own right; at best it was seen as a means to an end, and at worst a diversionary tactic which would weaken the case for an independent Irish parliament.

The subordination of the ideal of local self-government to other national objectives – political, economic and social – in the last quarter of the nineteenth century was to continue after 1898, with the result that local government in Ireland never assumed real significance in the public mind or in the minds of our political leaders. This was brutally demonstrated in 1924 when the Cumann na nGaedheal minister for local government, Séamus de Burca, promoted

---

1 61 & 62 Vict., c. 37. **2** The exhibition resulted in the publication D. Ferriter, *'Lovers of liberty'? Local government in 20th century Ireland* (Dublin, 2001). **3** M.J.F. McCarthy, *Five years in Ireland, 1895–1900* (8th ed., Dublin, 1902), p. 377.

legislation to abolish the rural district councils, only twenty-six years after their
establishment, because he viewed them as obsolete, uneconomic, inefficient, an
anomaly and a foreign imposition.[4] By the beginning of 1925, twenty other
elected councils had been temporarily removed from office by the minister for
a variety of reasons, under legislation enacted in 1923.[5] By 1934, the first Fianna
Fáil minister for local government, Seán T. O'Kelly, had come to believe that
even the county councils were largely redundant and submitted a memorandum
to the government in which he described them as 'a relic of British administration
… gradually becoming an expensive anachronism' whose functions could be
merged with those of the central government.[6] The county councils survived,
but there are many who would argue that real local government did not.

To understand what happened in 1898–9, and why it happened, it is necessary to look not only at the organizational arrangements which existed at local
level before the 1898 act, but also at the wider political context. Similarly, the
effects of the 1898 act can be judged both in practical administrative terms and
in broader political terms.

THE CASE FOR REFORMING THE GRAND JURY SYSTEM

The grand juries came into being for the purpose of acting as juries at major
criminal trials but, in addition to this judicial function, by the beginning of the
nineteenth century they had become responsible for a wide range of what was
called fiscal business, or what would be described today as civil or administrative functions. Under a series of acts passed during the seventeenth and eighteenth centuries, the grand juries were assigned functions relating to the construction and maintenance of public roads and bridges, the provision and
maintenance of courthouses, bridewells and gaols, the construction of minor
marine works and, in some counties, the maintenance of lunatic asylums, infirmaries and fever hospitals. The grand jury for each county was made up of
twenty-three members of landed society, all selected for the purpose by the high
sheriff, subject only to having one member from each barony. The jury assembled twice each year at the county courthouse for the spring and summer assizes

4 *Dáil Debates*, 7, 3 June 1924, cols 1783–6; Local Government Act 1925, section 3.   **5** Local
Government (Temporary Provisions) Act 1923; *Department of local government and public health,
first report, 1922–5*, p. 23.   **6** Quoted in Ferriter, *'Lovers of liberty'?*, p. 15. See M.E. Daly, *The
buffer state: the historical roots of the Department of the Environment* (Dublin, 1997), p. 298; also
E. O'Halpin, 'The origins of city and county management' in J. Boland et al. (eds), *City and
county management, 1929–1990: a retrospective* (Dublin, 1991), p. 14.

and transacted all of its fiscal business in the few days before the judges arrived
to begin the criminal trials. Until the 1820s, the procedure was for proposals to
be made on affidavit to the grand jury for presentments for particular works. If
these were approved by secret vote of the jury, and formally approved by the
judge, the works could be carried out either by the person who obtained the
presentment or by his contractor. When the works were completed, the cost
was levied on the county cesspayers and recouped to the person concerned.

By the early decades of the nineteenth century, there was widespread agreement that the grand jury system involved gross malpractice, inefficiency and
waste. In the house of commons on 2 May 1817 it was described as follows:
'Twenty-three gentlemen, or it might be twelve, in the midst of all the bustle
and business of an assize, without any previous examination to guide them, take
upon themselves to levy money, to an indefinite amount, for various purposes,
the items of which were almost innumerable.' This critic concluded that 'with
a view to doing justice, they might as well put the presentments and applications into a hat and draw out such number as they thought proper'.[7] In the
1820s, it was frequently alleged that corruption and jobbery were widespread,
with grand jurors themselves seeking presentments for works of personal advantage and works which would benefit their friends and associates. Landlords and
their agents often obtained presentments so that tenants could be engaged on
road repairs, not for a cash payment but so that the value of their labour could
be set off against their rents. There was no administrative or engineering organization for vetting the need for particular projects and the plans and cost estimates. Similarly, the arrangements for the supervision of work in progress and
for the inspection of the finished work were inadequate, with local landowners
and others, who might well have vested interests, acting as supervisors, overseers or conservators on behalf of the grand jury. In 1833 Daniel O'Connell
declared that he knew families 'who had made fortunes, and purchased estates,
out of their jobs in road-making, though the roads they made were now not
to be distinguished from the surrounding bogs'.[8]

The reform of the grand jury system was finally taken in hand in 1833 by the
chief secretary, Edward Stanley, who brought the necessary bill before parliament.
Most of the Irish members sought to have debate on the bill postponed to give
more time for its consideration. O'Connell was among those who took this line,
notwithstanding his dislike of the existing system under which, he said, 'favourites
of the grand jury were fattened'.[9] But the government were determined to push
the bill through and succeeded in doing so in August 1833, against the wishes

7 E.S. Cooper, MP for Sligo county, *Hansard* (1st series), xxxvi, 2 May 1817, 115. 8 *Hansard*
(3rd series), xix, 11 July 1833, 565. 9 Ibid., 561–5.

of many of the Irish MPs. The new act[10] established presentment sessions for each barony, the membership of which would consist of up to twelve of the major cesspayers, as well as the local magistrates: these sessions were to receive and consider all applications for presentments for public works in the area. County-at-large presentment sessions were also provided to deal with the relatively small number of matters of concern to the county as a whole. All presentments were to go before the grand jury itself for approval before any work could go ahead, but the jury was deprived of its earlier power to initiate projects or to alter presentments. The jury was required to sit in public when dealing with presentments, instead of retiring to the grand jury room from which the press and the public had hitherto been excluded. To enable this new and slightly more representative local government machinery to operate effectively, the act made provision for the appointment of a county surveyor for each county, except Dublin. In a remarkable departure from the patronage system, it was laid down that appointments to that new office were to be made by the lord lieutenant from a panel of persons whose qualifications had been examined and certified by a board of three civil or military engineers sitting in Dublin.

Grand jury law was consolidated in 1836,[11] and a large number of amending acts had been added to the statute book by 1898. However, notwithstanding the reports of royal commissions and select committees of the house of commons, occasional pressure from influential individuals, private members' bills in the 1850s and a long series of bills put down for discussion in later years by Irish Parliamentary Party members, the basic arrangements for county government, as laid down in the 1830s, survived to the end of the century. The grand juries continued to exercise their responsibilities for the construction of roads and bridges, but these functions declined in importance with the transfer of long-distance passenger and freight traffic to the railway system from the 1850s onwards. As a result, total spending on roads was no greater at the end of the century than it had been in the late 1830s. In 1877 the functions of the grand juries in respect of bridewells and county gaols were taken over by the central authorities; there were also a number of other losses of minor functions to the newly established classes of town authorities, to the poor law guardians and to central boards. Apart from their road expenditure of about £840,000 in 1898, the only other significant items of expenditure for which the juries were responsible at that stage were the asylums and infirmaries (£290,000) and subsidies to the railways in some of the southern and western districts (£100,000).[12] Long

10 The Grand Jury (Ireland) Act 1833: 3 & 4 Will IV, c. 78. 11 The Grand Jury (Ireland) Act, 1836: 6 & 7 Will IV, c. 116. 12 *Returns of local taxation in Ireland for 1898* [C. 9481], H.C. 1899, lxxxiii (Pt 1).

before their abolition, therefore, the grand juries had been completely bypassed as a dramatic expansion in the volume and range of local services was enabled by legislation. During the second half of the century, new functions relating to personal and public health, sanitation, housing, and what today would be called environmental protection were assigned in the rural areas to the poor law guardians whose expenditure on local services in 1898 (at almost £1.6 million) equalled that of the grand juries.[13]

Established originally in 1838 to administer the workhouse system, the 159 boards of guardians operated under a system of strict central inspection, audit and control, with a well regulated staffing structure, a detailed framework of procedures, regular meetings and power to raise revenue through the poor rate. Half of the members were *ex officio* and half were elected by owners and occupiers of property. By contrast, the grand juries had no corporate existence and very limited staff resources, and were dependent on small local contractors to carry out their functions. In addition, they were largely independent of the central authorities, even after the establishment of the Local Government Board for Ireland in 1872. The fact that successive governments opted, as a practical matter, to use the guardians rather than the grand juries to meet new needs is, therefore, understandable. In effect, the grand jury system was an anachronism long before 1898, being inefficient, ineffective, incapable of taking on new functions and politically indefensible. Members of successive administrations in London were ready to acknowledge these facts in private, and sometimes even in public, but political factors conspired to delay the overdue reform. It should not be forgotten, of course, that county government was in an equally unsatisfactory and undemocratic state in Britain throughout most of the nineteenth century;[14] the term 'local government' was not even in use there until 1858,[15] and there was no coherent nationwide system of directly elected local authorities in England or Scotland until the 1890s.[16]

THE POLITICAL CONTEXT

When reform of local government in Ireland eventually emerged onto the political agendas of the main political parties in Britain in the last twenty years of

13 Ibid. 14 A. Alexander, 'Local government in Ireland', *Administration*, 27:1 (Spring 1979), 3–29. 15 R.C.K. Ensor, *England: 1870–1914* (Oxford, 1936), p. 124. 16 County councils were established in England and Wales under the Local Government Act 1888 (51 & 52 Vict, c. 41) and in Scotland under the Local Government (Scotland) Act, 1889 (52 & 53 Vict, c. 50), while parish councils were established under the Local Government Act 1894 (56 & 57 Vict, c. 73).

the nineteenth century, it was not because of any particularly energetic campaigning by nationalist leaders in Ireland, nor because of the kind of pressure from mass movements and organized public campaigns which led to the enactment of the land acts. Neither was there a genuine belief among the majority of political leaders at Westminster in the intrinsic value of local self-government, or a conviction that a new system would bring major benefits in the delivery of services or in terms of social and economic development.

Beginning in 1875, and ending in 1897, a series of twelve bills to reform county government was brought forward by Irish Parliamentary Party members at Westminster. The earlier bills provided for county boards or representative councils, elected by the poor ratepayers, to take over the non-judicial business of the grand juries, while subsequent bills provided for county councils, elected by the parliamentary electors, and for district councils to replace the poor law guardians. The debates in the house of commons on these bills were generally rather tame, ritualistic affairs, with predictable points being made on both sides, and they inevitably ended in the defeat of the bill or deferral of further discussion on it. The promoters spoke of the grand juries as inefficient, anomalous survivors of another age, while government supporters and successive chief secretaries defended the *status quo*, or spoke of the difficulties of finding an acceptable alternative. As the century progressed, however, the reform of Irish local government at county level took on a new significance. It came to be seen by some English politicians as an alternative to home rule. It became part of the Conservative Party's policy of constructive unionism which was closely connected with the need of that party after 1886 to retain the support of the Liberal Unionists who had split from Gladstone in the wake of the first home rule bill; in effect, local government reform could be described as 'an unwanted child' of the liaison between the Conservatives and the Liberal Unionists.[17]

On coming into office as prime minister for the first time at the end of 1868, W.E. Gladstone pledged that his mission was to pacify Ireland.[18] His government implemented a number of significant reforms, including disestablishment of the Church of Ireland and the land act of 1871, but the establishment of the Local Government Board in 1872 was their only significant contribution in the area of local government structures. The succeeding Conservative government – the last to be led by the ageing Disraeli – was responsible for legislation to improve local services in Ireland, including a major public health act, but it did not concern itself with basic local government structures. No less than five

17 L.P. Curtis Jr, *Coercion and conciliation in Ireland, 1880–1892* (Princeton, 1963), p. 381.   **18** R. Jenkins, *Gladstone* (London, 1995), p. 290.

county government bills were brought forward by Irish members during the life of that government and routinely voted down at Westminster.

When the general election of April 1880 brought Gladstone back to power, the Land League was well established and Parnell was leading a strong Irish Parliamentary Party at Westminster. The Government was quickly forced to deal with agrarian distress and disorder and put through an important land act in 1881. However, support for the government was already ebbing away – due to the disasters in the Sudan and the death of General Gordon at Khartoum – when the government decided in early 1885 to take up the question of Irish county government reform which they had promised to address in the speech from the throne as far back as 1881.[19] Three more county government bills had been defeated in the previous few years and some members of the cabinet were still strongly opposed to dealing with the matter. Gladstone, however, seems to have been influenced by the fact that Parnell was reported to have expressed tentative support for the idea of proceeding with legislation to replace the grand juries, while being careful to state publicly that this was a matter quite distinct from the right of the Irish people to have their own parliament. And Cardinal Manning of Westminster had also suggested that the Irish Catholic bishops would be willing to support a local government reform scheme and to denounce the idea of a separate Irish parliament.[20] Against this background, the radical members of the ministry, Joseph Chamberlain, president of the Board of Trade, and Sir Charles Dilke, president of the English Local Government Board, were assigned the task of drafting a plan. Chamberlain had entered parliament after a successful period as mayor of Birmingham and was a committed supporter of local government reform in all parts of the United Kingdom. His proposals for Ireland involved elective county boards which would be co-ordinated by a central board formed from the elected members of the county boards. Functions relating to such matters as land law, poor relief, primary education and public works (but not judicial or police matters) would be transferred from Dublin Castle and the Custom House to the boards. But Chamberlain's central board scheme, as it came to be known, involving devolution as well as local government reform, was doomed to failure: Parnell came round to the view that acceptance of local government reform could weaken the drive for an Irish parliament and, quite apart from this, a majority in the cabinet were opposed to the scheme and formally rejected it in May 1885.

Gladstone resigned in June 1885, leaving it to the new Conservative leader, Lord Salisbury, to form a minority government. During the election campaign

19 *Hansard* (3rd series), cclvii, 6 Jan. 1881, 7.   20 F.S.L. Lyons, *Charles Stewart Parnell* (London, 1977), pp 272–9.

in the following November, the party committed itself to reforming local government throughout the United Kingdom, but Salisbury was careful to point out that Ireland would present special difficulties and that the integrity of the empire was paramount.[21] Thus, when the pledge was formally put on record at the opening of the new parliament in January 1886, it was qualified by a statement that a new system for Ireland would have to await more stable conditions there because 'no enlargement of the powers of local government in Ireland should be given which could be used as a lever to weaken the legislative union between Great Britain and Ireland'.[22] The government was, however, soon defeated in a house of commons' vote, leaving the way open for Gladstone, who had by then converted to home rule, to form his third ministry in February 1886.

In the debates on the home rule bill in the early months of 1886, the idea of reforming local government *as an alternative to home rule* was given concrete expression: Conservatives and Liberal Unionists tempered their opposition to the bill by making it clear that they could accept the extension to Ireland of the kind of local self-government principles which were being contemplated for the rest of the United Kingdom, but only if this were not a step to something very different. When the bill was defeated – after the defection from the Liberal Party of nearly one third of its members – a general election in July 1886 resulted in the return to office of the Conservatives under Salisbury with Liberal Unionist support and the re-emergence of local government on the political agenda. In the debate on the queen's speech in August 1886, Lord Randolph Churchill, who had again become chancellor of the exchequer and leader of the house of commons, outlined the three essential aspects of the government's Irish policy: social order (in effect, the suppression of disorder), the land question and local government reform. On the latter, Churchill said that the party wished 'to treat it as a question for the United Kingdom as a whole' – from which it followed that the 'great signposts' of Conservative policy were 'equality, similarity and, if I may use such a word, simultaneity of treatment as far as is practicable in the development of a genuinely popular system of local government in all the four countries which form the United Kingdom'.[23]

It appeared to many at the time that Churchill's August announcement had pre-empted full discussion and agreement in cabinet, though he stated quite explicitly in the house of commons two years later that his actual words had been approved in advance by the prime minister and the Irish secretary.[24] The fact is, however, that when Churchill resigned in December on a budget issue,

---

21 *The Times*, 8 Oct. 1885. **22** *Hansard* (3rd series), cccii, 21 Jan. 1886, 125. **23** *Hansard* (3rd series), cccviii, 19 Aug. 1886, 118–9, 132. **24** *Hansard* (3rd series), cccxxv, 25 Apr. 1888, 506.

he left behind a cabinet which was far from enthusiastic about local government reform and seriously divided on the question of whether an English bill
or an Irish one should come first. There was alarm in some quarters at the
prospect of handing over control of the poor relief system in Ireland entirely to
the representatives of the rural working classes and Salisbury eventually became
fed up of the whole business, telling one of his friends: 'I wish there were no
such thing as local government.'[25] Nevertheless, the government went ahead
in March 1888 with a bill to establish elected county councils in England and
Wales, even though Charles Ritchie, president of the English Local Government
Board, in introducing the bill, made the rather surprising statement that 'there
is no great or active force of public opinion behind us on this subject' and 'no
great or pressing public demand for it'.[26] The 1888 act was followed by a similar Scottish bill in 1889, bringing to the rural population of three of the four
kingdoms the kind of local government institutions which their counterparts
in the boroughs had enjoyed for more than fifty years.

In the initial debate on the English bill in 1888, Tim Healy and John Dillon
registered no more than formal protests at the departure from the principle of
simultaneity which had been laid down by Churchill less than two years earlier,
and none of the Irish Parliamentary Party members seem to have participated at
all in the six-day debate on the second stage.[27] Instead, the Irish members brought
forward another version of their county government bill and had it debated on 25
April.[28] Salisbury's nephew Arthur Balfour, who had become chief secretary for
Ireland in March 1887, opposed the bill on the grounds mainly of timing, arguing
that 'different circumstances and different behaviour' were essential before local
self-government could be proposed in Ireland with hope of success. The Plan of
Campaign was in full operation at that stage. As Balfour saw it, the bill if passed
would only be used to advance what he described as a state of social warfare in
Ireland and to 'carry out a political and social revolution'. Given that situation,
the promoters of the bill must have known that it had no prospect of acceptance,
although Gladstone had supported it and criticized those who spoke as if 'the Irish
people were under a curse of nature and had been improperly invested with the
civil franchise'; the introduction of the bill was probably designed as much to try
to split the Liberal Unionist–Tory alliance as to achieve its stated objective.[29]

Balfour is remembered for his ruthless approach to disorder and to the defeat
of the Plan of Campaign, which earned him the nickname 'Bloody Balfour',

25 Quoted in Curtis, *Coercion and conciliation in Ireland*, p. 153. 26 *Hansard* (3rd series),
cccxxiii, 19 Mar. 1888, 1641–2. 27 Ibid., 1695, 1700. 28 *Hansard* (3rd series), cccxxv, 25
Apr. 1888, 441. 29 C.B. Shannon, 'The Ulster Liberal Unionists and local government
reform, 1885–98', *Irish Historical Studies*, 18:71 (Mar. 1973), 413.

but his reforming instincts found expression in the land purchase acts of 1888 and 1891, the establishment of the Congested Districts Board under the 1891 act and the light railways act of 1889. And local government reform – once the time was opportune – was also to form part of his policy agenda of effective coercion coupled with conciliation and practical concessions, or 'constructive unionism' as it came to be known.[30] And so, having achieved his economic reforms and under pressure from the Liberal Unionists, Balfour urged his colleagues, before going out of office, to redeem the election promise of 1886 by setting up county councils in some form in Ireland. The ministry was still seriously divided on the subject, with Salisbury still heavily influenced by the opposition of landlords and loyalists to what they called 'raw democracy'. Even Professor A.V. Dicey, the noted authority on constitutional law and a bitter opponent of home rule, entered the fray, telling Balfour that his proposals were absurd, inconsistent with the policy of strictly enforcing the law and likely to break up the Unionist Party.[31]

Although he had ceased to be chief secretary, Balfour eventually got his way and was allowed to bring forward a bill in February 1892 to set up elected councils at county and at barony level. His proposals, however, did not meet the equality and similarity tests adumbrated by Lord Randolph Churchill six years earlier, but were hedged about with safeguards designed to pacify the landlords and unionists. The new county councils were to have limited functions (basically roads and bridges like the grand juries, but – unlike the grand juries – not police or poor law), and the non-elected grand jury was to retain a role in relation to capital spending and the appointment of officers. Besides, the bill was heavily weighted with other safeguards to prevent extravagant expenditure and to protect landlord and minority interests, and there was an extremely controversial provision – without precedent in the rest of the United Kingdom (but borrowed from the law relating to poor law guardians in Ireland) – allowing for the removal from office of an elected council for financial irresponsibility, breach of the law or other reasons.[32] The bill was derided in the house of com-

---

30 Not all commentators would accept that Arthur Balfour and his brother, Gerald (chief secretary for Ireland, 1895–1900), were influenced mainly by policy considerations. For example, Andrew Gailey – in *Ireland and the death of kindness* (Cork, 1987) – has argued that what was held out as a constructive reform policy for Ireland was nothing more than a strategy to achieve the support of the Liberal Unionists and retain power at Westminster. **31** Letter of 29 April 1890; quoted in Shannon, 'The Ulster Liberal Unionists and local government reform', 414. **32** As an aside, one might note that the very first piece of local government legislation enacted by the Dáil in 1923 contained a provision to allow the minister for local government and public health to remove an elected council from office, a power which was used freely in the 1920s, 1930s and 1940s.

mons by Irish Parliamentary Party members[33] and was withdrawn by the government. In effect, 'nobody cared a damn' about the bill, according to George Wyndham who had worked closely with Balfour on its preparation.[34]

When Gladstone's last government took office in August 1892, with the support of the Irish nationalists, local government reform was once again displaced on the agenda by a home rule bill which passed the house of commons in September 1893 but was overwhelmingly defeated in the house of lords. Gladstone left the political stage six months later, being succeeded by Lord Rosebury who had at least as much interest in the turf as he had in Irish affairs. And it was on the very day in May 1895 when one of the prime minister's horses won the Derby for the second successive time that the last debate on an Irish Parliamentary Party bill to set up county councils in Ireland took place in a sparsely attended house of commons.[35] The bill was extraordinary, essentially comprising only two sections that were designed to apply English law on county and district councils in its entirety to Ireland, subject to whatever amendments and adaptations the lord lieutenant might spell out in orders which he would be empowered to make. As a lawyer, Tim Healy, the author of the bill, must have known that these proposals were very unlikely to be taken seriously. He admitted as much in introducing the bill, declaring that he expected nothing by way of reform of county government from the Liberals – as this, he said, would leave them open to the charge that they were abandoning their home rule policy. However, with less than a month to serve before a general election, the government took the easy option and agreed to give the bill a second reading, knowing that it would lapse on the imminent dissolution of parliament.

The Conservatives under Salisbury returned to office in July 1895, with Arthur Balfour as chancellor of the exchequer and his younger brother, Gerald, as chief secretary for Ireland. Gerald was disposed to follow the policy and general strategy of his brother by promoting measures of economic and social progress in Ireland and, in October 1895, spoke publicly of the possibility of 'killing home rule with kindness'.[36] There was no indication that he regarded local government reform as an essential part of such a strategy, but the situation changed dramatically a year later following the publication of the report of the Royal Commission on Financial Relations between Great Britain and Ireland.[37] Immediate difficulty and embarrassment for the government was created by findings which gave substance to the oft-repeated allegation that Ireland was

---

33 *Hansard* (4th series), i, 18 Feb. 1892, 700–98.   34 Curtis, *Coercion and conciliation in Ireland*, p. 386.   35 *Hansard* (4th series), xxxiv, 29 May 1895, 538–87.   36 *Leeds Mercury*, 17 Oct. 1895.   37 *Royal commission appointed to inquire into the financial relations of Great Britain and Ireland* [C. 8262], H.C. 1896, xxxiii.

overtaxed by comparison with the rest of the United Kingdom, to the extent of about £2.5 million a year. The government's inept handling of the issue compounded their difficulties and led the Irish unionist and nationalist factions to combine forces in parliament, for the first time, in demanding an adequate response.

Faced with obstructionist tactics and imminent revolt at Westminster, Arthur Balfour, as chancellor, announced in the house of commons on 21 May 1897 that Ireland would receive a large grant in aid of agricultural rates (even though he had doubts about the real justification for this) and that a local government reform bill would be brought forward in the next session to set up elected county councils in place of the grand juries. The link between these two measures was justified, he said, because to have given such a grant without changes in the local government system would be like putting new wine into very old bottles. Quite apart from this, he acknowledged that the grand juries – even though they were doing honest, able and economical work – had now to be seen as antiquated political machinery. In effect, the statement demonstrated the government's lack of conviction that either the agricultural grant or the local government changes were fully justified; Balfour openly admitted that the overriding strategy had been to devise a response to the crisis which would gain the friendly support of every class in Ireland.[38]

The solution announced by Balfour was seen as a real coup by some of the government's supporters – the dangerous combination of unionists and nationalists would be nipped in the bud, the nationalists could hardly fail to welcome the local government reform element of the package, and opposition from the landlord and unionist side, on whose votes the government depended, would effectively be bought off by the new grant, coupled with the elimination of the landowner's share of the poor rate. As expected, the unionists expressed satisfaction at the announcement, with Edward Carson describing the scheme as 'statesmanlike'. On the nationalist side, the reaction of John Dillon was cautious, but John Redmond had no doubts – in fact, he could recall no government statement which was received with so universal an expression of agreement and satisfaction. William O'Brien (who was soon to establish the United Irish League but was not an MP at the time) went even further, claiming that the powers being given to the 'native race' could be the means of winning still wider ones and that thirty of the proposed new county councils could become 'simply thirty Irish parliaments'.[39] Sir Horace Plunkett (whose plans for legislation to set up a new department of agriculture would have to give way to the

38 *Hansard* (4th series), il, 21 May 1897, 1040–6.   **39** Quoted in P. Bull, *Land, politics and nationalism: a study of the Irish land question* (Dublin, London, 1996), p. 134.

local government bill) accurately described the whole business as a 'masterstroke
of statecraft', with Irish local government becoming 'a purely English necessity'
– effectively a pawn in an English political crisis.[40]

The Local Government (Ireland) Bill which emerged early in 1898 was modelled closely on the arrangements which had been introduced in Britain ten
years earlier and, for the first time, set out to create an ordered and systematic
set of local authorities in Ireland. For the larger built-up areas, it created county
boroughs, boroughs and urban district councils. For the rural areas, there was
to be a form of two-tier system comprising elected county councils and a network of rural district councils:

- The county councils were to take over the administrative business of the
  grand juries, but they were not to be entrusted with either education functions or control of the police, even though these were among the major functions of the English county councils.
- The new rural district councils were to take responsibility for most of the
  functions of the poor law guardians, including sanitary and public health matters, but not poor relief, and were to take the place of the baronial presentment sessions in making proposals to the county councils for road works,
  with the baronies ceasing to be administrative units.
- The grand juries were to continue to exist, but were to revert to their original judicial role.
- The poor law guardians were also to continue in being as separate legal
  entities, but the *ex officio* membership was abolished and the elected rural district councillors were in future to function also as guardians; in addition, the
  guardians were to return to a role close to that which they had performed
  before the expansion of their activities under the sanitary, housing and other
  legislation of the previous five decades.

There were no real surprises when the bill was introduced in the house of commons on 21 February 1898. Gerald Balfour explained, in a low-key address, that
the existing system was no longer in harmony with the spirit of the age and that
structural reform was a *sine qua non* for further reforms which he hoped to
achieve.[41] But he made it clear too that the new bodies were neither a step

40 Quoted in Gailey, *Ireland and the death of kindness*, p. 46. **41** *Hansard* (4th series), liii, 21

towards home rule nor were they intended to be a substitute for home rule: they were, he said, 'cribbed, cabined and confined' in every direction so that they would not become legislative bodies.

In the second stage debate in March,[42] John Dillon, leader of the anti-Parnellites, had very little to say about the broad principle of the bill but concentrated largely on points of detail. Overall, while objecting to the 'bribing' of the landlords, he took the view that the measure, with all its faults and shortcomings, would achieve 'a most beneficial and far-reaching revolution in the condition of Irish local government and Irish life'. John Redmond, the Parnellite leader, welcomed the bill, noting that Irishmen were practically united on the broad principle and that no serious section of English opinion was hostile. For the Ulster Unionists, Colonel E.J. Saunderson was inclined to dismiss the significance of the bill, noting that local government did not excite any emotion among the people of Ireland, nationalist leaders had never spoken out in its favour and his own party had been 'perfectly indifferent' on the subject. Another approach was represented by the historian W.E.H. Lecky who sat for Trinity College at the time and was a leading campaigner against home rule. Lecky believed that the grand juries were efficient, economical and fair, and that Ireland was as little suited to local democracy as any country in Europe, but even he felt obliged to accept that the arrangements proposed in the bill were inevitable because of pledges given since 1886 by all parties and 'the manifest trend of opinion both inside and outside the house'.

The bill received the royal assent on 12 August 1898, just three days before the major demonstration in College Green, Dublin, which was the high point of the 1798 centenary celebrations. According to Henry Robinson, who had become chairman of the Local Government Board for Ireland some months before that, Gerald Balfour had 'piloted the bill through the house with consummate skill, and his knowledge of the object of every line of it was so clear that he was unassailable in committee. It was therefore a terrible disappointment to him that, just when the work was finished, he broke down under the strain, and the final stages had to be taken by John Atkinson, the attorney general.'[43] On a technical level, it is worth noting that Balfour had admitted that the bill represented 'a new departure in draftsmanship'[44] in that it delegated extensive powers to the lord lieutenant to make orders for the application to Ireland of English and Scottish acts, for adapting existing Irish legislation so as to bring it into conformity with the bill, for regulating the procedure of the new councils and for transitional arrangements of various kinds. These unpre-

Feb. 1898, 1227.   **42** *Hansard* (4th series), lv, 21 Mar. 1898, 420–525.   **43** Sir H. Robinson, *Memories: wise and otherwise* (London, 1923), p. 127.

cedented shortcuts were essential because of the rush to complete the drafting and have the bill passed. But the pattern set in the act was adopted by parliamentary draftsmen at Westminster in the following thirty years to such an extent that the lord chief justice of England, Lord Hewart, was provoked to publish his classic essay *The New Despotism* in 1929, calling for resistance to the encroachment on the role of parliament by the growing bureaucracy.[45] The approach adopted in drafting the act also set a precedent for Irish local government legislation in the century which followed, leading to regular complaints in the Dáil and Seanad, even into modern times, about the extent to which, as the politicians saw it, ministers and civil servants in the Custom House were arrogating to themselves decisions and functions which were proper to the Oireachtas.

IMPLEMENTING THE ACT

As often happens, implementation of the act created even more work than had been involved in securing its enactment, and much of this fell to Henry Robinson who was to earn a knighthood for his efforts.[46] Apart from drafting the various detailed and lengthy orders already referred to, the Board had to set about a variety of other tasks. The boundaries of the 159 poor law unions (on which the new rural districts were to be based) were the only set of administrative boundaries in Ireland which had been drawn up on a fairly rational and scientific basis, the principle being to base the unions on towns of reasonable size and to form the towns and their hinterlands into administrative units, ignoring county and other existing boundaries. The result of this was that thirty-eight unions extended into two counties and another eight included parts of three counties. This had to be undone in 1898, so that each of the new rural districts would fall fully within a single county. To achieve this, county boundaries were altered in nineteen cases and a process of splitting some unions and amalgamating parts of unions with others had to be adopted.[47]

Next, in preparation for the elections, a new system of electoral areas had to be put in place. The poor law electoral divisions, numbering about 3,750 and dating from 1838, were retained as district electoral divisions and, as a rule, it was provided that two rural district councillors would be elected from each division; there was provision also for three co-opted members of each council and,

44 *Hansard* (4th series), liii, 21 Feb. 1898, 1245. **45** Lord Hewart of Bury, *The new despotism* (London, 1929). **46** See Robinson, *Memories: wise and otherwise.* **47** *Annual report of the Local Government Board for Ireland for the year ended 31 March 1899* [C. 9480], H.C. 1899, xxxix (1).

in the case of the first councils, three additional members were to represent the former *ex officio* guardians. In all, this made for a total of 9,456 district councillors. District electoral divisions were grouped to form new county electoral divisions, generally about twenty in each county and with populations averaging 3,000 to 10,000, depending on the size of the county. One councillor was to be elected from each division on the traditional 'first past the post' system for a three-year term and there was provision for two co-opted members of each council and for another three to represent the former grand jury members. In addition, the chairman of each rural district council was to be an *ex officio* member of the county council. Under these arrangements, the total number of the four categories of county councillors came to 1,055, of which 697 were to be directly elected. The 1898 act, therefore, set up the most extensive local representative system which ever operated in this country, one in which individual councillors were directly elected by, and identified with, very small areas. In all, the total number of county and district councillors added up to 10,500 and, with the members of the six county borough councils and the twenty-nine boards of town commissioners, the total number of elected members came to more than 11,000.[48] Today, there is only about one-fifth of that number in the entire island.

The parliamentary franchise, with the addition of peers and, for the first time, adult women who were otherwise qualified (that is, those who were householders or lodgers), was adopted for the new local government system, bringing the total number of county council electors to 760,210.[49] The 'one man, one vote' principle was also applied instead of the multiple property vote which had been in operation at elections of boards of guardians. The list of disqualifications for membership of the new councils was virtually the same as in Britain, but with an additional disqualification for ministers of religion of all denominations – a response to the active role played by clergy in political action in the previous twenty years and one which was generally favoured by both nationalist and unionist politicians. While men who were qualified to vote were also qualified to stand for election to a county council, women electors could stand for election only as urban or rural district councillors. Anna Maria Haslam, who had been a campaigner since the 1860s for the advancement and enfranchisement of women and who had played a leading part in securing the inclusion of these provisions in the act, wrote that they represented 'the most significant political revolution that has taken place in the history of Irishwomen'; she was not too disappointed about the exclusion of women from membership of the county councils because she felt that very few of them at that time would

48 *Return of the number of electors ... and numbers of councillors*, H.C. 1901, lxiv (2).   **49** Ibid.

be willing to undertake the duties involved.[50] In the event, less than thirty women were elected to serve on the new rural district councils.[51]

The work involved in implementing and overseeing the operation of the new legislation was to have a dramatic impact on the Local Government Board, which had a staff of less than eighty at the end of the 1890s. Until then, the Board – which had been established in 1872 to replace the Poor Law Commissioners – continued to be primarily concerned with the organization and financing of the poor law guardians and the supervision of their activities in respect of indoor and outdoor relief, public housing, and public and personal health services. With their wider responsibilities under the 1898 act for the organization of local government generally and for overseeing the operations of the new county and district councils and their services, including road construction and maintenance, the Board had increased its staff numbers to a total of about 230 by 1914. Like a cuckoo in the nest, the expanding organization forced the Office of Public Works to leave its traditional home in the Custom House in 1905 but, with the continuing growth in staff numbers, there was need for still more office space. Thus, when work began in 1913 on the complex of Government Buildings in Upper Merrion Street, the intention was that the north block would house the Board, while the south block would accommodate the department of agriculture and technical instruction which had been established in 1899. The buildings were not completed, however, until 1922. While the department of agriculture did gain possession of the south block, neither the Local Government Board nor its successor, the department of local government and public health, was allowed to take over the north block, even though the Board's existing headquarters at the Custom House had been burned down in May 1921. Instead, that block was pressed into use as the offices of the president of the executive council of the new Irish Free State and of the department of finance, and the room designed for Sir Henry Robinson came to be used as the cabinet room.

THE ELECTIONS AND THE RESULTS

The 1898 act fixed the day for the first elections as Saturday, 25 March 1899. However, the Local Government Board, which was allowed to fix an alternative date, opted for 6 April, the Thursday of Easter week, with polling set to take place from 10.00 am to 8.00 pm. Long before then, nationalists' election

50 Virginia Crossman, *Local government in nineteenth-century Ireland* (Belfast, 1994), pp 94–5.
51 Ibid., p. 96.

7 'The Grand National win'; cartoon from the *Weekly Freeman*, 25 March 1899.

campaigns were well under way – but there was considerable division as to how the elections should be fought. Speaking in Waterford in September 1898, John Redmond argued that the best men should be elected, irrespective of political or religious opinions, so as to ensure that local affairs would be administered efficiently and that the capacity of the Irish people for self-government would be demonstrated to the world.[52] Dillon, on the other hand, urged that no man should be allowed go into the county councils who was not determined to forward United Irish League principles; both William O'Brien and Michael Davitt advocated that only candidates who were firm supporters of home rule should be elected.

This latter view was to prevail and, before the elections, resolutions were adopted at meetings all over the country pledging votes only for candidates who were declared nationalists and members of the United Irish League. On the other side, the unionists knew that their days in power were numbered. Their leader, Colonel Saunderson, admitted publicly in March 1898 that those who had held county government in their hands would almost universally disappear and the gentlemen who had done the work so well would be replaced by others 'such as we now see on the poor law boards'.[53] In the house of commons, Gerald Balfour had urged the local gentry – 'the natural leaders of the people', as he called them – to seek election to positions which, he said, they alone were truly qualified to fill.[54] But these pleas fell on deaf ears, and many of the unionists

52 *Annual Register*, 1898. **53** *Hansard* (4th series), lv, 21 Mar. 1898, 494. **54** *Hansard* (4th

opted not to stand for election rather than, as one of them put it, 'make sport for the Philistines and part with what alone is left to them – their self-respect'.[55]

The election campaign in the first three months of 1899 was marked by large public meetings and processions, with bands and rousing oratory being deployed. Conventions had been held to select candidates with appropriate nationalist credentials and opposition to these was discouraged, so much so that there was no contest in a significant proportion of electoral areas – 8 out of 32 in Co. Cork, for example.[56] Meetings were organized not just to support particular candidates but, as in Charleville in March 1899, 'to protest against the pretensions of a candidate who was ever the aggressive, uncompromising opponent of national aspirations'; that particular meeting ended in a full-scale riot, with sticks and stones being used by opposing factions, and ended only when baton charges were resorted to by the RIC to disperse the crowds.[57]

The elections themselves seem to have passed off quietly almost everywhere, but the poll was low (fifty per cent was suggested in Cork) – partly because the day was very wet and wild, especially towards evening.[58] The Local Government Board reported that, although more than four thousand separate elections took place, 'there was no hitch of any kind'.[59] Once the votes were counted, it was clear that a dramatic shift in the location of political power was to take place in the counties, with the unionists and large landowners swept from office in three of the four provinces and nationalist councillors, many of them representing tenant farmers, labourers and small shopkeepers, becoming the dominant force in local affairs in most parts of the country. IRB men made up about ten per cent of county councillors, according to police reports.[60] Unionists who went forward for election suffered heavy defeat and humiliation in most parts of the country; the *Cork Constitution* noted with regret that not a single grand jury man, nor a single unionist or Protestant, had been elected to Cork County Council.[61] But there were some exceptions. In Limerick, the earl of Dunraven and Lord Monteagle won county council seats, as did Lord Emly who had nationalist leanings.

Whereas the last set of grand juries had 704 unionist members and only 47 nationalists, the figures usually quoted for the new county councils give unionists no more than 25 per cent of the total seats. The electoral rout is more apparent, however, if the figures for directly elected county councillors are viewed

series), liii, 21 Feb. 1898, 1248. **55** Letter dated 26 Mar. 1898; quoted in C.B. Shannon, *Arthur J Balfour and Ireland* (Washington DC, 1988), p. 101. **56** *Cork Constitution*, 6 Apr. 1899. **57** *Cork Constitution*, 27 Mar. 1899. **58** *Cork Constitution*, 7 Apr. 1899. **59** *Annual report of the Local Government Board for Ireland for 1899–1900* [Cd. 338], H.C. 1900, xxxv (1). **60** Shannon, *Arthur J Balfour and Ireland*, p. 308, n. 61. **61** *Cork Constitution*, 8 Apr. 1899.

in isolation. Nationalists took almost 83 per cent of these seats, leaving unionists with little more than one hundred seats. The fact that some 70 per cent of these unionist seats were in Ulster, and that the only four councils controlled by unionists were in that province, pointed up more sharply than ever before the division in political opinion that existed within the island of Ireland. In fact, Tom Garvin has argued that 'in a sense, the partition of Ireland dates from 1899 rather than from 1920', with a *de facto* acceptance that there were 'orange' and 'green' areas long before partition legislation was contemplated.[62] Perhaps this is what the editorial in the *Freeman's Journal* had in mind when it suggested that, for the nationalists, a victory of a less sweeping character would have served their purposes better.[63]

The transfer of power to the Catholic majority at county level was the culmination of a process which had been underway for some years but, as the late William L. Feingold argued in his detailed study of the poor law guardians in the last quarter of the nineteenth century,[64] it was not the real beginning of local self-government in the rural areas: the domination of the boards of guardians by the landowners had been broken by 1886 in much of the country outside Ulster as a result of the urgings of Parnell, the Land League and the Catholic church. By that stage, local self-government by the largely Catholic tenantry was already a reality in so far as the administration of poor relief and public health was concerned. Bearing in mind the wide range of functions exercised by the guardians in the 1890s and the relatively moribund position of the grand juries, Feingold's conclusion is significant. As he saw it, the 1898 act simply *completed* a democratizing process which had been going on for some time and which, in poor law administration, had begun to occur in the 1870s.

Many of the new generation of nationalist councillors who took power in 1899 continued in office until the 1920 local elections, the first to be held under proportional representation, when Sinn Féin candidates displaced the majority of them; while not achieving the virtual clean sweep the party had secured at the general election two years earlier, Sinn Féin won control of 28 out of the 33 county councils and nearly 90 per cent of the rural district councils at those elections. The majority of those who had participated in local government in the years since 1899 also failed to graduate to membership of Dáil Éireann in the early years. According to figures compiled by Professor J.L. McCracken,[65] only 10 per cent of the members of the First Dáil and 24 per cent of the mem-

---

62 T. Garvin, *1922: The birth of Irish democracy* (Dublin, 1996).   **63** *Freeman's Journal*, 10 Apr. 1899.   **64** W.L. Feingold, *The revolt of the tenantry: the transformation of local government in Ireland, 1872–1886* (Boston, 1984), esp. pp 113–16, 232–8.   **65** J.L. McCracken, *Representative government in Ireland: a study of Dáil Éireann, 1919–48* (Oxford and New York, 1958), p. 31.

bers of the Second Dáil had previous local government experience; the vast majority of the first deputies were graduates of other organizations, including the Gaelic League, the GAA, Sinn Féin and the Volunteers.

HOW THE COUNCILS PERFORMED

The first meetings of the new rural district councils were held on 15 April 1899; the first county council meetings took place on 22 April. Notwithstanding the political context and the inexperience of many of the new councillors, the initial transfer of power was generally so orderly that in May 1900 Sir Henry Robinson could tell Balfour that 'all is running smoothly, and our doubts and anxieties for the result are cleared up'.[66] It was obvious, of course, that the new councils would provide a platform for advocates of the nationalist cause and that many of them would be heavily influenced by the United Irish League strategy of making maximum use of existing institutions to give authority, and the appearance of legitimacy, to the activities and strategies of the League; some councils even considered a form of affiliation with the League, and there were suggestions that district councils should see themselves as its local branches.[67] From their very first meetings, many councils were passing resolutions that demanded home rule, recommended support for the Boers or dealt with the university question, railway rates and charges, or various other political and economic matters which did not come directly within their areas of responsibility. Councils also began to promote use of the Irish language, with resolutions being passed as early as 1905 to the effect that no one should be appointed to any local office unless he or she had a knowledge of Irish. Surprisingly enough, the Local Government Board, while objecting to this kind of extraneous political activity, seems to have displayed a greater degree of tolerance towards it than did ministers of the Irish Free State government in the 1920s and early 1930s.

The new arrangements did not lead to an increase in efficiency in the delivery of local services, or bring an end to the jobbery and petty corruption that had characterized the old regime. In fact, many of the nationalists who came to dominate local government after 1898 rapidly acquired a reputation for opportunism and graft – to quote Professor J.J. Lee, they 'dutifully attended to the three Fs of popular politics – friends, family and favours'.[68] As early as 1905 Arthur Griffith denounced the fact that efficient administration and moral stan-

---

66 Gailey, *Ireland and the death of kindness*, p. 28.   67 Bull, *Land, politics and nationalism*, p. 133.   68 J.J. Lee, 'Centralisation and community' in J.J. Lee (ed.), *Ireland: towards a sense of place* (Cork, 1985), p. 84.

dards were being impaired by the patronage system of appointments in local bodies and argued that patronage should only be exercised in the interests of the nation and not of the individual.[69] In 1919, when a vacancy for a county surveyor arose in Roscommon, Fr Michael O'Flanagan, a vice-president of Sinn Féin, preached a special sermon attacking not just the taking of money bribes for votes but, as he put it, the subtle insidious form of bribery which was commonly described by the expression 'scratch me and I'll scratch you'.[70] However, in spite of the declared policy of Sinn Féin, canvassing for posts at all levels in local government was to continue until 1926 when the Local Appointments Commission took over the function of selecting the persons to be appointed to senior professional and administrative posts.

IMPACT ON LOCAL STAFF

Grand jury staff numbers were relatively small in most counties – generally a secretary, a county surveyor, a small number of assistant surveyors, cess collectors and court-house attendants. Other positions, including those of solicitor, coroner and analyst, were held by legal or medical men in private practice in the area. The guardians, because of their much wider range of functions, had larger staff structures. Details of each member of the staff of the grand juries in March 1898 were given in a return presented to the house of commons in June of that year; similar details in relation to each employee who transferred to the new county and district councils were given in a report presented to the house of commons in August 1901.[71]

In practice, the new local government system had little impact on most employees, but it is interesting to look briefly at how the most senior men fared. The position of secretary to the grand jury was an influential one, the most senior office within the gift of the jury and, of course, a well-paid one, with a salary and fees of up to £1,000 in a number of the counties. The office-holders generally came from landed backgrounds, a significant proportion had military experience and many had been in office since the 1850s and 1860s. Special provision was made in the 1898 act for the county secretaries: they were to remain in office until 31 March 1900, and could then voluntarily retire or be removed by the council; in either event, they were to receive a pension on the civil

69 A. Griffith, *The resurrection of Hungary* (Dublin, 1905), p. 155. **70** *Roscommon Herald*, 1 Nov. 1919. **71** *Returns of officers in the service of the grand jury in each county in Ireland*, H.C. 1898, lxxxiv (237); *Return showing the names etc of all officials transferred by virtue of the provisions of the Local Government (Ireland) Act 1898*, H.C. 1901, lxiv (331).

service scale. Some of the secretaries continued in office well after this transitional period, but many of them resigned. In Cork, for example, Captain Noble Johnson, after thirty years' service, left the post which earned him about £1,000 a year and had to be content with a pension of £542. Others with shorter service did not fare so well. Lt Col. F.K. Izod of Kilkenny was awarded only £138 a year by way of pension and his colleague in Kildare, Mr De Laval Willis, got only £37. One case stands out: in Co. Down, Robert Gordon, who had been appointed as county secretary at the summer assizes in 1835, almost sixty-four years before the grand jury went out of office, died on 26 April 1899, just four days after his new council held its first meeting.

The county surveyors, who were permanent and pensionable officers of the grand juries, were also transferred to the new county councils, but with no special provision for early retirement. Many of them were worried about the impact of the new legislation and several publicly expressed their views on the subject at a meeting in Cork in August 1898.[72] John Horan of Co. Limerick spoke of the apprehension of his colleagues about the new councils but went on to say that 'we as loyal men will do our best to work under them, and we can only hope that the new bodies will rise to a sense of the increased responsibilities placed upon them'. And R.W. Longfield, then serving in Donegal but shortly to transfer to his native Cork, looked forward not only with apprehension but also with 'curiosity as to what these new bodies will do'; he anticipated a considerable amount of friction between the district and county councils, a considerable amount of trouble, and a considerable amount of odium thrown on the county surveyors. Some of the longer-serving surveyors decided to retire before the act came into operation; these included two of the three Cork surveyors, Nat Jackson and A. Oliver Lyons, F.R.T. Willson of Fermanagh and A.C. Adair of Londonderry. Adair, who had forty-four years' service, based himself on the Book of Exodus when he announced his retirement to his grand jury at their last meeting in March 1899, stating that he would prefer to have them fix the rate of his pension because, in a short time, there might be another king in power who knew not Joseph![73]

IMPACT ON SERVICES

A significant expansion of activity in the provision of water and sewerage schemes and in the provision of labourers' cottages was brought about by the new councils

72 *Proceedings of the Incorporated Association of Municipal and County Engineers*, 25 (1898–9), 28–38. **73** *Derry Standard*, 17 Mar. 1899.

in the early years, the rural district councillors being more willing to respond to the needs and demands of their constituents than their predecessors had been. The new county and district councils also had an immediate and lasting impact on the manner in which road construction and maintenance activity was organized and on expenditure priorities. Professor Mary Daly has well described what occurred as 'a triumph of local interests over central government' and a determination to use road expenditure as a form of social welfare system, rather than as a response to transport needs.[74] With the introduction of steam-propelled traction engines, bicycles fitted with pneumatic tyres and the motor car, there had been a revival of interest in road development from the 1890s onwards. There was intense discussion also of the organizational and practical arrangements for road maintenance and improvement – in particular, the contract system which had hitherto been used universally by the grand juries. The 1898 act and an order made by the Local Government Board in 1899 confirmed the traditional legislative bias by providing that public works undertaken by the county councils should normally be executed by contract rather than by direct labour. The majority of county surveyors were quite happy with this, arguing that any change would be financially unacceptable and operationally impracticable, and that substantial extra costs would arise from the purchase of plant and equipment and in respect of overseers, time clerks and pay clerks. Besides, as one of them said some years earlier, the main object of the hired labourer, as distinct from the contractor, was 'to put in his day'.[75]

   All of this changed dramatically in May 1901 when a Local Government Board order allowed a county council to introduce direct labour operations in any district where the council thought fit. This followed strong representations from a number of councils which were influenced more by the need to provide employment for rural labourers than by considerations of efficiency and effectiveness in road making or by pressure from the roads lobby. Limerick was the first county to change over fully to direct labour, under pressure from the labourers and their supporters. Schemes covering roads in ten other counties came into effect in the following three years; by 1908, the Local Government Board was able to report that the new method 'continues to find favour' and that 'the decrease in pauperism' in some areas was being attributed to the employment provided on the roads.[76] The movement to direct labour accelerated in the following years and county councils built up large direct labour organizations dedicated to road maintenance and improvement. By the mid-

74 Daly, *The buffer state*, p. 380.   75 P.J. Lynam (Louth county surveyor), *Transactions of the Institution of Civil Engineers of Ireland*, 17 (1887), 68.   76 *Annual report of the Local Government Board for Ireland for 1907–08* [Cd. 4243], H.C. 1908, xxxi (1).

1920s, a small army of more than twenty thousand road workers had come into existence and employment levels rarely dipped below that level until the 1960s.

The link between road work and employment provision went back, of course, to the Great Famine – and, indeed, to earlier periods of famine and distress – but, with the changes introduced by the first county councils, it was to become a dominant feature of road works policy and financing into the 1960s. In effect, job creation came first and transportation needs a poor second for much of that period. There was strong resistance among councils generally to the declaration of roads to be main roads and, even when grants were introduced in 1910 for the improvement of these roads, many councils were reluctant to take them up, preferring to continue to allocate available local resources to purely local roads in more remote areas. And there was opposition by councillors, even in the 1920s, to the introduction of steam-rollers and stone crushers, because of the view that all available funds should be used to employ additional local labour. Against this background, it is hardly an exaggeration to say that the approach to road expenditure chosen by the county councils in the first few years of the twentieth century, and followed by successive councils and governments for well over half of that century, left Ireland with an infrastructural deficit from which it is only now beginning to recover.

CONCLUSION

Whatever may have been the reasons for the reorganization of county government in 1898, the system then laid down has endured for a remarkably long time. The 327 baronies were swept away as administrative units in 1899, the boards of guardians had left the scene by 1923 and the rural district councils survived only until 1925. But the counties – which might well have been regarded as alien creations, first constituted in 1210 by King John – survived as administrative units, notwithstanding the huge differences in their size and financial capacity and boundaries which are often quite arbitrary and cut through natural communities. In 1969, a young civil servant – who shall be nameless – was assigned the task of preparing a first draft of a white paper on local government reorganization which, as published in February 1971, announced that the government still favoured the county as the basic unit of local government because 'it exists, powerfully supported by local sentiment and tradition and possessing already an established administrative organization with a considerable degree of competence in many functions'.[77] No government since then has even consid-

77 *Local government reorganisation* (Dublin, 1971: Prl. 1572), p. 25.

ered adopting a different position. And so, county councils are still with us, over 100 years after the Westminster parliament decreed that they should be created. How well the organizations themselves, and the successive generations of local councillors and local employees, have served Ireland is a debate for another occasion and another place. But it would be a brave or, perhaps very foolish, civil servant or minister who would now propose the abolition of county councils as Seán T. O'Kelly was tempted to do all those years ago.

The Irish college at Salamanca

Monica Henchy

WHEN FR ALEXANDER MCCABE, the last rector of the Irish college at Salamanca, led a group of the last surviving priests who had studied there in presenting their respects to King Juan Carlos of Spain on the occasion of his visit to St Patrick's College, Maynooth in July 1986, they were honouring the historical links that existed between the Spanish monarchy and the Irish colleges in Spain since 1592, when Philip II founded the first and most important of these colleges at Salamanca. The Irish colleges in Spain were designed to train students for the priesthood at a time when monasteries and Roman Catholic schools were suppressed in Ireland following the Reformation. The Council of Trent (1545–63) legislated that diocesan seminaries be established in Catholic countries as a means of raising clerical standards in the church. As that was not possible under the current political regime in Ireland, candidates for the priesthood were sent abroad to study in continental seminaries, either individually or in groups. Seminaries catering specifically for Irish students were established in cities and towns across continental Europe, amounting to a total of thirty by the 1690s. Among the more notable were those at Salamanca, Louvain, Rome, Paris and Prague.

From 1574 onwards, Irish students, lay as well as clerical, had been going to Salamanca and Valladolid in an effort to acquire through the generosity of Spain the education denied them at home; many of them were classed as *pauperes*, which gained them exemption from matriculation fees.[1] Fr Thomas White, a secular priest born in Clonmel in 1556 who settled in Valladolid in 1582,[2] was concerned at 'the many poor scholars having neither means to continue their studies nor language to make known their wants'.[3] He devoted himself to their care, maintaining them with money he earned from his teaching and by appealing to charitable citizens. In the meantime, Fr Robert Persons SJ established a college for English clerical students at Valladolid. Recognizing that it would be financially impossible to maintain two clerical colleges in Valladolid, Fr White

---

1 A. Huarte, 'Petitions of Irish students in the university of Salamanca, 1574–91', *Archivium Hibernicum*, 4 (1915), 96–130. 2 D.J. O'Doherty, 'Fr Thomas White, founder of the Irish College, Salamanca', *Irish Ecclesiastical Record*, 19 (1922), 579. 3 J. Coppinger, *Mnemosynum to the Catholics of Ireland* ([Bordeaux?], 1608), p. 268.

suggested amalgamating the English and Irish students in one college. When this proposal was rejected by Fr Persons, White decided to avail of the visit of Philip II to Valladolid in 1592 to request help in setting up an Irish seminary.

Philip II agreed to endow an Irish college, provided it was located at Salamanca and placed under the care of the Jesuits. He gave Fr White two letters, one for the rector of the university of Salamanca and the other for the city council, asking that the Irish students be 'regarded as highly recommended and be allowed a good annual stipend'.[4] Temporary accommodation was procured, and the Irish college (dedicated to St Patrick) was formally established. An old account book in the Salamanca Archives in St Patrick's College, Maynooth records that Fr White arrived in Salamanca on 10 August 1592; the number of students is listed as 'about ten'. The overall direction of the Irish college was entrusted to the superior of the local Jesuit college – seemingly to ensure that there were no irregularities or heretical teaching. Responsibility for day-to-day administration was given to three vice-rectors, Fr White, Fr James Archer SJ and Fr Richard Conway SJ, of New Ross.

Fr White can be credited with securing the foundation of the Irish college at Salamanca, but the consolidation and early development of the college were largely due to Fr Archer. Archer was born in 1550 in Kilkenny, where members of his family were legal advisers to the earls of Ormond.[5] He was educated at Louvain and later joined the Society of Jesus. In Flanders he had been chaplain to Sir William Stanley's Irish regiment which was attached to the duke of Parma. In December 1592 he travelled from Calais to Seville, where he met his fellow Jesuit Fr Persons who advised him on the future development of the college and on the steps necessary for securing financial support, especially how to cultivate the king's favour. In January 1593 Archer visited the royal court in Madrid; his efforts were successful and he left for Salamanca with increased financial aid. An astute diplomat, not only did he establish rapport with Philip II, but he also succeeded in fostering good relations with the university, the civic authorities and the Jesuit community in Salamanca.[6]

A major problem confronting Archer was the matter of revenue to support the day-to-day running of the college, partly because many of the Irish students were not financially self-sufficient – though they were almost all from the upper classes of Gaelic Irish society. Finance was a recurring problem as the royal grant (500 ducats per annum) was often delayed and was, in any case, inadequate. But

4 Letter in the University of Salamanca archives, signed 'Yo, el Rey', Valladolid, 2 Aug. 1592. **5** T. Morrissey, *James Archer of Kilkenny* (Dublin, 1979), p. 56. **6** T. Morrissey, 'The Irish student diaspora and the early years of the Irish college at Salamanca', *Recusant History*, 14:4 (1978), 246–54.

Spain was itself experiencing considerable economic distress in the period following the defeat of the Spanish armada in 1588. Fr White came to be particularly involved in raising revenue. He had left the Salamanca college in 1593
to help establish the Irish college at Lisbon, but soon returned to Salamanca
where he joined the Society of Jesus.[7] Between 1598 and 1602 he made visits
to Bilbao, Bayona and Santiago to collect funds from Irish noblemen and merchants for the fledgling Irish colleges of Salamanca and Santiago de Compostela.[8]

In 1596 Fr Archer was sent to Ireland to collect money and to explore the
possibility of reopening the Irish mission (that is, the systematic return of the
newly ordained priests to Ireland). Archer was a man of considerable ability,
which was most fortunate given the problems he had to face both in Spain and
at home in Ireland. In one letter to the general of the Society of Jesus in Spain,
Fr Aquaviva, he wrote of 'converting ten priests who were living in schism and
concubinage'[9] – which reflects the decadent state of the church in Ireland at
the end of the sixteenth century. The collapse of the political system of Gaelic
Ireland after the battle of Kinsale in 1602 caused additional problems for Archer,
which were exacerbated by edicts of James I forbidding Irishmen from sending
their sons to college abroad under threat of imprisonment and the confiscation
of their property. Irish merchants in Seville and Cadiz, however, promised to
pay the college a percentage of every pipe of wine exported to the British Isles.
In response to a petition from Archer, in 1605 the pope granted permission to
the fishermen of Galicia, Vizcaya and Portugal to fish on six Sundays or festi-
vals each year provided the fish were sold for the benefit of the Irish colleges.[10]
The papal licence was approved by Philip III, but later ran into trouble when
the ubiquitous tax gatherer insisted on taking a percentage of the proceeds.

Within a decade of its foundation the college faced a serious threat to its
reputation because of accusations made by certain disgruntled Irishmen. These
began in 1602, the main instigator being Florence Conry, a student in the early
years of the college who had been sent home for organizing opposition to Fr
White among his fellow students.[11] His dismissal must have rankled with Conry,
who later became provincial of the Franciscans in Ireland and archbishop of
Tuam *in absentia*. He alleged that, in the selection of students, Fr Archer and Fr
White had a strong bias in favour of Munstermen. He drew up a memorial to
the king in the names of Hugh O'Neill and Hugh O'Donnell, to whom he was

---

7 According to the private diary of the Jesuit residence at Salamanca, Fr White entered the
Jesuits on 11 June 1593. **8** O'Doherty, 'Fr Thomas White', 587–8. **9** W. McDonald, 'Irish
ecclesiastical colleges since the Reformation: Salamanca', part IV, *Irish Ecclesiastical Record*, 10
(1874), 554. **10** J. Corboy, 'The Irish college at Salamanca', *Irish Ecclesiastical Record*, 63
(1944), 249. **11** Morrissey, *James Archer of Kilkenny*, pp 38–40.

8 The Irish college at Salamanca; photograph (by courtesy of Monica Henchy).

chaplain. In the memorial he described White as 'an Irish father of the Society of Jesus, born in one of the provinces [Munster] subject to the queen, and consequently schismatical, who bears no affection towards Connachtmen or Ulstermen who are declared Catholics'.[12] Conry requested that half of the scholars admitted should be from Ulster or Connacht. An examination of a list in the archives at Maynooth College for the period 1592–1640 does indeed show that, of the twenty-two students in Salamanca up to 1603, all but one were from Munster. But the Jesuit provincial replied that if northern or western students were not admitted it was merely because not enough educated students from those areas presented themselves.

As a result of the dispute and subsequent investigations it was decided that, while the Jesuits should continue to administer the Irish college, it would be incorporated into the university of Salamanca where the students were already attending certain courses. It was also laid down that in future the rector and other superiors would be Irish, as that would best suit the students. Under the new

12 E. Hogan, *Ibernia Ignatiana* (Dublin, 1880), pp 106–8.

arrangements, Fr Richard Conway SJ was appointed to the office of rector in 1608. Two years later, Philip III presented the first dedicated residence for the Irish students. The college was then known as 'El Colegio Real de San Patricio de los Nobles Irlandeses' (the Royal College of St Patrick for Irish Noblemen), reflecting the fact that, as already noted, in the early years many of the students were members of Gaelic noble families. In addition to the yearly grant, Philip established a *viaticum* of 100 ducats for each student who finished the course and returned home.[13] The *viaticum* was a travel allowance, including a provision for secular dress, which was necessary as a disguise on returning to Ireland.

A particular problem for White, Archer and their immediate successors was that of inculcating a spirit of discipline and learning in the college, which was difficult as the students came from a country that had experienced extreme turbulence for more than a century. Such formal schooling as they had enjoyed in Ireland was provided by Catholic schoolmasters who taught in defiance of the law. As Fr John Howling of the Irish college at Lisbon noted of the Irish students in general, 'a spirit of obedience was lacking'.[14] Almost a century later Fr Walshe (rector, 1689–93) referred to the disposition of the Irish students when handing over to his successor, Fr Barnaby Bath: 'Have patience for they are mighty impertinent and never contented with anything.' He also threw in some practical advice in Latin for the new rector: 'Rector omnia videat, multa dissimulet et pauca castiget' (The rector should notice everything, but should overlook a lot of things and chastise only very little).[15] On the other hand, when Archer, three years after his arrival, was seeking increased aid for the college at the royal court, he was able to present a certificate from both the Jesuit college and the university of Salamanca praising the talent, virtues and learning of the Irish students.

The constitution of the Irish college laid down that students be of good disposition, be determined to lead a virtuous life and be of sound health. They had to be born of a legitimate marriage and both parents had to be Irish. They also had to be recommended by an eminent ecclesiastic or some other person of consequence who could testify that the parents were of good reputation, were not heretics and were not so poverty-stricken as to depend on the candidate's assistance for their survival. The course at Salamanca was of six years' duration. At the beginning of the course, each student had to sign three oaths: first, if he failed to take orders and returned to Ireland, he was to recoup the college for

13 W. McDonald, 'Irish ecclesiastical colleges since the Reformation: Salamanca', part II, *Irish Ecclesiastical Record*, 10 (1874), 457. **14** Morrissey, 'The Irish student diaspora and the early years of the Irish college at Salamanca', 248. **15** W. McDonald, 'Irish ecclesiastical colleges since the Reformation: Santiago', cont., *Irish Ecclesiastical Record*, 10 (1874), 253.

his maintenance at the rate of sixty Castilian ducats per annum; secondly, he was to obey all the college rules and strive after the perfection of collegiate life; thirdly, he was to take orders and return to the Irish mission as directed by his superiors.[16]

The curriculum consisted of Latin, philosophy and theology, with time also devoted to Greek, Hebrew and music. On Sundays and feast-days, when there were no lectures at the university, there was an hour's preparation for administering the sacraments, performing sacred ceremonies and teaching Christian doctrine on return to Ireland. Following the establishment of the Irish college at Santiago de Compostela in 1605, it was decided that the students would do their three-year course in philosophy there before going on to Salamanca to study theology for three years. This programme enabled the students to become acclimatized in the relatively temperate conditions of Galicia before facing the harsh extremes of heat and cold at Salamanca. Even as late as the nineteenth century, the Salamanca college diary records a high incidence of illness among the students. Unfamiliar Spanish food and the difficult climate on the high Castilian plateau affected the health of many of the students; some who failed to acclimatize had to return home. Health is an issue that features prominently in a letter written in August 1789 by a student named John Robinson, later parish priest of Clane, Co. Kildare, to his cousin Dan McRobin (that is, Robinson) in Dublin:

> We have a good many of our colleagues in a very indifferent condition, some with an ague and others with different complaints. This college, I dare say, is the first and best provided for of all the Irish communities in Europe; our fare is better than could be expected in a college, and we are under the protection of the king and council. We have a most excellent library, besides a globe, microscopes and an air pump which Mr Hussey bought ... In short, I should be as happy as any person in my situation were it not for the headache – but I hope it shall take its final leave of me before winter.[17]

As the students were forbidden from going abroad to study for the priesthood, many of them travelled to Spain in disguise, in some cases as sailors or merchants'

---

16 D.J. O'Doherty, 'Students of the Irish College at Salamanca, 1597–1619', *Archivium Hibernicum*, 2 (1913), 2–3. **17** M. Bodkin, 'Letters of a penal priest', *Irish Ecclesiastical Record*, 58 (1941), 177. The air pump referred to in this letter was presumably used for laboratory experiments: Professor Peter Mitchell, of the department of physics in University College Dublin, has kindly suggested that such experiments might have been concerned with the creation of vacuums or the pressure and temperature of gases as formulated by Boyle's law and Charles' law.

assistants. Similarly, on their return home as newly ordained priests, they also travelled in disguise and sometimes worked their passage. They usually sailed from Bilbao in a Spanish or Irish trading vessel, or else from Lisbon or one of the French ports; some availed of smuggling craft that slipped into secluded coves on the Irish coast under cover of darkness. In spite of the best efforts of the British and Irish authorities to prevent the return of the priests, the traffic continued. A report of the Irish privy council in 1608 confessed the failure of official measures to stem the flow, stating: 'The priests land here secretly in every port and creek of the realm and afterwards disperse themselves in such sort that every town and county is full of them.'[18] Another report denounced them as 'smoking firebrands and filthy frogs of the synagogue of anti-Christ'.[19] Following the Williamite re-conquest of the 1690s, Catholic bishops, religious orders and all who exercised ecclesiastical jurisdiction were banned by various penal laws. Any such persons found in Ireland after 1 May 1698 were to be deported; those who returned to Ireland were subject to the death penalty for the crime of high treason.

The correspondence in the archives held in St Patrick's College, Maynooth includes frequent requests to the Irish colleges in Spain for Irish-speaking priests. For example, in 1611 Fr Nicholas Lawndry, provincial of the Jesuits in Ireland, wrote to Fr Richard Conway, then rector of the Santiago college: 'If you can pick any of ours that hath the Irish tongue it will be well done to send him.'[20] If not all the priests were proficient in Irish, all certainly were in Latin. Indeed, Salamanca had an outstanding reputation for Latin scholarship. It was here that the *Janua Linguarum* (1611) was published. This Latin vocabulary designed for use by educated gentlemen was composed by Fr William Bathe with the collaboration of Fr Stephen White, professor of theology, and other members of the college staff. It was widely acclaimed and was reprinted several times.[21] The priests who returned to Ireland from Spain left few personal memorials or diaries, mainly because of security considerations. But it was recognized that they were the most cultivated men in their neighbourhoods and had brought with them, as one English official reluctantly admitted, 'a foreign culture and a foreign grace which did much to embellish Irish life'.[22] They acted as pastors, mentors and even notaries to their flocks; under their care some of the last remaining vestiges of classical learning continued to be preserved.

18 J. Brady, 'The Irish colleges in Europe and the Counter-Reformation', *Proceedings of the Irish Catholic Historical Committee* (1957), 7. **19** Ibid., 5–6. **20** W. McDonald, 'Irish ecclesiastical colleges since the Reformation: Santiago', app., *Irish Ecclesiastical Record*, 10 (1874), 291. **21** W. McDonald, 'Irish ecclesiastical colleges since the Reformation: Salamanca', part III, *Irish Ecclesiastical Record*, 10 (1874), 526. **22** Quoted in C. Tunney, 'Irish colleges on the Continent', *Tablet,* 24 July 1954, 81.

While the majority of the priests educated at Salamanca returned to minister in Ireland, a few were attracted by the mission fields in the New World opened up by the Spanish *conquistadores* centuries before. The first Irish priest from Salamanca to minister in North America was Fr Richard Arthur who went as pastor to the settlement of St Augustine in 1597; the Spanish hierarchy eventually appointed him vicar-general of the province of Florida. Almost two hundred years later, the Spanish council for the Indies approved the mission of two Salamanca priests, Fr Michael O'Reilly and Fr Thomas Hassett, to St Augustine, Florida in 1778. They were together responsible for the erection of the first Catholic cathedral in the region.

Salamanca priests were especially associated with Mexico. Fr Michael Wadding ministered to a flock of five thousand Indians in Mexico where his name is still honoured. Fr Peter French, a Dominican educated at Salamanca, also ministered to the Mexican Indians. His ministry lasted for thirty productive years, during which he composed a catechism in the language of his flock. He eventually returned to Ireland, where he died in 1693. Perhaps the most colourful of the Salamanca missionaries was Michael Muldoon (1780–1840) who went to Mexico in 1829. We may gauge something of his personality from the following announcement which was carried by the *Mexican Citizen* of 16 May 1831: 'Vicar-general Dr Muldoon begs to inform his beloved parishioners that on his visit through the colony he will baptize and marry the black race of both sexes.' He had an important role in civil and ecclesiastical affairs in the region of the Rio Grande, where he ministered.[23]

Throughout its history, funding was always a problem for Salamanca – as mentioned in this entry in the archives, dated 1652: 'I, Andrew Sall, gave Walter Henry expenses towards clothing and a *viaticum*, as this college has not received during 1649, 1650 and 1651 the dues assigned for *viaticum*.'[24] While the lives of many of the rectors have been described in detail, what appears to have been a discreet silence prevailed in the case of Fr Sall. This may be due to the fact that Sall, rector from 1652 to 1655 and later Jesuit provincial in Ireland, had gone over to the Protestant church in 1674. He then studied at Trinity College, Dublin, where he received a doctorate in divinity. In 1676 he became chancellor of Cashel.[25] The college was fortunate in securing a number of small bequests over the years, the most notable being that of the family of O'Sullivan

23 P. O'Connell, 'A Kilmore missionary in Mexico: Michael Muldoon, 1780–1840', *Irish Ecclesiastical Record*, 49 (1937), 252, 366. **24** D.J. O'Doherty, 'Students of the Irish college, Salamanca, 1619–1700', *Archivium Hibernicum*, 3 (1914), 105. **25** J.G. Simms, 'The Restoration, 1600–85' in T.W. Moody, F.X. Martin and F.J. Byrne (eds), *A new history of Ireland,* iii: *Early modern Ireland, 1534–1691* (Oxford, 1976), p. 435.

Beare. In 1654, Dermot O'Sullivan Beare – son of 'Dónall of the Long March', so-called in reference to his retreat to Ulster following the capture of his strong-hold in Co. Cork, Dunboy Castle, in June 1602 – made a will naming the Irish college at Salamanca his heir should his daughter Antonia die childless.[26] Dermot was a wealthy and influential Spanish citizen – chamberlain to Philip V, coun-cillor of the exchequer, member of the privy council and majordomo to Don Juan of Austria. When he died in 1659, Antonia was only ten years old. In a codicil to his will he had appointed her maternal grandfather, Don Fernando Cárdona, as her guardian. The latter married her off at age 15 to his natural son (this is, her natural uncle), the marqués de Belforte, who squandered the greater part of her inheritance. She eventually divorced him, but then married another squanderer – with the result that she died in poverty even though she had title to considerable property. As she was without issue, the college was the benefi-ciary of the estate. Establishing ownership and securing possession, however, involved a protracted lawsuit, which was not settled until August 1718. The judgment was that what remained of the estate was the property of the college; in addition, from that time onwards the title 'earl of Beare and Bantry' was to be borne by the rectors during their terms of office. The bequest included the famous portrait of Dónall O'Sullivan Beare which now hangs in St Patrick's College, Maynooth.

By the eighteenth century, the Irish college at Salamanca was so firmly estab-lished that, when Charles III expelled the Jesuits from Spain in 1767, it contin-ued under royal protection. The archives of the Spanish embassy in Rome, known as 'Fondo Santa Sede' – reports of Spanish ambassadors to the Holy See to the king of Spain, now housed in the ministry of foreign affairs in Madrid – show that the Irish college was allowed to continue and to receive its royal grant.[27] The only change was that from then on it was administered by Irish secular priests rather than Jesuits. The building vacated by the Spanish Jesuits was given to the Irish college; the building in which the college had been located since 1610 was sold in 1768.

In 1780, Dr Patrick Curtis, later archbishop of Armagh and primate of all Ireland, was appointed rector. He took over at a difficult period as the num-bers of students were beginning to decrease and the grants had fallen into arrears. The college records suggest that he was a strict disciplinarian. In 1802, two students, Benjamin Braughall and Dominic O'Hara, who had been punished for quarrelling and running up debts in the city, sent a petition to the king accus-

26 D.J. O'Doherty, 'Dónall O'Sullivan Beare, knight of Santiago', *Studies*, 19 (1930), 211.
27 Sr Benvenuta [Margaret] MacCurtain, 'Irish material in Fondo Santa Sede, Madrid', *Archivium Hibernicum*, 27 (1964), 48.

ing the rector of treating the students harshly, of being partisan in selecting scholars from the various provinces and of mismanaging the college.[28] The king ordered a visitation and the bishop of Salamanca carried out an exacting audit. The audit showed that not only had Dr Curtis been strictly honest in his accounting but that he was owed over £1,000 of his salary, which he had never drawn because of the impoverished state of the college. The dispute, one of many in the history of the college, might be seen as supporting Montesquieu's observation in his *Lettres Persanes* (1721) that the Irish abroad had 'un redoutable talent pour la dispute' (a formidable aptitude for argument).

By the end of the eighteenth century the political climate in Ireland had changed considerably from that of the 1590s. The penal laws had been relaxed and the Catholic hierarchy was free to establish seminaries at home, the first being set up at Kilkenny in 1782. Nevertheless, Salamanca and a number of the other overseas seminaries continued to educate priests for Irish dioceses, in some cases well into the twentieth century. At around the same time, the French Revolution ushered in a troubled period in the history of the Salamanca college. Following the French invasion of Spain in 1807, the college had to be closed because of the disturbed state of the country. Sir John Moore reached Salamanca on 13 November 1808. The college diary records that a number of the Irish students joined his forces as interpreters.[29] During the French occupation the college was looted and lost nearly all its property, including deeds of mortgage – a loss which was later to have particularly serious repercussions. A large part of the archives, including a lengthy series of account books, was also destroyed. Eventually, in 1817 Fr Patrick Mangan returned from Mexico to become the new rector. He and his students lived as best they could in various lodgings until, in 1821, the town council gave them the magnificent building known as 'La Casa del Arzobispo', after its founder, Archbishop Fonseca.

In 1830 the town council claimed the building as part of the university of Salamanca, and Fr Mangan and the students were evicted. Rector and students retired to their summer villa in Aldea Rubia; in effect, the college carried on there until 1837 when it was reinstated in 'La Casa del Arzobispo' – mainly through the good offices of the British ambassador in Madrid, George Villiers.[30] Fr James Gartlan, who was then rector, successfully campaigned for the rights of the college during the difficult period of the Carlist war, when ecclesiastical property was seized by the state. Fr Gartlan was succeeded by Fr William

28 D.J. O'Doherty, 'Students of the Irish college, Salamanca, 1776–1837, 1855', *Archivium Hibernicum*, 6 (1917), 17–18. **29** W. McDonald, 'Irish ecclesiastical colleges since the Reformation: Salamanca', part VI, *Irish Ecclesiastical Record*, 11 (1874), 112. **30** O'Doherty, 'Students of the Irish college, Salamanca, 1776–1837, 1855', 21.

McDonald, Monsignor Michael O'Doherty, later archbishop of Manila, and his brother Fr Denis J. O'Doherty – all of whom made valuable contributions to the history of the college.

The college enjoyed a period of peace until the outbreak of the Spanish civil war in July 1936. The 'Radharc' film *Spanish Ale,* shown on RTÉ television in November 1982, features a still of the last group of students at Salamanca. Among them is Michael Lane, later parish priest of Kenagh, Co. Longford, who has given a humorous eyewitness account of the evacuation of the Irish students from Spain.[31] Lane – from Shannonbridge, Co. Offaly – was among the sixteen students at the college's summer villa in Pendueles in Asturias where the students were on holiday. He was delegated by his fellow students to ask the vice-rector, Fr O'Hara, if they could be sent home. The morning after Michael Lane had made his request, the British consul informed Fr O'Hara that, if the students wished to avail of the protection to which they were entitled because of their British passports, he would arrange for their evacuation. Next day, a bus arrived to take the students to Santander. Miniature Union Jacks were pinned to their lapels, and they were flanked by the communist flag. They were instructed to give the communist salute going through the towns, and they complied with gusto. In Santander they boarded HMS *Valorous* and were transported to St Jean de Luz on the French coast, just north of the Pyrenees. They took a train from there to Paris, where the Irish consul gave them each an *ex gratia* payment of fifty francs for the journey home. Meanwhile, in Ireland de Valera's government and the bishops were monitoring the situation. When de Valera thanked the British Navy for evacuating the students, *Dublin Opinion* featured a cartoon depicting Nelson coming down from his pillar to inspect a notice pinned to the base reading: DEV THANKS BRITISH NAVY. Nelson stares at the notice in amazement, exclaiming: 'Gosh, I thought I was losing the sight of my one good eye!'

The rector, Fr Alexander McCabe, from Drumkilly, Co. Cavan, was on holidays in Ireland at the time of the withdrawal. On returning to Salamanca, he found that General Franco had established his headquarters in the town and that the college was being requisitioned by the military. McCabe resolutely opposed this, as he also opposed the request by the Irish brigade to use the college as its headquarters. This refusal must have rankled with General Eoin O'Duffy: at a meeting in the Irish college at which he announced his intention of leading the Irish brigade home, he muttered darkly to McCabe that 'we'll close the Irish college too'. The rector dryly replied: 'General, you look after the brigade and I'll look after the college!' McCabe was determined that outsiders, of whatever

---

31 *Longford Leader,* 19 Nov. 1982.

political hue, would not be allowed to take over the college. In his memoir *In Franco's Spain*,[32] Francis McCullough has an amusing anecdote of McCabe's diplomacy in this regard. At a time when Salamanca was crowded and many people were looking for rooms, the Conde de Esteban y Cañongo, a descendant of O'Sullivan Beare, approached the rector to see if he could put him up. McCabe invited him to the college, divested him of his fur coat, and took him on a tour of the building in which the central heating had been turned off. The count returned from the tour frozen to the bone and decided this was no place for him. Other would-be lodgers were similarly frozen out.

When the Spanish civil war ended, it was hoped to recall the students, but soon the Second World War began. Because of the danger of invasion, Spain mobilized her forces and the college was occupied by the military. Fr McCabe enlisted the help of the bishop of Salamanca, who was also chancellor of the university: the bishop promised that, if the college were handed over to the university to house his clerical students, he would have the soldiers removed. The Irish bishops agreed to this as a temporary arrangement. When the war ended, however, they realized they had a serious problem. As the building was then over 400 years old, it was in need of extensive repairs which would require considerable expenditure. It could house only thirty students, so the necessary expenditure was hard to justify; on the other hand, if it were to be extended, there was the difficulty that the college might be hard to fill as vocations in Ireland were already in decline. Nevertheless, Fr McCabe – who had spent thirty years in Spain as student and rector at the college, and was proud of its record – urged the bishops to make a national collection for the restoration of the building. But, though it could have raised considerable funds as every diocese in Ireland had sent students to Salamanca at one time or another, this was not followed up. The only solution seemed to be to abandon the college and sell the building. The Spanish hierarchy maintained that the Irish could not do this as ecclesiastical property in Spain belonged to the state. The Irish bishops claimed that they were in a special position since they held the original college as the gift of the Spanish monarchy, and that as recently as August 1914 Alfonso XIII had recognized their rights to the college and its investments. Estéban Madruga Jiménez, former rector of the university of Salamanca, has written that he was surprised that the bishops considered themselves owners of the building since in 1939 Fr McCabe had acknowledged that the university was the owner so that he would be liable for taxes only on the lands and investments.[33]

32 Francis McCullough, *In Franco's Spain* (London, 1937), pp 158–61. **33** E. Madruga Jiménez, 'Los últimos días del Colegio de los Irlandeses en Salamanca', *Publicaciones de la Asociación de los Amigos de la Universidad de Salamanca*, 10 (Salamanca, 1972), 65.

Moreover, McCabe has stated in his private notes that the agreement given to the Irish college by the town council in 1821 listed all the entitlements of the Irish but that the last proviso was 'salvo el derecho de propiedad' (except the right of ownership). This contract, he says, was kept in a secret drawer in his desk.[34] A joint committee of two Irish bishops – Dr Michael Browne of Galway and Dr John Kyne of Meath – and two Spanish bishops was established to arbitrate on the matter. General Franco was against the closure as he feared that it might be interpreted as displaying a lack of confidence in the political situation in Spain; both he and the Spanish hierarchy urged the Irish bishops not to close the college.

By 1951 a compromise was agreed, which gave the college building to the university of Salamanca. The proceeds of the sale of the summer villa, lands and investments realized 20 million pesetas (about £20,000), which was to be used for the Irish college in Rome and to establish two Salamanca scholarships.[35] Following the closure, transcripts of the college archives were brought to St Patrick's College, Maynooth where they are housed in the library. Fr McCabe donated his unpublished journals to the National Library of Ireland:[36] they are a valuable source for the history of the college and were used very effectively by Dermot Keogh in his book *Ireland and Europe, 1919–89*. Keogh describes McCabe as 'a liberal-minded man with little time for cant or rhetoric, who was critical of the conservative, distant, aloof Spanish church'.[37] I am eternally grateful to Fr McCabe for having allowed me access to his papers.

34 The late Fr A. McCabe, in a letter to the author.   **35** M. Browne, 'The Irish college at Salamanca: last days', *Furrow* 22 (1977), 699–702.   **36** National Library of Ireland, Acc. 4872. **37** D. Keogh, *Ireland and Europe, 1919–89* (Cork, 1990), p. 294.

Book

You come to me with such avid eyes
I wonder what you expect to find.
When you turn my pages

It is not me you see, but you.
Is there anywhere in the world
You do not meet yourself?

What the rain writes on the ground is for you alone.
What the rain screams between the houses
Cannot so be heard by any other man.

You see and hear the wind and rain
And never know the pain
That made me.

Something has sentenced you to yourself.
Your only world is where you are,
What your eyes look at,

Open or shut.
You are an unspeakable secret,
A prison that walks about.

When you consider me
You involve me in your secret.
I extend and deepen it,

I enlarge you as I lose myself, word by word.
I am part of a story you invent
Like a rumour you once heard

And decided to make your own.
When you believe you possess me
You are most alone.

BRENDAN KENNELLY

Remembering the future, imagining the past: how southern Irish Protestants survived

Ian d'Alton[1]

TEHERAN, APRIL 1929: a package arrives at the Imperial Bank of Persia, addressed to an employee. That employee, William d'Alton, is the essayist's great grand-uncle. He has awaited the d'Alton family history, researched and written by a firm of London genealogists. Funds have now run out, and Musset & Co has reached the limit of its commission. In immaculate copperplate, here chronicled is the story of a family in Co. Clare, Ireland, from sometime in the late seventeenth century – unexceptional minor gentry, with the usual clutch of justiceships of the peace and deputy lieutenantships. The agricultural depression after the Napoleonic wars did for the d'Altons economically, the decline being exacerbated by the coincidence of a tragic alcoholism and an injudicious Catholic marriage in 1835, albeit to the daughter of a well-to-do Limerick merchant. The lands eventually sold, the family moved to Dublin, where they became middle-class professionals – lawyers, doctors, public servants. As 'Castle Catholics', they were loyal, fighting in both World Wars. And as such, they naturally mixed with urban Protestants. The writer's grandfather duly married back into the Church of Ireland in 1918 after surviving the carnage at Gallipoli. Subsequently this branch of the family – in characteristic defiance of the 1908 *Ne temere* decree – was baptized as Anglican, back to its southern Protestant roots. Loyalties were complex; for example, my grand (in every way) aunt saw no contradiction between her devout Catholicism and acquaintanceship with Archbishop John Charles McQuaid and the proudly displayed war medals of her brother who died at the military hospital in Étaples in 1917. This complexity of loyalties determined, in many ways, the two modes of relating to Ireland – engagement and exclusivity – into which

1 No historian of Ireland could work without the National Library of Ireland and its collections, so well husbanded by Dónall Ó Luanaigh. It is appropriate, therefore, that this essay – illustrated largely, but not exclusively, by a long-standing research interest in Cork Protestantism – had its genesis in a paper read to the National Library of Ireland Society on 26 February 2004. Writing it has been much like a butterfly trying to pin itself to a display case, so my grateful thanks are due to Bishop Richard Clarke, Tom Dunne, Jim Hehir, Felix Larkin and Robert Tobin for reading it in draft and for their insightful comments thereon.

southern Irish Protestantism fell, and by which the d'Altons and their ilk – a once-dominant minority – affected to maintain morale, survive and remain relevant.

* * *

Some four years before the family history arrived in Persia, W.B. Yeats had electrified the Irish Senate with his take on Irish Protestants: 'We are one of the great stocks of Europe ... If we have not lost our stamina then your victory will be brief, and your defeat final, and when it comes this nation may be transformed.'[2] His was not the first magisterial voice with such sentiments: Lecky had written in similar terms at the time of the first home rule bill, Dicey at the second.[3] But the context in which Yeats spoke was radically different, the grandiloquence of his language in direct inversion to the position of powerlessness that southern Protestantism now occupied. In this brilliant, carefully-crafted and dangerous speech, he captures a truth from the reality he perceived Irish Protestantism to be. Sublimating an entire people into an imagined past, the poet sends them into a stern and predetermined future. Never mind that it is doubtful whether he had the majority of southern Protestants on his side in 1925, or even that many understood what he was up to. Stating a reason for existing was the point, *contra* Daniel Corkery who argued later (in 1931) that Protestant culture was always an impermanent structure.[4]

It seems to me, however, that the assertions of Yeats and Corkery can both be legitimized; it depends on perspective. Irish Protestants, from the earliest times, needed to reassure themselves, constantly, that they mattered, and not only to themselves. The Yeats worldview articulated this, grandly, in cultural terms. Corkery's narrow and exclusive polemical vision, representative for its time of a great swathe of Catholic and nationalist opinion, explained why this was a continuing necessity. Cultural relevance was a key determinant of survival: 'We cannot tell what political change lies before our country', sermonized the newly-elected archbishop of Dublin in July 1920, 'but one thing is certain, the Church of Ireland must never let itself be a stranger in Ireland.'[5] And southern Irish Protestants – despite persisting in seeing Ireland as 'a country, rather than a nation'[6] – could often show, as in the empathetic words of Somerville and Ross, why they should not be considered strangers:

2 D.R. Pearce (ed.), *The Senate speeches of W.B. Yeats* (London, 1961), p. 99. 3 W.E.H. Lecky, 'A "nationalist" parliament', *Nineteenth Century*, 19 (Apr. 1886), 636–7; A.V. Dicey, 'The protest of Irish Protestantism', *Contemporary Review*, 62 (July 1892), 3. 4 R.F. Foster, *W.B. Yeats: a life,* ii: *The arch-poet* (Oxford, 2003), p. 300; D. Corkery, *Synge and Anglo-Irish literature* (Cork, 1966), pp 4–7. 5 G. Seaver, *John Allen Fitzgerald Gregg, archbishop* (Dublin, 1963), p. 105. 6 J.M. Hone, in *The Bell*, 2:6 (Sept. 1941), p. 26.

9 'Ceilidhe in the Kildare Street Club'; cartoon by Charles E. Kelly, reprinted in *Forty Years of Dublin Opinion* (Dublin, n.d.).

The very wind that blows softly over brown acres of bog carries per-
fumes and sounds that England does not know: the women digging the
potato-land are talking of things that England does not understand. The
question that remains is whether England will ever understand.[7]

Yet, even if 'England does not know', Ireland did; an acute awareness of difference and minority is inherent in Irish Protestant history almost as soon as the
'old world colony' is founded. As an illustration, while the Protestant population of Cork city increased by about 30 per cent between 1736 and 1834, this
was dwarfed by the almost 200 per cent increase in Catholic numbers over the
same century.[8] Such relative change did not go unnoticed. Cork city in the seventeenth and eighteenth centuries was 'a contested space, with Catholic and
Protestant groupings vying for superiority and recognition within the landscape'.
After the insecurities of the half-century from 1641, a wave of church construction and renovation in this 'contested space' commenced in 1693 with the
rebuilding of St Peter's in the city centre. Lasting for about a hundred years,
matching the high-water mark of Protestant patriotism, it ended in 1788 with
that same church being demolished and built again. In between, several others
were reconstructed and a new cathedral was erected in 1738, resources coming
not only from taxes and levies, but also, voluntarily, from the Protestant community. At the end of the eighteenth century, the latter still largely prevailed;
as late as 1800, the city had thirteen Protestant churches, in contrast with nine
Roman Catholic.[9]

The eighteenth century really is a time of 'confident opposition'; placing it
– as Buckland (1972) and Jackson (2001) have done – in the period from the
1880s to the First World War is too late.[10] In truth, nerves were shot to pieces

7 E. Somerville and M. Ross, *Some Irish yesterdays* (London, 1906), p. 249. 8 K. Bowen,
Protestants in a Catholic state: Ireland's privileged minority (Dublin, 1983), pp 7, 20–1, 26; *An
abstract of the number of Protestant and Popish families in the several provinces and counties of Ireland
taken from the return made by the hearthmoney collectors … in the years 1732 and 1733* (Dublin,
1736, rep. 1785), p. 5. These carry a health warning – see S. Connolly, *Religion, law and power:
the making of Protestant Ireland, 1660–1760* (Oxford, 1992), pp 144–5; D. Dickson, 'Second city
syndrome: reflections on three Irish cases' in S. Connolly (ed.), *Kingdoms united?* (Dublin,
1999), p. 104; C. Gibson, *The history of the county and city of Cork*, 2 vols (Cork, 1861–4), ii,
201; *First report of commissioners of public instruction, Ireland, with appendix*, H.C. 1835 (45, 46)
xxxiii, 1.829, 124c, 136c, 138c, 140c. 9 M. Costello, 'A symbolic geography of church construction in Cork city from the early seventeenth to the mid-nineteenth century' (unpublished MA thesis, University College, Cork, 1994), pp 92, 99–100, 103–7, 136–45; S. Hood
(ed.), *Register of the parish of Holy Trinity (Christ Church), Cork, 1643–69* (Dublin, 1998), p. 9;
Gibson, *History of Cork*, ii, 301; J. O'Shea, 'The churches of the Church of Ireland in Cork
city', *Journal of the Cork Historical and Archaeological Society*, 48 (1943), 30–5. 10 P. Buckland,

well before the flower of southern Protestants, of all classes, suffered the same fate in the muddy hell of the trenches. Morale had started to crumble a century earlier. The amendment of a toast in 1830 at Cork's mansion house from 'Protestant ascendancy in church and state' to 'the memory of Protestant ascendancy' was a straw in the wind. By 1833, the fantasy world of the mad earl of Kingston saw Daniel O'Connell leading an army to invade Britain. More prosaically, the sense of powerlessness is captured in the 1837 comment of a defeated election candidate in Cork that 'it is almost useless for any *Protestant* of conservative principles to hope for success'.[11] From the 1880s there is no shortage of the analysis of decline by insiders and outsiders in the intellectual periodicals – *New Ireland Review, Nineteenth Century, Contemporary Review, Blackwood's Magazine, Fortnightly Review.* By the beginning of the twentieth century, the angst was in full flood, typified by the self-deprecatory and bewildered doggerel of a 1907 Co. Clare unionist:

> Sweet land, farewell; sweet land, farewell;
> Where loyal and leal no more may dwell.
> For over the seas and far away
> The poor West Briton must sadly stray.
> He is out of fashion and out of date,
> And the deeds of old are forgotten of late.
> He brings no votes and he counts no more,
> And little is thought of the days of yore.
> And rare as the dodo, as all may see,
> A loyal West Briton full soon will be.[12]

Some nationalists thought this meant that Protestants would fall, like ripe cherries, into their political laps. 'It should be left to England to snub them', wrote Count Plunkett to Redmond in 1897: 'That should make them Irishmen.'[13] But this overemphasized the degree to which Protestant loyalty was conditional and passive; individuals and families still had to make their way in Ireland, and they knew it. As one of the founders of Cork Grammar School put it in 1882: 'It is a great pity that Irish parents, who labour at home and expect

Irish unionism, i: *The Anglo-Irish and the new Ireland, 1885–1922* (Dublin, 1972), p. 1; A. Jackson, 'Irish unionism, 1870–1922' in D. Boyce and A. O'Day (eds), *Defenders of the union: a survey of British and Irish unionism since 1801* (London, 2001), p. 119. **11** D. Dickson, *Old world colony* (Cork, 2005), p. 499; J. Chatterton to Sir R. Peel, 13 Aug. 1837, British Library, London, Peel papers, Add. MS 40,424, 63–4. **12** *Poems of a county of Clare West Briton* (Limerick, 1907), p. 27, 'Lament of a West Briton'. **13** Plunkett to Redmond, 7 Mar. 1897, National Library of Ireland, Redmond papers, NLI MS 15,220(6).

their sons will live in the country for wear or woe, will not see how desirable it is to keep up the connection during the time of their education with the people amongst whom they are to live subsequently ... They did not want to make Englishmen of their boys. There was much to admire in the Irish character and they wanted to maintain it.'[14]

Here is willing and enthusiastic engagement. We might expect this from an urban Protestant source. The notion of landed Protestantism, on the other hand, as nothing but unimaginative, state-subsidized, incompetent, repressive whinging is deep-seated.[15] Yet it, too, is not the whole story. There were many exceptions – and Arthur Hugh Smith Barry was one of them. On 22 February 1925 this Anglo-Irish landlord lies dying in his London town-house near Berkeley Square. Inheriting his Irish and English estates as a minor, the first (and last) Baron Barrymore had become one of the youngest MPs ever at 24 when elected a Liberal MP for Cork county in 1867. In 1900, he was still representing the Cork Protestant interest in parliament, but now perforce as a conservative unionist from an English shire. Smith Barry chose to revive an extinct Barrymore title when offered a peerage in 1902.[16] The title had resonance, and anchored his family firmly to an historic Ireland rather than a contemporary England.

Yet Smith Barry was a man of his own time, 'with a number of virtues which he hides with reprehensible industry'.[17] History has remembered him as the prime mover in an effective opposition (Cork Defence Union) by landlords to the nationalist land agitation in the 1880s and 1890s. But he was more than this – an improving landlord, supporter of the extension of the franchise, in favour of Irish Church disestablishment and of denominational education, and chairman of the Irish Unionist Alliance between 1911 and 1913. His will was proved at nearly £500,000, an enormous sum in 1925. Substantial cash was supplemented by the remains of once-great estates in Cos. Cork and Tipperary in Ireland and extensive lands in England. The point about Smith Barry is that an Irish landlord, provided the conditions were right, could leave the world a wealthy man. Many like him, with competence and some luck, were able to survive the political foundation of the Irish Free State, their economic and social

---

14 W. Goulding, conservative MP for Cork city 1876–1880, quoted in the *Cork Constitution*, 21 July 1882. **15** For a view of landlordism as inevitable tragedy, see J.S. Donnelly Jr, *The land and the people of nineteenth-century Cork: the rural economy and the land question* (London and Boston, 1975), esp. pp 377–84. K.T. Hoppen, *Elections, politics and society in Ireland, 1832–1885* (Oxford, 1984), p. 170; W. Vaughan, *Landlords and tenants in mid-Victorian Ireland* (Oxford, 1994); and L.P. Curtis Jr, 'Landlord responses to the Land War, 1879–97', *Éire–Ireland* (Fall–Winter 2003) all provide a corrective. **16** *Burke's Irish family records* (London, 1976), p. 77; *Burke's dormant, abeyant, forfeited and extinct peerages* (London, 1883), pp 24–5. **17** *Vanity Fair*, 31 Aug. 1910.

privileges virtually intact. In 1925, Lord Barrymore was at the apex of Cork county society, just as his forebears had been a century earlier.[18]

Smith Barry was not afraid to engage with nationalist and Catholic Ireland; but politically, in an age edging towards democratization, such engagement often invited humiliation. At the 1885 general election, encouraged by the recently formed Irish Loyal and Patriotic Union, loyalists in various guises (conservatives, independents, liberals) contested many southern Irish constituencies. Head-on confrontation with nationalism only served to demonstrate starkly the weakness of southern unionism. In Ireland, fifty-two contests resulted in fifty defeats. In eight Cork constituencies, loyalist candidates amassed a total of 3,136 votes, against more than ten times that number for the nationalists.[19]

As it became progressively more local, though, Protestant/unionist attempts at meaningful political participation in the period after the mid-1880s were more successful. Cork city politics demonstrates how unionists used the Parnell split to sow divisions amongst nationalists and further their own political agenda. In 1841, in the dark days following municipal reform, it had seemed that local influence had gone forever. Only six conservatives, in sixty-four seats, were elected to Cork city's new council. But by 1844 numbers had increased to sixteen and by 1849 to twenty-two.[20] With one-third of the seats, the conservatives/unionists were potentially in a powerful position. The Parnellite split in the 1890s gave them the opportunity to use that power. It was graphically illustrated on 12 December 1895, when Sir John Harley Scott, a unionist, was elected mayor of Cork for 1896. How was this achieved? Scott, one of the city's leading shipping merchants, saw that a nationalist split could be exploited. If this were to be fruitful, though, it would require constant adaptation and occasionally distasteful political alliances. It helped that southern unionism was possibly a 'frame of mind' rather than an immutable political constant.[21] Successful for a time, Cork city political Protestantism was elevated to an eminence that its numbers did not really warrant. So, allying first with Parnellites, then with anti-Parnellites, the unionist bloc on the corporation manoeuvred to improve its numbers and morale. Scott had become high sheriff in 1892; his election to the mayoralty in 1895 followed, as a result of a deal with the anti-Parnellites.

18 I. d'Alton, 'Keeping faith: an evocation of the Cork Protestant character, 1820–1920' in P. Flanagan and C. Buttimer (eds), *Cork: history & society* (Dublin, 1993), pp 771–5; Smith Barry's will, proved 16 Dec. 1925. **19** B. Walker (ed.), *Parliamentary election results in Ireland, 1801–1922* (Dublin, 1978), pp 130–6; I. d'Alton, 'Cork unionism: its role in parliamentary and local elections, 1885–1914', *Studia Hibernica*, 15 (1975), 149. **20** *Cork Constitution*, 28 Oct. 1841; I. d'Alton, *Protestant society and politics in Cork, 1812–1844* (Cork, 1980), p. 191. **21** P. Buckland, 'Irish unionism and the new Ireland' in D. Boyce, *Revolution in Ireland, 1879–1923* (Dublin, 1988), p. 75.

During 1896 Scott took every opportunity to advertise his views, prompting the *Cork Examiner* to say at the end of it that Cork unionists, at least, could not complain that he had 'abandoned his political allegiance'.[22]

Scott's city unionists rode the surf of Irish politics in the 1890s: exhilarating, but always potentially unstable. In 1899, local government reform removed substantial economic power from the gentry with the abolition of the grand juries. In the first elections under the new regime, unionists did better than expected. In Cork county, although none won a seat, their average vote was 17 per cent, nearly three times the proportion received in the 1885 parliamentary elections. Several received votes in excess of 25 per cent, though at the price of considerable fudge in relation to the issue of home rule. The pattern of 'more local, more successful' is demonstrated at urban district council and town commission level; the January 1899 elections produced eleven unionist councillors in ten different towns, a respectable showing.[23]

In Cork city, a divided nationalism continued to pay political dividends for city unionists. At the time of the first local government elections for the new city corporation in 1899 and during the O'Brienite phase of the early 1900s, Cork unionists played a pivotal role in local politics. Yet all this was relative. In 1900, outside the current boundaries of Northern Ireland, 131 unionists had seats on county councils. After the local government elections of 1905, that number had shrunk to 23.[24] By 1911 the game was up; a unionist party in Cork corporation had ceased to exist as such, its erstwhile members emerging as independents, ratepayers' representatives and – prefiguring support for Cumann na nGaedheal and later Fine Gael – a surprising number as All-For-Ireland League supporters.[25]

However, if engagement and the shape-shifting that necessarily went with it was one mode in which southern Protestants dealt with the other Ireland, another was to ignore it and retreat into exclusivity. In their separate worlds, 'nationalist and unionist Ireland confronted each other, politically speaking,

---

22 The 1895 election took seven hours to complete as a result of a filibuster by Parnellites (*Cork Constitution, Cork Examiner*, 3 Dec. 1895; *Cork Examiner*, 24 Oct. 1896). **23** Full results are in *Cork Examiner*, 18 Jan. 1899 (towns) and 8, 9 and 10 Apr. 1899 (county divisions). See C. Shannon, 'Local government in Ireland, the politics and administration' (unpublished MA thesis, University College, Dublin, 1963), *passim*; also B. O Donoghue, 'From grand juries to county councils: the effects of the Local Government (Ireland) Act 1898' in this volume. **24** G. Arbuthnot, 'How local government is worked in Ireland', *Nineteenth Century*, 61 (June 1907), 1027; of rural and urban district councils, there were 167 nationalist chairmen and only 5 unionist. **25** I. d'Alton, 'Southern Irish unionism: a study of Cork city and county unionists, 1885–1914' (unpublished MA thesis, University College, Cork, 1972), pp 236–52.

from positions of monolithic security; competition was unnecessary'.[26] In the public sphere, existing organizations were adopted and adapted, such as the freemasons and the Cork Church of Ireland Young Men's Association. Some were created to meet special conditions, like the Brunswick Clubs in the 1820s, the Protestant Operative Association in the 1830s, the various metropolitan conservative societies between 1830 and 1853, and the Primrose League in the 1880s.[27] One voluntarist institution thrust upon an unwilling Anglicanism was a disestablished church:

> Look down, Lord of Heaven, on our desolation!
> Fallen, fallen, fallen is now our country's crown,
> Dimly dawns the New Year on a churchless nation,
> Ammon and Amalek tread our borders down

lamented the wife of the bishop of Derry in 1870[28]; and even fifty years after the event, the trauma still had the power to evoke hurt. 'The dark clouds of disestablishment were gathering thickly around the Irish Church in the sixties; men's hearts were failing them for fear ... But faith triumphed', wrote the bishop of Cork, Cloyne and Ross in 1920. And when in doubt, build. Thus, as in the eighteenth century, 'the answer of Cork churchmen to the gloomy forebodings ... was the erection of a beautiful and stately cathedral' (St Fin Barre's, consecrated in 1870). Disestablishment was not, however, the administrative meltdown feared by its opponents. It set free the men of business to run the church, and gave clerics confidence. The lay members of the new Diocesan Council for Cork, Cloyne and Ross appointed in June 1870 were doughty veterans of grand juries, boards of guardians and the city corporation.[29]

As in the public, so in the wholly private sphere, Protestants and Catholics 'could live side by side, as they frequently did, and still live in completely

26 R. Foster, *Modern Ireland, 1600–1972* (London, 1988), p. 434.   **27** J. Hill, *From patriots to unionists* (Oxford, 1997), p. 371; M. Maguire, 'The Church of Ireland and the problem of the Protestant working-class of Dublin, 1870s–1930s' in A. Ford, J. McGuire & K. Milne (eds), *As by law established: the Church of Ireland since the Reformation* (Dublin, 1995), pp 196–7; Jackson, 'Irish unionism, 1870–1922', p. 122; d'Alton, *Protestant society and politics in Cork*, pp 200–14; J.H. Robb, *The Primrose League, 1883–1906* (New York, 1942), *passim*; Irish Unionist Alliance, *Notes from Ireland No. 49* (1894), p. 149; *Cork Constitution*, 1 Oct. 1890, 28 Jan. 1891, 16 May 1898 (reports of typical League meetings). Cork Corporation produced a fine bronze medal in 1814 (by Thomas Wyon) to celebrate the centenary of the accession of the House of Brunswick to the throne of Great Britain.   **28** E. Alexander, *Primate Alexander, archbishop of Armagh: a memoir* (London, 1913), p.183; D. Stevens, 'Protestants in the Republic' in E. Longley (ed.), *Culture in Ireland, division or diversity?* (Belfast, 1991), p. 144.   **29** K.T. Hoppen, *Ireland since 1800: conflict and conformity* (London, 1989), p. 154; C. Webster, *The diocese of Cork* (Cork, 1920), pp ix–x, 358.

different worlds'.[30] One physically discrete world was that of the landed classes;
here exclusivity is taken to its conclusion. Reflected in the Big House – the
last redoubt – a sense of isolation sets in. 'Nothing counted for about three
miles on any side of us', wrote Lionel Fleming of his childhood in west Cork
before the First World War, 'because there were no Protestants until then.'[31]
The retreat into an essentially private existence was one in which social ritual,
often pointless and tedious, was acted out as if to a script, with Catholics and
lower-class Protestants (and, in Cork, nine military garrisons) playing the walk-
on parts and supplying the bit-actors. It was a world which involved a great
deal of snobbery – Timoleague's tiny tennis club was open only to Protestants,
'and not to all of those', and Smith Barry's Royal Cork Yacht Club was a
bastion of the Protestant political establishment – and in which 'family trees
were meticulously composed'. Elizabeth Bowen immortalizes, like a fly in
amber, one otherwise ordinary event – the 5 August 1914 garden party at
Mitchelstown Castle. Here, the flower of north Cork Anglo-Irish society met,
'this first day of the war', incongruously doing what it did best – 'comings-
and-goings, entertainments'. And here, in the introverted miniature worlds of
The Irish RM and *The Real Charlotte* of Somerville and Ross, the landed classes
wove an intricate social filigree and indulged, amongst themselves, in a
'narcissism of small differences'.[32]

If there was a script governing this private world, it was incumbent upon
the participants to learn it. This 'remembrance of the future' was what largely
drove the life of the gentry in the years from the 1880s. It emerges, blinking,
in the spate of Protestant memoir and chronicle that appears from the 1920s
onwards. As the poet Thomas McCarthy writes: 'The gentry, and southern Irish
Anglicans in general, were born for remembrance. Their children took to autobiography as naturally as they'd taken to horse-riding' – from Edith Somerville,
Sir Henry Blake and Lennox Robinson through the likes of Thomas Rice
Henn, L.A.G. Strong and Hubert Butler to Peter Somerville-Large and Joan
de Vere.[33] If, in Oliver MacDonagh's words, 'the physical precincts were now
central to identity', in many instances they *were* identity.[34] Biography often has
an elephant in the room – another 'person', the Big House. Elizabeth Bowen

---

30 D. Akenson, *Small differences: Irish Catholics and Irish Protestants, 1825–1922* (Montreal, 1988),
p. 126.   **31** L. Fleming, *Head or harp* (London, 1965), p. 36.   **32** D'Alton, 'Southern Irish
unionism', p. 45; Fleming, *Head or harp*, pp 17, 36; *General rules and regulations of the Royal
Cork Yacht Club: corrected to 1st May 1904* (Cork, 1904), pp 8–10 (persons to be admitted as
honorary and *ex officio* members); E. Bowen, *Bowen's Court & seven winters* (Virago ed.,
London, 1984), pp 259, 436; Akenson, *Small differences*, p. 149.   **33** T. McCarthy,
'Introduction' to E. Bowen, *Bowen's Court* (repr., Cork, 1998), p. xi.   **34** O. MacDonagh,
States of mind: a study of the Anglo-Irish conflict, 1780–1980 (London, 1983), p. 28.

personalizes it in *The Last September* (1929); those who fire it are its 'execu-
tioners' – and similarly Yeats, in his play *Purgatory* (1938):

> Great people lived and died in this house;
> Magistrates, colonels, members of parliament,
> Captains and governors, and long ago
> Men that had fought at Aughrim and the Boyne.
> Some that had gone on government work
> To London or to India came home to die,
> Or came from London every spring
> To look at the May-blossom in the park ...
>
> But he killed the house; to kill a house
> Where great men grew up, married, died,
> I here declare a capital offence.

Bowen goes one step further. 'A Bowen, in the first place, made Bowen's
Court', she writes in *Bowen's Court*: 'Since then, with a rather alarming sure-
ness, Bowen's Court has made all the succeeding Bowens.' And, in the same
vein, Bowen's house had, as against her father's long drawn-out death, 'a clean
end. Bowen's Court never lived to be a ruin.'[35] Many of these houses, their
economic justification largely gone by the early 1900s, were already dying. As
Robert Tobin points out,[36] this led to 'the readiness with which many Protestant
writers have embraced, or at least acquiesced in, the imagery and language of
extinction'. That extinction is one of black hole; saddled with their genealogy,
prisoners of their futures, the gentry struggled with the often overbearing and
centripetal force of their houses.

In my view, the most effective articulation of these houses' imaginative force
is to be found in the work of the poet and the novelist. Writers as diverse as
Molly Keane, William Trevor and Jennifer Johnston are free to mine memoir
but not be entombed under it. Elizabeth Bowen's *Bowen's Court* is family chronicle written with a literary sense – superb story and subversive history. In it the
individual Bowens in each generation, the family, the ancestral home, become
almost of one substance. It is significant that Bowen gives the name of the house
to her history of her family: this really tells you who she *was*. You couldn't really
divine her bizarre marriage with Alan Cameron, or her intelligence work for
Lord Cranborne during the war, or her love affairs, or her ambivalent sexual-

35 Bowen, *Bowen's Court*, pp 445–6, 459. **36** R. Tobin, 'Tracing again the tiny snail track:
southern Protestant memoir since 1950', *Yearbook of English Studies*, 35:1 (Jan. 2005), 172.

ity, or her fascination with American glitz from the book; but to know Bowen's Court the house – possibly the child she never had, or the father who was never 'quite there' – was to know the essence of Elizabeth Bowen. The subversion lies in a portrayal of the decline of her caste as predetermined grand tragedy: intense, emotional, inevitable, the introverted integrity of a lost cause, Protestants (and Catholics) 'caught inextricably in the web of their tragic history'.[37]

If over the nineteenth century place becomes identity, it also substitutes for time. In retrospect, this both dealt with and reinforced irrelevance – as seen, for instance, in the life of 'Big George', third earl of Kingston. As ruefully put by an impecunious descendant, he 'ushered in an era of folly and disaster which led finally to the ruin of the great Mitchelstown inheritance of the Kings'. The outward sign of this catastrophe was the gothic castle, built in 1823 and burnt down a century later. More Mervyn Peake's *Gormanghast* than Mr and Mrs Hall's 'modern castellated mansion', it was modelled on Windsor Castle and indeed built for a visit from the earl's friend, George IV, which never happened. Everything about the new castle was grand. It cost possibly close to £220,000 and was staffed lavishly (one of the chefs was young Claridge, later of London hotel fame). Tocqueville said that by the 1830s the earl found himself burdened with £400,000 of hopeless debts. Eventually he broke down from the strain of trying to balance the unbalanceable. He was declared publicly insane in 1833 and died in London in 1839.[38]

But money troubles seemed to be too prosaic to explain Kingston's spectacular fall. Elizabeth Bowen's novelist's eye divined that Big George

> epitomizes that rule by force of sheer fantasy that had, in great or small ways, become for his class the only possible one. From the big lord to the small country gentlemen we were, about this time, being edged back upon a tract of clouds and of obsessions that could each, from its nature, only be solitary. The sense of dislocation was everywhere. Property was still there, but power was going. It was democracy, facing him in his gallery, that sent Big George mad.[39]

Lord Kingston, popularly known as 'The Chief of the Galtees' in the early 1820s, saw himself as a fusion of the great Irish chieftain and the feudal baron. Almost

37 F.S.L. Lyons, *Culture and anarchy in Ireland, 1890–1939* (Oxford, 1979), p. 177. 38 B. Power, *White knights, dark earls: the rise and fall of an Anglo-Irish dynasty* (Cork, 2000), pp 39–94; R. King-Harman, *The Kings, earls of Kingston* (Cambridge, 1957), p. 79; Mr and Mrs S. Hall, *Hall's Ireland*, ed. M. Scott (London, 1984), pp 1, 40. 39 Bowen, *Bowen's Court*, p. 258.

certainly the last earl of Kingston to exercise a *droit de seigneur* against the wom-
enfolk of his tenants and hankering after the title of White Knight borne by his
mother's Geraldine ancestors, he pestered chief secretary Robert Peel for its
royal *imprimatur*. A final refusal brought forth the imperious claim: 'I shall be
satisfied with a recognition of the people and *that* nothing can deprive me of.'[40]

Clearly, Lords Kingston or Barrymore never thought they were irrelevant
to their Ireland. But if irrelevance was indeed the outcome of the long decline
from the 1780s, and if that irrelevance can be characterized as failure, then in
this 'failure' of southern Protestantism, paradoxically, lay the seeds of survival.
The great legacy of the British regime, from Catholic emancipation to the
Treaty, was unplanned and serendipitous, but 'the Ireland that *we* made', as
Balfour later proudly claimed,[41] was one in which the vital issues – land, local
government, education, the church – had been effectively settled by the end of
the Union. Duty may have continued for a time to tug insistently at Protestant
sleeves; until 1921, the gentry still dispensed justice and involved themselves in
poor law administration. Ultimately, though, they were no longer needed.
Southern Irish Protestants (and certainly the landed classes) had, despite Yeats'
protestations, simply become unnoticed and their remaining public functions
were close to vanishing point – 'in the life of the new Ireland … the lives of
my own people become a little thing.'[42] Increasingly, there are only conversations with themselves – Lord Glenavy, speaker of the Senate, gently chiding
Yeats in 1925 is sadly typical. No one else is really listening. The rest was already
in another dimension. Like Lewis Carroll's Cheshire Cat, eventually only the
grin – in this case the southern Protestant badge of loyalty – was left. Or, to put
it another way, in Foster's words about the poet's family: 'The Yeatses had had
money, social influence and a history in Ireland. By the later nineteenth century all they were left with was the history.'[43]

If irrelevance had any value, it surely meant that Protestants should have
been left in peace. Yet that did not happen. The cascading effect of land
agitation, Parnellism, Catholic religious aggression and, above all, the Gaelic
cultural revival had led to an Ireland that inexplicably demanded the adherence
of Protestants to the nation and their exclusion from it at one and the same time.
Both perplexing and maddening, they were looked upon, in the words of a
Protestant novelist in 1916, as 'illegitimate children of an irregular union between

40 Kingston to Peel, 10 Jan., 10 Feb., 14 Dec., 30 Dec. 1822, Peel to Kingston (copies), 19
Dec. 1822, 20 Jan., 13 Mar. 1823, British Library, London, Peel papers, Add. MSS 40,353,
174, 203, 243, 245; 40,354, 124; 40,355, 90, 92. **41** B. Dugdale, *Arthur James Balfour*, 2 vols
(London, 1936), ii, 392. **42** Bowen, *Bowen's Court*, p. 437. **43** R. Foster, *W.B. Yeats: a life*,
i: *The apprentice mage, 1865–1914* (Oxford, 1997), p. 1.

Hibernia and John Bull'. Edna Longley contrasts the reality that 'Protestants have to work their passage to Irishness' with the perception that 'Catholics are born loving the country'.[44] Protestants were trapped in involvement whether they liked it or not. For a time, around independence, this dichotomy could not be sustained. The result was violence: it cannot be gainsaid that nearly half the Protestant population of Cork was driven out or left in the period from 1920 to 1926. Between 1920 and 1923 a spate of shootings, burnings and evictions of prosperous Protestant tenant farmers, professionals and small-town shop-keepers occurred around Bandon and Dunmanway, although they had seemed to have been relatively well-integrated with their Catholic neighbours.[45] A massacre of ten Protestants took place in three days in April 1922, well *after* the Treaty. Something quite similar had happened before, elsewhere: the 1920–23 period echoes 1798, especially Co. Wexford.[46]

This violence has been characterized[47] as nothing short of ethnic cleansing, comparable to that in Armenia and the Balkans in the twentieth century. But if so, it was a very targeted cleansing indeed. No Bosnia, this. In retrospect, it seems to have been much more an opportunity to get rid of those individuals and families that most provoked the particularity of animus from the other side, for whatever specific reason – personality, land, politics, religion. Thus, the execution of the fictional Sir John Hamilton by volunteers in Ken Loach's 2006 film, *The Wind That Shakes the Barley*, is represented as being due essentially to Hamilton's being an informer, rather than just a Protestant landlord.[48] And the real-life murder of Vice-Admiral Boyle Somerville at Castletownshend, Cork in March 1936 was explained at the time in terms of his alleged recruiting activities for the British forces. Joseph O'Neill, in a remarkable family memoir, reduces the reason for the murder to the sole fact of Somerville being a

44 S. Day, *The amazing philanthropists* (London, 1916), p. 16; E. Longley, 'The separation of political Irishness and culture in Ireland', *Irish Times*, 9 Aug. 1989.   **45** P. Hart, 'The Protestant experience of revolution in southern Ireland' in R. English and G. Walker (eds), *Unionism in modern Ireland: new perspectives on politics and culture* (London, 1996), pp 81–94. See also Hart, *The IRA and its enemies: violence and community in Cork, 1916–1923* (Oxford, 1998), pp 272–93, 307, 309, 314; T. Dooley, *The plight of Monaghan Protestants, 1912–1926* (Dublin, 2000).   **46** See T. Dunne, *Rebellions: memoir, memory and 1798* (Dublin, 2004), pp 128, 186, 247–264. **47** Hart, 'The Protestant experience of revolution', p. 94; J. O'Neill, *Blood-dark track: a family history* (London, 2000), p. 326. My thanks to Felix Larkin for drawing my attention to this latter work. Its powerful and imaginative writing carries it towards what seems a predetermined conclusion; as O'Neill notes, 'families and nations have self-serving editions of their past' (p. 327). In this, it replicates the subversion of *Bowen's Court*.   **48** P. Laverty, *Screenplay of 'The wind that shakes the barley'* (Cork, 2006), pp 66–7, 78–9, 84–6. See also perceptive reviews of the film by R. Foster, *Dublin Review*, 24 (Autumn, 2006), pp 43–51, and B. Hanley, *History Ireland*, 14:5 (Sept.–Oct. 2006), pp 50–1.

Protestant, on the grounds that many others – priests, councillors and the like – could equally have been targeted for assisting in recruitment. Yet that does not necessarily invalidate the 'particularity' argument. The fact cannot be ignored that Somerville wasn't just *any* Protestant – he was a former high-ranking British military officer and thus, in the eyes of an IRA desperate at the time for a military revival, a 'legitimate' target. His being a Protestant could not have been in itself the only justification for killing him.[49]

'Particularity' is an explanation of why hatred ran out of fuel so quickly; it was not sustained by community memory. In any case, 'hardships sustained by the southern loyalists were on the whole not excessively severe nor long-lasting.'[50] Furthermore, those who remained were the beneficiaries of the tragedies of those who had fled. Catharsis eventually produced normality. Curiously, as after 1798, it suited the folk-memory on both sides to be wiped selectively clean.[51] For Protestants, a kind of soporific fatalism took over, and a further retreat into the private realm. A chronic loss of confidence arrived at its logical destination – shame – in the early 1920s. Lennox Robinson has one of his characters in *The Big House* (1926), set in 1921–3, declare 'we were ashamed of everything, ashamed of our birth, ashamed of our good education, ashamed of our religion, ashamed that we dined in the evenings, and that we dressed for dinner'.[52]

This is the nadir. Struggling out of it, it helped that southern Irish Protestantism did not try to maintain a separate, irredentist and aggressive political identity. If it had, its integration with, and acceptance by, the new regime might have been painful indeed. To those for whom the Irish Free State was anything but free – economically, socially, culturally – departure was the only option, and many did leave. But those who remained, or who, like Smith Barry and Bowen, travelled back and forth across the Irish Sea in the 'perpetual transits'[53] between Anglo and Irish, found that they could manage. 'Acquiescence seemed the only course open to them, and they adjusted themselves to the new conditions more quickly and with less difficulty than might have been expected.'[54] It may be thought that this is about 1922; but here the historian J.C. Beckett was referring to those Protestants who were opposed to the Act of Union after 1801. This offers the clue to coping. Southern Protestants, in 1922, had been in this place, this time, before. They could be there again, or

---

49 O'Neill, *Blood-dark track*, pp 127, 132–3, 328–9. **50** R.B. McDowell, *Crisis and decline: the fate of southern unionists* (Dublin, 1997), p. 159. **51** See O'Neill, *Blood-dark track*, pp 295–6, 327–33 for a fascinating discussion about why southern Protestant memory is so selective – essentially a defence mechanism, he maintains. **52** C. Murray (ed.), *Selected plays of Lennox Robinson* (Washington, 1982), p. 195. The d'Altons continued to 'dress for dinner', for family Christmases at any rate, up to the mid-1960s. **53** Bowen, *Bowen's Court*, p. 447. **54** J.C. Beckett, *The Anglo-Irish tradition* (London, 1976), p. 85.

so it seemed. Echoing Yeats, history was cyclical; 'the soul of man lived many lives'.[55] The future could be remembered, even if this time furtively. Symbol, relatively harmless, took the place of substance. A spontaneous rendering of *God Save the King* at the Armistice Day remembrance in the Phoenix Park in 1931 was a rare public manifestation of loyalty usually kept close to the chest. Up to the 1960s, southern Protestants might still have listened to the Queen's Christmas message – but this was done strictly in private between consenting adults. Only in the revision of the Church of Ireland's *Church Hymnal* in the year 2000, in contrast to previous editions, did the hymn *God Save the Queen* acquire a rubric: 'For use in Northern Ireland'.

The generation that bridged loyalty to crown and republic had to decide how it was to deal with the new state of things. Characteristically, one option was a private response: my pregnant grandmother was brought to Belfast in 1925 to ensure that the child she bore would be indisputably a subject of George V. The public warning was no less salutary. 'Singularity is never popular', advised the archbishop of Dublin in October 1921.[56] He was right. Southern Protestants learnt quickly in the period from 1920 to 1923 that keeping your head down was a sound policy. Cowed by the strident voices of Catholic triumphalism in the 1920s and 1930s, as evidenced by legislation in favour of the Irish language and censorship and restrictions on liquor sales, divorce and contraception,[57] southern Protestants were encouraged to keep a low, nay cringing, profile right through to the 1970s. An illustration is that in 1958 the General Synod of the Church of Ireland decided not to use the term 'Anglican', as suggesting 'a vague West British sound'.[58] And it helped that, even in Cork, up to the 1970s, it was still possible to live a Protestant life without necessarily entering the Catholic world – born in the Victoria hospital, attending Cork Grammer or Rochelle schools, dating and mating in church socials, employed by the Central Garage or Lester's chemists, socializing among the freemasons and the choir of St Fin Barre's cathedral, spending old age in St. Luke's home, buried by Bogan's undertakers.[59]

'I believe in its promise' was Elizabeth Bowen's cautiously conditional verdict[60] on the Treaty – over forty years after it was signed! It is typical of an approach – check for the cat before venturing out of the mousehole – adopted

55 F.S.L. Lyons, 'Yeats and the Anglo-Irish twilight' in O. MacDonagh, W. Mandle and P. Travers (eds), *Irish culture and nationalism, 1750–1950* (Canberra, 1983), p. 232. **56** Seaver, *John Allen Fitzgerald Gregg*, p. 117. **57** J. Whyte, *Church and state in modern Ireland, 1923–1970* (Dublin 1971), pp 38–9. **58** *Church of Ireland Gazette* (30 May 1958), 2. I am indebted to Dr Robert Tobin for this reference. Identification boards outside Church of Ireland churches now (2007) confidently use the term 'Anglican' to describe the religious denomination. **59** I am grateful to the Revd Peter Hanna for this insight. **60** Bowen, *Bowen's Court*, p. 453.

by southern Protestants. 'We merely exist and even that we do with increasing unobtrusiveness' was Hubert Butler's pessimistic judgement.[61] But from the perspective of the early 1920s mere survival could be considered a kind of triumph. It is not surprising, therefore, that with a few exceptions – writers in the *Irish Statesman, The Bell, The Church of Ireland Gazette*, Butler himself, Yeats and some prominent, but totally atypical, churchmen – southern Protestants chose not to confront and engage. Indeed, in the 1920s and 1930s, their public representatives often displayed a rather distasteful fawning attitude to the Free State.[62] An essential obeisance to the current power? Yes, in part. They had much to lose, and had nearly lost it. Perhaps 'as a vestigial population in the new nation-state' they instinctively felt that 'their citizenship was a matter of indulgence and not of right'.[63] But it may have been a little more than this. Southern Protestants, at least up to the 1950s, were not much less illiberal than Catholics when it came to matters like divorce and abortion.[64] If Yeats and Butler – as far removed from many of their co-religionists as from the mass of Catholics – imagined they led an army, it was mainly a conscript one, reluctant and uncomprehending.

* * *

Engagement and exclusivity have elided into a comfortable invisibility for the southern Irish Protestant. What was once a contemporary political issue then became fodder for the historians, and is now of almost archaeological interest. Within a single generation, arguing the proposition of Protestant and Catholic conflict in southern Ireland has become, well, somewhat detached and unreal. When Dónall Ó Luanaigh was starting his career in the National Library in 1963, the fault-lines of Irish identity still ran clearly through a Protestant/Catholic landscape. No more. As early as 1983 the historian G.C. Bolton dared to assert that 'the time has now come when the role of the Anglo-Irish is a question which needs no further attention as such'.[65] If that seemed a provocative statement then, it was not difficult to justify it on the basis that southern Protestants appeared to be 'dwindling … towards a painless extinction' and in the process of accepting 'the need to live quietly and passively in their dying culture'.[66] But today – even if recent census numbers suggest a numerical revival – perhaps Bolton's assertion is more acceptable. The proposition is really that, since the 1800s at least, the

---

61 H. Butler, *Escape from the anthill* (Mullingar, 1985), p. 114.   **62** C. O'Halloran, *Partition and the limits of Irish nationalism* (Dublin, 1987), pp 79–85.   **63** O'Neill, *Blood-dark track,* pp 326–7.   **64** J. Regan, *The Irish counter-revolution, 1921–1936* (Dublin, 1999, 2001), p. 254.   **65** G. Bolton, 'The Anglo-Irish and the historians' in MacDonagh, Mandle and Travers (eds), *Irish culture and nationalism*, p. 254.   **66** Beckett, *The Anglo-Irish tradition*, p. 152; Bowen, *Protestants in a Catholic state*, p. 210.

Protestant-Catholic axis was the visible part of the iceberg. At the pinnacle of a much deeper discussion about Irish identity, it was a proxy fight between nationalists and imperialists, colonists and natives, liberals and conservatives, those who had and those who had not, revisionists and traditionalists, believers in a religiously ordered society and secularists. That discussion has at last moved on. But it is not Protestants alone who have had the 'stamina': it is by a global community that Ireland has been opened up. I rather suspect that today's budding historians will, in time, be debating the place of Poles rather than Protestants in twenty-first-century Ireland. Nevertheless, for southern Protestants, can we say that the outcome is satisfactory, the question resolved, the journey ended? Perhaps. But if we can, if Bolton is right, this is more than a tiny triumph, a small victory. An historic accommodation has been reached:

> The unseen descent of the sun behind the clouds sharpens the bleak light; the band, having throbbed out *God Save the King*, packs up its wind-torn music and goes home.[67]

67 Bowen, *Bowen's Court*, p. 437; the reference is to the aftermath of the Mitchelstown Castle garden party, 5 Aug. 1914.

On first meeting the marquess of Lansdowne

Listowel castle, 21 April 2005

THE MARQUESS OF LANSDOWNE is the direct descendant of Patrick Fitzmaurice, son of Thomas Fitzmaurice, 18th Lord Kerry. Patrick was five years old when Listowel Castle, the last Fitzmaurice castle to hold out against Queen Elizabeth I, was besieged by Sir Charles Wilmot in November and December 1600. He was smuggled out of the castle upon its surrender. Patrick, 19th Lord Kerry, was subsequently captured, educated in England and raised in the Protestant faith.

'Which line do you belong to?' I don't know.
Too poor to trace, there's no record of my line.
Somewhere, somehow, long ago
Someone, a Fitzmaurice, one of mine
Left it all behind him and now I
Can't trace my line to castles. All I know
Is we left all that behind us, I don't know why
But know myself a poet, proudly low.
A rich man with a title finds his place
In history. It was ever so.
The rest of us are hard pressed to trace
Our great grandparents. It's enough to know
That, rooted in this place where I belong,
I turn our common history to song.

GABRIEL FITZMAURICE

Public monuments in Ireland, 1840–1950: barometers of political change

Síghle Bhreathnach-Lynch[1]

WHEN CONSIDERING THE role of art in establishing the identity of a nation, one art form is especially important, that of sculpture. This form – which includes portrait busts, relief decoration and public monuments – has long been employed by governments and political movements to attract and maintain public support for their particular ideologies. It is generally believed, even in the present day and age, that the celebration of milestone events or the commemoration of national heroes in marble or bronze ensures a measure of immortality for the subject. Commemorative monuments also serve as exemplars for successive generations and suggest that, should the need arise, the deeds of the past can be emulated in the future – 'cometh the hour, cometh the man'.

Public monuments are a means of expressing national identity because they represent cultural and political concepts and may signify national aspirations. An examination of a representative selection of Irish public statuary from the mid-nineteenth century to the mid-twentieth century demonstrates that this art form may have as important a role as written documents in enabling us to interpret and understand the world in which it was created. Indeed, public statuary constitutes a significant source of information for social, cultural and political historians. In the period of over one hundred years with which we are concerned, the greater part of Ireland underwent dramatic political change, being transformed from what was virtually a colony to a free and independent republic. The change in political and constitutional status is reflected in contemporary public monuments, which both shaped and articulated the emerging national identity. We will proceed to study a variety of political, literary and religious monuments erected during this period, concentrating on issues of patronage, location, scale and choice of style. A reading of the selected sculptures on levels other than the solely aesthetic sheds considerable light on the ideological concerns of Ireland and the Irish in the decades before and after independence.

[1] A section of this essay is based on an article published by the author in 1992: 'Public sculpture in independent Ireland, 1922–72', *Medal*, 21 (1992), 44–52.

The first call for the erection of patriotic memorials came from the ranks of the Young Ireland movement in the early 1840s. The issue was discussed in the pages of the Young Ireland newspaper, the *Nation,* where it was noted that not a single statue to an Irish patriot adorned the streets of the capital city.[2] Nothing was done to rectify the situation, however, for two decades, mainly due to the Famine and its difficult economic and social aftermath. It was not until 1862 that nationalists in Ennis, Co. Clare, led the way by raising a monument to Daniel O'Connell, designed to commemorate in particular his famous victories in the 1828 and 1829 Clare by-elections. Two years later, the foundation stone of what was to be Dublin's most elaborate and imposing monument to 'the Liberator' was laid in the principal thoroughfare of the city, Sackville Street (now O'Connell Street, renamed 1924). It was not, however, erected until 1882. By that time other monuments were in place in Dublin, including three in honour of literary icons: Thomas Moore, Oliver Goldsmith and Edmund Burke. Statues of political figures such as Henry Grattan and William Smith O'Brien also now occupied prominent positions on the streets of the capital.[3]

In the case of Dublin's statues of nineteenth-century British worthies, their location – and at times relocation – acted as a barometer of national feeling in relation to colonial rule. For those who opposed colonial rule, they offered a means of expressing their opposition – usually by attempts to destroy them. Thus, while all the newly-commissioned nationalist monuments were located in public spaces where they were highly visible, new monuments representing the crown and British imperialism tended to be placed on the outskirts of the city or in places remote from the public gaze. For instance, statues to Lord Gough and the earl of Carlisle were consigned to the Phoenix Park on the outskirts of the city, as was the obelisk commemorating the victories of the duke of Wellington. The earl of Eglinton and Winton was indeed located in the city, but only in what was then the private park of St Stephen's Green, where it was railed off from easy access. When one considers the fate of earlier British statues in the city centre, the reasons for situating the new arrivals well away from an increasingly hostile public becomes obvious.

Grinling Gibbons' statue of King William III, erected in College Green in 1701, was the focal point for an annual declaration by loyalists. Every year a

2 *Nation*, 24 Mar. 1843. **3** For a more detailed discussion on nineteenth-century monuments see G. Owens, 'Nationalist monuments in Ireland, *c.*1870–1914; symbolism and ritual' in B.P. Kennedy and R. Gillespie (eds), *Ireland: art into history* (Dublin, 1994), pp 103–17; also P. Murphy, 'The politics of the street monument', *Irish Arts Review Yearbook* (1994), 202–8. *From O'Connell to Parnell: the conservation of O'Connell Street's monuments* (Dublin, 2006) contains much valuable information about the monuments in O'Connell Street, Dublin.

commemorative procession culminated in the decoration of the statue with a sash and orange lilies: by 1836 Irish radicals had already blown it up three times. Nelson's triumphal column (1808), soaring like a powerful phallic symbol above Sackville Street, was controversial from its inception, being eventually blown up in 1966 to coincide with the fiftieth anniversary of the Easter Rising, the beginning of the end for British rule in Ireland. Other statues were also moved from their original locations to less prominent sites to avoid becoming targets for nationalist spleen. In 1753 an equestrian statue of George I was moved from Essex Bridge to the relative safety of the Mansion House. Two centuries later the statue of Queen Victoria's consort, Prince Albert, was relocated within Leinster Lawn to make way for the second cenotaph. The fate of Victoria herself was decidedly more ignominious: she was removed from her prime location outside Leinster House, dismantled, forgotten and left to languish in storage for many years before being eventually donated to the Australians – rather in the manner of a recycled unwanted gift.[4]

The conflicting reactions to newly commissioned public statues, particularly at the time of unveiling, provides another indication of the growing strength of nationalist feeling as the nineteenth century drew to a close. When the monument to O'Connell was first mooted in the 1860s, he was almost universally regarded by his countrymen as a glorious Irish hero. However, by the time of the unveiling twenty years later, public opinion had undergone a sea-change; by then a more militant brand of nationalism held sway, a nationalism very different from that espoused by O'Connell in his constitutional crusade for repeal of the union. A strong anti-O'Connell element now existed, so much so that the *Freeman's Journal* felt it needed to remind its readers to behave with decorum on the occasion of the unveiling. Its editorial of 14 August 1882 declared:

> One word and one word only have we now to say to the people. It is to remind them that order ought to be and is their first law … The critic eye of a watchful world views their display with as great severity as the review of troops at the march past … Let each man act as if the peace of all depended on him alone.

The unveiling passed off peacefully – but days later a large mob attacked the statue of William III, damaging it once again.

The unveiling of the monument to William Smith O'Brien in 1870 attracted a crowd of over 20,000 people and turned out to be a rowdy, rather raucous

---

4 For a full account of the history of this monument, see S. Bhreathnach-Lynch, 'The chequered fate of a queen', *History Ireland*, 9:4 (Winter 2001), 5.

affair. O'Brien had been the leader of the doomed rebellion of 1848, and had fallen out with O'Connell because of their differing views on the issue of physical force. Now, over twenty years later, the city authorities feared that the unveiling might become an excuse for incitement to riot, and not without cause: O'Brien, after all, had once represented armed resistance to British rule. The unveiling was used by the committee responsible for the memorial, mainly O'Brien's former followers, as an occasion for the expression of nationalist feeling. The fact that such a monument had been put up, they argued, was an indication that Ireland was ready for self-government: 'Free peoples erect such monuments as this [to those] who were loyal to the national cause of their country.'[5]

In 1899 the laying of the foundation stone for the monument to Charles Stewart Parnell in Sackville Street was accompanied by rowdy behaviour between former followers of Parnell and those who had opposed him. Parnell was not long dead and the level of feeling about his treatment by Gladstone's Liberal Party and the Irish bishops because of his relationship with a married woman was still running high.

Caution generally governed the involvement of the city fathers in the commissioning of statues and also in the choosing of locations for those raised by private subscription. Thus Thomas Davis, another Young Ireland leader, was regarded as too controversial a figure to be placed in a very prominent position outside his old alma mater, Trinity College. Instead, the more 'politically safe' Edmund Burke and Oliver Goldsmith, also old boys of the college, were preferred for this prime location. Wolfe Tone, who had played a remarkable role in Irish revolutionary politics over half a century earlier, was also thought to be a potentially troublesome subject. As a result, a foundation stone for the Tone memorial was not laid until his centenary year in 1898. In contrast, a statue to the great eighteenth-century parliamentarian Henry Grattan, erected in 1876, appears to have created no particular problems. Subscriptions for the commission had been raised privately, but Dublin corporation was quite happy to offer a choice location in front of the old parliament building (now the Bank of Ireland) on College Green. The reason is possibly that Grattan's brand of politics offered something for everyone, as he was both a loyalist and a renowned advocate of an independent Irish legislature.

The 1890s were marked by a growing public interest in Ireland's history and traditions, an interest directly related to the desire to foster a distinctive national identity. One manifestation of this was a craze for erecting monuments to notable patriots whose methods found favour with the more advanced nation-

5 Quoted in Owens, 'Nationalist monuments in Ireland', p. 105.

alists of the day. The most spectacular expression of the trend was in the raising of monuments commemorating the United Irishmen and the 1798 Rising.
These memorials celebrated armed resistance, many of the figures being represented in militaristic pose.

Following independence, the first political monument was the cenotaph,
which was intended as an expression of Irish Free State mourning and triumph.[6]
It was commissioned early in 1923 by the Free State government, then only a
year in power. Although embroiled in the Civil War, the government yet
devoted time and energy to the planning and erection of this public monument.
Its purpose was to commemorate the two prime architects of the new state who
had died in August 1922 – Arthur Griffith, who had died after a brief illness,
and Michael Collins, who was shot by republican forces. It would later be used
also to honour Kevin O'Higgins, following his assassination in 1927.

Because the government was anxious to have the monument erected in time
for the first anniversary of Griffith's and Collins' deaths, a temporary edifice of
wood and plaster was constructed; this was replaced in 1950 by the permanent
– and very different – structure in stone which we can see today. The temporary monument was erected with remarkable speed, mainly because in that
period of great political upheaval the government was desperate to stabilize its
position. It believed that the promotion of Griffith and Collins as founding
fathers and national heroes would tend to validate and legitimize the government and foster respect for the fledgling Free State, then under attack from
republicans. The monument was located in a conspicuous position on Leinster
Lawn beside Leinster House, the seat of government. It was placed adjacent to
busy Merrion Square so that it would be on view not only to parliamentarians
– of all political persuasions – but also to the general public.

The design for the memorial – by George Atkinson, of the Dublin
Metropolitan School of Art – made manifest the official version of the Irish hero
under the new dispensation. It featured a stylized Celtic cross with a Gaelic
inscription in the centre. This read *Do Chum Glóire Dé agus Onóra na hÉireann*
(For the glory of God and the honour of Ireland). Relief medallions of Griffith
and Collins by the distinguished sculptor Albert Power were set into the rect-
angular base on either side of the cross. These were made of plaster but painted
to look like bronze. The overall effect was of a simple, rather stark edifice of
no particular artistic merit.[7] The government press handout described the Celtic

6 For an in-depth analysis of this monument, see ch. 1: 'The elephant on Leinster Lawn: a
cenotaph to civil war' in A. Dolan, *Commemorating the Irish civil war: history and memory,
1923–2000* (Cambridge, 2003), pp 6–56. **7** Dolan calls it a 'sham' because of the temporary
nature of the materials used in its creation, but criticizes art historians for disparaging the

cross, however, as 'symbolic of the faith of the men commemorated'.[8] It went on to say that their strength of character was symbolized in the single pylon on either side of the cross. Not only did the new vision of the Irish hero provide for the traditional heroic attributes, but his religious beliefs were also stipulated: the message to the nation and to the outside world was that henceforth the Irish hero was Roman Catholic.

The design – assertively Christian, indeed Roman Catholic, in the use of a cross and with a Gaelic rather than English inscription – can also be read as a visual expression of the official self-image of the newly independent Ireland as a sovereign nation. That identity was firmly linked to contemporary Roman Catholicism on the one hand and to an ancient pre-conquest past, with its Gaelic traditions, language and culture, on the other. The roots of this construct lay in a deep-seated longing to resume a former pre-colonial identity and to be as different as possible from the former ruling power. Britain was perceived as urban and industrialized, while Ireland regarded itself as predominantly rural and agricultural. Britain was largely Protestant, so Ireland emphasized its Catholic heritage. As Britain's mother tongue was English, it was imperative that Ireland's first official language be Irish. The location of the monument is also significant. Statues of Queen Victoria and Prince Albert, prime symbols of British rule, were already in the grounds of Leinster House. As the new monument was a symbol of contemporary Ireland – now a sovereign nation – its positioning in the vicinity of the British royals triumphantly signalled their political overthrow.

The longing of post-colonial societies to see themselves as homogeneous nations, forever united against their former rulers, was shared by the new state. Yet over 200,000 Irishmen had fought for the United Kingdom of Great Britain and Ireland in the First World War.[9] As a result, there was a considerable problem in reconciling service in the world war with the new political reality. The scenario of Irishmen fighting on the side of the former ruler did not conform with the prevailing notion of what constituted a 'true' Irishman. He was now perceived as a man who was willing to lay down his life for Ireland, not Britain. This conflict of identity underlines the problems surrounding the erection of the monument commemorating Thomas Kettle.

Thomas M. Kettle had had a distinguished career as MP for Tyrone East from 1906 to 1910 and then as the first professor of economics in the Dublin college of the National University of Ireland from 1908 onwards. He had supported home rule, and had become an authority on the economic implications

artistic merit of its design (*Commemorating the Irish civil war*, p.12).   **8** The handout was published in the *Irish Times*, 14 Aug. 1923.   **9** See K. Jeffery, *Ireland and the Great War* (Cambridge, 2003), p. 6.

of Irish self-government. Critical of what he regarded as narrow-minded concepts of Irishness, he believed that to achieve a true national identity Irish people should cultivate and absorb European and other foreign influences. A gifted
orator and a talented poet and essayist, his death as a volunteer soldier at Guinchy
in the battle of the Somme in 1916 was regarded as a great loss to Irish political
and intellectual life. A committee of dedicated friends quickly raised money for
a memorial.[10] Taking the form of a splendid bust by Albert Power, it was completed by 1921 and the Commissioners of Public Works agreed to have it erected
in St Stephen's Green, now a public park. The inscription decided on by the
committee included some lines of poetry written by Kettle himself: 'Died not
for flag, nor King, nor Emperor / But for a dream born in a herdsman's shed /
And for the secret Scripture of the poor.' The words 'Killed in action in France'
were to be appended.

The erection of the monument was delayed, mainly due to the ongoing
political crises arising from the Civil War and a strike in the Stradbally quarry
that was to supply the limestone plinth. Finally, after an interval of six years, all
was ready and the unveiling was set for 25 March 1927. Shortly before the
appointed day, however, the Commissioners of Public Works suddenly saw fit
to object to the proposed caption 'Killed in action in France'. It seems that the
seemingly innocuous wording intimated all too clearly that Kettle had died
while serving in the British army: the authorities feared that the unveiling might
offer an excuse for extreme nationalists to make a public protest directed against
the many other Irishmen who had served in the British army during the war.
Significantly, it was requested that 'Killed in action in France' be changed to
'Killed at Guinchy, 9 September 1916', a wording that gave no indication as to
where Guinchy actually was or what Kettle might have been doing there. The
family had also tried to play down the British army dimension as it had decreed
that the portrait bust depict Kettle without his uniform. Compliance with both
stipulations finally enabled the authorities to permit the erection of the monument. There was, however, no unveiling ceremony.[11]

Another memorial which raises similar issues about Irish identity is the War
Memorial at Islandbridge, in the western suburbs of Dublin, which was commissioned by a group wishing to honour all those who died in the First World
War. When the idea for a memorial was first mooted, several different schemes
were proposed. For one reason or another, all were found to be impracticable
or to be inconsistent with the requirement that the memorial be public, visible

10 National Library of Ireland, W.G. Fallon papers, NLI MS 22,598; this collection includes
an almost complete set of minutes, accounts and correspondence detailing the commission.
11 Letter dated 6 Feb. 1923, Fallon papers.

and monumental. Eventually, in 1924 an eminently suitable scheme emerged. This provided for the erection of a memorial centrepiece incorporating gates to the park in Merrion Square, to be located directly opposite Leinster House. When a bill to put the scheme into effect was placed before the Oireachtas, however, it was heavily defeated – with forty votes against to only thirteen in favour. A speech by the minister for home affairs, Kevin O'Higgins, throws light on the reasons why the project failed to get Oireachtas approval. He stated that it would be wholly inappropriate to place a memorial of that kind so close to the seat of government. It would 'give a wrong twist as it were, a wrong suggestion to the origins of the State'. Those viewing it might erroneously conclude that the 'origins of the State were connected with the park, and the memorial in that park, and with the lives that were lost in the Great War'.[12] Independence, he declared, had not drawn its birth from the deeds of the 200,000 Irishmen who had fought for the allies in the Great War, but from the sacrifice of the men of the 1916 Rising.

Within two years, however, the leader of the government, W.T. Cosgrave, showed a more conciliatory spirit.[13] In a letter to the memorial committee relating to the impasse, he wrote: 'There are many schools of thought now, but this is in the main a big question of remembrance and honour to the dead and it must always be a matter of interest to the head of the government to see that a project which is dear to a big section of the citizens be a success.'[14] He then outlined his scheme for a memorial park to be laid out on the banks of the Liffey at Islandbridge. The choice of Islandbridge, well away from the city centre, recalls the strategies used in the previous century when memorials were located away from adverse public attention. Predictably, there was no great public airing of the decision by the Cosgrove government to go ahead. In spite of some republican opposition, the project proceeded without any major delays. The English architect Edwin Lutyens was duly engaged to design the memorial.

The myth that the only 'true' Irishman was one who had fought in the Easter Rising or the War of Independence continued to exercise a powerful and long-lasting influence. Until fairly recently, no Irish government openly commemorated the dead of the First World War, either at Islandbridge or elsewhere, in case it would be construed as an affirmation of British imperialism. As a result, the November commemoration ceremonies became the preserve of Protestant Ireland – the wearing of the poppy is unusual for Irish Catholics, even to this day. Instead, successive Irish governments have concentrated on celebrating the

12 *Irish Times,* 30 Mar. 1927.   **13** See Dolan, *Commemorating the Irish civil war,* pp 40–1, for an analysis of the issues that lay behind this benign decision.   **14** See Lieut. Col. Boydell, *The Irish National War Memorial: its meaning and purpose* (Dublin, n.d.), p. 6.

Easter Rising of 1916. Two memorials associated with this event, both in Dublin city, particularly stand out. The first is a bronze statue of Cú Chulainn which depicts the legendary Ulster hero tied to a stone pillar so that he can fight to the bitter end. With one arm he is wielding a sword, while his shield has slipped down from his breast. A raven, a symbol of death, is perched on his shoulder. The bronze is located in the General Post Office in O'Connell Street, the head-quarters of the provisional government during the Rising, outside which Patrick Pearse read the Proclamation of the Irish Republic on Easter Monday 1916. The building itself was set on fire and suffered severe damage during the fol-lowing week's fighting. When it was rebuilt in 1935, it was decided to erect the Cú Chulainn statue in the main hall as a memorial to those who had fought and died in the Rising.

A highly significant aspect of the memorial was that it was erected in 1935 and not in 1936, which would have been the twentieth anniversary. This was a case of Eamon de Valera stealing a march on his opponents.[15] The general perception was that de Valera and Fianna Fáil, then in government, had hijacked the occasion and appropriated this historical cornerstone of national commem-oration and identity. As a result, some of the opposition Fine Gael TDs refused to attend the unveiling. The republican opposition also expressed displeasure. Subsequent to the figure of Cú Chulainn being deemed suitable for the memo-rial and the decision to use it made public, this faction objected – largely on principle, but also because it was genuinely felt that the wrong mythological hero had been selected as a symbol. The radical newspaper *United Ireland*, which expressed the republican view, claimed in an editorial that Cú Chulainn was not as true a Gael as Fionn Mac Cumhaill.[16] The latter was reputed to have fought much more courageously against foreigners. The newspaper declared: 'There is nothing told of Cú Chulainn that would make a representation of his death a suitable symbol for the struggle and sacrifice of 1916.' In addition, the editorial pointed out that there was a certain ambiguity in choosing the cham-pion of Ulster as a symbol of nationalist ideology. Later loyalist murals which show Cú Chulainn defending Ulster against the Republic would seem to bear this out.

In spite of the arguments put forward, de Valera did not change his mind and the project went ahead. The formal unveiling of the memorial was marked by elaborate ceremony, featuring an evocative pageant, a review of soldiers of the national army and a parade by surviving members of the Irish Volunteers.

15 A similar criticism was laid against the government with regard to the re-establishment of elaborate public ceremonies for the ninetieth anniversary of the Rising. 16 *United Ireland,* 20 Apr. 1935.

At the ceremony, de Valera declared that the statue symbolized 'the dauntless courage and abiding constancy of our people'.[17]

The second memorial to those killed in the cause of Irish freedom is the Garden of Remembrance in Parnell Square. This garden was commissioned by the Irish government in the 1940s following a competition, though it was not completed until 1971. The wording of one of the conditions for the competition is worth noting:

> To be worthy of its purpose the Garden of Remembrance should symbolize, in a setting of solemnity and repose fitting to the memory of the dead, the high courage and nobility of endeavour which inspired the nation's struggle for freedom ... The layout of the Garden should provide an architectural setting as a focal point for a memorial.[18]

The design by the winning architect Daithí Hanley sticks closely to this brief in that every aspect of it is symbolic, from the entrance gates and protective railings to the central sculptural feature in bronze, the work of Oisín Kelly. Relying on a blend of religious motifs and a strong element of Celtic imagery, Hanley created a garden which not only commemorates the dead but also represents peace and hope for the future. The garden is sunk to a depth of over two metres, which almost completely eliminates the noise of passing traffic, and provides a relatively secluded sanctuary and a retreat from the bustle of city life. The sense of calm and serenity is enhanced by a pool of water, designed in the form of a Latin cross, which occupies the centre of the garden. An imaginative series of motifs on the floor of the pool links those who are commemorated with Celtic warriors of the ancient past. A design consisting of six groups of weapons inset into a mosaic background of blue-green waves recalls the Celtic practice of placing weapons in lakes or pools of water after battle. The weapons depicted here are based on Irish designs from the early iron age. On the railings, a repeating motif of an Irish harp surmounted by an olive branch gracefully evokes the concept of peace.

The central feature of the garden is the bronze group, the *Children of Lir*. The ancient Irish legend of four children who were changed into swans represents the transformation of Ireland's destiny as brought about by the valour and self-sacrifice of her sons. The swan – graceful, powerful and heroic – seems a particularly appropriate image to represent national resurgence and ultimate triumph, tinged inevitably with undertones of sacrifice, sadness and isolation. It

---

17 *Irish Times*, 22 Apr. 1935. **18** *General conditions for competition for designs for a Garden of Remembrance* (Dublin, 1946), p. 2.

appears that for the sculptor, Oisín Kelly, the swan represented the idealism and heroism of all those who had given their lives in the cause of Irish freedom down through the centuries. He had originally considered presenting the group in a semi-abstract and stylized form, but being very much aware that the Irish public was notoriously conservative with regard to modern *avant-garde* styles and might reject that visual language, he opted for this realistic representation – which culminates in the concept of upward flight symbolizing the future.

Another aspect of the monument that is worth noting is the inscription in Irish, English and French. The placing of the English is particularly significant. Despite the fact that the whole population spoke English almost exclusively, the French inscription is placed above the English. This reveals the deep-rooted ambivalence with regard to English at the highest political levels, English being perceived as having forcibly replaced Irish as the spoken language during the centuries before independence. The reality that over ninety per cent of the population still spoke English as the mother tongue some decades after independence was a matter of grave concern to a government totally committed to the revival of the Irish language, as it regarded the language as a prerequisite for a truly authentic 'Irish Ireland'.

The importance accorded to the Irish language in establishing a national identity can also be gauged in the official enthusiasm generated by the monument dedicated to the Irish writer Pádraic Ó Conaire who died in 1928. The Gaelic League entrusted the commission to Albert Power. The monument was erected in Eyre Square, Galway, and the unveiling ceremony was scheduled for Whit Sunday, 9 June 1935. Extra trains were put on to allow people to come from all over Ireland to join in the celebrations. There was considerable newspaper coverage, de Valera's *Irish Press* proudly declaring that the occasion represented 'a great hosting of Gaels'.[19] As leader of the government, de Valera performed the unveiling ceremony. His speech from the platform stressed the Irishness of the occasion.[20] He reminded those present that Galway was the capital of the Gaeltacht, and that it was on the big towns that the future of the Irish language would depend. If the people of that city made Irish the language of business and everyday life, they would make Galway not alone the first city of the Gaeltacht but of the whole of Irish Ireland. He also said that the committee could not have found a more suitable sculptor for the memorial than Albert Power. The reason for this accolade lay in Power's public statements on the need for a distinctive Irish art. In pursuance of this ideal, he used Irish stone wherever he could: he chose a Durrow limestone for the Ó Conaire statue. In a letter to the *Irish Press* on 17 January 1935, Power explained that, while his

19 *Irish Press,* 10 June 1935. **20** *Irish Times,* 10 June 1935.

statue was not the first attempt at sculpture in the medium of Irish limestone, it was the first attempt at portrait sculpture – the possibilities of this stone having been quite overlooked in Ireland. 'Irish limestone', he wrote, 'lends itself particularly to sculpture, it is native of the soil, harmonized with our climate, and its warmth of colour gives life to a figure carved from it which is seldom seen in imported white marble. In other words, our Irish crystalline limestone is our own white marble.'

Another cornerstone of national identity in this period was Roman Catholicism. Its role in Irish life had become inextricably linked to the 'Irish Ireland' ideology. In the decades after independence the biggest patron of the arts was the Catholic Church. The hierarchy, clergy, lay organizations and pious individuals all wanted art and artifacts: altars, pulpits, baptismal fonts, memorials, statues. An interesting consequence of this link between Catholicism and national identity was the treatment of some religious monuments as quasi-political icons. For instance, the wayside crosses which dotted the countryside the length and breadth of Ireland were invested with a meaning beyond that of the simply spiritual. Traditionally such crosses marked a local site with religious associations, and passers-by were encouraged to stop and pray. The crosses erected in the years following independence, however, were mainly dedicated to patriots involved in the War of Independence and the Civil War. They usually marked the spot where participants had died in combat. On one level, the appropriateness of a wayside cross as a memorial is self-evident – but the cross with its crucified Christ held a second, much deeper significance for those erecting such monuments. The dead to whom they were dedicated were now popularly regarded as Irish martyrs, along with those executed by the British following the Easter Rising. The cross was perceived as a symbol of their ultimate sacrifice.

Such sentiments were articulated by Countess Markievicz when she unveiled one of these wayside crosses in 1926. She proclaimed:

> The cross is the noblest symbol that we know. It stands for our faith and when we bow before it we call to mind the terrible death Christ died to save us. We think of the shame, the suffering and torture of those hours he passed, nailed to it, tortured in body, tortured in spirit, tortured in soul ... This implement of his death is a symbol of undying love, of steadfast courage and of deathless hopes ... What further symbol could there be for those tortured for what they love?[21]

21 *An Phoblacht*, 17 Dec. 1926.

10 'Madonna and child' by Albert Power, at All Hallows' College, Dublin, 1922;
with an insert showing a detail of the back (by courtesy of
Síghle Bhreathnach-Lynch).

When one considers that those on the republican side in the Civil War had been excommunicated by the Catholic Church, such a speech is not without irony. At the time of the split in early 1922 the Church had come down strongly in favour of those who opted for the Free State compromise.

An examination of religious statuary in this same period offers a fascinating insight into how the Irish Free State perceived itself in relation to the outside world. This is especially true in relation to the numerous Christ the King monuments dotted around the countryside. They had become very popular following the International Catholic Eucharistic Congress held in Dublin in 1932, an event that engendered considerable religious fervour throughout the country. In the main, the Christ the King figures were depicted full-length, with mantle, crown and scepter. Many were cheap mass-produced works, although on occasion sculptors were commissioned to carve individual figures. The concept of Christ the King has its roots in the prophecies of the Old Testament on the coming of Christ: 'And all kings of the earth shall adore him: all nations shall serve him ... All nations shall magnify him.'[22] In the years between the two worlds wars, the Vatican was aware of a general weakening of religious belief and moral conviction in western Europe. It was felt that a spiritual reawakening was needed, in the cause of which a special feast-day in honour of Christ the King was established. This was seen as a modern equivalent to the Crusades of the middle ages; the new crusade under the leadership of Christ the King was designed to rescue the hearts and minds of Christians from the growing secularism of modern life.

When Pope Pius XI summoned the world to rally to the standard of the new king, no country responded with more alacrity and fervent enthusiasm than Ireland. Churches were built under the patronage of this spiritual king and monuments were raised in his honour in cities, towns and villages throughout the country. On the occasion of the opening of a new cathedral dedicated to Christ the King in Mullingar in 1936, Archbishop John Glennon of St Louis, Missouri, shed light on the reasons why the concept of Christ the King had caught the imagination of the Irish people.[23] He reminded his listeners that Ireland had come through centuries of subjugation and strife under colonial rule. In spite of strenuous efforts on the part of its British rulers to discourage Catholicism, the people had clung tenaciously to their own religious beliefs. He appealed to the congregation to make Ireland 'a veritable city and citadel of God, a beacon of light to this storm-tossed humanity, whereby it may, if it will, reach some harbour of rest where it shall find peace with God'. In other words, he saw it as

22 Ps 71:11–17. **23** The sermon was published in a souvenir booklet marking the occasion.

an opportunity for the Irish state to make its mark, albeit a spiritual one, on the world stage. The underlying reason behind this somewhat optimistic view was an uncomfortable realization that Ireland lacked any real power or influence, surrounded as it was by large and powerful states with great resources and political prestige. It was, therefore, imperative that Ireland forge a distinctive identity as a nation, that it make its voice heard on the international stage, and above all that it be seen as absolutely separate and different from its nearest neighbour and former colonial master. An overwhelming declaration of unswerving loyalty to a spiritual king was regarded as furthering this agenda.

Christ the King was not the only popular subject for sculpture at the time, as there was also considerable demand for statues of the Virgin Mary and of the Madonna and Child. While Mary had been traditionally venerated in Ireland, she was now assiduously promoted as an exemplar for women. In the new state, her attributes of chastity, submissiveness and unquestioning piety usefully coincided with the 'official' construct of the female: the role of women was decidedly domestic, with business and politics being the preserve of men. The majority of the new statues were located inside churches, but many were also placed in the grounds of churches or in wayside grottos where they were more publicly on view and would have greater impact. The artistic quality of these representations was, however, generally very poor. The designs harked back to the figurative tradition of the best of European religious art since the Renaissance, but almost all were executed in an utterly hackneyed format. The figures appear to have depended on a kind of simpering prettiness for devotional effect. To a nation largely untutored in the visual arts, the 'prettified' doll-like figures were attractive to look at and easy to relate to in prayer. Their general lack of any semblance of sexuality – or even gender, being flat-chested to a degree – was especially acceptable in a repressed society which zealously tried to control women's sexuality through its legislation.

This creation of a link between the Virgin and the women of Ireland is best expressed in a statue of the Madonna and Child carved in 1922. It was commissioned by Fr Tom O'Donnell, president of the All Hallows' seminary in Dublin, and was intended to commemorate two distinguished past members of the Vincentian community at All Hallows' College. It was located in the grounds of the seminary, which were open to the public. Fr O'Donnell allowed the sculptor Albert Power a free hand in the design. Power produced a religious image which reinforced that supposed spiritual bond between the Madonna and the women of Ireland by imbuing her with characteristic Irish traits; for instance, he portrayed her wearing the cloak traditionally worn by married women in Munster in earlier generations. Moreover, he used his wife and son as models.

As it turned out, the group looked unmistakably Irish – a welcome relief from the typical Madonna and Child of the period.

The first public monument erected in the new Irish state was, as already mentioned, the cenotaph honouring Griffith and Collins, and later Kevin O'Higgins. That edifice – erected in 1923, with the addition of a medallion of O'Higgins in 1928 – was a temporary structure, and was intended to be merely temporary. It was duly removed to make way for the modern memorial. This was erected in 1950, the year after Ireland was formally constituted a republic. The new cenotaph consists of a columnar obelisk which, in comparison with the original, is less overtly 'Irish' in its design. In analyzing this stylistic modification, it could be argued that by the 1950s – in the more stable political situation – the need to express an exclusively Celtic and Roman Catholic identity was no longer imperative. By then, there was a greater degree of national self-confidence and a more realistic sense of national identity which did not require bolstering with iconographical symbols to the same extent. The more generalized design of the new cenotaph reflects this transformation and visually attests this maturation in national self-awareness.

Our study of a representative selection of public sculpture from the mid-nineteenth century onwards suggests that this art form manifests the concerns of the political and religious establishment of the day in developing and articulating an appropriate self-image. Public monuments express political and cultural concerns, especially those relating to national identity. Until the recent past, it was the practice among Irish art historians to give public monuments in Ireland a rather superficial reading, assessing the subject mainly in terms of art and style. As many of the subjects were somewhat dull and prosaic, they were considered unworthy of intensive study. Yet even the most humble monument may well be a veritable fount of information on the ideology, outlook and aspirations of those involved in its creation and on the social, cultural and political preoccupations of the age.

'Love's rock-built tower':
the Ulster tower at Thiepval

Wesley Hutchinson

The Tower of Hate is outworn, far and strange;
A transitory shame of long ago,
It dies into the sand from which it sprang;
But thine, Love's rock-built Tower, shall fear no change.
God's self laid stable earth's foundations so,
When all the morning-stars together sang.

Robert Browning, 'Helen's Tower'.[1]

THIS ESSAY DEALS WITH the Ulster memorial tower at Thiepval on the Somme using articles from the Belfast press in the period between the conception of the project in 1919 and its realization in 1921. This monument commemorates those of Ulster origin who died during the First World War, and particularly those men who fought in the 36th (Ulster) Division, formerly the Ulster Volunteer Force (UVF), which lost a considerable number of men on the first day of the battle of the Somme on 1 July 1916.[2]

The UVF had been created in January 1913. It was made up of men who had signed the Ulster Covenant in September 1912. The signing of the Covenant had been organized by the unionists in the North of Ireland as a focus of resistance to the third home rule bill which was then going through parliament. The militarization of unionism was an inevitable result of the commitments of those who had signed the Covenant which foresaw the use of 'all means which may be found necessary' to oppose what unionism saw as a perfidious attempt by the Liberal government to force them into a home rule Ireland under a predominantly Catholic Dublin parliament.

The tension in the North over the home rule issue was to be sidelined, however, by the outbreak of the First World War. Edward Carson, the unionist leader, offered the services of the UVF to Kitchener who was engaged in putting together the new armies to fight on the continent. His offer was accepted

---

1 R. Browning, 'Helen's Tower' in W. Sharp (ed.), *Sonnets of this century* (London, 1886), p. 31. 2 For the 'official' account of the battle, see C. Falls, *The history of the 36th (Ulster) Division* (London, 1996 [1922]), pp 41–63.

and forthwith large numbers of UVF men signed up, joining the British Army's new 36th (Ulster) Division, Carson having successfully convinced the British authorities to maintain the UVF as a recognisable unit – another significant propaganda coup for the unionist leader. After completing training in England, the 36th was moved to France and saw its first major action at the Somme on 1 July 1916, during which the division suffered some 5,000 casualties after what was unanimously hailed as a heroic advance from their base in Thiepval wood across no-man's-land and deep behind German lines. The emotional impact of the day's losses was all the more important in the North of Ireland in that at this point in the war the troops in the division were still overwhelmingly of Ulster origin – belonging, what is more, to the same Protestant community.[3]

When the war ended, it was Carson who suggested that some kind of battlefield memorial should be built. As usual wasting no time, he published a letter in the local press on 16 November 1918 – 'a few days after the signing of the Armistice'[4] – suggesting the setting up of a committee which would organize and finance the project.

The *Belfast Newsletter* of 20 October 1919 informed its readers that an exhibition of models of designs for war memorials that had been organized by the Royal Academy was to open at Burlington House in London the following day. The British authorities, like their French counterparts, were keen to keep some measure of control over the commemorative statuary that was about to spring up all over the country.[5] However, the *Belfast Newsletter*'s anonymous commentator was clearly unimpressed by the models on show: 'As a whole … it is rather a disappointing collection and leaves one with the impression that our artists have derived little inspiration from the war.'[6] Several members of the

---

3 See recent research into the 'demography of deaths' in the 36th (Ulster) Division over the course of the war by Y. McEwen, 'What have you done for Ireland? The 36th (Ulster) Division in the Great War: politics, propaganda and the demography of deaths', *Irish Sword* 24:96 (Winter 2004), 194–218. **4** *Northern Whig and Belfast Post*, 19 Nov. 1921, 'History of the memorial'. **5** As D. Sherman explains in 'Le discours de l'art et le commerce de la mémoire' in P. Rive et al. (eds), *Monuments de mémoire: les monuments aux morts de la première guerre mondiale* (Mission Permanente aux Commémorations et à l'Information Historique, 1991), pp 131–7, the French ministry of the interior, while refusing to accede to requests from some local officials to propose models for 'monuments aux morts' that would be 'bon marchés, sans vulgarité', directed prefects in September 1920 to set up 'review commissions including the departmental architect and others with competence in design matters to evaluate local proposals for monuments' (p. 131). The commissions sought to discourage work that was too mass-produced and to promote original material from trained artists and sculptors, a luxury many of the smaller of France's 38,000 communes could not afford. **6** *Belfast Newsletter*, 20 Oct. 1919, 'Our London letter'.

committee, including Sir James Craig, had been present at that exhibition and it is interesting to note that these comments were to confirm what was to be their own lukewarm reaction to the models proposed.

The meeting of those subscribing to the memorial project organized in the old town hall in Belfast the following month (on 17 November 1919) followed Craig's advice when he rejected the 'government-approved' models and stated that he would prefer a monument that would be more immediately and more recognizably 'Ulster' in origin. He suggested that they should think in terms of some Ulster landmark that would give a greater sense of immediacy and identity, one of the possible models being Helen's Tower at Clandeboye in Co. Down.

The explanation most usually put forward for the choice of Helen's Tower as a model for the Ulster memorial is that many of the men of the 36th (Ulster) Division, especially those from Belfast and neighbouring areas, had done their basic training in a camp that was opened at the outbreak of the war at Clandeboye in the grounds of the estate of the marquess of Dufferin and Ava.[7] In an article dating from the opening of the completed memorial in November 1921, the *Northern Whig and Belfast Post* points out that this design was 'far more appropriate than … a conventional "victory" trophy with sculptured battle scenes upon its faces and groups of dead and engines of death clustered around its base'.[8] It continues: 'To many of [the men who died] … "Helen's Tower" had been a familiar landmark from boyhood. It met the gaze of the Belfast boys on their frequent train trips to Bangor. Not a man from Co. Down and few from Antrim or Derry or Armagh but had seen the tower and heard or read of its story.'[9]

All of the commentators insist heavily on the 'story' of Helen's Tower. The tower had been built in 1861 by the first marquess of Dufferin and Ava as a tribute to his mother, Helen, Lady Dufferin, some six years before her death.[10] Quotations from Dufferin himself reproduced in the *Belfast Newsletter* of 19 November 1919 make it clear that the son idolized the mother whose 'nobility of character' was such that 'there was no quality wanting to her perfection'.[11] Dufferin was the personal friend of Tennyson and Browning, each of whom at his request wrote a poem on what Dufferin called 'Helen's Tower'. The way in which the poets imagine the original tower would clearly influence how the

7 See P. Orr, *The road to the Somme, men of the Ulster Division tell their story* (Belfast, 1987), pp 54–60. The first marquess of Dufferin and Ava was governor-general of Canada (1872–8), ambassador to Russia (1879–81) and governor-general of India (1884–8). 8 *Northern Whig*, 21 Nov. 1921, 'The Ulster war memorial'; see section 'The soldiers' cemeteries'. 9 Ibid., see section 'A bit of Ulster in France'. 10 See I. Adamson, 'Helen's Tower', *Battle Lines*, 1 (1990), 9. 11 *Belfast Newsletter*, 19 Nov. 1919, 'Ulster Division war memorial: the Helen's Tower design'.

11 The Ulster tower at Thiepval; photograph (by courtesy of Wesley Hutchinson).

Ulster tower in Thiepval was to be read. The Tennyson poem insists on the intensity of the relationship between mother and son:

> Helen's Tower, here I stand,
> Dominant over sea and land.
> Son's love built me, and I hold
> Mother's love in lettered gold.
> Love is in and out of time,
> I am mortal, stone and lime.
> Would my granite girth were strong
> As either love, to last as long!
> I should wear my crown entire
> To and thro' the Doomsday fire,
> And be found of angel eyes
> In earth's recurring Paradise.[12]

The Browning text, on the other hand, takes a slightly more sulphurous angle in that it compares Lady Dufferin's beauty to the charms of Helen of Troy: 'Lady, to whom this tower is consecrate / Like hers, thy face once made all eyes elate / Yet unlike hers, was bless'd by every glance.'[13]

As far as the unionist elite was concerned, it is obvious that it was the Tennyson text that was the more appreciated of the two. Apart from the fact that, as one commentator pointed out, Tennyson was poet laureate – a guarantee of quality poetry if ever there was one – the sentiments in his poem, focusing as they do on the undying nature of filial affection and on the promise of eternal life, are particularly appropriate to the commemorative function of the Thiepval tower. As far as Craig was concerned, there was no doubting the matter: 'A memorial so designed would constitute a connecting link with Ulster, and the people of the province, knowing the filial affection which Helen's Tower symbolizes, would appreciate the beauty and significance of such a monument.'[14] But, of course, this is just one element in a highly complex constellation of factors that was to ensure that Helen's Tower would soon take on a truly iconic status.

* * *

12 *Poetical works of Alfred Lord Tennyson, poet laureate* (London, 1935 [1899]), p. 574. 13 Browning, 'Helen's Tower'. 14 *Belfast Newsletter*, 19 Nov. 1919, 'Ulster Division war memorial: the Helen's Tower design'.

What was chosen, therefore, was a replica of Helen's Tower. Craig's choice of monument – specifically his decision to build a replica – has come in for a considerable degree of criticism. Keith Jeffery, for example, in his study *Ireland and the Great War*, attacks what he sees as an illustration of a 'distinct aesthetic conservatism and lack of artistic imagination'.[15] It is true that some of the monuments being erected in Europe at the same time showed evidence of a more radical aesthetic – for example, the monument by Gropius in memory of the nine workers killed during the Kapp putsch and unveiled just a few months after the Thiepval monument in 1922.[16] Other commentators, like Michael Stedman, while less severe on the unionist establishment's aesthetic judgment, complain that the tower is 'not however unique'.[17] However, these criticisms miss the point. The tower is interesting precisely because it is not unique, because it is a copy!

The resulting discourse is highly ambiguous. Looked at in one way, the mirror effect between the original in Co. Down and the copy in north France can be seen as obliterating the distance between the two. The tower erected in Thiepval becomes the centrepiece of an imagined landscape, the result of a seamless fusion between the two – as the *Belfast Telegraph* puts it, 'this corner of France that is for ever Ulster'.[18] Looked at in a different way, the replica could be seen as extending the imaginative co-ordinates of (unionist) Ulster into France. Unionism in Ireland had been undergoing a contraction in terms of the space it could claim to occupy, a shrinkage that was moving it from an imperial perspective towards a narrower, regional logic. The threat of home rule had forced unionism to face the possibility that the 'idea of the Union' might migrate from the frame of the unitary British state to relocate on the periphery, in Ulster. The Somme tower allowed unionism to look beyond what it saw as a notoriously unstable centre to map out an emotional geography beyond the British Isles, whose central feature would be the 'graveyard in Europe' that belonged to Ulster by right of sacrifice.

In any case, the way the space of the memorial is read merely picks up on what had been a reality on the day of the battle itself when the men of the 36th were given military objectives bearing the names of the towns and villages of

---

15 K. Jeffery, *Ireland and the Great War* (Cambridge, 2000), p. 107. **16** See J. Willett, *Les années Weimar: une culture décapitée* (Paris, [1984]), p. 85. **17** M. Stedman, *Somme: Thiepval* (Barnsley, 2000 [1995]), p. 134. **18** *Belfast Telegraph*, 19 Nov. 1921, 'Ulster's thoughts are there today'. See also *Northern Whig*, 21 Nov. 1921, 'The Ulster war memorial', in particular the section 'The soldiers' cemeteries': 'But it seemed to us that it must be soothing to [the widows and friends of those killed] to know that, though buried on the field of glory where they fell, their soldier heroes are sleeping in this little bit of transplanted Ulster and under the shadow of Helen's Tower awaiting the great reveille.'

their native province. In climbing out of the trenches and crossing no-man's-land, they were to a very real extent going home – to Enniskillen or Bundoran, to Portadown or Strabane, names that had been given to the various objectives behind the German lines. What we have is an imagined space, an explicitly Ulster space, superimposed on a French space – two systems of toponyms existing side by side in the valley of the Somme, a truly bi-lingual landscape. The memory of their native geography quite literally 'translates' the French landscape – at least what is left of it – into a parallel, familiar geography. The unidentified – indeed unidentifiable – space of the front is made familiar through renaming. As the *Newsletter* puts it: 'The Thiepval tower, built of white stone ... [is] in the centre of a ... district, which the merciless guns of the Germans ... have reduced to a barren wilderness – black, desolate and chaotic.'[19]

The lynchpin of this collective, multiple re-invention of Ulster space would be the tower itself, the copy generating a reality as real as the original. Whatever about Craig's alleged aesthetic conservatism, his choice can be read as a perfect illustration of the triumph of the simulacrum, the clone of the original tower – itself, of course, an architectural pastiche – generating a series of parallel, independent and infinitely fluid landscapes. As one reporter pointed out, referring to the impressions of some of those present at the opening ceremony: 'Some of the travellers fancied that they could recognize in parts of the area features reminding them of Down and Antrim and Derry and Armagh.'[20] The tower acts as a catalyst, producing, from the *tabula rasa* of an obliterated landscape, a multiplicity of remembered, highly personal, intimate, domestic spaces.

So what we have is a commemorative space that, although highly public in its function, remains essentially intimate in the way it is to be experienced. Reports on the opening of the Thiepval tower focus on two particular features: the room at the base of the tower containing a commemorative plaque to the men of the 36th (Ulster) Division and the parapet at the top of the building.

The very design of the building seeks to attract the visitor 'inside' itself, to have him enter the shell of the building. This is not a monument to be contemplated from outside, rather one to enter and explore. The strategy by which the building draws the visitor inside is in itself evidence of a very undemonstrative culture. Indeed, we need to be prepared to envisage a certain degree of intimacy if we are to understand the significance and function of the building – because there is nothing outside to tell us what this structure is about. The 'special correspondent' of the *Times* described the scene at the official opening of the tower on 19 November 1921. After completing his speech, Field Marshal

19 *Belfast Newsletter*, 21 Nov. 1921, 'To the glorious dead'.   **20** *Northern Whig*, 21 Nov. 1921, 'The Ulster war memorial'; see section 'The soldiers' cemeteries'.

Sir Henry Wilson, who was standing in for Carson (unable to attend due to a bout of flu),

> was met on the steps leading up to the tower by Major Boyle, who handed him the key of the inner sanctuary. The little chapel, within which General Weygand then performed the brief unveiling ceremony, contains nothing but a marble tablet. On it is inscribed King George's tribute to the Ulster troops ... Beneath the oaken beams of the ceiling, shields bearing the badges of the Inniskillings, Irish Rifles, Irish Fusiliers and the other units of the Division have been placed.[21]

This room – which incidentally contains the engraving of an adapted version of the above-mentioned Tennyson poem – is sixteen foot square. It is tempting, of course, to see the measurements as having a particular significance, an echo of the date, the fatal year in which the battle took place. Given the tradition from which many in the Ulster Volunteer Force came, a tradition heavily influenced by the ritual of the Loyal Orders, it is hardly surprising that the building itself should carry a message, making space significant. But beyond the question of the dimensions, what is more important is that the 'inner sanctum' should be a square – a perfect space, a balanced space, an ordered space. According to Chevallier and Gheerbrant :

> The square is an anti-dynamic geometrical figure firmly fixed on four sides ... The square implies an idea of stagnation, of solidification, indeed of stabilisation in perfection. Such is the case of the new Jerusalem. Whereas easy, circular movement is linked in to roundness, stability is associated with ideas of angularity.'[22]

What we have, therefore, is a perfect, balanced space contained inside the otherwise flamboyant shell of the building. That space, sacred by virtue of its geometry, imposes immobility and invites the visitor to contemplate the emblems of the regiments that fought at the Somme, their emblems arranged in carefully ordered rows. The careful arrangement of this 'inner sanctum' is all the more eloquent in that it has been effected in spite of the 'black, desolate and chaotic'

21 *The Times*, 21 Nov. 1921, 'Thiepval ridge: a memorial for ever'. 22 J. Chevalier & A. Gheerbrant, *Dictionnaire des symboles* (Paris, 1982), 'carré': 'Le carré est une figure anti-dynamique ancrée sur quatre côtés ... Le carré implique une idée de stagnation, de solidification, voire de stabilisation dans la perfection. Ce sera le cas de la Jérusalem céleste. Tandis que le mouvement aisé et circulaire arrondit, la stabilité s'associe avec des idées anguleuses.'

wilderness outside, the mathematical precision of the architecture and the display making the tower a symbol of a new order emerging out of chaos.

The second key feature of the building is the platform on the roof from which it was claimed you could see up to thirty miles. By its very nature, the tower structures movement within itself along a vertical axis, up the spiral stair-case, up the wooden ladder leading out of the tower on to the parapet. It is, of course, difficult not to think of Bachelard's lovely passages on his '*maison onirique*'. According to Bachelard, the stairway to the bedroom may be imagined going up and going down, the stairway to the cellar invariably goes down whereas the ladder to the attic invariably goes up: 'Finally, as for the stairs to the attic – steeper, less elaborate – you always go up. They mean movement upwards towards the most peaceful solitude. When I go back to dream in the attics of long ago, I never see myself coming back down again.'[23]

The verticality of the design is fundamental. In this regard, Major General Simms, a Presbyterian minister and principal chaplain to the British forces in France, published a very interesting piece entitled 'On Pilgrimage' in the *Northern Whig and Belfast Post*. In this article, he encourages people from Ulster to come to France and to visit the graves and, in particular, the tower: 'May our monument be a Pisgah height from which to view the Promised Land from afar which they were not permitted to enter, where, like Moses too, so many of them rest in unknown sepulchres at our feet.'[24] Simms is here referring to the passage in the Book of Deuteronomy which tells of how God allows Moses to see the Promised Land:

> And Moses went up from the plains of Moab unto the mountain of Nebo, to the top of Pisgah, that is over against Jericho. And the Lord shewed him all the land of Gilead, unto Dan … And the Lord said unto him, This is the land which I sware unto Abraham, unto Isaac, and unto Jacob, saying, I will give it unto thy seed: I have caused thee to see it with thine eyes, but thou shalt not go over thither. So Moses the servant of the Lord died there in the land of Moab, according to the word of the Lord … but no man knoweth of the sepulchre unto this day.[25]

Those who climb the stairs onto the roof of the tower are invited to look out over a land, a Promised Land, where so many of their fellow-countrymen now lie in unmarked graves.

23 'Enfin, l'escalier du grenier plus raide, plus fruste, on le monte toujours. Il a le signe de l'ascension vers la plus tranquille solitude. Quand je retourne rêver dans les greniers d'antan, je ne redescends jamais' (G. Bachelard, *La poétique de l'espace* (Paris, 1994 [1957]), p. 41). 24 *Northern Whig and Belfast Post*, 21 Nov. 1921, Major-General Simms, 'On pilgrimage'. 25 Dt 34: 1–6.

This notion that the tower constitutes a favoured axis of communication between the two worlds of the living and the dead was most forcibly expressed in an extraordinary passage in which the 'special representative' of the *Belfast Telegraph* described the end of the religious ceremony:

> It was a moving ceremony. Perhaps the most tense moments were reached in the closing paraphrase, 'How bright those glorious spirits shine', and as the company came to the last verse:
>
> > They climbed the steep ascent to heaven,
> > Through peril, toil and pain;
> > O, God, to us may grace be given
> > To follow in their train,
>
> many could endure the strain no longer, and mingled their tears with those of the simple French folk who had come from the ruins of the neighbouring hamlets … It was one of those occasions that brought us into the presence of the eternal, and as the strains of 'St Asaph' rose to heaven in the glorious sunshine, one could feel that the noble army, men and boys, of whom they were singing were not far away. Nor were they. Their mortal bodies lay all round. Within three hundred yards were two of our cemeteries – but their spirits seemed in very truth to be hovering round.[26]

Just as the ziggurat was designed to bring man closer to God, so the Thiepval tower acts as a place of communication, exchange, transfer between two realities – a space that offers an intimacy, a communion of a very special kind.

* * *

But if the tower as panopticon offers a vantage point from which to see, it is also a point from which to be seen. Although from the start Craig had argued for the tower on the basis of its visibility, claiming 'this would be something that at a distance would catch the eye',[27] the 'visibility' we are concerned with here has more to do with the function of the tower as a focus for symbolic activity – such as, for example, that offered by the inauguration ceremony in November 1921.

---

26 *Belfast Telegraph*, 21 Nov. 1921, 'Place of glorious memories: Thiepval ceremony: singing that moved to tears'. **27** James Loughran, '"For the fallen" (The story of Ulster's war memorial)', *Battle Lines*, 8 (1993), 4.

As is inevitably the case, the project as it developed slotted into the wider framework of ongoing events in Ireland during the period between its initial conception at the end of the war and the opening of the tower in November 1921, a few weeks before the signing of the Treaty that brought the War of Independence in Ireland to an end. When it was decided in 1919 to construct the tower, the Northern Ireland parliament had not come into existence. The tower had, therefore, been conceived initially as a purely regional initiative. However, by the time the tower had been completed and inaugurated, it had become the symbol of a new political entity – Northern Ireland. Given that the Belfast government had been in the eye of the storm since its creation in June 1921, it was a particularly welcome coincidence for the unionist establishment that the inauguration of the tower should offer them an opportunity to remind all concerned – the British, the French and the nationalists at home[28] – of the sacrifice of the 36th Division, thus generating sympathy, in Britain at least, for the unionist cause. The inauguration came at a particularly delicate moment in the negotiations between Sinn Féin and the British Government, as it is clear that the principle of partition had by no means been won definitively at this stage.

The papers – including *The Times* and the *Irish Times* – all record the high degree of tension in political circles at the time the tower was opened. It is interesting to note, for example, that on the very day of the opening ceremony Seán T. O'Kelly, 'Envoyé extraordinaire of the Irish Republic at Paris', was making a declaration to the French press on the Anglo-Irish peace negotiations – a coincidence that did not go unnoticed by the *Belfast Newsletter*, which reported that O'Kelly claimed that there was no question that the Irish delegates would 'agree to recognize the sovereignty of the king of England, and … accept as a settlement of Ireland's claims a modified form of Dominion home rule'.[29]

Carson's message, read out by General Ricardo, made no bones about the Thiepval inauguration being a ceremony for unionist Ulster. Interestingly, he made an oblique reference to ongoing political tension in Ireland when he said: 'Let us reverently today … resolve in our hearts that those that come after [the 'splendid troops' of the UVF] will at all costs follow their example and maintain their freedom from the aggressor whether at home or abroad which they won at such a heavy cost.'[30] Craig's reference to the exact identity of the 'aggressor … at home' was left unspecified.

---

28 For (a remarkably succinct) coverage of the events in Thiepval from a northern nationalist perspective, see *Irish News*, 21 Nov. 1921, 'Memorial in France to Ulstermen'.   **29** *Belfast Newsletter*, 19 Nov. 1921, 'Independence claim reasserted in Paris: statement by so-called "Irish Republican envoy": press reports denied'.   **30** *Northern Whig and Belfast Post*, 21 Nov.

Indeed, the unionist press as a whole was quite unrepentant in its denunciation of what it sees as potential government treachery. The *Belfast Telegraph*,
for example, recalling the 1916 Easter Rebellion and what it sees as its happy
suppression, announced to its readers:

> Today the British cabinet is closeted with some of the men who took
> part in that shocking betrayal of their country, and are bartering the rights
> of those who fought for them to those who fought against them. They
> seem to think that by so doing peace can be brought to Ireland. Mr
> Asquith was universally denounced because he visited some of these men
> in jail shortly after the uprising. Mr Lloyd George is receiving them at
> Downing Street and Mr Austen Chamberlain has spoken of them as men
> of honour. We wish the prime minister better company.[31]

Clearly, unionism's relationship with London was anything but stable. In these
circumstances, the choice of Helen's Tower, and specifically what we might call
its cultural genetic code, takes on added significance. Helen's Tower is in what
is called the Scottish baronial style. The site of the original tower, the Ards
peninsula, has always been an interface between Ireland and Scotland, with particularly intense exchanges from the early seventeenth century, a period in which
such large numbers of Scots settled in Down and Antrim. Furthermore, there
was – thanks to Balmoral – a fashion for this style of architecture in the mid-
nineteenth century, as witness a building such as Belfast Castle, completed in
1870. But, while these factors may explain why the original tower was built,
they do not explain why Craig's committee should have been so attracted to it
as a model for his project. Admittedly, the early part of the century had seen the
development of a considerable renewal of interest in the Ulster-Scots
tradition as evidenced by an upsurge in publications in this field. Of more
immediate significance, perhaps, was the fact that central figures in the unionist
community had already shown their strong sense of identity with Scotland at
another key point in their recent past. When it was decided to mobilize unionist resistance to home rule, the document chosen as the model for the text of
the Covenant was, as Stewart explains, that of the old Scottish covenant of 1580.[32]

This explicitly Scottish tradition underlying the aesthetic preference of the
new Northern Ireland authorities may be explained by a number of other factors. In a period of intense political instability, unionism was – and this is still

1921, 'Message from Lord Carson: the prowess of Ulster's sons'. **31** *Belfast Telegraph*, 21
Nov. 1921, 'Ulster and Thiepval.' **32** A.T.Q. Stewart, *The Ulster crisis: resistance to home rule,
1912–14* (London, 1979 [1967]), p. 61.

true today – faced with a considerable dilemma: the need to demonstrate a distinct regional identity that was sufficiently 'British', while at the same time – given the very real risk of being rejected by Westminster – being careful to avoid too close an identification with an explicitly English heritage. This is a high-risk strategy and it is clear that the unionist authorities could not afford to go too far. Hence the systematic appeal in the newspapers sympathetic to the unionist position to the theme of a parallelism of affection. The *Northern Whig*, for example, makes it clear that:

> Helen's Tower commemorates in Ulster the love of a son for his mother. The Helen's Tower at Thiepval commemorates a mother's love for her sons … How freely they gave their life for their motherland. And what was their motherland? It was Ulster, but it was also for the larger motherland of Great Britain and the British empire that they died. Those Ulstermen who thus nobly died did not think in their hearts' devotion of Ulster only, although they loved Ulster, nor of Ireland only, although they loved Ireland too, but of all those passionate and unutterable things which move in the hearts of all true Britons when they think of what their country is to them and what it stands for in the world.[33]

So this is very much 'Mother Ulster', but a Mother Ulster that the *Northern Whig* is careful to place in a series of Russian dolls, unionist-style, each one fitting inside the next on an ever-expanding scale: Ulster, Ireland, the United Kingdom, the empire.

Unionist papers are very interested in emphasising also the role that France plays in the ceremonies. They point out that the Union Jack and the French tricolour are unfurled together from the top of the Ulster tower by the duchess of Abercorn. They underline the key role played by General Weygand, Marshal Foch's chief-of-staff – in Carson's absence, he is invited to unveil the tablet inside the tower;[34] Sir Henry Wilson delivers his speech in French and, addressing the French in the audience, he says: 'You stand this day on a sacred little bit of Ulster – that far distant land whose sons came running to help you – and you see a beautiful building whose foundations we trust will go deep down into the heart of France.'[35] There is the guard of honour from the French army, as well as the presence at the ceremony of the mayors of the local towns and villages, various prefects and the minister responsible for devastated areas. The

33 *Northern Whig and Belfast Post*, 21 Nov. 1921, 'What Thiepval means: contrast to "Easter Week"'. **34** *Belfast Newsletter*, 21 Nov. 1921, 'To the glorious dead'; see section 'General Weygand's part'. **35** Ibid.; see section 'The Thiepval ceremony: Sir H. Wilson's tribute'.

extent of the involvement of the representatives of the French state in the inauguration of what was a regional monument was a considerable propaganda coup for the new Belfast authorities.

Ultimately, however, it is clear that the increased visibility that the tower gave unionist strategists was directed, as always, towards the government in London. Despite the perennial cries of impending treachery by Liberal politicians, unionism was using the occasion to send out a series of messages. Not surprisingly, the first of these was a reminder of the debt owed by Britain for unionist commitment in the nation's hour of need.[36] More interestingly, the construction and inauguration of the tower also allowed the Belfast authorities to place Northern Ireland on a par with other countries of the empire and the other members of the United Kingdom who were at that time constructing memorials to their dead.[37] Perhaps most important of all, the unionist authorities were giving an active demonstration of their impressive organizational abilities, not only as regards the running of the ceremony – the only jarring note of the day had been the tearing of the French flag as it was being hoisted alongside the Union Jack[38] – but as regards the organization of the entire project, completed as it was in record time. Indeed, the building was opened two years almost to the day after the initial decision to build it had been taken at the meeting in the old town hall in Belfast. Even *The Times* admitted: 'The Ulster memorial is ... the most imposing of the monuments as yet erected on the Western Front.'[39]

The ongoing project in the Somme had become tangible proof that the unionist authorities were capable of wresting order out of chaos and of constructing in record time an edifice of quasi-national importance. The implications were clear for those who had eyes to see – if they could construct an ordered space in the midst of the desolation of the western front, they would also be capable of imposing order in their home province if only the British government decided to give the unionist authorities even their qualified support. It is perhaps this message that the poem 'Reveille' that featured in the

36 Interestingly, this aspect was often linked to a determination to carry on where the dead had left off. One of the most interesting examples of this line is to be found in a text by an Ulster exile living in Paris, a certain Ella Davis, who, in an article in the *Belfast Weekly Telegraph,* quotes at length from the Gettysburg address, reminding her readers that 'it is for us the living rather to be dedicated here to the unfinished work which they who fought here have thus far so nobly advanced' (*Belfast Weekly Telegraph*, 26 Nov. 1921, Ella Davis, 'Thiepval pilgrimage: Ulster woman exile's visit'). **37** See K. Inglis, 'Les mémoriaux dans les pays anglophones' in Rive et al. (eds), *Monuments de mémoire,* pp. 123–5. **38** *Belfast Weekly Telegraph*, 26 Nov. 1921, Ella Davis, 'Thiepval pilgrimage: Ulster woman exile's visit'. **39** *The Times,* 21 Nov. 1921, 'Thiepval ridge: a memorial for ever'.

Newsletter on the same page as the accounts of the opening ceremony of the Thiepval tower is trying to put across: 'We have builded firm in our province fair / and a smiling land is everywhere, / Let us hold it for those who follow.'[40]

In conclusion, it is interesting to note that by a curious coincidence, on the day before the inauguration of the tower, *The Times* carried the following notice:

> Sir J. Gilmour stated, in a written parliamentary reply, that the first commissioner had invited Mr Ralph Knott FRIBA to design and execute the public offices in connexion with the civil service of the northern Irish government. He had also invited Mr Arnold Thornley to execute the parliament house. Both these architects had consented to undertake the work, which would be begun as soon as circumstances permitted.[41]

Clearly, Sir James Craig – who had less to worry about than he thought – was soon going to have another, infinitely more important, building programme on his hands.

---

40 *Belfast Newsletter*, 21 Nov. 1921, A.N.M., 'Reveille'. **41** *The Times*, 18 Nov. 1921, 'Ulster government building: the architect chosen'.

On publishing, *a rhapsody*

A writer's life? Thrice-distilled folly,
Hours, years, aeons of melancholy,
That passionate joy of true creative vision
Reduced to *product* by shareholders' option:
Beckett's plays seen as merely bums on seats,
Obscene fixation with end-of-year receipts.

Your lover says she merely feeds you,
Children exclaim that they still need you,
Friends cease to call, your writing takes
Precedence over all their sakes.
Locked in a room of small dimensions,
Too hot, too cold, you reek pretensions
Of the grinding Grub Street trade,
A life unkempt, a bed unmade,
Sheets trashed in *Tracey Emin* squalor.
Here no *coy mistress* will devour
With kisses all your angst-wracked wishes:
She's downstairs now amongst the dishes.

Practitioners of those useful arts,
Plumbing and prostitution, torts,
Advance the cause of their professions
As hedges secure against recession.
Utility, propinquity and law provide
Attractions to the seeking kind
Of youthful aspirants who may discover
Promising careers, chameleon cover
For lifetimes spent in wealth – or poverty:
Determining which, now that's the novelty.

The writer's trade appealed, its hours
Are flexible, its misty bowers
Attractive to reclusive spirits.
In bookshops no one keeps the minutes

Of conversations, languid, intellectual,
Involved, pellucid, polysexual,
Where 'book in all of us' would out
As secret name in *Turandot*,
Without enduring *Puccini*'s twist,
Life sacrificed to conquer it.

Now banks send rude and threatening letters,
Your mortgaged soul exists in tatters,
Base economics for a writer
Involve the belt being always tighter.
You've sold your *Shakespeare and Company* edition
Of *Ulysses*, its Aegean blue and mint condition
Cover has always brought you joy:
Joyce now buys schooling for your boys.
He would have doubtless empathized
That literature, though vanquished, lives,
But then, possessed of *silence, cunning,*
With *exile* he made a *Second Coming*.

Manuscript complete, you heave a sigh,
Its writing, an eternity.
Exhausted, stressed and out of pocket,
You descend bleakly from your garret,
The laptop now can gather dust,
E-mails unread, for now you must
Attempt to act the penitent sinner
And cheerfully appear at dinner,
Remember each your children's names,
Appease your lover's strong disdain
For all that marks the writer's trade:
Ego and absence, promises betrayed.

A year has passed, the manuscript sent
By agent to publishers of fair intent,
But back it comes: *the editor doubts*
A market for existential thoughts,
Suggests you write a book of riddles
For four-year-olds or witless ninnies.

Another thanks for your submission,
Declines the honour: *try revisions.*

A scream escapes mid strangled swears
When agent soothingly declares
That *Purloin Press*, mandarin, august,
Are expanding their non-fiction list
And will accept your book profound
As codpiece to their New Age mound.
It might be worse, you can discern
No saviour on the horizon:
Ideal worlds would be more lavish,
A Sylvia Beach in every parish.

A lunch at *Smash*, the guests are wined,
Agent and publisher, yourself resigned,
The contract signed, advance arranged,
Now baseless optimism descends,
Your manuscript is praised by all:
We'll certainly publish in the Fall.
Smashed, into the night you wander,
A modest cheque on which to ponder
Warms in your pocket for a while:
You are, it seems, quite gullible.

Vanessa, pert at twenty-five,
Edits your manuscript at *Verve*
(Coffee-shop cacophony by *Catatonia*,
Mies van der Rohe chairs from Barcelona).
In margins narrowed for economy
She lays down laws like *Deuteronomy*,
In *Weidenfeld* she learned her letters,
Hiberno-English she dismisses,
She hates your prose, can't understand
Why anything you writ should stand:
Even devotees of the Oxford Dictionary
Will not be familiar with your vocabulary,
Sentences should more simple be,
Cut every single par. by three.

Vanessa phones, now in a bar:
Your manuscript's too long by far,
Cut chapter seven, reduce nine,
I need revisions, Tuesday's fine.
By Tuesday, Vanessa is, it seems, 'unwell',
Or one, two, many *drinkies* tell,
On Thursday e-mails she has 'revised
All of chapter twenty-five':
Your hand goes to the telephone,
You only get a ringing tone.

Your agent counsels patience, tact.
In your dim brain has dawned the fact
That editors can with impunity alter
That which you burnished to a wafer,
Destroy the harmony of your prose,
Make nonsense of your noted 'nose',
Render absurd your erudition,
Reduce your words to repetition,
Prefer a cliché to a well-turned phrase,
Annihilate your stylish ways,
Make ignorant your every utterance,
Accept your work merely on sufferance,
Tax simple thoughts with wordy dross:
Your editor, *Coleridge*'s albatross.

Stella, eighteen, now joins the scene,
Intern, ambitious, faced with *Gleam.*
Vanessa's on maternity leave
And texts to Stella all her brief,
Who soon announces her opinion:
Your text is quite beneath derision.
To publisher, agent, you appeal:
Spare me this further round of hell.
Stella retracts, but will decree
Your *title* must change, instantly.

Lemuel, copy-editor of Anglo mien,
A *Gaeilgeoir-fascist* long has been,

His *pukka* rendering of your name
Not that your parents smiled upon:
I've gouged from your forename the fada
But four to your surname I have shackled.
Orthography rigid as Soviet *diktat*
Thought by a fool as literary *panache*:
Language politics can like scorpions sting,
Locust swarms of fadas will not a Gaelic Ireland bring.

The proofs arrive with one week deadline:
Sooner if poss., Ibiza's divine.
The text showcases Stella's hand,
Typos to fill the space expand.
Vanessa left nothing to fortuity
And slashed your failing continuity,
Words which in other times had grace
Computer hyp-henated in each place
Which usage, language, sense forbids.
You loudly mouth a *Jeremiad*:
Never, since English prose began
Did editors create parallelog-ram,
Nor wit permit a teenage doxy
Britannica to render poxy.

The proofs complete, you've compromised
On everything just to survive,
Your text, now barely recognisable,
Its highbrow tone reduced to babble.

Chloe, a nymph of fifty-three,
Your publicist, has a degree
In marketing; it might as well
Be toxic waste she has to sell,
Or condoms, doubtful potions for
Noisy bowel syndrome, roofing tar.
You shudder when she ethics utter,
Her standards hover near the gutter:
We pile 'em high, and sell 'em fast,
Spare me your 'Books are meant to last'

Delusion of the eighteenth century
Promoted by the leisured gentry.
You know the adage about the kitchen?
We have three months to sell t'edition.
Copies then will be advertised
In pound shops, almost nationwide.

A publisher's aesthetic sense
Dictates a jacket's munificence.
Like camel of popular legend,
A horse, by committee intended,
The firm's directors sit en masse,
Make of your jacket, a jackass:
Inept typography, a hideous image,
As ordered as a rugger scrimmage.
Where professional wisdom would disdain,
Amateurism is the gain.
Unlettered in the visual arts,
They chose the worst in all its parts:
The world your work will greet with yawns,
Clad in uncouth and purblind tones.

Your book is launched, reviews peremptory,
C. Ricks in *TLS,* complimentary.
Media interviews are tricky,
You lose the run of self on *Kenny.*
Signings in *Waterstones* are slender,
A sales assistant blames the weather.
Then sales improve: the *Irish Times*
Best-seller list has numinous lines,
Your book is there at number two;
Next week – but fate can good undo –
Next week you drop to number five.
How does that wretched *Truss* survive?

Not chick-lit miss by fame beguiled,
Nor eminent author of a tome on Wilde,
Nor youth whose modish, mannered prose
Has missed the *Booker* by a slender nose,

Nor scholar – you have read his paper,
Cloacal witterings from Drapier ? –
Nor author dropped, his work endangered
And left in stacks to be remaindered,
Can hope, for all their sweated labour
And contract clauses in their favour,
That when their royalties are paid
The sum will buy a walking aid.

Then authors, in your vain attempts
A decent living to invent,
May sell your books on 'Connell Bridge
Or dump the volumes in a ditch,
But Irish publishers avoid:
Their soothing blandishments are cloyed.
To Thames or Hudson, Amazon go,
Your precious manuscripts in tow,
Display them not around the Liffey
And poorer grow with publishers iffy.

There published be in *Stubbs Gazette*
To rival authors' merriment,
Defeated by your publishers' whims,
Incompetence, duplicity and madcap scams.
You often spoke of foreign tours,
Of books of yours which won awards,
They greet you now in *Eason*'s window
Two copies gratis with the '*Indo*'.

Pride (they say) cometh before a fall,
The dole (they say) it leveleth all,
The best-sellers list is rigged (they say),
Be published, and be damned today.

BRIAN LALOR

Míl Espáine and links between
Ireland and Spain

Fergus Gillespie

IN 1692 DON BERNARDO O NEILL, an army officer in the city of Santiago de Compostela, published a pamphlet for submission to the king of Spain, Charles II.[1] Some time before this Don Bernardo – or Brian, for he states that he was born in Aughnacloy, Co. Tyrone – was nominated as a knight of the Military Order of Santiago. The pamphlet was essentially a petition requesting that the king dispense with certain costs arising from the knighthood as Don Bernardo had no money apart from his salary as an army officer.[2] He gives an account of his army career, and mentions other soldiers of his kindred in the king's service and a number who had died in active service for Spain and the Catholic church. The most notable feature of the pamphlet is that Don Bernardo reminds the king of the blood ties that existed between the Spanish people and the O'Neills, because, as he says, the Irish were descended from Míl Espáine or Milesius of Spain, who lived long before the time of Christ. He goes on to list fourteen authorities to support his Milesian genealogy. These include Isidore, archbishop of Seville in the early seventh century, Florián de Ocampo, sixteenth-century chronicler to Charles I of Spain, and Pilib Ó Súilleabháin Bhéara, author of *Historiae Catholicae Iberniae Compendium*, published at Lisbon in 1621.

The king would almost certainly have known the story of the sons of Míl and their supposed conquest of Ireland. It is likely that he had it in mind when he issued a proclamation in 1680 confirming that the Irish who resided in Spain were to have the same rights and privileges as Spaniards in respect of the obtaining of offices or employments.[3] The proclamation declares: 'No obstacle has ever

---

1 Bernardo O Neill, *Relación de los cavalleros irlandeses de la casa de O Neill, Condes de Tiron, en el Reyno de Irlanda, sus parientes, y séquito en la Provincia de Ultonia, que han servido, y muerto en defensa de la Corona de España desde el año de mil quinientos y catorce à esta parte, que en la real consideración de su Magested haze memoria Don Bernardo O Neill, sargento mayor de la civdad de Santiago, Cavatos de Arçua, Mellid, Guititis, y sus Partidos, en el Reyno de Galicia* [n.p., n.d]. The pamphlet is in the manuscripts department of the Biblioteca Nacional, Madrid.   **2** For an account of Don Bernardo and his petition see M. Kerney Walsh, 'Don Bernardo O Neill of Aughnacloy, Co. Tyrone', *Seanchas Ard Mhacha*, 10:2 (1982), 320–30.   **3** Kerney Walsh, 'Don Bernardo O Neill', 320.

been placed in the way of their obtaining political or military appointments in their turn with Spaniards. Such has always been the custom and this is what at present is being observed.'[4] The proclamation largely reiterated the provisions of the Hapsburg-Desmond treaty of Dingle (1529) in which Charles I of Spain granted full rights and the graces and privileges of citizenship in the Spanish *monarquía* to the Irish.[5] The supposed ancestral link between the two peoples was also forthrightly acknowledged in a letter of 1602 from Count Caracena, governor of Galicia, to Philip III, in which he refers to the Irish as *nuestros hermanos irlandeses, los españoles del norte* (our Irish brothers, the Spanish of the north).[6]

Don Bernardo O Neill was not the first Irishman who made reference to his remote Spanish origins when seeking assistance or royal favours from the Spanish crown. Petitions preserved in the Archivo General de Simancas in Valladolid and in other Spanish archives attest that from the sixteenth to the eighteenth century various Hiberno-Norman and Gaelic notables made particular mention of Míl Espáine and the Spanish origin of the Irish when petitioning the monarch for political and military assistance against the English. Most notably perhaps, Aodh Ruadh Ó Domhnaill, lord of Tirconnell, referred to the connection on a historic occasion shortly after the battle of Kinsale. An Irish army led by Hugh O'Neill, earl of Tyrone, and Aodh Ruadh suffered a crushing defeat (24 December 1601) at the hands of Lord Mountjoy, Queen Elizabeth's deputy in Ireland, after they failed to rendezvous with their Spanish allies who were besieged by the English inside the town of Kinsale. Following the withdrawal of the Spaniards, Aodh Ruadh set sail for Spain to seek further assistance for the Irish cause from Philip III. He landed near La Coruña in northwest Spain. The Annals of the Four Masters take up the story:

> They came to port the fourteenth day of the same month [January 1602], near La Coruña, a famous town in the kingdom of Galicia in Spain. Breoghan's tower, called Brigantia, was located there. It had been built long before by Breoghan, son of Bráth, and it was from there that the sons of Míl of Spain ... had first come to conquer Ireland ... When Ó Domhnaill landed at La Coruña, he went around the town and went to see Breoghan's tower. He was very happy to have landed there, for he deemed it a good omen of his success that he should have come to the

4 Untitled typescript by Patrick McBride in possession of Concha Castells, p. 2. The late Professor McBride was founder and first director of the Overseas Archives at University College, Dublin. **5** D. Downey, 'Purity of blood and purity of faith in early modern Ireland', in A. Ford and J. McCafferty (eds), *The origins of sectarianism in early modern Ireland* (Cambridge, 2005), pp 223–4. **6** Ibid., p. 225.

place from which his ancestors had obtained dominance and power over Ireland in former times. It was clearly a moment of great emotion and hope for Ó Domhnaill, but his hopes were not to be realised: he died the following September on his way to meet King Philip at Valladolid.[7]

The tower that Aodh Ruadh visited still stands. It was originally a Roman lighthouse known as the Torre de Hercules. In Spanish tourist literature it is sometimes called Torre de Breogan. A large statue, a modern representation of Breoghan with drawn sword and round shield, now stands at the beginning of the path leading to it. The lighthouse, as it is today, is depicted on the flag in the illustration on page 273.

The most complete account of the story of Míl Espáine and the conquest of Ireland by his sons is to be found in *Leabhar Gabhála* (The Book of Invasions), a Middle Irish text which dates from the eleventh century and survives in various recensions.[8] *Leabhar Gabhála* provides a genealogical tree of the Gaelic Irish beginning with Noah. It explains the origins of such words as *Féni*, *Gaedhil* and *Scotti* (all meaning 'the Irish') by reference to such invented personages as Fénius Farsaid, who took the Irish language from the Tower of Babel, and Scotta, daughter of Pharaoh, and her son Gaedheal Glas from whom the Gaels (*Goídil*) are supposed to have descended. Like the Israelites, the descendants of Gaedheal Glas are said to have fled from Egypt to escape persecution by Pharaoh. After wandering for many generations they finally settled in Spain, where Míl was born. Míl's grandfather Breoghan had built the city of Brigantia (that is, La Coruña) in northern Galicia which he adorned with a lofty tower. Breoghan's son, Íth, was the first to see Ireland from the top of the tower as he gazed out across the ocean north-eastwards on a winter's evening. The adventurous Íth afterwards sailed to Ireland accompanied by 150 warriors, but was killed by the Tuatha Dé Danann, a mythical people said to have been dominant here before the Milesian invasion. The sons of Míl then invaded Ireland to avenge Íth's death; they landed in the south-west at a location named Inber Scéne, literally 'the mouth of the river Scéne'.

According to *Leabhar Gabhála*, Míl's sons, Éremón, Éber and Ír, were the ancestors of a number of the more prominent Irish dynasties or tribes. In this scenario, Éremón was ancestor of the Connachta, the Uí Néill of the midlands and the north, the Déssi of Munster, the Dál Riata and Dál Fiatach of Ulster and the men of Alba (Scotland). The second son, Éber, was ancestor of the

---

7 Annals of the Four Masters, 1602; translation by the author. **8** *Lebor Gabála Érenn: the book of the taking of Ireland*, ed. and trans. with notes by R.A.S. Macalister, 5 vols (Dublin, 1938–56).

12 Flag flown by the yachts of the Irish Cruising Club on their visit to Galicia in 1998, incorporating allusions to the Milesian story and the pilgrimage to the shrine of St James at Santiago de Compostela: design by Fergus Gillespie, drawing by Katy Lumsden (chief herald painter in the National Library of Ireland).

Éoganachta of Cashel and of Munster as a whole, and of the Lemnaig of Scotland. The third son, Ír, was presented as the ancestor of the Ulaid (men of Ulster), and so on. The names of all three appear to be represented in early nomenclature: Éremón in *Ériu* (later *Éire*), Éber in *Iberia* (Spain) and Ír in *Írland* (Old Norse for Ireland). Although *Leabhar Gabhála* contains some genuine tradition, most of it is pseudo-history and is ultimately based on the chronicle of Eusebius of Caesarea, who flourished in the fourth century. It was compiled by the Irish learned classes to give a place to Ireland in world history. For example, the synchronised list of pre-Christian Gaelic kings incorporates the names of biblical kings and kings of ancient Greece, among others.

The *Leabhar Gabhála* was first written down in the eleventh century and is the culmination of the *Seanchas Coitchenn* or accepted doctrine of the official historians of early medieval Ireland. It claimed that the genealogical lines of Irish dynasties, great and small, emerged long before the Christian era from the Gaelic line which descended through the common ancestor, Míl Espáine/Milesius. This doctrine first sought to legitimize the hegemony of supposed Gaelic dynasties such as the Uí Néill of the midlands and the north and the Eóganachta dynasties of Munster, which had subdued earlier population groups such as the Érainn. As time passed, the older population groups, including the Érainn, the Dál Riada, and the Déssi, were also given Milesian genealogies, thus assimilating them into the Gaelic genealogical scheme that provided a racial and cultural homogeneity for all prominent pre-Norman and non-Viking tribes and families.[9]

The myth of the taking of Ireland by the sons of Míl goes back, however, long before *Leabhar Gabhála* and the Middle Irish period. It features in a long poem in Old Irish, 'Cad a mbunadhas na nGaedheal' (What is the origin of the Gael?), written by Máel Mura, abbot of Fahan in Donegal, who died in 887. This is substantially the story as in *Leabhar Gabhála*, but it deals only with the Connachta (Uí Néill) and the Eoganachta of Munster.[10] A slightly earlier version appears in the *Historia Brittonum* by the Welshman Nennius, a work dated to the early decades of the ninth century.[11] Míl is also referred to in the seventh- or eighth-century grammatical work *Auricept na nÉces*[12] and in seventh-century genealogical poems relating to the kings of Leinster.

The myth appears to have originated in Spain rather than Ireland, the germ of it being found in the writings of two Spaniards – Orosius, a fifth-century scholar who compiled a history of the world, and Isidore of Seville, author of a number of important seventh-century texts. Orosius is believed to have been born in Braga in modern north-west Portugal, close to the border with Galicia. His *Historiarum adversum Paganos Libri Septem* (completed in 418) has an account of Ireland which claims that Spain can be seen from the mouth of the river 'Scena' (*ostium fluminis Scene,* Early Irish *Inber Scéne*) in the west of Ireland.[13] Some manuscripts of the text, however, give 'Sena', suggesting the mouth of the Shannon.[14] This identification is supported by Ptolemy's geography of Ireland (*c.*AD 150): Francis John Byrne's reconstruction of 'Ptolemy's map' places

9 F. Gillespie, 'Irish genealogy and pseudo-genealogy', *Proceedings of the First Genealogical Congress* [Dublin, 1991], pp 123–37.   **10** Máel Mura Othna, 'Cad a mbunadhas na nGaedhel' in *The Book of Leinster*, ed. R.I. Best et al., 6 vols (Dublin, 1954–83), iii, 516–23.   **11** *Nennius, British history and the Welsh annals*, ed. and trans. by John Morris, History from the Sources (London, 1980), pp 20–21, 61–62.   **12** A. Ahlqvist (ed.), *The early Irish linguist: an edition of the canonical part of* Auricept na nÉces, *with introduction, commentary and index*, Commentationes Humanarum Litterarum 73 (Helsinki, 1983), pp 36–7, 47–8.   **13** Paulus Orosius, *Historiarum adversus paganos libri septem*, ed. C. Zangmeister (Leipzig, n.d.), p. 12.   **14** R.M. Scowcroft, 'Leabhar Gabhála: part II', *Ériu*, 39 (1988), 15, n. 38.

Senos at the mouth of the Shannon.[15] The same location was probably also intended as the supposed site of the Milesian landing.

In his account of Spain, Orosius stated that there was a lofty lighthouse in Brigantia in Galicia that was directed *ad speculam Britanniae*.[16] The Irish would have understood from this that Britain was visible from Galicia; since Orosius also said that Ireland was situated between Spain and Britain, they took it that Ireland was also visible from the lighthouse.[17] Two centuries later, Isidore of Seville repeated much of Orosius' account of Ireland in his great work the *Etymologiae*, but he also added something new: the word *Hibernia* (Ireland) derives from *Iberia*, the Latin word for Spain.[18]

As the germ of the story in *Leabhar Gabhála* is to be found in the works of Orosius and Isidore, both of whom were Spaniards writing in the fifth and seventh centuries respectively, questions arise as to how the Irish, living on the edge of the world, came to know their works so well and why they used these works as the basis for their origin story. A partial and rather fanciful answer to the question is presented by a text in the twelfth-century Book of Leinster, 'Do fhallsigud Tána Bó Cuailgne', which relates to Senchán Torpéist, *ardollamh* (chief learned man) of Ireland, who died about the year 650.[19] It claims that Senchán convened a meeting of his fellow learned men to determine if any of them could recite the Ulster epic poem *Táin Bó Cuailgne* (The cattle raid of Cooley), which tells of the incursion by Medb, queen of Connacht, into the territory of the Ulaid or Ulstermen which was defended by the Ulster hero Cú Chulainn. The learned men could not oblige, and Senchán discovered that it was because the *Táin* had been taken to the Continent and given in exchange for the *Culmen*, a work which had been compiled there shortly before. It may be relevant that the sympathies of *Táin Bó Cuailgne* do not lie with the Gaelic dynasties descended from Míl, but rather with the Érainn who, according to T.F. O'Rahilly, had been in Ireland long before the Gaelic peoples arrived here and had been subjected by them; for example, the Ulaid, or people of Ulster, were subjected by the Connachta (Uí Néill) from the fourth or fifth centuries onwards.[20] The implication may have been that the Gaels had little interest in the *Táin*, and so exchanged it for the *Culmen* which had important associations.

15 T.W. Moody, F.X. Martin, F.J. Byrne (eds), *A new history of Ireland*, ix: *Maps, genealogies, lists: a companion to Irish history, II* (Oxford, 1984), p. 16; see also T.F. O'Rahilly, *Early Irish history and mythology* (Dublin, 1946), p. 4. **16** Orosius, *Historiarum adversum paganos libri septem*, p. 11. **17** Ibid., p. 12. **18** *Isidori hispanalensis episcopi etymologiarum sive originum*, ed. W.M. Lindsay, 2 vols (Oxford, 1913), i, liber XIV, par. 6. Isidore's account of Ireland is to be found in the oldest redaction of *Leabhar Gabhála*, the *Mínugud* (the explanation). **19** 'Do fhallsigud Tána Bó Cuailgne' in *The Book of Leinster*, v, p. 1119. **20** O'Rahilly, *Early Irish history and mythology*, pp 75ff, 222ff.

Tomás Ó Máille has shown that the *Culmen* was none other than Isidore of Seville's most famous work, the *Etymologiae*. Indeed, Isidore was often called 'Isidór in *Chuilmein*' (Isidore of the *Culmen*) in Irish.[21] The story suggests that Isidore's works were already available in Ireland in the first half of the seventh century. It also probably means that in the early seventh century the learned classes were becoming increasingly interested in the new Latin learning that was being introduced from abroad. There is certainly considerable evidence that Isidore's *Etymologiae* was studied in Ireland from an early date. For example, the archaic genealogical poems of the early seventh century mentioned above contain genealogies that go back to Míl of Spain, and from him to Gomer, son of Japheth, son of Noah. One of the poems provides a list of the peoples of Europe – the descendants of Japheth – which is taken straight from Book IX of Isidore's *Etymologiae*.[22] James Carney has dated the Milesian part of the poems to the first half of the seventh century. He has also argued that it was the poet Senchán Torpéist, writing about 630, who developed the ideas of Orosius and Isidore and formulated the Milesian origin legend which appeared in its final form in the eleventh-century *Leabhar Gabhála*.[23]

In addition to Orosius and Isidore, the Irish also had the works of other Spanish authors to hand. Columbanus (*c.*561–615), chief reader at the monastic school of Bangor and founder of the monasteries of Luxeuil in France and Bobbio in northern Italy, mentions Juvencus, a fourth-century Spanish priest who wrote a version of the four gospels in verse.[24] One of Columbanus' poems, 'Ad Hunaldum', which was written for a pupil or a former pupil, borrows a line from Juvencus.[25] The editor of the collected works, G.S.M. Walker, believed that the poem was written before Columbanus left Ireland for the Continent in 590.[26] The circulation of Juvencus' works in Ireland is further attested by the manuscript tradition: the earliest extant manuscript – of which only a fragment remains – was written here in the seventh century, the next earliest being an eighth-century Spanish manuscript.[27]

It is significant that Columbanus is the first Irishman known to have called the Irish 'Spaniards'. Writing from Milan to Pope Boniface IV in 613, at the time of the Arian heresy, he makes the claim: 'For all we *Irish*, inhabitants of the world's edge, are disciples of Saints Peter and Paul … and we accept noth-

21 T. Ó Máille, 'The authorship of the Culmen', *Ériu*, 9 (1921–23), 71–6. He cites the Book of Ballymote (*c.*1400) as a source for his identification.   **22** M.A. O'Brien, *Corpus genealogiarum Hiberniae* (Dublin, 1962), pp 2–7.   **23** J. Carney, 'Three old Irish accentual poems', *Ériu* 22 (1971), 65–73, esp. p. 73.   **24** G.S.M. Walker (ed.), *Sancti Columbani opera*, Scriptores Latini Hiberniae 2 (Dublin, 1970), p. lxvii.   **25** Ibid., pp 184–7.   **26** Ibid., p. lvii.   **27** J.N. Hillgarth, 'The east, Visigothic Spain and the Irish', *Studia Patristica*, 4 (1961), 447–8.

ing outside the evangelical and apostolic teaching.' Rather than using the usual term *Scotti*, or even *Hibernici*, for the Irish, Columbanus uses *Iberi* ('Spaniards'), which must have given rise to some initial confusion in Rome.[28] Likewise, in a letter in defence of his Irish customs addressed to a French synod ten years earlier, he wrote: 'For we are all joint members of one body, whether Franks, or Britons or Spaniards (*Iberi*).' The context here suggests that he meant 'Irish'.[29] Columbanus' references to the Irish as Spaniards predates Isidore's *Etymologiae* (written between 612 and 620), suggesting that at least some aspects of the Milesian myth were current in Ireland in an earlier period.

Among the other Spaniards whose works were studied in Ireland in the seventh century were Priscillian, the Spanish theologian and bishop of Ávila who was put to death for heresy in the fourth century, Martin of Braga who founded the monastery of Dumio in the sixth century, and Julian of Toledo who wrote the *Ars Grammatica* in the seventh century.[30] Notable evidence of Spanish influence is also provided by the famous letter of Cummian Foto, abbot of Clonfert, to Segéne, abbot of Iona, concerning the proper computation of the date of Easter. The letter advocated the adoption of the 19-year Roman cycle and the abandonment of the traditional Irish 84-year cycle still observed by Iona and in the northern part of Ireland.[31] Among the sources used by Cummian in developing his argument were theses written in Africa and later used in Spain; they appear to have been introduced to Ireland from Spain some time before Cummian compiled his letter in 632–3.[32]

Of the Spanish texts circulating in Ireland in the early middle ages, those of Isidore were most familiar. Isidore was born about the year 560 and was archbishop of Seville from 600 to 636. He was a theologian, a doctor of the Church and a prolific writer. During his lifetime he saw great changes in the political and cultural life of Visigothic Spain, especially in relation to the church. One of the more notable events of the period was that in 587 the Visigothic King Reccared abandoned Arianism and adopted Catholicism. Throughout the seventh century Spain had no equal in spirituality and classical learning in the western world, with the exception of Ireland.[33] Among the works of Isidore known and studied in Ireland were a grammatical lexicon (*De Differentiis Verborum*), a discourse on cosmology and meteorology (*De Natura Rerum*), and religious works (*Sententiae* and *De Differentiis Rerum*). But the work most used by Irish scholars was his *Etymologiae*. Arranged in twenty books, this great

---

28 Walker, *Sancti Columbani opera*, pp 38–9. **29** Ibid., pp 22–3. The synod was probably that held at Chalon in 603. **30** Hillgarth, 'The east, Visigothic Spain and the Irish', 447–8. **31** D. Ó Cróinín, *Early medieval Ireland, 400–1200* (London, 1995), pp 152–3. **32** J.N. Hillgarth, 'Ireland and Spain in the seventh century', *Peritia*, 3 (1984), 10. **33** Ibid., 3ff.

encyclopaedia summarizes all the knowledge of the sciences and the humanities available from classical sources. Each book concerns itself with a particular branch of learning – grammar, medicine, the church, peoples, languages, and so on. As mentioned above, the *Etymologiae* (Book IX) was a source for an early seventh-century genealogical poem, and also for the seventh- or eighth-century *Auricept na nÉces*, which is attributed to Cenn Fáelad who died in 679. As it has come down to us, the *Auricept* is mostly in Middle Irish (post 900), but the oldest part, according to Anders Ahlqvist, could date from the seventh century.[34] This part includes a description of the taking of the Irish language from Nimrod's Tower, the biblical Tower of Babel, which was later used in *Leabhar Gabhála*.[35]

Isidore is more widely attested in Hiberno-Latin texts than in Irish texts, and here also the *Etymologiae* was the work most commonly used as a source. For example, Laidcenn Mac Baíth Baindaig (died 661), scholar of Clonfertmulloe, Co. Laois, availed of it for his exegetical treatise *Ecloga de Moralibus Job*, as did Malsachanus in the compilation of his grammar. It was very obviously a model for the pseudo-Isidorian *Liber de Ordine Creaturum* which was compiled between 680 and 700.[36] It can also be identified as a source for *Hisperica Famina*, a satire on the schools written in experimental and curious Latin and compared by E.K. Rand to *Finnegans Wake*.[37] It would appear that the interest in Isidore continued well into the eighth century. For example, the early eighth-century *Collectio Canonum Hibernensis* used six of his works, and he was also a source for the grammatical text *Anonymous ad Cuimnanum*, which dates from *c*.740.[38]

In contrast to the widespread transmission of Isidore's works in seventh-century Ireland, it would seem that they did not reach Italy until the eighth century, when they were introduced following the Moorish invasion of Spain. There is no evidence that they were known in France before the end of the seventh century, and the same is true for England. Aldhelm (640–709), abbot of Malmesbury in Wiltshire, who began writing late in the seventh century, appears to be the first Anglo-Saxon to refer to Isidore.[39] It may be significant that Aldhelm was educated under the Irishman Máeldub, who founded the monastery of Malmsbury. In the case of Ireland, it appears that there was considerable contact with Spain in the seventh and eighth centuries and that Isidore's works were introduced directly from Spain.

34 Ahlqvist, *The early Irish linguist*, pp 36–7.   **35** Ibid., p. 47.   **36** M.C. Díaz y Díaz (ed.), *Liber de ordine creaturum; un anónimo Irlandés del siglo VII: estudio y edición crítica* (Santiago de Compostela, 1972), p. 20 *et passim*.   **37** E.K. Rand, 'The Irish flavour of the *Hisperica Famina*' in *Studien zur Lateinischen Dichtung des Mittelalters: Ehrengabe für K. Strecker*, ed. W. Stach and H. Walther (Dresden, 1931), pp 134–42.   **38** Hillgarth, 'The east, Visigothic Spain and the Irish', 451–2.   **39** Hillgarth, 'Ireland and Spain in the seventh century', 6–7.

J.N. Hillgarth has claimed that it was from Galicia that Spanish literature was brought to Ireland. He has also drawn attention to the manner in which the liturgical rite in that region came under Irish influence and to similarities between aspects of monasticism there and in Ireland. According to Hillgarth, Spanish manuscripts were first acquired by monasteries in the south of Ireland, such as Lismore and Clonfertmulloe. Geographically, these monasteries were closer to Spain than those in the northern half of the country, but they were also closer in terms of observance and spirituality.[40] For example, the southern monasteries adopted the Roman dating for Easter around 630, bringing themselves into line with practice in Spain and elsewhere, while their northern counterparts do not appear to have conformed until considerably later.

Nevertheless, the north of Ireland seems also to have been subject to Spanish influence, as suggested, for instance, by the Greek inscription on a cross at Fahan in Inishowen in Donegal which is a copy of a doxology first used in 633 at the Fourth Council of Toledo.[41] The date of the Fahan cross is uncertain, but the style indicates that it is probably eighth century. In addition to the various writings already referred to, a number of prayers for use in the Mass and in the monastic office have also been identified as being of Spanish origin, which suggests that liturgical writings were introduced from Spain at an early date. Among the more notable examples of Spanish influence on Irish liturgical literature is the Antiphonary of Bangor (Co. Down), preserved in a manuscript in the Ambrosian Library in Milan and thought to be one of the earliest surviving liturgical manuscripts from western Europe.[42] The editor of the antiphonary, Michael Curran, has shown that at least four of the collects (short seasonal prayers) are of Spanish origin, four are of probable Spanish origin, one is of possible Spanish origin, and a strong Spanish influence can be detected in others.[43] According to Curran, complete liturgical texts were not imported from Spain but individual prayers were copied by Irish monks visiting or resident there. He concluded that Spain was the predominant influence on seventh-century Irish liturgy. Like Hillgarth, he believed that the church in Galicia was in turn influenced by Irish monasticism, particularly in relation to penitential discipline and community rule.[44]

In 711 the Moors invaded Spain and it was not long before most of the peninsula was under their control. It would seem that there was little contact

40 Hillgarth, 'The east, Visigothic Spain and the Irish', 454–5. **41** F. Henry, *Irish art in the early Christian period (to 800 A.D.)* (Ithaca, NY, 1963), pp 126–7; she claims that the Spanish formula 'Glory and honour be to the Father and to the Son and to the Holy Ghost' was known in Ireland in the seventh century. See also R.A.S. Macalister, *Corpus inscriptionum insularum Celticarum*, 2 vols (Dublin, 1945–9), i, 118–20. **42** The antiphonary was written into the manuscript towards the end of the seventh century. **43** M. Curran (ed.), *The antiphonary of Bangor and the early Irish monastic liturgy* (Dublin, 1984), p. 151. **44** Ibid., pp 153–4.

between Ireland and Spain in the centuries that followed, although Isidore and
other Spanish writers continued to influence Irish writers for many centuries.
Following the invasion, many Spaniards fled the country and manuscripts were
taken to other parts of Europe; it is possible that some of them reached Ireland.

Returning to the Milesian origin legend, the sixteenth-century historian and
chronicler to Charles I, Florián de Ocampo (1499–1554), has provided echoes
of the story. In his *Crónica General de España*, Ocampo refers to the mythical
Brigo, king of Spain, who is mentioned in the chronicles of Spain:

> Others, however, say that Brigo settled people on a great island which is
> now called Irlanda but which in earlier times was called Ibernia. This island
> is near England and it is said that it was once also called Yerna and that
> Brigo was its king. And when these people came to this country [Ireland]
> they were called Brigantes because there was a great river flowing through
> the country that was called Brigo. I remember once when we arrived by
> good fortune from the sea. We came ashore at a city called Catafurda
> (Waterford?). The citizens, with some others who came from outside,
> showed great joy on meeting the Spaniards, taking us by the hand as a sign
> that they knew who we were, and saying that they were of Spanish origin,
> which for me was something new. But then I recalled what I had heard
> about this matter in the chronicles of Joannes Annius de Viterbo. I also
> recalled that when the Arabs and the Moors conquered the Spanish in the
> time of Don Rodrigo, king of the Goths, many Spaniards fled to ... that
> island ... Although many returned to Spain, it is possible that many
> remained on the island mingling with the natives ... and this resulted in
> the kinship that exists between the Irish and the Spaniards.
>
> They have a tradition which has come down from father to son about
> a Spaniard who lived in olden times in the north coast of Spain, who
> was called Iberno or Hierno. While voyaging on the sea he was caught
> in a great storm ... which brought them in only three days of journey-
> ing to that island, which had no inhabitants. Their boat was wrecked in
> the storm. They remained there, as did some women they had brought
> there. And because of that Hierno, or Iberno, they first called the island
> Yerno or Ibernia. These are all the ways in which the above mentioned
> kinship could continue, a kinship of which the Irish are so proud.[45]

Ocampo's *Crónica* was published in 1578, twenty-four years after his death.
It was one of the sources cited by Don Bernardo O Neill in his petition to

---

45 F. de Ocampo, *Los cinco libros primeros de la crónica general de España* (Alcalá, 1578), pp
20v–21r; translation by the author.

Charles II mentioned above. Don Bernardo was installed as a knight of the Military Order of Santiago in September 1692. His parents were given as Don Diego O Neill of Aughnacloy and Doña Magarita Maguierr of Clogher. Among his nineteen sponsors were Felipe Patricio, ensign in the Spanish service, Juan Chloe of Galway, Tomás O Lanan, Augustinian, of Tipperary, Ambrosio O Conor, Dominican, Reimundo Tuite of Leinster, Guillermo Geraldino of Kildare, and Guillermo Morfi, knight of Santiago, who was later a general in the Spanish army.[46] The first Irishman to be created a knight of Santiago was Domhnall Ó Súilleabháin Bhéara (Dónall O'Sullivan Beare), who is named as Don Daniel O Sulivan de Bearhaben. His sponsors, like those of O Neill, were of Old English as well as Gaelic Irish stock. One of them was the count of Puñoenrostro, member of the Spanish Supreme Council of War, who is titled Protector of the Irish in Spain.[47]

The Irish were not just given protection by the Spanish. Philip III (reigned 1598–1621) made no distinction between the Irish and Spaniards, and in 1680, as already noted, a royal decree confirmed that the Irish in Spain were to be accounted Spaniards. In April 1701, when another royal decree granted special rights to Irish and English Catholics resident in Spain for more than ten years, the Irish protested at their being mentioned in conjunction with the English, fearing that their ancient privileges were being disregarded. A new decree was promptly published the following June, confirming their ancient rights. As late as 1792, a resolution of the Spanish Council of State again affirmed that the Irish, unlike other foreigners resident in Spain, were to be accounted Spanish. There is no evidence that these privileges were ever revoked. The Irish and their descendants were extraordinarily successful in Spain, being ambassadors to Austria, England, Russia, Sweden and many other countries; they also provided prime ministers and ministers of war and external affairs. In the seventeenth and eighteenth centuries no less than 150 generals were Irish or of Irish origin. It is surely a matter of some significance that no other foreigners in Spain reached these heights with such frequency and regularity.[48]

---

46 M. Kerney Walsh, *Spanish knights of Irish origin*, 4 vols (Dublin 1960–78), i, 30–1. **47** Ibid., i, pp 1–2. **48** Typescript by Patrick McBride cited in fn. 4 above, pp 1–4.

'A gruesome case':
James Joyce's Dublin murder case

Adrian Hardiman

THE GRUESOME CASE which is the subject of this essay is the meeting point of three separate story lines. One is of a Dublin family of three brothers, the money they made or lost, two wills, a violent death and the trial of one brother for the murder of another in 1899. The second story line concerns a young man who attended the trial and later became the most influential writer of the twentieth century,[1] and who incorporated the case into his greatest work. The third is the story of two lawyers who jointly conducted the defence at the trial, one of whom provoked the enmity and the other the admiration of the writer. The former, after a brilliant if unorthodox career, became the first governor general of the Irish Free State.[2] The latter, a scion of two of the most prominent Protestant families of the nineteenth century, was enveloped in a scandal of his own and left Ireland within a few years of the trial.[3]

On 3 September 1899, when James Joyce was 17 years old, a wealthy old man of impeccable background was found bludgeoned to death in his house beside Glasnevin cemetery. He lived in 5 Bengal Terrace, a sombre place still extant, whose dinginess belies its exotic name.[4] Joyce knew the area well: a relative lived next door and since he was 11 years old he had accompanied his father, who was an assiduous funeral-goer in the Dublin tradition, to many burials in the great Catholic necropolis. Both the crime and the subsequent trial for murder of the dead man's brother, Samuel Childs, a retired accountant from Brooks Thomas (a well-known Dublin firm of builders' providers), fascinated the writer for years. Like other events of his youth, it is refracted frequently and unpredictably in Ulysses, that most prismatic of novels.

At 11.00 a.m. on the original Bloomsday, 16 June 1904, Joyce has Mr Leopold Bloom with three other solid citizens of Dublin, including Mr Power, a Dublin Castle official, sitting in a horse-drawn carriage making its way, as part

1 R. Ellmann, James Joyce (Oxford, 1982 [1959]), p. 91. 2 F. Callanan, T.M. Healy (Cork, 1996), passim. 3 M. Healy, The old Munster circuit (repr., London, 2001) pp 46, 246 and passim. 4 All Dublin newspapers of the time carry accounts of the crime, investigation and trial. I have used principally the Daily Express.

of Patrick Dignam's funeral procession, from 9 Newbridge Avenue,
Sandymount, to Glasnevin cemetery. It is the 'Hades' episode of *Ulysses*. The
mood in the carriage is melancholy as befits the occasion. As the procession
approaches the burial ground, it passes on the right-hand side a row of six wide
but dingy houses of dirty red brick, Bengal Terrace:

> Gloomy gardens then went by: one by one: gloomy houses.
> Mr Power pointed.
> – That is where Childs was murdered, he said. The last house.
> – So it is, Mr Dedalus said. A gruesome case. Seymour Bushe got
> him off. Murdered his brother. Or so they said.[5]

They go on to consider the difficulties of circumstantial evidence.[6]

This is the first mention in *Ulysses* of the Childs murder case. In one way
or another, the case or its protagonists are referred to up to twenty times in the
text, sometimes very plainly, at other times obscurely. The case thus emerges
as one of the numerous threads, often submerged but constantly recurring, which
form the fabric of the great novel.

George Orwell famously lamented 'the decline of the English murder'[7] from
its heyday in late Victorian and Edwardian times. The Childs case, a sensation
in the Dublin of the day, was of that classic time and in the classic mode. The
victim was Thomas Childs, a wealthy old man with, so crown counsel later said,
the reputation of a miser. Much earlier in the century, his father, Alexander
Childs of Arran Quay, Dublin, had been carver and gilder to the lord lieutenant.
Thomas lived alone and very modestly in the unprepossessing six-room, three-
storey house beside Glasnevin cemetery: the lead prosecutor, Mr Serjeant Dodd
QC, pointed to the unusual feature that he 'transacted his own domestic business'.[8] He died in his front parlour on the night of 2 September 1899, a Saturday.
The room and the rest of his house were filled with books, 'the ancient classics
and the fine old classics of English literature', according to prosecuting counsel, as well as religious books. The books had mostly been inherited from the
deceased's brother, the Revd Edmond Childs, a clergyman of the Church of
Ireland. But the deceased, too, had been a reader and Dodd emphasized as
'somewhat pathetic' the fact that on his table was the *History of the Bible* with

5 *Ulysses*, 6. 467ff. All references to *Ulysses* are to the chapter and line numbers given in the
Corrected Text edited by Hans Walter Gabler (London, 1993, Bodley Head). **6** *Ulysses*, 6.
473. **7** George Orwell, 'The decline of the English murder' in *Shooting the elephant* (London,
1950). **8** Newspaper sources: the trial is comprehensively reported in the *Daily Express*
(Dublin), 20, 21, 23 Oct. 1899, and the following account is based largely on these reports.

the dead man's spectacles resting on two heavily blood-stained pages (1316 and 1317). There were two pools of blood near the victim's chair, a leg of which was broken off, and several splatters elsewhere. There was a kettle of water on the burnt-out fire, and glasses and a decanter of whiskey elsewhere in the room. The fire irons – poker, hammer and tongs – were around the room: the hammer was broken and the knob of the tongs was found elsewhere on the floor. The body, however, was not in the room. It had apparently been dragged from the parlour to another room across the hall. When examined, the dead man was found to be fully dressed, though with slippers on his feet, and to have two grievous wounds to the head, one overlying a depressed fracture, and a wound to the left forearm, suggesting an attempt to ward off a blow to the head.

Two features of the scene drew suspicion on to Samuel Childs, the dead man's brother. Samuel lived at 51 St Patrick's Road, Drumcondra, about a mile from Bengal Terrace. He was an accountant by profession who had retired in February 1899 as a result of a 'scheme of reorganization' with a pension of only one pound per week after many years with Brooks Thomas. Samuel was the only key holder apart from the dead man; the house, the Dublin Metropolitan Police (DMP) concluded, had not been entered forcibly. It was, in fact, virtually sealed against anyone but a key holder, or someone the occupant might admit. True, there was a back door but it was double-bolted and so badly cobwebbed that, the DMP thought, it could not have been opened for months. Furthermore, they said, Samuel Childs had met one of the constables investigating the case by chance on Tuesday afternoon, 5 September, at Dunphy's corner and had said to him in some distress: 'Suspicion points to me. Oh, that unfortunate latchkey.' Samuel said that he had found the body when he called to the house just after noon on Sunday, 3 September, when he had let himself in after getting no reply. He had alerted the neighbours and set off for Mountjoy DMP station. The previous night, he said, he had been home from 6.00 p.m. except for a few minutes around 8.00 p.m. when he had gone around to Cotter's grocers for a pint of whiskey to make punch.

If the latchkey showed that Samuel had the opportunity to commit the crime, the second discovery the DMP made seemed to show motive. In the parlour where Thomas Childs died, his business papers were found on a table and on several chairs. They showed him to be an active and methodical businessman, though he was in his seventy-seventh year. There was a cash box, open, three account books, dividend warrants, bank books, share certificates and deposit receipts. The accounts showed numerous small advances to Samuel Childs since 23 February 1899, about the time he had left Brooks Thomas' employ. Two-thirds of them had been repaid. There was also paper showing that Thomas Childs had just capitalized a loan society, the New Century Loan Society, with offices in Batchelor's Walk, of which Samuel Childs was secretary and a neighbour of Thomas, Mr Hilferty, was treasurer. But most telling of all, under the *History of the Bible* was the dead man's will, showing Samuel Childs as the principal beneficiary.

Accordingly, the police concluded, Samuel Childs was a newly poor man, with a wife and three children aged from 12 to 3 to support (though he was 61 years old) and in need of constant small loans. He had only one source of financial expectation, his brother's estate, and he possessed the only key to the virtually sealed house where the murder took place. Over the next few weeks, evidence was gathered showing that he had spent the afternoon preceding the crime in and out of various public houses, and had been seen opposite Hedigan's Brian Boru House, at Cross Guns Bridge, at 8.30 p.m. on that day. When, a few weeks later, a gravedigger and retired soldier called Norton came forward to identify Samuel as a man he had seen entering the house at 11.30 p.m. on the Saturday night, the noose tightened – literally and metaphorically.

Samuel was arrested and charged with the murder and lodged in Mountjoy jail to await his trial. This trial was, as his counsel Seymour Bushe QC was to point out in a fine Victorian flourish, 'to determine the aye or nay of that appalling alternative, whether he went hence to the home where wife and children awaited him, or on the other hand, whether from the cell in which he awaited his trial he merely passed to that other cell in which the convict awaited his doom – the vestibule of the grave'.

The trial took place between Thursday and Saturday, 19 to 21 October 1899. The case against Samuel, though circumstantial, seemed very strong. In opening the case for the crown, Serjeant Dodd said:

> The surrounding circumstances, the defendant's own conduct on the Saturday, his own motive for the crime, his own relationship to his brother and the fact that nobody else could have been in a position to commit the crime that night save the prisoner pointed irresistibly to one conclusion, that the hand that caused the death of Thomas Childs was the hand of Samuel Childs, the prisoner at the bar.

In this passage, counsel was describing precisely what is required before a conviction on circumstantial evidence can take place: the evidence must exclude any reasonable hypothesis other than the guilt of the accused.

Nevertheless, the prosecution case unravelled and Samuel Childs was acquitted. How did that happen? The answer Joyce gives is a simple one: he was acquitted by reason of the brilliant oratory of his leading defence counsel,

Seymour Bushe QC. In the 'Aeolus' chapter, which immediately follows the 'Hades' episode, the case comes up for discussion during an argument between a number of gentlemen – including Stephen Dedalus – assembled in the offices of the *Evening Telegraph* as to whether there are any contemporaries who could rival the great figures of the eighteenth and nineteenth centuries in polemical writing or in parliamentary or forensic oratory. The editor thinks not, but the broken-down barrister J.J. O'Molloy takes him on:

LINKS WITH BYGONE DAYS OF YORE

– Grattan and Flood wrote for this very paper,[9] the editor cried in his face. Irish volunteers. Where are you now? Established 1763. Dr Lucas. Who have you now like John Philpot Curran? Psha!

– Well, J.J. O'Molloy said, Bushe K.C., for example.

– Bushe? The editor said. Well, yes. Bushe, yes. He has a strain of it in his blood. Kendal Bushe or I mean Seymour Bushe.

– He would have been on the bench long ago, the professor said, only for … But no matter.

J.J. O'Molloy turned to Stephen and said quietly and slowly:

– One of the most polished periods I think I ever listened to in my life fell from the lips of Seymour Bushe. It was in that case of fratricide, the Childs murder case. Bushe defended him.[10]

A purported sample of Bushe's speech in the Childs case is subsequently quoted by O'Molloy:[11] the audience is awed.

Joyce's view of the Childs case – that it had been won by the sublime eloquence of Seymour Bushe – is repeated on several occasions in *Ulysses*. In the 'Oxen of the Sun' episode, the medical students attached to Holles Street hospital discourse, somewhat less than soberly, on various aspects of medicine and life. Bushe's compelling speech and the rightness of the verdict are acknowledged during a discussion of fratricide.[12] Later on, in the 'Ithaca' episode, Seymour Bushe KC is listed with Rufus Isaacs KC as an exemplar of the eminent barrister.[13]

Joyce is, however, radically wrong in his crediting of Seymour Bushe with the acquittal of Samuel Childs. The case was very fully reported at the time, both in the police court and in the court of trial. To anyone who reads these accounts, it is immediately clear that the credit for the acquittal belongs to Childs' other leading counsel, Timothy Michael Healy QC, MP. Healy, a shrewd, brilliant,

9 The *Freeman's Journal*, 'parent' paper of the *Evening Telegraph*, was established in 1763; the *Evening Telegraph* began publication only in 1871.   **10** *Ulysses*, 7. 737ff.   **11** *Ulysses*, 7. 766ff.   **12** *Ulysses*, 14. 955ff.   **13** *Ulysses*, 17. 786.

bitter and flamboyant figure whose political career stretched from his election to parliament as an acolyte of Parnell in 1880, through his subsequent ruthless leadership of the anti-Parnellite faction and on to a maverick parliamentary career in the early twentieth century – during which, however, he earned the wary respect of both the British establishment and of the emergent Sinn Féin. This unique position lead to his appointment (without much enthusiasm on anyone's part, it is true, but *faute de mieux*) as the first governor general of the Irish Free State in 1922. T.M. Kettle called him 'a brilliant calamity'.[14]

Healy was a very tough-minded barrister who took no prisoners. He appeared for Childs both in the police court and in the court of trial. It appears that from the first he noted the fundamental flaw in the crown case: they had allowed themselves to be so convinced that the crime must have been committed by Samuel Childs that they brought him to trial without considering the weaknesses of their case, or even whether there were any weaknesses. In fact, there were several. First, the house was not so hermetically sealed as the crown believed. This was revealed when the crown called a small boy called Richard Corcoran who lived next door to the deceased to say that he had seen him alive in his front garden at about 6.00 p.m. on the Saturday evening. The defence, however, cross-examined him about whether or not there was running water in the houses in Bengal Terrace. The crown's desperate objection to this very simple question suggests that they could see their theory unravelling. The boy said there was no running water in the houses but that each had a tap in the back yard. Each had a toilet there as well, and an ash pit. He, the boy, often went into the deceased's garden to play with Samuel Childs' children when they were on their weekly visit to the deceased with their father. He had personally seen the back door open not long before the crime.

This effectively ended the 'hermetically-sealed-house theory' but, like the Austrian cavalry defeated by Napoléon, the crown were unable to change front. The police witnesses at the trial continued to insist that the back door could not have been opened for a long time. Healy pointed to the fact that, on the crown case, the deceased had been boiling a kettle in his parlour when attacked. He asked where the water came from and a stolid sergeant of the DMP replied that he did not know where it came from, but that the back door had not been opened. The crown case then went from bad to worse. A scale model of the house, which they had prepared for the trial, had to be withdrawn in humiliating circumstances because it was incomplete. It did not show the rear of the house and left out several features of the front. It was admitted that the defendant had borrowed small sums from the deceased, but it transpired that the

14 Quoted in Callanan, *Healy*, p. 740, fn. 152.

deceased owed him a much larger sum. It turned out that when their clerical brother died about twelve years previously, he had left his estate to his two surviving brothers in equal shares. Samuel Childs, however, had allowed his brother to take his share, about £580, asking only that the sum be a first call on Thomas' property. Samuel's generosity in this was acknowledged in Thomas' will.

Then the identification evidence collapsed. First, the witness had not come forward for weeks after the alleged sighting; he said that his wife did not want him to. Secondly, he could not identify the defendant at an identification parade, but picked him out only when the men on the parade were asked to walk: he said that he identified him because he 'walked like a tailor'. He gave an elaborate description of the man's features in court but had to admit that he had not been able to give any such description to the police. Finally, when challenged by Healy to say, knowing the consequences of his evidence, whether he was sure the prisoner was the man he had seen, he said he could not say that. The man claiming to have seen Samuel at 8.30 p.m. was, manifestly, a drunk.

The DMP suffered a further, and possibly fatal, blow during the evidence of Superintendent Dempsey. The defence produced a letter from the commissioner of the force addressed to the deceased, written in reply to a complaint Thomas had made in July 1898 about 'corner boys' hanging around the area and breaking glass in windows. Although the commissioner said that Thomas' letter had been passed to superintendent, D Division, which was himself, Dempsey said he had never seen it. He had been told of it by an inspector, however, some days after the murder, but its existence had not been disclosed to the defence. The letter, when produced, turned out to contain a request for police protection because of the congregating of corner boys around the house and in the lane behind. This presented the prosecution with a serious problem in the form of the possibility of an opportunist small-time criminal hanging around the area. Their difficulty was worsened by defence cross-examination of their engineer. Perhaps shaken by having to admit the inaccuracy of his model and plans, he conceded that if one were in the laneway at the back of the garden there would be no difficulty in getting into the garden. Still worse, he said that if anyone said the back door opening into the garden had not been opened for years, it would be 'rank nonsense'.

All of this opened the possibility that the deceased might have left the house through the back door to visit the outside toilet or to get water from the tap, allowing a casual intruder entry into the house. There was no evidence that this had occurred and it is, of course, unlikely that an intruder would have left cash and valuables, including the deceased's watch, untouched. But the prosecution had committed themselves to the theory that the house was sealed against intrusion. Not only had that theory been exploded, but the deceased's request for police protection, never mentioned by the crown until the defence produced the commissioner's reply, raised the possibility at any rate of a lurking intruder. The fact that the crown concealed the letter added substance to the point.

The dramatic speech attributed to Seymour Bushe KC in *Ulysses* is not reflected in the contemporary records at all. He did make the opening speech for the defence, and made it very well. In addition to the points mentioned above, he emphasized that the crown's doctor conceded that the killer must have a lot of blood on him but none had been found on the accused. He was able to call highly respectable Protestant businessmen, doctors and clergymen to testify to the caring and affectionate relationship which existed between the Childs brothers. Indeed, a prosecution witness, Mr Hilferty who lived in 6 Bengal Terrace, positively stated that Thomas Childs had set up the New Century Loan Society in order to give employment to Samuel. In this way, the crown's theories as to Samuel's allegedly exclusive opportunity to commit the crime, and his motive for doing so, were very gravely damaged in the course of the hearings. Most of this process of destruction was achieved by hard, pointed and continuous cross-examination, nearly all of which was done by Healy. It appears also that it was Healy who advised the proofs for the defence – that is, directed the steps to be taken by the defendant's solicitor by way of investigating the case and securing evidence. There were, for example, photographs taken on behalf of the defendant which led the judge to disallow the prosecution's scale model of the house.

Why then did Joyce give the credit for the acquittal to Seymour Bushe? The reasons appear to be both political and literary. Joyce nourished a life-long hatred of Tim Healy by reason of the leading role he played in the downfall of Parnell. Joyce's very first literary work, now lost, was a bitter anti-Healy poem entitled, in a reference to the dying Caesar's words to his assassin Brutus, 'Et tu, Healy?'. This work was written at the age of 9 or 10 and his doting father, John Stanislaus Joyce, was so proud of the poem that he had it privately printed.[15] Accordingly, Joyce was most unlikely to give Healy any credit for anything. The Childs acquittal was very popular with the public and the newspaper accounts show that the 'not guilty' verdict was greeted with cheers for Healy, but Joyce allowed him no credit at all. Though Healy is mentioned in *Ulysses*, unfavourably, it is not in connection with the Childs case.[16] Yet Joyce must have been aware of his leading role.

The literary reason for downplaying Healy's role relates to the nature of that role itself. As we have seen, it was based on mastery of detail, painstaking preparation and dogged cross-examination. Joyce was not interested in that aspect of the case at all and the one detail he has Mr Power give of the case, other than

15 See J. Wyse Jackson and P. Costello, *John Stanislaus Joyce* (London, 1998), p. 170. **16** *Ulysses*, 7. 800 ff.

that it was one of fratricide, is wrong: the Childs house was the second last and not the last house in Bengal Terrace. Joyce was interested in quite different, and disparate, aspects of the case: first, in the abstract question of how one can ever know what really happened in the past, and secondly, in fratricide as a thing in itself. Besides, he was interested in the public perception of the case, how it was spoken of in Dublin five years after it happened, and how it had entered the public consciousness. Part of that consciousness was a recollection of the case as a gruesome one, as Mr Dedalus said; but another part of that consciousness was the linkage of the trial in the public mind with the kindly, louche, liberal and histrionic character of Seymour Bushe QC. For Bushe had been the subject of his own quite separate scandalous notoriety. This is hinted in the 'Aeolus' chapter by the Professor's remark 'He would have been on the bench long ago, only for … But no matter'.[17]

Seymour Bushe QC was the epitome of a well-connected Protestant Irishman of the late nineteenth century. He was descended from Charles Kendall Bushe, an opponent of the act of union who adapted himself to the new regime and eventually became the lord chief justice of the king's bench. Charles's daughter married a son of Lord Plunkett who had had a similar but still more successful career to that of Bushe, having been an anti-union lawyer and parliamentarian who dramatically signalled his conversion to the government side by prosecuting Robert Emmet in 1803. He went on to become lord chancellor and the greatest nepotist in nineteenth-century Ireland. By the late nineteenth century prominent descendants of these men included William, fifth Lord Plunkett, archbishop of Dublin (1884–97) and David, Lord Rathmore, the Tory Party's principal Irish organiser. The archbishop's statue stands in Kildare Place; Rathmore's portrait hangs in the Kildare Street and University Club. Of this distinguished lineage, it would have to be conceded that Seymour Bushe was to be found away on the left fringe. He was a liberal, a supporter of causes such as women's suffrage and a man about town. He had the reputation, confirmed by many contemporary sources, for exalted forensic eloquence. His speech for the defence in the Childs trial, from which an extract has been quoted above, was an eloquent speech in the high Victorian style. Joyce may, however, have embroidered it a little in the 'Aeolus' episode:

ITALIA, MAGISTRA ARTIUM

– He spoke on the law of evidence, J.J. O'Molloy said, of Roman justice as contrasted with the earlier Mosaic code, the *lex talionis*. And he cited the Moses of Michelangelo in the Vatican.[18]

17 *Ulysses*, 7. 744. 18 *Ulysses*, 7. 754ff.

If Bushe spoke about Moses the law-giver, or the statue of Moses by Michaelangelo, no reference to it has survived in any of the contemporary sources.

The defence's principal point on the law of evidence, which Bushe urged with great vehemence and eloquence, related to the inadmissibility of the testimony of Mrs Samuel Childs. It will be recalled that Samuel told the DMP that he had spent the evening at home, apart from a brief trip to the off-licence about 8.00 p.m. Police witnesses made a point of saying that they had taken a statement from Mrs Childs; the suggestion was that her statement did not support the alibi. Mrs Childs was not, however, a competent witness for the prosecution as she was the defendant's wife. But she was not a competent witness for the defence either, because under the law of evidence then prevailing in Ireland neither the defendant nor his or her spouse was competent to give evidence. The law in this respect had been altered in England only the previous year.[19] After the passing of that measure the defendant or his spouse could give evidence in a criminal trial in England, but the act did not apply to Ireland. The law was not altered until 1924.[20] Bushe complained eloquently and bitterly about the absence of the wife's evidence and the irrationality (in the context of the then United Kingdom of Great Britain and Ireland) of holding the wife's evidence admissible in one part of the kingdom and inadmissible in another. Healy could not have made this point. As an MP he had successfully opposed the extension of the new act to Ireland. He feared that innocent Irish peasants would be bamboozled by crown counsel into convicting themselves out of their own mouths. In this he was supported by Edward Carson. Bushe could possibly have referred to ancient legal codes by way of contrasting them with the law then applied in Ireland, but the record is silent on this. The defence, however, arranged for Mrs Childs to sit in court throughout, as near the dock as possible. She was accompanied by her brother and by the Revd Mr Gibson, chaplain to the McGeogh Home in Cowper Road, Dublin, who gave character evidence for the defence and then ostentatiously returned to his place in court beside Mrs Childs. All this, combined with Bushe's complaints about the law which kept her out of the witness box, was intended to suggest that she knew him to be innocent and could have said so but for the silly prohibition against receiving her evidence, or his.

Whether Bushe referred to Moses and to Roman law or not, there is no doubt that his eloquence made an enormous impression on the young James Joyce. He went to the trouble of finding out quite a bit about Seymour Bushe.

19 Criminal Evidence Act 1898 (61 & 62 Vict, c. 36). 20 Criminal Justice (Evidence) Act 1924.

His cryptic reference to the reason Bushe was never appointed to the bench is addressed in a note of October 1970 by the late Mr Colum Gavan Duffy, librarian of the Incorporated Law Society:

> It seems that a certain Sir — Brooke and his wife were rather estranged, and that on a certain occasion the husband followed his wife to Dublin. He eventually found his wife in the room of Mr Bushe and threatened to take proceedings against him. As there was no divorce in Ireland, these proceedings would consist in the tort of criminal conversation, whereby the husband would sue the alleged co-respondent for damages for adultery. It is for this reason that I understand Mr Bushe left ... He also drank heavily.[21]

Seymour Bushe's tragedy was that a well-born married woman transferred her affections to him in 1885 and her husband took condign and very well-publicized revenge. This husband was Gerald Richard Brooke, of Kellystown House, Clonsilla, Co. Dublin – there is no support for Mr Gavan Duffy's view that he was a knight or baronet. On 25 June 1886, Mr Brooke procured a parliamentary divorce by the passage of a private act at Westminster.[22] Although judicial divorces had been available in England since the 1850s, this facility did not extend to Queen Victoria's Irish subjects. If they wanted and were entitled to a divorce, and had the means to do so, they had to seek the passage of a private act of parliament dissolving their marriages. This is what Mr Brooke did, and in the preliminary recital to the act he sets out what occurred. He says that he married the Hon. Kathleen Maude, daughter of the Rt. Hon. Viscount Hawarden, on 10 April 1875, in Donnybrook. They had three children aged between 6 and 9 at the time of the bill. Mr Brooke went on to recite that his wife 'did on 2 October 1885, elope ... with Seymour Bushe, of Ely Place, Dublin, Barrister-at-law, with whom she hath since lived and cohabited in a state of adultery'.

Mr Brooke's bill then goes on to describe the extent of his revenge. On 20 October 1885, he commenced proceedings for criminal conversation (that is, adultery) against Seymour Bushe. Bushe did not enter a written defence to this claim, presumably because he had none. This omission allowed Brooke to 'mark judgment' against him in the offices of the high court without proceeding to a full hearing. Under this procedure, all Brooke had to do was to prove that he had issued the proceedings and that Bushe had failed to file a defence, whereupon he became entitled to have judgment entered or 'marked' in the books

---

21 D. Giffard, with R.J. Seidman, *Ulysses annotated* (revised ed., Berkeley, CA, 1988), p. 145.
22 Brooke's Divorce Act 1886 (49 & 50 Vict, c. 181).

of the high court. But the damages could only be assessed by a jury. Accordingly, on 15 January 1886, a jury in the common pleas division of the high court in Dublin awarded damages of £1,000 against Bushe; the bill recites that the costs and damages were paid by Bushe. Moreover, on 24 October 1885, Brooke sued his wife for 'divorce from bed and board and mutual cohabitation'. He obtained a final decree against her on 14 January 1886, the day before the damages against Bushe were assessed. This divorce, however, was not a divorce *a vinculo* (that is, one that permitted remarriage).

Having succeeded in these two actions, Mr Brooke promoted his parliamentary bill in which he claimed that 'the said Honourable Kathleen Brooke … hath by her said adulterous and criminal conduct dissolved the bond of matrimony on her part'. The act was passed. Section 2 recited that the bond of matrimony, 'being violated and broken by the manifest and open adultery of the said Honourable Kathleen Brooke, shall be and is hereby from henceforth wholly dissolved, annulled, vacated, and made void'. Seymour Bushe, therefore, was in the awkward position for a professional man in late Victorian Dublin of having the fact that he had committed adultery publicly proclaimed in an act of parliament. He continued, however, to practise law in Dublin for the next eighteen years. In 1904 he migrated to London, was admitted king's counsel in England and endeavoured to establish himself at the parliamentary bar.

Joyce's reference shows that Bushe's embarrassment was comparatively well known amongst the chattering classes in Dublin after an interval of almost twenty years. It is not possible at this distance in time to know why precisely Bushe left Ireland. Joyce's reference to the scandal as a reason for Bushe's failure to be promoted to the bench is, however, suggestive: in the Ireland of the 1880s, and probably for a long period thereafter, a scandal of this kind would have interfered with promotion either on the bench or in politics.

A photograph of Bushe survives in a book by Michael McCarthy, an Anglo-Irish journalist;[23] there is also a line drawing in A.M. Sullivan's first autobiography.[24] In both, he appears as something of a dandy, with wide tapering moustaches, and is distinguished by a very large nose. These features also claim Joyce's attention when, in the 'Circe' episode, Bloom is arraigned in a surreal court on charges of concupiscence on the complaint of Mrs Yelverton Barry, Mrs Bellingham, and other ladies.[25] J.J. O'Molloy appears to defend him and is described as assuming 'the avine head, foxy moustache and proboscidal eloquence of Seymour Bushe'.[26] He delivers a much shorter reprise of the speech

23 M.J.F. McCarthy, *Five years in Ireland: 1895–1900* (London, 1902). **24** A.M. Sullivan, *Old Ireland: reminiscences of an Irish KC* (London, 1928). **25** *Ulysses*, 15. 859ff. **26** *Ulysses*, 15. 999ff.

attributed by him to Bushe in the Childs trial, and his client proceeds shamelessly and suggestively to drop names saying 'I have moved in the charmed
circle of the highest ... Queens of Dublin Society'.[27]

Bushe and one or two other persons mentioned in the 'Aeolus' chapter are
for Joyce prototypes of eloquence – forensic, parliamentary or demagogic. A
large part of the 'Aeolus' chapter is an examination of eloquence with quite
lengthy examples. At one point Stephen wonders in his interior monologue:
'Could you try your hand at it yourself?'[28] This perhaps is a reference to one of
two paths not taken by Joyce when he devoted himself to writing. As a student
at University College, Dublin, Joyce did a good deal of public speaking in the
Literary and Historical Society, the university's debating society. His success at
this led his father repeatedly to suggest that he should become a barrister.[29] Joyce
himself, though he attended some law lectures, preferred to follow in his father's
footsteps by enrolling as a medical student, but also by dropping out at a very
early stage. *Ulysses*, however, contains numerous references to legal and medical practitioners, eminent and otherwise. Rufus Isaacs, later Lord Reading, and
Sir Thornley Stoker,[30] the great Dublin physician and brother of Bram Stoker,
are examples of the eminent. But equally interesting to Joyce were the struck-
off solicitor O'Callaghan selling shoe laces for a living,[31] the broken-down barrister, J.J. O'Molloy,[32] and Dr O'Gargle of the Mater Misericordiae hospital,
who is said to 'chuck the nuns there under the chin'.[33]

The Ireland of Joyce's youth in the last eighteen years of the nineteenth
century and the very early twentieth century is the seedbed of his great works,
the unfailing source of his themes and of the events and narratives that are
reflected in the books. Those decades are, as time passes, increasingly inaccess-
ible even to people who are historically aware. History, like landscape, has its
folds and hidden places. The twenty-odd years after the fall of Parnell in 1891
is such a place, obscured between that dominating event on the one hand and
1913, the Great War and 1916 on the other. The period evokes for most
people no immediate picture or sense of social texture. In Yeats' phrase (used
by Constantine Curran as the title of his volume of early recollections),[34] those
years have passed 'under the receding wave' of time which leaves only the great
prominences clearly visible. The Childs case, saved from utter obscurity only
by Joyce's mention of it, is like a time capsule preserving accurately – because
incidentally – some of the texture and details of life in the years 1899 and 1904.

---

27 *Ulysses*, 15. 1008/9. **28** *Ulysses*, 7. 836/7. **29** Jackson and Costello, *John Stanislaus Joyce*,
p. 237. **30** *Ulysses*, 15. 1030. **31** *Ulysses*, 6. 229ff. **32** *Ulysses*, 12. 1022ff. **33** *Ulysses*, 14.
810. **34** C.P. Curran, *Under the receding wave* (Dublin, 1970); the phrase is taken from Yeats'
poem 'The nineteenth century and after'.

Elegiac occasions

Maurice Harmon

LEGIES MEDIATE BETWEEN the living and the dead. They may bring order
to the confusion of grief and replace the void of loss with the life-substance
of the poem. Traditionally, they have been reflective and formal. The poet has
had time to consider the significance of the death, to sort out private or personal grief from a more general loss, to give it a context – philosophical, religious, natural, social – and to find a form through which to express feeling.
Elegies offer consolation. As relatives or readers we may be moved and healed,
our experience of death given an ordered imaginative context and alleviated.
The poet, too, may be affected; his grief may be assuaged in the process of composition. He also responds as an artist. The better he writes, the greater the comfort and healing he may experience. Although they belong to the same genre,
the first two elegies I want to consider –'In Memory of Major Robert Gregory'
by William Butler Yeats and 'Martha Blake at Fifty-One' by Austin Clarke –
differ from each other in approach and treatment. While a particular death is
central to each, other elements, such as style, structure, language, tone and the
degree of personal attachment, are different. I want to consider the nature of
the relationship between the poet and the dead, and to assess to what extent
each elegy becomes more than a lament for a particular person.

Elegiac occasions may, however, encompass more than a particular death. The
poem may respond to a more general loss. Patrick Kavanagh's depiction in 'The
Great Hunger' of the unfulfilled lives of a small farming community in Co.
Monaghan is in effect an extended elegy. So, too, is John Montague's response
in 'The Rough Field' to a culture that has been eroded in Co. Tyrone, as is my
poem 'The Doll with Two Backs' on the disappearance of Native American tribes.

The qualities of W.B. Yeats' elegy, 'In Memory of Major Robert Gregory',
are distinctive: courtesy of manner, dignity of tone and a personal voice. We
return to it as to a masterpiece that pleases us for its many particular accomplishments and for its overall achievement. It is characterized by a disarming
civility. Its combination of dignity with conversational simplicity is heard at
once in the poet's address to his wife: 'Now that we're almost settled in our
house'. The eight-line stanza flows in one courteous, rhyming sentence and this
is the hallmark of the entire poem:

> Now that we're almost settled in our house
> I'll name the friends that cannot sup with us
> Beside a fire of turf in th' ancient tower,
> And having talked to some late hour
> Climb up the narrow winding stairs to bed:
> Discoverers of forgotten truth
> Or mere companions of my youth,
> All, all are in my thoughts to-night being dead.[1]

This reflective persona may use the language of ordinary discourse, but what he reflects upon and what he has been shaped by are no ordinary considerations. He appreciates the thinking man, Lionel Johnson, investigator of the occult, respects his pursuit of sanctity and classical learning, and tolerates his weakness, because he loved abstract thought. He values John Synge, who had the capacity to be in tune with natural man, and is warm towards George Pollexfen, who combined riding skills with an interest in astrology. He values above all personal accomplishment, which the poem itself confirms in its own delicate negotiations and procedures.

One of the poem's achievements is the encapsulating ease by which the persona creates the portraits of particular friends – 'Discoverers of forgotten truth / Or mere companions of my youth' – and then, midway, yields graciously to the crowding memory of Robert Gregory, whom Yeats regarded as the most accomplished man he had ever known. He makes him the epitome of the other three, combining action and contemplation. A Renaissance man in his versatility and grace, he exemplified all the virtues that the others had individually. Because of the 'discourtesy' of his death, Yeats can proceed with the aesthetic courtesy of the poem, a gracious acknowledgement that the elegist needs the death. The more distant sorrow associated with the deaths of Johnson, Synge and Pollexfen has been replaced by lament for the recent loss of Robert Gregory which leads in a process of natural logic to explanation as to why the poet should feel so strongly about his death. 'Imagination', Yeats says, 'was stirred by a better idea.' This, too, is consoling, since it implies that the recent more personal loss and the realization of Gregory's superb and varied potential absorbed Yeats' imagination to the exclusion of all else. Robert Gregory looms large because he is the ideal.

By associating Robert Gregory with the scene about the tower, Yeats draws him closer, making him more real and more intimate. What Gregory saw and valued in this landscape, the poet sees and values. Each has made artistic work from it. The rhythm gathers pace now to portray Gregory as daring horseman,

1 W.B. Yeats, *The poems*, ed. R.J. Finneran (Dublin, 1983), pp 132–5.

first in the hunt, superb over a perilous jump, and leads smoothly to declare that his intellectual pursuits were even more daring: 'his mind outran the horse's feet'. The changing rhythms of this stanza on instances of nerve and physical courage mimic the theme of intellectual curiosity at full tilt:

> When with the Galway foxhounds he would ride
> From Castle Taylor to the Roxborough side
> Or Esserkelly plain, few kept his pace;
> At Mooneen he had leaped a place
> So perilous that half the astonished meet
> Had shut their eyes; and where was it
> He rode a race without a bit?
> And yet his mind outran his horses' feet.

The panegyric is mirrored in the alteration in rhythm through the three stanzas on Robert Gregory from the smoother flowing, reflective nature of the previous stanzas devoted to particular people. Yeats praises his artistic abilities:

> We dreamed that a great painter had been born
> To cold Clare rock and Galway rock and thorn.

Alliteration, repetition and dominant monosyllabic words mimic the certainty of that conviction. Speaking as an artist about a fellow artist whose potential he identifies – 'stern colour' and 'delicate line' – the poet implies that his poem aspires to the same virtues. It is the tribute of high-level imitation, a bonding that helps to persuade us of their closeness as artists. In addition, Gregory had what Yeats has – 'our secret discipline': the ability to contemplate the depths of one's own mind. The poem achieves its ease of manner because the choice of word and the control of line are as exact and disciplined as line and colour in Gregory's paintings. That 'intensity', as Yeats calls it, lies behind the casualness of the voice. Robert Gregory, the consummate Renaissance man, would have been the 'bride's heartiest welcomer', where heartiest includes warmest, as well as genuine or unequivocal. Since his artistic abilities, in Yeats' portrayal, were impeccable, he would have advised them, with authority and to their satisfaction, on domestic decorations – 'all he did done perfectly'.

In a daring move from panegyric to consolation, the poem descends from these evocations of high achievement, skills of hand, eye and mind, to conclude that such vitality was destined to consume everything, including itself. Because he was the epitome of fulfilment – 'Soldier, scholar, horseman' – he was doomed. Yeats has moved from expectancy to regret:

> Some burn damp faggots, others may consume
> The entire combustible world in one small room
> As though dried straw ...

That argument, too, takes some of the sting out of the grief. Because his life flared so vividly, we are left with the blackness of the empty grate, but one balances the other. The poem, also, alleviates the darkness of grief by the brilliant light of its aesthetic.

'In Memory of Major Robert Gregory' sets a standard. It recalls and celebrates the dead man's virtues and capacities so eloquently that it helps to assuage the grief occasioned by his early death. It laments the waste when one so richly talented and so full of promise dies and raises that consideration to a tragic level. Great men die – Oedipus, Hamlet, Lear. Once evoked, the tragic paradigm crowds into our minds. The poem's aesthetic success, all its elements of tone, persona, allusion, development, structure so perfectly managed, is serenely consoling. Not the least part of its mastery is the intensity and precision with which Yeats manages the twelve eight-line stanzas almost all of which move forward in one unbroken movement. But there is another important aspect: Yeats raises his lament to a higher, more inclusive level and gives intellectual and cultural contexts to his meditation. This elevation is characteristic of many elegies. Within his observations on the achievements of his chosen figures he evokes a whole wide range of human aspiration – the Renaissance ideal of the well-rounded man, the possibility of personal growth, the fact of artistic achievement – and the ancient paradox of achievement so rare that it leads to personal tragedy. This consideration encompasses the sadness at the heart of things, the sad realization of our humanity, not only capable of aspiring to and achieving greatness, but mortal and prone to failure. The effects of these extensions, internal complexities and enlargements secure 'In Memory of Major Robert Gregory' as a major artistic achievement. We return to it as to a masterpiece that endlessly rewards our affection.

Although it is one of his best poems, Austin Clarke's elegy is not as well known. It is much less elevated in language, is involved more personally with the subject and is Joycean – rather than Yeatsian – in its naturalistic use of detail. Written in twenty-four rhymed stanzas, 'Martha Blake at Fifty-One' is a descriptive, narrative portrait of a pious woman of no importance who lived a banal life and suffered a harrowing division of body and soul, a Yeatsian dichotomy, but treated with none of the symbolic resonance and grandeur he favoured. Her daily life is made up of trivia, her spiritual life is superficial as is shown in her response to the sacrament of Holy Communion:

Waiting for daily communion, bowed head
    At rail, she hears a murmur.
Latin is near. In a sweet cloud
    That cherub'd, all occurred.
The voice went by. To her pure thought,
    Body was a distress
And soul, a sigh. Behind her denture,
    Love lay, a helplessness.[2]

Prosaic details of her lonely life and her digestive distress illustrate the abject nature of her body. She daydreams about saints and miracles in Italy and France. Clarke contrasts the shallowness of her religious sense with the passionate, self-transforming love of God experienced by mystics St Teresa of Ávila and St John of the Cross which Martha cannot appreciate:

She thought of St Teresa, floating
    On motes of a sunbeam,
Carmelite with scattered robes,
    Surrounded by demons,
Small black boys in their skin. She gaped
    At Hell: a muddy passage
That led to nothing, queer in shape,
    A cupboard closely fastened.

The language – 'floating / On motes of a sunbeam', 'Small black boys in their skin', and 'queer in shape' – shows Martha's failure to comprehend. When compared with Teresa's own account of her horror vision of a claustrophobic hell, these lines reveal how sanitized Martha's perception is. Teresa's erotic mysticism, unmistakably carnal in the saint's own account, is also beyond Martha's understanding.

The description of the bridal night of St John of the Cross works to the same effect. Drawing from St John's poem, 'The Living Flame of Love', Clarke refers to the physical transformation of the mystic union: the saint's wasted flesh 'flowers', his senses soar close to God –

Paler than lilies, his wizened skin
    Flowers. In fifths of flight
Senses beyond seraphic thought,

---

2 A. Clarke, *Poems, 1955–1966*, ed. L. Miller (Dublin, 1974), pp 264–70.

> In that divinest clasp,
>   Enfolding of kisses that cauterize,
>   Yield to the soul-spasm.

In the case of St Teresa and St John of the Cross, body and soul are joined in ecstatic union with God. Martha's body denies her the possibility of reaching a comparable spiritual transcendence of the physical. They swoon and soar in blissful union with God; she is tormented by dissolution of the flesh – 'Ill-natured flesh / despised her soul.'

The poem descends to its conclusion with further delineation of the prosaic details of her life. The emphasis is on disappointment. In order to avoid the pain of purgatory she joins the Third Order, and she imagines an idealized form of dying in which she will be cared for in a 'quiet sick-ward' and nuns 'with delicious ways' will console her. What actually happens is heart-rending: she is shut away in a hospice for the dying, there is no doctor, the place is noisy. She cannot sleep, worries – 'O how could she be saved?' The nuns give her purgatives. 'Only her body lived.' The soul loses out. She is refused Holy Communion, the food is revolting, the field outside is rented as an amusement park so that she has to endure dizzying noises, movements and bright lights. 'How could she pray to God?' Alone, ignored, unloved, her ending is miserable:

> Unpitied, wasting with diarrhoea
>   And the constant strain,
> Poor Child of Mary with one idea,
>   She ruptured a small vein,
> Bled inwardly to jazz. No priest
>   Came. She had been anointed
> Two days before, yet knew no peace:
>   Her last breath, disappointed.

'Martha Blake at Fifty-One' is a powerful delineation of a type of pious, non-intellectual woman. In a sense, she was a nobody whose life was narrow, whose spirituality brought little comfort, whose Christianity lacked force. Yeats regretted the waste of potential when Robert Gregory died. Clarke's elegy cannot do so on the same terms. Martha Blake was not a great person, not a figure of distinction or promise. Nevertheless, a life has been wasted. Line by measured line, detail by objective detail, Clarke builds her portrait. Just as James Joyce amassed his portrait of the little man, Leopold Bloom, so does Clarke and in the process makes Martha Blake important. She is significant now and representative in this literary rebirth. Clarke brings her to life in sympathetic, unflinching detail, makes her memorable and exemplary through the actuality of her life, her gross physical distress, her hollow spirituality. A life has been wasted not in ennobling or admirable endeavour but in division, suffering and foolish sentiment.

Clarke gives the lament its own universality. This is the tragedy of the little woman. There is no appeal to a greater moral power. The mystics serve not as exemplars, but as metaphors. Martha Blake as victim is manipulated by higher authority, deceived and self-deceived. Clarke does not describe what he values, her opposite: the self-reliant, thinking Catholic in a church that respects her, the integrity of an individual moral code. In this he was unlike Yeats, who often dramatizes the warring of antinomies.

Yeats' poem transcends its occasion, the voice is attractively humane, cultured and civilized. Clarke's voice is embittered and non-consolatory. Yeats' intensity was the controlled intensity of the rational imagination; its passion infused the technique. In Clarke, the intensity is part of his bitter rage and grief that Martha – who is partly modelled on his sister, Eileen – had suffered so terribly, betrayed by an institution she trusted completely.

By focusing on the death of an individual the poet heightens the sense of loss one experiences on such occasions. Sometimes, an elegiac poem is infused with a more general realization that an entire community or an entire civilization has died. In 'The Great Hunger' Patrick Kavanagh recreates a hauntingly realistic portrait of existence on a small farm. Written from the point of view of a man who has left, it is a sad reflection on what conditions are like for the man who remains. Ironically, Patrick Maguire, the bachelor farmer, devotes his life to cultivating his small fields while his own life remains unfulfilled. As Kavanagh pithily says: 'For the strangled impulse there is no redemption.'[3] The years go by, life goes by and the hope of change dies. 'Life dried in the veins of these women and men.' The pity is that Maguire has the capacity to enjoy the cycle of the seasons and the beauty of nature – 'yellow buttercups and the bluebells among the whin bushes' and 'goldfinches on the railway paling'. At the heart of Kavanagh's response is the knowledge that man is capable of more and deserves better. Like Yeats, he regrets a man's failure to reach his potential.

Death is also a consideration for Maguire. The fact that he will feel at home in the grave makes the history of his limited and circumscribed life all the more moving. Kavanagh disguises the sadness with wry sarcasm:

> ... he'll understand the
> Quality of the clay that dribbles over his coffin.

3 P. Kavanagh, *Collected poems*, ed. A. Quinn (London, 2004), pp 63–89.

> He'll know the names of the roots that climb down to tickle his feet.
> And he will feel no different than when he walked through
>   Donaghmoyne.

The humour is macabre but tellingly accurate. His death is not much different from his life.

Circumstances deny Maguire his natural right to love and joy. Conditioned by his mother's advice to make the field his bride and his church's teaching against sexual sin, he is afraid of women:

> He was suspicious in his youth as a rat near strange bread
> When girls laughed; when they screamed he knew that meant
> The cry of fillies in season. He could not walk
> The easy road to his destiny.

In the culture of the small farm there is little intellectual nourishment and the virtues of respectability and righteousness have an increasing influence as Maguire grows older. 'Ignorance' gives him 'the coward's blow':

> And he cried for his own loss one late night on the pillow
> And yet thanked the God who had arranged these things.

The similarity with Martha Blake as a person is striking. Both their lives are guided by the same church; both have the kind of passive personalities that Clarke and Kavanagh deplore. Their unthinking, unquestioning natures ensure that they remained trapped. Nature provides models for Maguire:

> The fledged bird is thrown
> From the nest – on its own.
> But the peasant in his little fields is tied
> To a mother's womb …

The pity is that he and others like him have the ability to experience finer feelings, have at times a mystical sense of the natural world:

> Yet sometimes when the sun comes through a gap
> These men know God the Father in a tree:
> The Holy Spirit is the rising sap,
> And Christ will be the green leaves that will come
> At Easter from the sealed and guarded tomb.

But, as the poem recurrently reveals, Maguire does not have the strength to effect change nor to leave the circumstances that inhibit him. He resembles James Joyce's characters in *Dubliners* who lack the will-power to alter their lives; even when given the opportunity to escape, they hold back, so conditioned are they by circumstances. George Moore's *The Untilled Field* provides even more relevant examples of a similar lack of mental or spiritual decisiveness in the dispirited years after the Famine. Kavanagh's 'The Great Hunger', in which the title is a conscious echo of the Great Famine, describes the hunger of the failed imagination. His is the tragedy of the little man; this is 'the weak, washy way of true tragedy'. Life is a 'procession [that] passed down a mesmerised street'.

John Montague's 'The Rough Field' is more intellectually aware than 'The Great Hunger'. Whereas the latter ignores the historical associations of Inniskeen, the former sees Garvaghey, his home-place, within historical contexts, in the immediate and more distant past. Just as William Carleton, who also grew up in Co. Tyrone, lamented the weakening of its cultural memory, particularly after the Famine, so Montague regrets what time and change have done to his own place. An entire region has been altered, a language silenced, a culture fatally weakened. His poem is written as a return, a circling back to what he came from, but also a circling outward from that centre to take in a wider landscape and a circling backward to define historical disruptions. In the process the local is not only identified, not only described in affectionate terms, but given permanence through the power of the poetry. As the traditional elegy can memorialize the life and achievements of a particular person, so the general elegy can give permanence to particular places and events. Both 'The Great Hunger' and 'The Rough Field' give an enduring record of what is disappearing. Montague writes about diminishment and erosion and in doing so rescues what remains – places, people, events, a landscape, a culture, his own experience – from oblivion. He does it with tenderness and precision, raptly attentive to what is on the brink of existence:

> ... For two hundred years
> People of our name have sheltered in this glen
> But now all have left.[4]

Like an archaeologist examining 'shards of a lost culture', Montague retrieves and itemizes the signs of what once existed, what once formed a community, what once was whole before it was broken by process, by political violence, by emigration and by the great collapse of the O'Neill dynasty at the end of the

4 J. Montague, *Collected poems* (Loughcrew, Oldcastle, Co. Meath, 1995), pp 3–81.

sixteenth century. A powerful emotion stirs behind the quiet delineation of loss.
What holds this long poem together is the understanding of events and the passion of the response – rage at what has happened; compassion for those affected;
an elegiac, minute attention to details of person and place; and acceptance that
he too must leave what no longer sustains. It is a farewell to Tyrone as well as
a lament for Tyrone –

> ... a half-life in this
> by-passed and dying place.

This is harshly accurate, and at times the strength of feeling breaks through:

> I assert
> a civilisation died here;
>   it trembles
> underfoot where I walk these
>   small, sad hills.

So emotionally involved is he that the poem at times threatens to explode
into angry rhetoric or to descend into sentimentality. But Montague is too disciplined and self-aware for that to happen. He can be delicately responsive, as
in the tribute poems about the selfless old women who minded him as a child:

> Old lady, I now celebrate
> to whom I owe so much;
> bending over me in darkness
> a scaly tenderness of touch
>
> skin of bony arm & elbow
> sandpapered with work:
> because things be to be done
> and simplicity did not shirk
>
> the helpless, hopeless task
> of maintaining a family farm.

He can be sturdily objective as he deals with 'the sadness of a house in decay'.
The poem is a kind of catharsis. Just as the old people in the glen are encysted
on the landscape in 'Like dolmens round my childhood', so these elegiac

revelations about person and place are memorialized in the poem, distanced and dignified.

At the heart of the conflict in my poem 'The Doll with Two Backs'[5] is the inability of outsiders to understand the culture and traditions of insiders, whether it be the Tudor colonists when they invaded Ireland or the white men when they took possession of Native American lands. The notion of incomprehension is inherent in the metaphor of the doll found by the Indian girl who has become friends with an Irish academic:

> Discovering driftwood wedged
> beneath a log she pried it loose
> then exclaimed, 'It's the doll. It looks
> in both directions, the faces never meet.
> Neither can ever see or understand the other'.

It is manifest in Francis Parkman's impressive account in *The Oregon Trail* of the shooting of the buffalo:

> Feeding alone, apart from the herd, the old
> bull moves massively above the plains
> while the man crawls through the long grass.
>
> The buffalo stares at the spot, grazes again, but abruptly
> attacks. Stops short. The gunman aims
> at the thin shield of bone above the nose.
>
> Sights the chest matted with coarse hair
> thick horns blunted and split to the skull
> nose and forehead marred with white scars.
>
> They watch and wait under the hot sun.
> The man thinks, my friend, if you'll let me off
> I'll let you off. The animal turns.
>
> Little by little the width of his side appears.
> The gun explodes. The old bull spins
> about like a top, gallops away, drops.

---

5 M. Harmon, *The doll with two backs, and other poems* (Cliffs of Moher, Co. Clare, 2004), pp 15–47.

For a moment it seems possible that a degree of mutual understanding might exist between animal and human, but the hunter-historian wilfully destroys the beast and has no conception of the consequences of such destruction for the native peoples. Nor has he any notion of the close affinity Indians feel with the buffalo, as with the earth itself. The wanton killing is symptomatic of the cruel mind-set of the intruders.

Irish and Native American experiences of colonialism fuse. Even the names of those who push the extermination of the Indians have a familiar ring (Kearny, Carleton, Connor), while the incidents are the same – intrusion, harassment, broken treaties, dispossession and massacre. The expulsion of Irish families across the Shannon in the time of Oliver Cromwell and the plantations of Munster and Ulster are mirrored in the forced marches of Indians in the Long Walk and the Trail of Tears. Historical associations overlap:

> The bull that tore at *Carraic-an-phuill*
> pawed the ice at Bear River.
> What rid the land of lord and chief
> put paid to Modoc and Chinook.

An earlier passage in the poem makes the same associations. When President Thomas Jefferson's pioneers, Meriwether Lewis and William Clark, opened the land route to the west coast, their *Journals* record their journey down the great Columbia river and their first sight of its 'great falls – / Horsetail, Latourell, Wahkeena, Multnomah – / spilling through God's hands upon their passage'. But the journey ended badly, and their treatment of the Indian tribes was dishonest. They camped not far from the aptly named Cape Disappointment and deceived an old native woman by buying her daughters with bits of ribbon. It was a bad bargain. The girls gave them syphilis. The tawdry scene is far removed from Emerson's reflections on his country's tenuous links with the old country:

> 'Ocian in view! O! the joy!' At journey's
> end Cape Disappointment
> an old Baud, ribbons, a bad exchange
> frail links with king and courtly muses.

When the girl and the Irish academic camp at Yachats, an Indian place on the Pacific coast, the past presses down upon them so much that she is consumed by it and fiercely summarizes forces that have disrupted and weakened Indian culture – the covered wagons, the trains, the telegraph, the prospectors and others who took Indian lands:

> Once she scratched upon the ground
> scoring, digging, jabbing. The stick
> she used shaped whitetops, iron horses, talking wires
> grubbers, grabbers, panners, pedlars.

On one level, the poem – over thirty pages long – is an extended lament both for the destruction of Native American civilizations and for the failure of a friendship that had been promising and mutually enriching. The realization of that potential makes their growing apart a matter of regret. But there is also the failure of the imagination to absorb Indian myths, legends and storytelling. Storytelling itself is a value, frequently evoked both in the allusions to myths of origin and to various stories from both Indian and Irish sources. These, too, contain incidents of division and misunderstanding. The academic tries to understand the history of the Oregon territories, realizing that those with whom he works are strangely silent about the past. For him, the girl – part tree spirit, part water nymph – is the best connection he has with that past.

Their friendship ends. She disappears. He feels the loss as 'bereavement'. The sixteenth-century poem – with its echo of Yeats' 'The Second Coming' – which ends the work refers to the loss of control between the falconer and the falcon:

> 'Wo ho ho he cries, awaie she flies,
>   and so her leaue she takes.
> This wofull man with wearie limmes,
>   runnes wandring round about.'

It is another example of failed connection, the theme that has permeated the poem and underscored its elegiac nature.

Elegies often include regret for a loss of potential, and so are closely related to tragedy in which the belief that the hero might have achieved greatness is a persuasive matter. The idea is clearly voiced in W.B. Yeats' sense of what the gifted Robert Gregory might have achieved had he not been cut down prematurely. It is less evident in Austin Clarke's response to Martha Blake's death – no expectation there that she might have distinguished herself had she lived, but regret that without the pressure of a restrictive religion she might have had a different and more complete life. Patrick Kavanagh's perception of Maguire and his kind is that they had moments of insight when they transcended the stunted conditions of their lives. John Montague's feelings about his family suggest not so much that they were capable of fulfilment, but that events and circumstances have worked against them. In my consideration of friendship between two people from different cultures, their failure to deal with what separates them results in personal loss and is symptomatic of the waste when civilizations cannot exist together. Most elegiac occasions contain this idea of unfulfilled potential.

The library of adventure

Dennis O'Driscoll

> I rarely feel happier than when I am in a library – very rarely feel more soothed
> and calm and secure; and there, in the soft gloom of the stacks, I feel very much
> in my element – a book among books, almost.
>
> Randall Jarrell.

I AM A FAST READER who became a slow reader. I started in the fast-reading
lane in the sense that I learned to read unusually young and was treated as a
freak show for visitors to the Presentation Convent school in Thurles, where
my schooling began. No guest – lay or clerical, church canon or department
of education inspector – was spared what was no doubt a cringe-making display,
as I gave command performances from *Pears Encyclopaedia* or a gold-edged *Lives
of the Saints*. My greed for words gathered momentum in secondary school
with essay competitions, radio scripts, a verse-speaking medal, slogan and
caption entries. I read with the obsession of an addict in the grip of an
uncontrollable urge. Whatever had been written, I wanted to read. Whatever
there was to read, I wanted to have read. Eventually, what there wasn't to read,
I wanted to write.

At some point in my childhood, I began to ruefully realize that one book a
day – adventure novels, biographies of the great inventors, stories of everyday life
in distant lands like Norway and France, heroic accounts of missionaries and
lifeboat men – would make only a small dent in the stock of the local library. I
therefore resolved to double the dose and increase my intake to two books a day,
as though I needed a book for each of my avaricious eyes. My favourite reading
position was in a large tea chest propped against the smooth bark of a mature
laburnum tree, close enough to the backyard rose beds to catch their wafting
scent and near enough to the proliferating blackcurrant bushes to warily monitor
their progress. The currants, which seemed to increase and multiply at a prodigious
– even promiscuous – pace, would need to be picked for jam-making before their
plum-coloured skins reached seam-bursting ripeness. My tea chest was rendered
comfortable by deft deployment of borrowed cushions and a deaf ear to the
demands that I clamber out of my shell and – instead of risking cabin fever – help
to weed the long thin lettuce and cauliflower beds.

I have never lost my sense of urgency about reading, any more than I have gained a sense of urgency about weeding. I sometimes want to bypass the reading process altogether and – reverting to the metaphor of addiction – simply *inject* knowledge into my veins so that they might course with whatever wisdom or insight the reading of Proust or Plato, Maria Edgeworth or William Faulkner would confer. But reading is a gratifying act in itself and one pleads for more time, more life, to get through everything: Amichai to Zabolotsky, Zozimus to Aristotle. My older brother Frank once remarked: 'Whenever someone buys a book, they also imagine they are buying the time to read that book' – a sage insight which encapsulates not only the pleasurable anticipation that accompanies the buying of a book but also the depth of our illusions. We feel more learned simply for having bought Tacitus' *Agricola* or Juvenal's *Satires*. The volume is handled and fondled, sniffed and shelved, never again in many instances to be disturbed: a bibliographical example of 'dust to dust'. If living authors received royalties for books read rather than books bought, they couldn't hope to balance their own books. 'A poem is never finished, only abandoned', Paul Valéry famously remarked of the writing process. And – of the reading process – one might similarly claim of our frenzied, distracted age: 'No book is ever started, only anticipated.'

When I say I was a fast reader, I don't mean that I read carelessly or skipped pages. Skipping was an activity in which my sister and her friends specialized – the metronymic beat of their rhymes and the rhythmic thud of their sandalled feet as much a defining part of summer as hoverfly hums and horsefly bites. As a reader, I absorbed every page, eking out the pleasure; but – displaying a youthful conflict of interests – I also relished the prospect of conquering the next column of books and was limbering up in expectation. It was as if reading was childhood itself, as if I sensed that my days under the pendulous laburnum, with everything coming up smelling of roses, were numbered. Time was running out. Evenings dissolved too quickly into a red-skied night. Relatives were quizzing me with increasing seriousness about what I would do when I left school. Certainly, I indulged in a lot of daydreaming about time and infinity. I would take the sudden notion to jot down the time as shown in Roman numerals on the classroom's pendulum clock. Later, I would ruminate on the fact that the particular second I had taken such careful note of was now gone forever and a day:

TEMPUS FUGIT

X to III by the school clock;
a pendulum paces its cage.
Now I know what time means:

at III, I will be older by ten minutes,
this moment will have passed.
A singsong teacher lists
the industries of Wales.
The fly Glossy Gleeson freed
from a red Elastoplast tin
scales the chalky blackboard ...
I never saw my friends again
once we had walked out
together, backwards,
through the wrought front gates
– all that remains of the school.

If we chanced to meet
what would there be to say?
What would we have in common
(crow's-feet; grey hairs landing
like some migratory birds)?

Another sense in which I was a quick reader – and an anticipative one – was that I would sometimes check the book's ending before I embarked on the first chapter. As speed-reading experts tell us, it is always easier to follow the plot of a story when its outcome is known. Advance notice of how the characters in the book would fare whetted my gratification more than it spoiled my suspense. Happy endings are one of the great impulses for childhood reading – and, of course, they are normative too in great literature of the order of Shakespeare's comedies and Jane Austen's novels – because of the assurance they offer that 'all shall be well and all manner of thing shall be well'. In a fractious world – where a volatile teacher would suddenly whip the leather strap from its scabbard and lash out, and where family life was not without tension either – it was salutary to enter a space where good invariably triumphed and adversity was overcome. If books revolved solely around their dénouements, few would re-read them, whereas – in Hazlitt's words, which I recently re-read – 'when I take up a work that I have read before (the oftener the better), I know what I have to expect. The satisfaction is not lessened by being anticipated.'

In poetry, re-reading is the whole point. Stanza means room; and the first familiarization with the poem is a way of getting a feel for its rooms, exploring their ambience, gauging their proportions, deciding whether or not one would want to linger in them. If the poem has real merit, it will reveal more and more features – tonal, emotional, linguistic, rhythmical, metaphoric – on each subsequent visit. Eventually, you live in the poem and it lives in you. As the American poet C.K. Williams has brilliantly expressed it:

> A poem is meant to be read and read again and again, to be run through the mind until it is part of the mind, until the mind recites it as it recites itself … Mind becomes doubled in its dealings with the formal arts. We aren't satisfied to 'know' a poem, a painting, or a piece of music by being able to describe it to ourselves, to paraphrase it. There has to be the incorporation of the actual object, of the precise notes in a piece of music or the precise words in a poem, so that we hear the music or the poem when we think it, so that we hear our own actual voice, the voice we speak our own lives with, drawn into and fused with its melodies and rhythms.

Hazlitt rightly emphasizes the fact that to re-read a book we love is not only to savour the work itself but also to enjoy the added 'pleasures of memory': 'It recalls the same feelings and associations which I had in first reading it, and which I can never have again in any other way.' As a schoolboy, I remember instructing myself more than once: 'Don't *ever* say your schooldays were the happiest days of your life' – a command to which I have remained unswervingly faithful. But school holidays are not schooldays, as such; and to think of the balmy Easter break from fifth year – a secondary school year free of exam woes – still warms what Thomas Kinsella humorously terms 'the yolk of my being'. It was not Easter eggs but Easter reading that brought about this fulfilment. No longer nesting in a tea chest, my brooding took place on a maroon-coloured kitchen chair, transported to the garden where I was revelling in the little Oxford Classics edition of *The Vicar of Wakefield*. It was as simple as that.

As a younger child, though, I had been less keen on classics, resisting in particular the nineteenth-century novels which my parents wished on me: *Swiss Family Robinson*, *Children of the New Forest* and so on – and on. These were printed on yellowing pulp paper of a North Korean standard, which soaked up blotchy ink the way 'Great Leader' Kim Il Sung soaked up the adulation of his 'Progressive People'. I read them (one read *everything*), but only as an interim measure, an emergency ration, on those still, starched days out of school with asthma, pending my return to full health – and to further raids on the library, where I would find volumes aplenty that were worthy of the high status I assigned to books. Many of the disparaged hairshirt productions were not so much true classics as out-of-copyright stories which happened to be known to, and sanctioned by, parents and grandparents – a factor which only increased the child's sense that they (the books rather than the grandparents!) were a bit musty and antiquated. What I loved beyond price were lively, brightly illustrated tales from World's Work or Blackie's; ever-reliable Antelope Books; an exotic American production, solid and shiny – illustrated with plaid lumber-jackets and crew cuts and left-drive gas-guzzling cars that swept all before them; anything at all by Enid Blyton, whose signature on her front covers represented a quality mark equivalent to the logo lettering on a Coca-Cola bottle (a lesson not lost in a town where County Cola from Dwans on Parnell Street just didn't offer the same fizz or frisson as the 'real thing').

A 7-year-old bibliographer and short-lived child diarist in 1961, I recorded a few highlights from my past reading, including titles like *The Little House in the Woods* and *The Sleepy Lion*, along with Rupert Bear annual and – as befitted a veteran of convent readings – *Pears Encyclopaedia*. The following year, on his tenth birthday, my brother Frank used some of the blank diary pages to catalogue what he called 'The O'Curry Private Library at Galtee View, Mill Road, Thurles'. Ever the historian, and now editor with his wife Mary of the scholarly *Tipperary Historical Journal*, Frank had named the library after Eugene O'Curry, the nineteenth-century historian and manuscripts scholar – an astonishingly esoteric and precocious choice for a 10-year-old. As well as true classics by writers like Robert Louis Stevenson and Jules Verne, the books he listed – having presumably salvaged them about our child-disordered house – ranged from a well-balanced pair of bipolar biographies (those of rivals Michael Collins and Eamon de Valera) to *Blackcock's Feather* and a biblical tome. The fifty-six books deposited in the O'Curry Library were divided into sixteen categories – many of which, such as 'Rilegon', 'Soldering' and 'Love' contained no more than two or three volumes. The 'History' section, with nineteen titles, was much the best stocked; 'Fiction' and 'Potery' had six volumes each. Books could only be borrowed 'when charman is present' and, with an entrepreneurial eye on expansion of the enterprise, he added 'books will be bought secondhand (on conditions)'.

It is a measure of how centrally important the public library could be for children of our generation that a home equivalent would be created by a bright 10-year-old in an austere rural home that might in some respects have been a Haworth parsonage. Our household offered no television, no record player, no musical instruments; background music came from valve radio programmes on the BBC Light and Home services and Radio Éireann: waltzes from Brighton tea-rooms and Rhoda Coghill accompaniments from the Henry Street studios in Dublin, brass bands and céilí bands, Jeanette MacDonald and Nelson Eddy, John McCormack and Jim Reeves, The Clancy Brothers and The Tulla Céilí

Band, 'I dreamt I dwelt in marble halls' and 'Kevin Barry gave his young life
for the cause of liberty'. I don't suppose it would have occurred to anyone in
my circle that music or visual art could be at the core of an education; they
were hobbies, entertainments, pastimes – and the implication was that only a
waster, a shaper or a cissy would want to study them at a boy's school.

I received not a stroke of instruction in art (though I displayed some slight
flair and had won a couple of small Caltex – now Texaco – prizes for my
doodles); not only were drama and music not taught to my class, our secondary school had no assembly room or hall in which to present a play or musical,
even had such a frivolity been contemplated. The education provided was as
rudimentary as the school's facilities: a narrow preparation for the roles in church,
bank, teaching and the civil service into which most of us drifted. We may not
have been cultivated, but we must have been courteous in a manner that
anticipated the era of 'customer service'. One of the peculiarities of my education was that, for a year or two in secondary school, my class – swains and
townies alike – was treated to a weekly lesson based on a book by our head-
master called *Courtesy for Boys and Girls*.

Glimpsing a favourite book from childhood, I shamelessly indulge in rose-
tinted memories of some red-letter day when I was the first borrower of some
similarly coveted title from the library. The pages open with an agreeable creak,
like the sound – on which every young reader becomes expert – of a door
slowly and stiffly opening to reveal hidden treasure. The print is invitingly large.
The cover foregrounds an Edward Ardizzone illustration perhaps, warm colours
washing over the bold drawings of characters whose boldness, in a different
sense, is fundamental to their charm and fascination. The smell of the book, the
feel of the paper, the allure of the illustrations, the excitement of the plot: one
delight is heaped on another. I may not know what happiness is, but I know it
smells very like a newly opened children's book. I have been following that
scent all my life, recognizing that – whereas, for adults, happiness occurs by
happenstance – bliss can be summoned, sustained, even guaranteed by the child
reader. Seamus Heaney notes that 'everybody recollects their earliest life as
somehow in the middle of a space that is separate and a little sorrowing'.
Reading provides the necessary solace and escape:

> A rose window, buried
> since Cromwellian times,
> was unearthed in the henhouse
> of a children's adventure story.
> I read about it, waiting in the car

for my father, as a shivery evening
descended on the village like an Asian flu.

(from 'Family Album')

Sorrowings notwithstanding, the obliviousness that is a synonym for happiness – we are never more contented in life than when we are out of it – triumphs regularly in childhood like the happy endings of the stories. Reading acts as a literate means of achieving pre-literate states of primary contentment – insofar, that is, as one can actually speak of happiness except retrospectively. As Hans Magnus Enzensberger remarks, 'the moment / when the word *happy* / is pronounced / never is the moment of happiness'. Books can prove as infectious as measles or mumps, the fever of the stories becoming one with the fervour of childhood itself. Here is Brandon Robshaw's encapsulation of the glowing Enid Blyton world:

> Days are always sunny; adventures take place almost entirely out of doors; food is constantly consumed (ham, cheese, hard-boiled eggs, salad, sandwiches, cakes, ice creams and, of course, lashings of ginger beer), usually in the form of picnics or high tea ... There is a clear moral structure; bad characters are punished and flawed characters learn their lesson.
>
> Most notable of all is the near-total absence of grown-ups. Uncle Quentin may hover around at the beginning of the story and he tends to pop up again right at the end, but in between he is entirely dispensed with. The children are allowed a degree of liberty which would be considered the height of parental irresponsibility today: they climb mountains, find their way into ruined castles, go swimming in the ocean, even drive motor-boats around, and all without a smidgen of adult supervision. This must be a vital part of the appeal – the vicarious sense of independence and control the books give to children, at a time when they are beginning to be old enough to realise how little power they have in reality.

Independence was certainly a well-thumbed theme in my childhood reading. After all, if childhood had been unfailingly blissful in itself, one would scarcely need the escape which books provided: escape from dependency; from being herded as a large family *en masse* to Mass; escape from adult gloom and conflict, from childhood fears and dreads. Little wonder that a book like Eleanor Graham's *The Children Who Lived in a Barn* (1938), in which five young brothers and sisters manage without their parents (and without Childlines and social workers too, as Jacqueline Wilson observed), made an unforgettable impact.

A book that has remained with me all my life – the physical object as well as the favourable recollection – is Philippa Pearce's *Tom's Midnight Garden*, a first edition hardback of which (published in 1958) I received as a gift from my aunt Eileen – Sister Gabriel of the Ursulines, one of the guardian presences of childhood. In Pearce's atmospheric book, the lonely hero – lodging with childless relatives while his brother is quarantined with measles – begins travelling through time when the clock in the hall strikes 13. It was in homage to this dysfunctional grandfather clock, living on borrowed time, that I named a recent sequence of prose poems 'Fifty O'Clock'. And time is of the essence in reading: the arresting of time and – by allowing us to live other lives in other eras – the imaginative and emotional enlargement of our own lives. The alternative lives I imagined were ones I could identify with. This preference for what I regarded as 'realistic' books would lead me to poets like Philip Larkin, Seamus Heaney and Douglas Dunn, poets whose collections were among those I bought from my first teenage pay packets. I related to wardrobes more than witches, lions more than hobbits, just as – in visual art – I came to prefer Munch to Picasso and the unflinching Northern Renaissance school over the more voluptuous Mediterranean schools.

As a young hurling heathen, in a Thurles where almost everyone was a fervent believer, I was often banished to the sidelines for games. Scrawnily built and sporting few attributes – not even a knowledge of the rules – that would make for glory on a hurling field in the very town where the GAA had been founded, my only goal was to make myself dispensable. Eventually, at the age of 14 or so, I received a welcome transfer indoors as the school's first librarian, date-stamping and card-indexing book loans to younger students when my own class was – there being no accounting for taste – flogging a ball fervently in the mud with an ash stick. While the library included high-minded, inspirational material – which, of course, remained in mint condition – the cowboy books (Zane Grey's purple sage prose especially) were 'Wanted, Dead or Alive', equalled in popularity only by the Hardy Boys mysteries. I staked a claim on a narrow seam of more valuable stuff by middlebrow authors who could write stylishly – Somerset Maugham, Saki, Steinbeck, Carson McCullers, even the forgotten Neville Shute of *Trustee from the Toolroom* – and who led the reader onwards to better things in bigger libraries. As a reader, I was gaining altitude but losing my taste for adventure. The Hardy Boys seemed synthetic, every chapter ending implausibly in a frenzied cliffhanger. I tried Agatha Christie's most famous detective story and found myself utterly bored with its thin language and a plot that creaked in all the wrong places.

It is autumn 1968. I am standing, aged 14, in a long, slowly-moving snake of schoolboys waiting for the Intermediate Certificate results when I decide to give up, there and then, on the Agatha Christie book I am reading. I can't muster the slightest interest in whodunnit. My days of trailing detectives – amateur or professional – were over. A literary puberty was well advanced. The town's, if not the world's, most zealous reader of Enid Blyton stories – of which her 'find-outers' series and her 'adventure' books reigned supreme – was in search of new adventures in words. The founder and most assiduous member of the Thurles branch of the Lone Pine Club, inspired by Malcolm Saville's gripping stories with picturesque rural settings, was in search of more taxing adventures. The only smugglers I would encounter from then on would be real ones, known to me through my job in Customs – criminals who didn't conveniently wear the crew-neck sweaters and shifty expressions that made them so immediately recognisable in an identity parade of Enid Blyton characters. December 1967 had been my last fling. My Christmas gift from my parents had included eight Malcolm Saville paperbacks. By 1969 Samuel Beckett and Henry James were at the head of my reading list; and some nimbus of forbidden fascination surrounded the hazy name of James Joyce – if only because of the tongue-lashing meted out to Frank by our mother for sullying our household propriety with *A Portrait of the Artist as a Young Man*.

Thurles having no bookshop to browse in, I continued to rely for reading material – non-fiction mainly at this stage: essays by George Orwell, poems by Austin Clarke, a biography of Rubens – on the same single-storey, multi-story library on Castle Avenue which I had first joined as an infant. A prim, trim, well-proportioned whispering gallery, set back from the street and never, of course, painted in a loud colour, it discreetly but firmly stood its ground not far from the technicolor rival attractions of The Capitol, one of the town's two cinemas (establishments known to everyone simply as 'the wan above' and 'the wan below'). Whereas the craved-for excitement of the Sunday afternoon matinee was rarely sanctioned by my parents, and I have to this day watched fewer films in my lifetime than many people see in a year, library visits – like savings stamps purchases – were a long-running Saturday morning serial:

> Saturday morning, our father ferries us to town.
> A pound of this, a scoop of that, from fragrant sacks
> of seeds, pellets, phosphates, feeds in Sutton's yard.
> A pair of brass hinges at Molloy's hardware.
> The library's squeaky-clean linoleum for Enid Blyton's
> Secret Seven, a doctor-and-nurse story for our mother,
> our father wavering between two gory wars.

Salmon-coloured stamps licked into savings books.
The sweet, addictive smell of pulped sugar beet
wafting our way on a raft of factory steam.
Bills to pay for clothes we'd tried on appro.
Then back to the car, pulling faces at passers-by,
while our father eyes a rival's cabbage plants,
doused and counted into hundreds at the market.

A busker plays a tarnished trumpet. Hawkers gesture.
Capped men off country buses check used suits for thickness.
Half-heads, teaty bellies, hard-salt flanks, smoked streaky
grace Molony's bacon window. My brothers and I caffle,
tire, then face out racing clouds until the world begins
to spin – like when our father swings us to dizziness,
sets us down on the kitchen's unstable ground.

(from 'Family Album')

You knew the library in Thurles was open when its heavy wooden double-doors, with raised panels resembling square books, were pinned back like wings and the display case of new arrivals could be tantalisingly glimpsed from the entrance path. The most sought-after children's titles, not least among reluct-ant readers who wanted an experience akin to a cinema on the page, were the comic-book annuals. A small boy is rushing home to Kickham Street, pressing an annual possessively to his duffel coat. 'What have you there?' I ask, curiosity getting the better of me. 'The Harold Harry Annual', he informs me victoriously, displaying the trophy cover on which Harold Hare is grinning – like the lad himself – from ear to velvet ear. Annuals and weekly comics like *The Topper, The Beano* and *The Beezer* brought colour to all our lives in a monochrome age of black and white opinions, black and white TV screens, and the black and white clerical dress that set the tone for a town of two seminaries, two convents and a Christian Brothers' monastery. While the service of God was seen as a job for the afterlife, I opted at sixteen for a civil service 'job for life'. Three years of legal studies and thirty years in offices dealing with specialized technical legislation would make a crucial impact on my reading pace and practice.

During secondary school holidays, I had been sampling the library copy of the cobalt-blue Oxford Standard Authors edition of Wordsworth: seven hundred double-column pages in small print. The fact that the volume opened with a poem 'composed in anticipation of leaving school' heightened my sense of being at the threshold of some vital lifelong commitment to this poet and to poetry. I was quickly, as it were, becoming a slow reader, savouring words and images and rhythms and ideas rather than story lines. Just as I am a tedious companion in an art gallery, where I wear down the canvases with staring, so I am a very deliberate reader, turning the pages hesitantly and staring over my shoulder in case I missed anything first time round. I collect and publish literary quotations. I note down sources. I cross-reference articles. I file and index reviews. For about ten years, much of my work in the stamp duties office in Dublin Castle pivoted around a relief for company amalgamations and reconstructions which the standard textbook on the topic, *Sergeant on Stamp Duties*, characterized as 'one of the longest and most complicated sections in revenue legislation'. Only a slow reader, prepared to outstare each individual word and to tease out every possible implication, could survive for long in such a job. There are worse groundings for a poetry critic than the study of law.

Poets – seldom found in civil service offices nowadays – are increasingly employed in creative writing departments of universities. Michael Donaghy once remarked that saying you studied English because you love poetry is 'like saying I studied vivisection because I loved dogs'. But there is a vast difference between a student being systematically walked through great poems and novels by a sympathetic English department mentor and having those works treated as plastic bones for aspirant writers to cut their creative teeth on. Instead of being read for their own sake, for enjoyment, enlightenment and a fresh angle on reality, the great works are degraded by the creative writing industry into a kind of booster rocket to be discarded once the would-be author has been launched into an inspirational orbit.

One of the most popular internet sites summarizes its advice to teenage writers in three words, 'read, read, read'. 'Reading', it goes on, 'can teach you to write better and it can teach you how not to write. It can give you ideas, topics to write about, tidbits and facts to work into your fiction or poetry …' Having continued in breathless vein, the instructor paused for a 'But'. After this potentially pregnant pause, I naively expected a peroration exhorting people to read for pure pleasure; or for the understanding of the world reading fosters, the language it finds for our losses and joys, the insights it offers into the human condition, its capacity to break and lift our hearts at once. Instead, teenagers were warned that those who spend too much time reading – albeit in pursuit of creative kindling – will be depriving themselves of time for their precious writing. Robert Hass, probably America's finest living poet, has confessed that, while there are times when he reads poetry 'only in the hope that it will inspire me to write', it 'crosses my mind that what I do write will be read, if it is, by poets who are only reading it so that they will be inspired to write'. Addressing his deeper reading of poetry – 'out of need' – he concludes that not only will reading 'clarify and focus inchoate feeling', it will sometimes 'not help me live my life, but make living it seem impossible'.

Only when we are prepared to be challenged and resisted and appalled as well as charmed and cheered and inspired by what we read are we engaging deeply with literature, opening ourselves fully to its scope. But for many writers, whose attention span is conterminous with the responsive click of the internet pointer and the flick of the TV zapper, serious reading may be a very difficult discipline to master. All those small-print pages, all that tiresome concentration. Here's what an American professor – himself a writer – told me recently about his students: 'As for reading, they would rather write, which is the product of the computer age, of course. Banging away on the computer, giving vent to TV notions of the world, is like a playstation.' The drawback, however, in being a slow reader, taking poetry and prose at a pre-TV and -DVD pace, is that – at this leisurely rate – one will leave so much great literature unread. Books I once gazed on with avid anticipation, I now contemplate with something akin to elegiac dread; books I had virtually taken as read and imagined re-reading in old age still elude me. I revise some famous lines of Keats to say, 'I have fears that I may cease to be / Before my brain has gleaned those teeming books'. I try to half-heartedly convince myself that some of these volumes would have proved disappointing; but I – who have squandered my way through so many Sunday newspaper supplements and literary periodicals and mediocre books and reviews of mediocre books – repudiate my self-serving propaganda.

It is difficult to state precisely why reading is so essential. It is impossible to disentangle the linguistic pleasures from the moral insights, the wisdom from the knowledge, the cadence from the characterization. One may quickly forget the details of a plot or the premises of a philosophy and yet feel changed forever by having read the book. 'Education is what remains after one has forgotten what one has learned in school' is Albert Einstein's formulation. The nearest adult experience I know to being a child, eagerly turning pages in the kitchen while my mother – hands gloved in a dishcloth – takes from the oven a sugar-dusted apple pie that is sweating cinnamon through its pores, is being a slow reader of a great book, entering a zone of timelessness. I suspect that it is only in such a state that we are detached enough from the attachments of the everyday to gain access to those profound truths and poignant yearnings that are the ultimate goal of serious readers and the richest reward a writer can bestow. And it is significant that, in writing poetry, what is remembered with uncanny intensity is often some experience one hadn't realized was being even casually registered at the time. If we want to see the world with a clarity and amplitude denied us by the dazzle of our electronic screens, we must take a step beyond chronological time and enter the 13 o'clock world of *Tom's Midnight Garden*.

The realization that – despite having renounced TV, cinema, DVDs, pubs, thrillers, golf, morris dancing and just about everything else – the odds are stacked against my being able to tick off as read all of the books that anyone half-civilized should know fills me with panic. It is as if we are barely granted a sidelong glance at the world when it is time to leave it again. Life, I have always said derisively, is too short to accommodate this or that trashy book; but how am I to cope with the creeping awareness that it is literally too short to allow for nearly enough of the great poetry, fiction, essays, journals, memoirs, letters, criticism, travel writing, art history and all the rest of it to be absorbed? I contemplated writing my way out of this frustration. Could my not having read, say, Hobbes' *Leviathan* really become raw material for a poem? Why not just devote time to reading the book and spare the world my moans about not having bagged it? However illogical or contradictory, the inner pressure to explore my word-craving in words proved so overwhelming that I felt compelled to succumb, eventually making not just one but *two* stabs at the topic. The first, called 'Classic Days', was itself in two parts:

I

What a day to be alive,
on leave from work, free
to sit out among sun and flowers,
a renewable supply of song birds
perched on birch and beech and yew.

I want to catch up with an unread classic,
some book of hours, long
looked forward to, one of those
sessions of sweet silent thought
last granted as a schoolboy

when an aromatic tea chest,
stamped 'Ceylon', was my
wood-panelled reading room,
the garden unwinding around me
like a delayed-action nature programme.

Having had it to up to there with worldly
life, what I now want is the right
to plunge headlong into books,

to clear space for another run at Proust,
dust off *Buddenbrooks*, take on Boswell's
Life of Johnson, re-discover *Adam Bede*.

A rueful sense of wasted time afflicts me,
reading an advertisement for Loeb Classics:
a 'freshly-edited' version of Valerius Maximus

to die for; a new two-volume Virgil (*Georgics*,
Eclogues and the *Aeneid*) to gorge on.
The backlist's Aristophanes and the Horace *Odes*.

Sometimes a creaky fragment of school Latin
or a fleeting tale of seafaring Greeks will surface
in my mind, like driftwood floating in a wreck.

'492 books strong', the Loeb announcement boasts.
What a long leisurely life I could have done with.
And what a happy life it might have been.

When a letter from John Lucas, the English critic and poet, brought an invitation to contribute to a book celebrating Anne Stevenson's seventieth birthday, I decided to offer 'Classic Days': it seemed thematically well-suited to a poet as widely-read and as attuned to literary tradition as Anne. By the time the Lucas book had been published and noticed in the *Times Literary Supplement* – where the reviewer was enormously encouraging about 'Classic Days' – I had unravelled the entire poem as ruthlessly as Penelope's shroud and started again. I wanted to home in even closer on the joys of childhood reading and to counterpoint the mortal pangs I feel when – if I may again redistribute Keats' words – standing before 'high-piled books', knowing I will never harvest their 'full ripen'd grain'. I'm not sure that my second effort, 'Book Sale', is any more definitive than the first:

Seizing, as if in panic,
armfuls of reduced-price classics,
  bound in sombre, artful jackets,
he is determined at last to take
  a stand on *Crime and Punishment*,
come to terms with *The Rights of Man*,
  surrender to the power of *Leviathan*,
renew youth like a library book:
  remembered times past when,
cushioned from hardship, lying astride
  an easy-chair or in the wood-panelled
reading room of a summer garden lair,
  an aromatic tea chest marked *Ceylon*,
he plunged headlong into adventure,
  knowing contentment like the back
of his page-turning hand, oblivious
  to the rota of household chores,
the squeegee singing of a thrush,
  the tennis ball's monotonous crush
on a gable wall, the canter
  of an empty meat tin blowing
like perpetual motion near the bin,
  cows ripping out chapters of grass.
He expects more substance from
  his reading now, of course,
and these books he stacks up
  at the cash desk have a weighty feel:
You must change your life is what
  he wants to hear them say,
There is still time to begin.
  They will fill his shelves like resolutions,
tasks he must get round to some day soon:
  that leaking tap, that creaking door,
that bathroom fungus needing close attention.

When I was a schoolboy, my classmates pitched some of their reviled text-books into the river Suir at the end of the Leaving Certificate exams, a gesture like that which Prospero promises at the close of *The Tempest*. But the school-boys had little Prospero-like sense of the magic that was contained in anth-

ologies of prescribed prose and poetry, the very books on which Patrick
Kavanagh's precocious but precarious talent had been nurtured in his Inniskeen
hedge school. I didn't drown any texts 'deeper than did ever plummet sound'.
Having shut my favourite childhood books in the preceding years, I had begun
to give primacy to poetry, abandoning in the distance *The Island of Adventure*
by Enid Blyton, *Strangers at Snowfell* by Malcolm Saville, *The Wind on the Moon*
by Eric Linklater, Biggles, Jennings, Billy Bunter, William. Long cured too was
the ache to pack a trunk for public school, to have mortar-boarded 'beaks' as
teachers and quads and removes instead of a rough gravel schoolyard, to plot
midnight feasts washed down with ginger beer, to while away summer hols on
some island of adventure where mysteries were the norm and crimes that
baffled policemen could be solved by a few inquisitive, independent-minded
children and their laterally thinking dog.

I have no access now to the 'library of adventure'; in fact, I haven't even
been a member of a library for a decade. But something of the hushed pleasures of libraryhood are still accessible on days when I am fortunate enough to
have set aside time for reading and my book-lined study, overlooking a formal
garden, is as soundproofed and trouble-proofed as the most cushioned tea chest
from monsoon-drenched Dimbula. In Montaigne's words: 'It is my throne, and
I try to rule here absolutely, reserving this one corner from all society.' Am I
aged 50 o'clock or 13 o'clock? My God, look at the time – and I need to be up
at 6 for work.

By the close of *Tom's Midnight Garden*, the clock hands have stretched well
beyond 13 and Hatty, the girl befriended every night by Tom in his visionary
garden, is an old woman. Even in children's books, the pages of time must finally
turn and 'the end' be greeted with a bereft but satisfied sigh:

> A village clock struck across the darkened countryside, and Tom thought
> of Time: how he had been sure of mastering it, and exchanging his own
> Time for an Eternity of Hatty's and so of living pleasurably in the gar-
> den for ever. The garden was still there, but meanwhile Hatty's Time
> had stolen a march on him, and had turned Hatty herself from his play-
> mate into a grown-up woman.

On seeing the old director's office derelict

5 February 2003

THE DIRECTOR'S OFFICE had moved from the main National Library building to the newly refurbished 4 Kildare Street, and the former office was being converted to a passageway linking the main building and the new wing where the exhibition centre and lecture room are now located.

> Transient our fiefdoms –
> To this plundered space,
> This bare, abandoned spot,
> Historians, poets, scholars
> Once beat a path.
> Sunlight of early spring
> Illumines carvings,
> Sumptuous,
> Of the fireplace,
> Round whose flame, long dead,
> Ghosts hover:
> Lyster, Hayes, Henchy,
> And those who served them.
> On the dusty mantel
> Sits a stone,
> Sculpted,
> From the façade,
> Broken.

GERARD LYNE

The Roman triumph

Mary Beard[1]

O N 1 MAY 2005, the British *Independent on Sunday* newspaper published a cartoon by Peter Schrank – reproduced on page 329 – in which Tony Blair was portrayed as a victorious Roman general on his triumphal victory parade. Dressed in a sort of toga, he was shown making his way towards a very Napoleonic triumphal arch on which waved the flag of a 'third term'. We now know that Blair was triumphant and that he did make it to his third stretch as prime minister; but at the time it was not so clear and the spectre of the continuing war in Iraq seemed to be undermining his chances of re-election. Hence, the figure of Death behind, his scythe blazoning the name of the country that promised to be Blair's nemesis. This grim figure suggests that the cartoonist knew more about the triumph and its darker side than we might imagine. But first, what is this ritual represented here?

* * *

We tend, I think, to take the idea of triumph for granted. It is a familiar word in our own usage: people triumph over adversity; movie performances are an absolute triumph; once upon a time a Triumph Spitfire was the car to die for. It has come to stand for more or less any kind of victory. But it goes back to something much more specific in ancient Rome. There the triumph was a clearly defined ceremony. It involved a procession by a victorious general with his troops and prisoners and booty through the streets of Rome, up to the temple of Jupiter on the Capitoline hill.[2] It was an honour not granted to just any victorious general: according to one Roman tradition, in order to claim a triumph it was necessary to have secured a victory in which there were at least five thousand enemy casualties.[3] It was intended for very great successes – or massacres.

---

1 This essay is a lightly edited and footnoted version of the inaugural John O'Meara lecture I was honoured to give to the National Library of Ireland Society in Dublin on 14 Sept. 2005. The research on which it is based was mainly the outcome of a senior research fellowship awarded by the Leverhulme Trust; it is to be published in full by Harvard University Press. 2 Clear introductory accounts of the ritual in English can be found in K. Hopkins, *Conquerors and slaves* (Cambridge, 1978), pp 26–9; see also E. Champlin, *Nero* (Cambridge, MA, 2003), pp 210–15. 3 Valerius Maximus, *Facta et dicta memorabilia* 2, 8.

In Roman imagination the ceremony went back to the earliest days of the city, back to the founder Romulus. It was calculated that there had been 320 triumphs between the foundation of Rome in the eighth century BC and the first century CE, which means a triumphal procession roughly every two or three years.[4] The institution lasted right up into the Byzantine period, or on some definitions even longer. For there has hardly been a dictator, monarch or dynast in the West who has not continued or recreated the tradition of the triumph. Napoléon had a definite fondness for triumphal imagery, as we might guess from his famous Arc de Triomphe. But there are some rather less predictable inheritors of the Roman tradition. Admiral Dewey celebrated his victory over the Philippines in the early twentieth century with a triumphal parade down Madison Avenue in New York, complete with a cardboard triumphal arch. And it was not just a phenomenon of the West. Saddam Hussein had a variant on a triumphal arch erected in Baghdad.[5]

Roman writers tell us a great deal about the triumphal procession, describing the ceremonies of famous generals with often graphic details: Pompey the Great in 61 BC who defeated the Eastern King Mithridates and cleared the Mediterranean of pirates; Julius Caesar who a few years later held a mammoth celebration for campaigns in Gaul, Africa and the East (it was during this triumph that he displayed on placards his famous slogan *veni vidi vici* – I came, I saw, I conquered).[6] From these accounts it seems clear that triumphal parades were generally divided into three parts. At the front came the captured prisoners and the plunder acquired from the war. Occasionally, we are told, there was so much booty that it took two or even three days to trundle it through the city. In the middle was the general himself with his entourage. The victorious soldiery brought up the rear, behaving in the way that squaddies might be expected to do: they sang ribald songs about their general. Some of the most famous of these verses were sung at the triumph of Julius Caesar: 'Romans look out for your wives, the bald adulterer's back home' – a piece of ribaldry which would not, I imagine, have unduly perturbed the general.[7]

A closer look at some parts of the procession shows what an impact it must have had. Directly in front of the general's chariot, we are told, came the prisoners and captives. These could not possibly have included all of those who

---

4 The figure 320 is given by Orosius, *Historiae adversum paganos* 7, 9, 8. **5** The Dewey arch will be discussed in M. Malamud, *New Romes for a new world* (forthcoming). Saddam's arch (known as the 'Hands of Victory') was made in the form of two crossed swords. **6** Key ancient accounts include: Plutarch, *Pompey* 45 and Appian, *Mithradatic war,* 116–7 (Pompey); Appian, *Civil war* 2, 101–2 and Suetonius, *Divus Julius* 37 (Caesar); Appian, *Punic war* 66 (Scipio Africanus, 201 BC). **7** Suetonius, *Divus Julius* 37.

were taken during the campaign, of course; the vast majority was probably sold into slavery in the war zone. The triumphal procession would have featured the most glamorous, famous or dastardly. There was a certain competition between generals here. On one occasion, for example, Pompey is said to have stolen a particularly striking captured pirate from one of his Roman rivals in order to decorate his own procession.[8] Captured kings and queens were a particular draw. In the third century CE, the queen Zenobia made a tremendous impact, loaded with so many golden chains that she had to have servants to carry them for her.[9]

It was understandable that many of the most notable prisoners were keen to avoid such public humiliation, and the nasty execution that might also be their fate. For the story was that, as the general reached the last stretch of the procession and was about to climb the Capitoline hill, the key captives were hauled off to be killed. Anticipating this, there was a predictable series of suicides by captured monarchs – most famously by Cleopatra after the death of Mark Anthony.[10] But even then, they did not altogether escape exhibition in the procession. If a prisoner were unavoidably absent, the general would often have a painting or model made instead. Caesar displayed some extremely gory pictures of his opponents' final moments – and there was a famous model made of Cleopatra herself, apparently in the attitude in which she had died, complete with an asp or two.[11]

The booty of war seems to have been mixed in with the prisoners or carried in front of them at the very head of the procession. Sometimes this was on a stupendous scale. Roman writers list vast quantities of bullion and coin carried through the streets on wagons and carts: in the triumph of Pompey in 61 BC there were what is described as '75,100,000 drachmas' of silver coin on show.[12] This was more than the entire tax revenue of the Roman world at the time – or, to put it another way, enough to keep two million people alive for a year. But no less important than the cash were the works of art, the curiosities and the bric-a-brac picked up on campaign. At Pompey's triumph again, there were said to be 'vessels of gold and gems, enough to fill nine display cabinets, three gold statues of Minerva, Mars and Apollo, thirty-three crowns of pearl' and 'the first vessels of agate ever brought to Rome'. And this is not to mention an out-sized gaming board, three feet by four, made out of two different types of precious stone – and on the board, apparently, a golden moon weighing thirty pounds.[13] There might be exotic flora and fauna too from

8 Dio Cassius, *Histories* 36, 19. **9** Scriptores Historiae Augustae, *Aurelian* 34, 3. **10** Horace, *Odes* 1, 37, 29–32; Plutarch, *Mark Antony* 84. **11** Propertius, *Elegies* 3, 11, 53–4; Dio Cassius, *Histories* 51, 21. **12** Appian, *Mithradatic war*, 116. **13** Pliny, *Historia naturalis* 37, 13–14; 18 (agate).

13 Cartoon by Peter Schrank, in the *Independent on Sunday*, 1 May 2005.

the conquered territories, elephants or even rare trees. Most modern scholars have seen this whole array as more than just a display of booty and wealth. It is almost as if the procession represented a microcosm of the very processes of Roman imperialism, literally bringing the world – the *orbs* – into the city – the *urbs*. New discoveries, new profits were brought from the very edge of Roman territory into the cosmopolitan centre, for theatrical display.[14]

The most notorious booty ever brought to the city raises rather different issues. In AD 71, the Roman emperor Vespasian and his son and heir, Titus, celebrated a triumph for the quashing of the revolt of the Jews and the destruction of the Temple in Jerusalem.[15] In the course of this, they paraded the holy objects from the Temple – as is described by a Jewish turncoat witness and portrayed in a large sculptural relief on the arch put up in the Roman Forum to commemorate the occasion. Usually the fate of the booty after the procession remains frustratingly unknown to us, or is a matter of guesswork. This is one of the few cases where we have some idea of what happened next to these objects. Josephus, the Jewish turncoat witness, carefully notes that the

14 P. Hardie, *Ovid's poetics of illusion* (Cambridge, 2002), p. 310; T. Murphy, *Pliny the Elder's natural history: the empire in the encyclopaedia* (Oxford, 2004), pp 155, 160. **15** This triumph is fully discussed in M. Beard, 'The triumph of Flavius Josephus' in A.J. Boyle and W.J. Dominik (eds), *Flavian Rome: culture, image, text* (Leiden and Boston, 2003), pp 543–58.

majority of them went into Vespasian's new Temple of Peace – except for the scrolls of the Law and the purple hangings from the Temple, which were kept in the imperial palace itself.[16] But what happened after that, especially to the famous menorah (the seven-branched candlestick), has been the subject of controversy for centuries. Different hypotheses have it crisscrossing the Mediterranean through the middle ages, being moved by the first Christian emperor Constantine to his new capital of Constantinople, being robbed by the Vandals, returned to Jerusalem but plundered again later, and so on. One particularly picturesque version has the menorah lost in the river Tiber on 28 October 312 CE, falling into the river from the Milvian Bridge during the flight of Maxentius from his victorious rival, Constantine.[17] Quite how Maxentius is supposed to have got his hands on it is not stated. An alternative idea, with a strong following even now, contends that the object never left Rome at all and remains to this day in the storerooms of the Vatican. We have no idea which of these stories, if any, is right. Yet the continuing conflicts around this single piece of Roman plunder are a wonderful proof of how the moral, religious and cultural controversies of the triumph continue even today.

At the centre of the procession, between the prisoners and the spoils in front and the troops behind, came the general himself. It is he who has most captured the imagination of modern scholars. He was dressed for the show, more or less, in the costume of the statue of the god Jupiter Optimus Maximus in the Capitoline temple, his face was painted red just like the statue and he was decked out with a series of divine or kingly attributes. He held a sceptre, a branch of laurel or perhaps palm in his hand; he had a laurel wreath on his head. His young children travelled with him in the chariot, to give them a taste for glory. Underneath the chariot was hung a phallus – to ward off the evil eye, it was said. Behind the general – just where we see the grim presence of Death in the Blair cartoon – stood a slave who held a golden crown over his head and, it is said, constantly reminded him in a whisper throughout the whole procession that he was only a man: 'look behind you, remember you're a man, remember you're a man.' The idea was that, at this his greatest hour, he was all too likely to forget that he was human.[18]

It is fairly clear why he has been the subject of such modern interest. His divine attributes – his straddling of the boundary between god and man – have

---

16 Josephus, *Jewish war* 7, 158–62. 17 The controversies are summarized in L. Yarden, *The spoils of Jerusalem on the arch of Titus* (Stockholm, 1991). 18 These features are variously attested in Pliny, *Historia naturalis* 28, 39 (phallus); 33, 111 (red paint); Tertullian, *Apologeticus* 33 (slave); Tzetzes, *Letters* 107 (slave); Livy 10, 7, 10 (clothes of Jupiter); 45, 40, 7–8 (children).

been grist to a whole range of theories of religion, from James Frazer and *The Golden Bough* to the present day.[19] But whatever theory of this we decide to adopt, the key fact is that, in the competitive culture of Rome and the Roman elite's relentless search for glory, the victorious and triumphant general was the closest thing to a god that Roman man ever came. If little boys at Rome closed their eyes and thought about the best thing that might happen to them, it is a fair bet that, nine times out of ten, that would be a triumph.

The idea of triumph seeped widely through Roman culture, even if not in such an attenuated sense as in our own. Roman intellectuals speculated on the origins of the ceremony and the reasons for some of its characteristic oddities, while there were notable re-enactments on the Roman stage. Roman poets, too, imagined how the ceremony might have taken place in the time of myth. In one epic poem of the first century CE, for example, we find the Greek hero Theseus celebrating a Roman-style triumph over the warrior women Amazons.[20] And in the second century CE the powers that be were so keen to give the emperor Trajan a triumph even though he had died that they hosted a procession with a wax model of the emperor in the chariot.[21] But there is clear evidence of its impact on 'popular' Roman culture too. We know of a gladiator called 'Triumphus' and a town in the province of Spain going under the name 'Triumphale'.[22] For one racy Roman poet, the triumphal procession was an excellent place to pick up a girl. The idea was that the girl would not understand what all the material was that was being trundled past her and that it was an excellent start to a chat-up routine to help her out by explaining – even if you didn't quite know yourself.[23] There are also all kinds of other stories and anecdotes that revolve around the ceremony. During Rome's war against Hannibal, two prodigious infants were supposed to have uttered the words traditionally chanted in the triumphal procession *io triumphe*: the first, aged six months; the second – even more incredibly – *in utero*. The triumph stood at the heart of Roman culture.[24]

* * *

Yet the triumph was not so simple as this account makes it seem. There are, in fact, all kinds of questions that can be raised about this apparently clear picture. The first, to put it straightforwardly, is how far should we believe what we are told about the ceremony. In many respects that is now impossible to judge, but

---

19 H.S. Versnel, *Triumphus: an inquiry into the origin, development and meaning of the Roman triumph* (Leiden, 1970), pp 56–93 reviews the various theories, as well as providing further documentation of the appearance of the general. **20** Statius, *Thebaid* 12, 519–98. **21** Scriptores Historiae Augustae, *Hadrian* 6. **22** Seneca, *De providentia* 4, 4; Pliny, *Historia naturalis* 3, 10. **23** Ovid, *Ars amatoria*, 1, 217–21. **24** Livy 21, 62; 24, 10.

some of the figures of the riches on display must surely be the product of a good deal of exaggeration – or at least of over-optimism about what Roman power could launch. Only a very few of the accounts we have are from eyewitnesses – not that eyewitnesses are especially reliable when it comes to describing lavish processions, as those who have looked at their accounts of modern spectacle have shown. Many of the most detailed descriptions are by those writing, with no doubt rose-tinted spectacles, hundreds of years after the events they describe. Is it really feasible, for example, that Pompey's triumph included a solid gold statue of Mithridates eight cubits (roughly four metres) tall?[25] But, even supposing we were to believe that, there are other indications that the picture we are sometimes offered hardly adds up. What kind of balancing act, for example, would be required of a general simply to stay upright in a horse-drawn chariot travelling over the bumpy Roman streets, both hands full with a sceptre and laurel branch, sharing the ride with a couple of children and a slave? Surely this picture of the triumphing general is the celebratory photo-graph image, not the real life triumph. It is a bit like imagining that university students frolic around their campuses wearing the gowns and mortar board in which they are seen in the photo on their Mum and Dad's piano.

The next question is to wonder quite how typical these big blockbuster affairs that dominate our image of the Roman triumph actually were. The basic template with which we work is drawn from those over-the-top, multi-day spectaculars overflowing with spoils, troops, glamorous prisoners and elaborate artistic recreations of the general's successful encounters. A moment's thought should prompt some hesitation. It is not just that these mega-ceremonies could only have been feasible relatively late in Roman history, once Roman imperialism was drawing in the wealth of the Eastern kingdoms. It is more than a question of chronology. Even after the period when lavish celebrations were possible, they certainly were not all like that. And some ancient writers do occasionally note that there were no spoils or no prisoners on show.[26] Out of the total of 320, the 'average' triumph was probably a much more modest affair: a token squad of troops, a couple of unfortunate prisoners and half a wagonful of loot.

But the major point that challenges the standard view of the ceremony concerns the image of the general himself, the fragility of the triumph's success and the version of Roman culture that the parade presents. My argument is that if you look more carefully at the triumph, it appears not only as a vehicle of Roman imperialist aggression, but also as a ceremony which raised all kinds of doubts and problems about victory, glory and personal status. That is to say that

25 Appian, *Mithradatic war*, 116.   **26** For example, Livy 31, 49, 3; 45, 42, 2.

Roman accounts of triumphs repeatedly challenge the glory that they appear to celebrate.

The first issue is triumphal *failure*. We tend to tell the story of triumphs as a story of success: the great general secures his massive victory and comes home to be granted a triumph by senate and people. The only failure we notice is the failure of those generals who – despite what they regarded as an entirely triumph-worthy rout – were not granted the glory of a triumphal procession. This is, however, a woefully one-sided reading of what Roman writers have to say about triumphal ceremonies. For a prominent theme also is concern with the failures, disasters and upsets in even the grandest parades.

Spectacle is always a risky business. Great public celebrations can go wrong as well as right – and the greater they try to be, the 'wronger' they can go. Ancient writers on the triumph stress this, time and again. Sometimes the practical arrangements go embarrassingly awry. For example, according to Plutarch and others, Pompey got above himself at one of his triumphs and chose to yoke elephants, and not horses, to his triumphal chariot – he was supposedly imitating the god Bacchus. Everything went fine till he had to pass through a gate, where the elephants ignominiously got stuck; he tried a second time and it was still no good, and everyone had to hang around while they were replaced with horses.[27] The moral was obvious. Julius Caesar too, on one of his triumphal occasions, was forced to interrupt proceedings after the axle of his chariot broke and a replacement had to be quickly rustled up.[28]

Sometimes, even if the procession itself went off smoothly, the nature of what was on display scored an own goal for the triumphing general. There was a very fine line between splendour and excessive luxury, between the proud parade of victory and frankly bad taste. There was, we are told, considerable shaking of heads at those pictures of his enemies' final moments that Caesar displayed at one of his triumphs, including a painting of the noble Cato disembowelling himself.[29] Pompey too raised anxieties with one particularly extravagant object carried in his procession in 61 BC. This was a portrait head of the great general himself made entirely of pearls. The elder Pliny, that curmudgeonly and moralizing encyclopaedist who died when his curiosity got the better of him at the eruption of Vesuvius, used all the advantages of hindsight to draw the moral here. This was not just effeminizing luxury, though it was certainly that – no decent Roman male had themselves modelled in *pearl*; it was more than that, since for Pompey to have his head on display without a body was a nasty presage of his own death by decapitation on the shores of Egypt.[30]

27 Plutarch, *Pompey*, 14. **28** Suetonius, *Divus Julius*, 37, 2. **29** Appian, *Civil war*, 2, 101.
30 Pliny, *Historia naturalis*, 37, 14–16.

The triumph, in other words, boded Pompey's downfall as much as it celebrated his success.

Even when nothing went wrong in that sense, triumphs brought into focus
much bigger questions about Roman status, values and heroism. Roman writers
repeatedly ask us to reflect on the nature of the glory that the triumph celebrates.
Are these lavish processions a decent and proper reflection of Roman
achievement? Or are they mere baubles, not the real thing? As often, Pompey
is the key example. In an epic poem on the great civil war between Pompey and
Julius Caesar – after Caesar has 'crossed the Rubicon' – written a hundred years
later, Pompey is portrayed not as enhanced by his triumphs but as repeatedly
dogged by his triumphal career and his own obsession with the superficial allure
of triumphal glory. On the night before the final, disastrous battle, the poet Lucan
has him taken back in his dream to the day of his first triumph and the applause
of senate and people on that occasion – here turned, as with the pearly head,
into an uncanny presage of his imminent defeat. And when it comes to his funeral
pyre, it is not his body that is thrown onto the flames, but his triumphal togas.[31]
It is not just the cynical Lucan who takes this line. Cicero has much the same to
say about Pompey's preoccupation with his triumphal fancy dress.[32]

But the final twist in the triumphal tale comes with the repeated slippage or
even confusion we find between triumphal victor and triumphal victim. The
basic paradox is a straightforward one: military victory against feeble opposition
is never worth boasting about; the more impressive the prisoners, the greater
the glory that accrues to the victor – but, at the same time, the greater the risk
that the strikingly noble and worthy captives will upstage the noble and
worthy general. Time and again ancient writers reflect on and explore this
paradox – to the extent that triumphal narratives come to represent some of the
sharpest questioning from inside Roman culture of the very nature of Roman
success. For example, the mere sight of the Egyptian princess Arsinoe in Caesar's
triumphal procession moved the audience to tears and, so it is said, caused them
to reflect on their own misfortunes – rather, that is, than on Caesar's glory.[33]

Occasionally a much more elaborate story is woven. Here the key example
concerns the general Aemilius Paullus and his triumph over the Eastern king
Perseus in 167 BC. Part of this story is one of Arsinoe-style upstaging. It was,
one writer insists, the young children of the king walking as prisoners in the
procession who captured the attention and provoked the tears of the audience.[34]
But the ambivalence between victor and victim informs accounts of this
triumph in a much more detailed way, explicitly subverting the hierarchy of

31 Lucan, *Pharsalia*, 7, 6–28; 8, 175–9. **32** Cicero, *Ad Atticum*, 1, 18, 6. **33** Dio Cassius,
Histories, 43, 19. **34** Plutarch, *Aemilius Paullus*, 33, 4.

success between Paullus and the defeated Perseus. For, at the very height of his apparent glory, Paullus was afflicted by a disaster that struck at the heart of his household: one of his two sons died five days before the triumph, the other three days after. Of Perseus' children, on the other hand, one at least survived to learn metalworking and Latin, and became a secretary to Roman magistrates – a job, we are told, he carried out with skill and elegance. Livy, writing more than a hundred years after the events, puts the obvious comparison into the mouth of Paullus himself:

> Both Perseus and I are now on display, as powerful examples of the fate of mortal men. He, who as a prisoner saw his children led before him … nevertheless has those children unharmed. I, who triumphed over him, mounted my chariot fresh from the funeral of my one son and, as I returned from the Capitol, found the other almost breathing his last … There is no Paullus in my house except one old man.[35]

And the theme is echoed several times in Roman moral and philosophical writing, which insists that you could show equal virtue whether you were the triumphant general or the prisoner dragged in front of the triumphal chariot, provided you were 'unconquered in spirit'.[36] Those are extraordinary claims in a culture that is often seen as having nothing but contempt for defeated opponents.

The message is clear. Triumphal glory was a perilous and greasy pole. The triumph prompted the question of who was really the victor – and so what really constituted virtue and heroism. Roman triumphs and their narration were not only jingoistic celebrations of military success; they also provided a framework within which the fault lines and the uncertainties of Roman militarism were explored.

* * *

This brings us back to the cartoon with which I started. It is clear enough that the figure of Death here replaces that of the slave in the triumphal chariot, whispering to the general 'remember you're a man, remember you're a man'. But the cartoonist is not simply offering an in-joke for the classically trained. For this cartoon also picks up and rubs home the darker aspects of triumphal culture that have been discussed in this essay. It hardly needs saying that there are messages here about our own world as much as the Roman world – even

35 Livy 45, 40, 7–8; 41, 10–11; Plutarch, *Aemilius Paullus*, 35, 1–2; Valerius Maximus, *Facta et dicta memorabilia*, 5, 10, 2. **36** Seneca, *Letters*, 71, 22.

more uncomfortably sombre messages than when the cartoon was first published in Spring 2005. In a nutshell, triumphalist rhetoric – whenever, wherever – always sows the seeds of its own subversion; triumphs are never quite what they seem.

The purchase of the Irish embassy in Paris, 1954

J. Anthony Gaughan

THE IRISH EMBASSY IN PARIS stands at one of the most prestigious locations in the French capital. It is at the corner of Avenue Foch, formerly Avenue du Bois de Boulogne, and rue Rude. The latter street is named after the sculptor of the Arc de Triomphe, just two hundred metres distant at the Place de l'Étoile. Notwithstanding its location, the purchase of the embassy in 1954 was the subject of considerable controversy.

The first Irish permanent diplomatic presence in Paris was at 37 bis rue Paul Valéry. This residence was leased in 1929 and housed only a foreign mission until 1950 when the government raised the status of the legation to ambassadorial rank. In 1953 Cornelius C. Cremin,[1] the first Irish ambassador to France, suggested that the embassy be moved to another premises. He pointed to the changed environment of the neighbourhood and the inadequate office accommodation for himself and the staff. Moreover, it seems that large expenditure would have been necessary to make the existing premises suitable.

In November 1953, at the request of the minister for external affairs, Frank Aiken, who was also acting minister for finance, the government authorized Raymond McGrath, then principal architect at the Office of Public Works, and a colleague to inspect a premises at 17 rue du Conseiller Collignon, which were on offer for approximately £102,000. The principal architect recommended against the purchase of these premises for a new embassy. However, while in Paris, he and his colleague also inspected the Hôtel de Breteuil on Avenue Foch. This was at the suggestion of the ambassador who had been alerted by his wife – by a curious coincidence, a friend of the owner – to the fact that this desirable property was for sale.

McGrath reported favourably on the Hôtel de Breteuil and indicated that it was on offer for approximately £158,000. The department of external affairs requested sanction to acquire it, and also for a further visit to Paris by McGrath to facilitate its purchase. In mid-December Frank Aiken, in his capacity as acting minister for finance, approved its purchase. His approval carried three conditions:

---

1 Cremin (1908–87) was one of the leading Irish ambassadors of his generation. For more, see Niall Keogh, *Con Cremin, Ireland's wartime diplomat* (Cork, 2006).

no more than 155,000 francs were to be paid for the building; the purchase was to be negotiated by the ambassador and a local lawyer; and the building was not to be acquired before 1 April 1954, the beginning of the state's next financial year.[2]

* * *

The Hôtel de Breteuil was built for Henri–Charles, eigth marquis de Breteuil, in the early 1890s. He came from a long line of diplomats, soldiers and ministers. He had an Irish connection: in 1720 his ancestor, Claude-Charles de Breteuil, married Lady Laura O'Brien de Clare who was from an Irish Jacobite family. Henri-Charles was a career officer in the French army. He married an American, Marcelite Garner, a cotton heiress, whose fortune funded the construction of their new home. The architect was Ernest Sanson, well known for his classical constructions.

The four-storied Hôtel de Breteuil has no less than thirty-one rooms and a small garden on the Avenue Foch frontage. Among its features are some remarkable examples of French *boiserie*. This gilded panelling – in the grand salon, dining room and library on the first floor – had initially enhanced an early eighteenth-century mansion, long since demolished. The de Breteuil family entertained some of the most famous people of the time there. Among these were Marcel Proust and the 18-year-old Edward VIII who, as prince of Wales, spent a number of months as a guest of the family in 1912. Of his time at the Hôtel de Breteuil he later recorded in his autobiography: 'I had a suite to myself there, far superior to any accommodation I had previously known at home.'[3] After the marquis died in 1916, the house was sold to the Saint family. They in turn sold it to Princesse de Faucigny-Lucinge et Coligny, a Hungarian socialite, in 1937.[4]

The *princesse* and her two daughters put the mansion up for sale in 1953, and in January 1954 Ambassador Cremin indicated that the Irish government was interested in purchasing it. At the subsequent negotiations Princesse de Broglie, the elder daughter, and Madame Boeg represented the vendors. Cremin and McGrath made a number of offers well below the 155,000 francs at which the family valued their property. Madame Boeg proved to be as astute a negotiator as her Irish counterparts. She told Cremin and McGrath that Argentina, Brazil and Venezuela, who were also on a quest for an embassy in Paris, had shown an interest in the mansion. In addition, she claimed that one government had made an offer of 160,000 francs, but that this was still to be confirmed. The

2 National Archives of Ireland, department of finance file S2/8/54. 3 *A king's story: the memoirs of HRH the duke of Windsor* (London, 1951), p. 89. 4 *Irish Times*, 28 Oct. 2006.

Germans, whose embassy in Paris had been confiscated, were also interested and had, she stated, 'offered payment in hard currency'.

The Irish increased their offer to 150,000 francs, and this was accepted. However, at that stage a further difficulty arose. Princesse de Broglie stated that she and her sister 'had immediate commitments on behalf of their mother' and wanted a substantial part of the purchase price as soon as possible. After further discussions, the Irish paid over £11,000 – with a guarantee of final payment soon after 1 April. In return, they would secure not only the building but also its fittings and furnishings. In the event, the balance of the purchase price – about £142,500 – was not paid until May. Possession of the premises was obtained at the end of that month.[5]

The Hôtel de Breteuil did not appear to be as splendid a purchase in Dublin as it did in Paris. Persons who were not aware that a *hôtel particulier* in France was a private town house asked why it was necessary to acquire a hotel rather than a residence to accommodate the Irish ambassador! Frank Aiken, briefed by the ambassador and officials in the department of external affairs, was at pains to point out what a valuable asset the building was – and that a suitable embassy was required for the ongoing growth in work in Paris relating to Ireland's membership of the Organisation for European Economic Cooperation (OEEC) – later, the Organisation for Economic Cooperation and Development (OECD) – and the Council of Europe, as well as Irish-French trade. However, the Fianna Fáil administration was presiding over a stringent economic situation at home, characterized by high unemployment and almost unprecedented emigration. In these circumstances, the price paid for the new embassy – in today's terms about €4.5 million – must have seemed excessive to the frugal-minded Taoiseach, Eamon de Valera. The government was only too aware that the purchase of the embassy would not have popular support. In fact, the contract for purchase was formally concluded on 14 May, four days before the 1954 general election. The total cost of the premises, its contents, legal fees and bank charges amounted to £153,568 1s. 7d. With support for the government waning, information about the purchase and its cost was not made public until after the general election.

When the acquisition of the embassy was eventually made public, there followed a flurry of references to it in the press. The *Irish Times* of 20 May reported the purchase of 'the four-storey, 35-room [*sic*] Hôtel de Breteuil' for £150,000 and described its prestigious location and the duke of Windsor's glowing reference to it in his autobiography. A more critical article, headed 'Elephant

5 National Archives of Ireland, department of finance file S2/8/54.

House', appeared in that newspaper on the following day. It concluded: 'It is fitting that Ireland should present a brave face to the world; but in her present budgetary circumstances, the face that she proposes to offer Paris is more than brave; it is positively brazen!' In response to these and other press comments, Aiken on 25 May published a comprehensive statement setting out the reasons why the government had bought the new embassy.[6]

Fianna Fáil continued to govern until 2 June, though they had lost the general election to a coalition of the opposition parties. On 26 May, eight days after the election, a postponed poll was held in the Wicklow constituency. On the hustings Gerard Sweetman, who was to be minister for finance in the incoming administration, severely criticised Fianna Fáil for 'squandering £150,000 on the purchase of a house in Paris'.[7] In a press briefing after he had taken office Sweetman continued to criticise the previous government on this issue, particularly for the manner in which they had until after the general election 'deliberately hidden it from the people' because of the effect they believed it might have.[8] Indeed, the new government availed of every opportunity to embarrass their predecessors in this vein. For example, on 15 June in Dáil Éireann, Michael J. O'Higgins TD – a government backbencher – requested a statement on the purchase of the Paris embassy. This was given by Liam Cosgrave, minister for external affairs, and prompted the irrepressible James Dillon, minister for agriculture, to exclaim gleefully: 'That is no fish barrel.'[9]

* * *

Time has more than justified the purchase of the Hôtel de Breteuil. The role of the ambassador of the day, Cornelius C. Cremin, in its purchase was crucial. From the outset he was determined that the government should acquire this imposing and strategically-located building – if for no other reason than to signal Ireland's wish to be taken seriously in European affairs. Apart from the diplomatic business conducted in the building, it has been a centre for commercial and cultural events and exhibitions. It has undoubtedly advanced the profile of Ireland and has been a source of pride for many Irish delegations and visitors. Cremin's successors have been meticulous in attending to its proper maintenance – none more so than the present ambassador, Anne Anderson. With Patrick Mellett, a Paris-based Irish architect, she initiated and supervised a major refurbishment of the building in 2006 – the aim of which, as she has stated, was 'to enable the building to show its age beautifully'.[10]

6 *Irish Independent, Irish Times*, 25 May 1954. 7 *Irish Independent*, 24 May 1954. 8 *Irish Press*, 16 June 1954. 9 *Dáil Debates*, 146, 15 June 1954, cols 81–2. 10 *Irish Times*, 28 Oct. 2006.

Notes on contributors

MARY BEARD is a professor of classics in the University of Cambridge and a fellow of Newnham College, Cambridge.

SÍGHLE BHREATHNACH-LYNCH is the curator of Irish paintings in the National Gallery of Ireland.

MICHAEL COMYNS is a poet and an expert in Irish heraldry.

L. PERRY CURTIS JR taught Irish and British history at Brown University, Providence, RI, for over twenty-five years before retiring in 2001. He is the author of *Images of Erin in the Age of Parnell* (2001), published by the National Library of Ireland.

IAN D'ALTON is the managing director of the Housing Finance Agency in Dublin. He has published a number of historical studies on Cork Protestant society.

THEO DORGAN is a poet and broadcaster.

OWEN DUDLEY EDWARDS is an honorary fellow in the school of history and classics at Edinburgh University. His latest book is *British Children's Fiction in the Second World War* (2007).

GABRIEL FITZMAURICE is a poet and teacher in his native Moyvane, Co. Kerry.

ADRIAN FRAZIER is a professor in the English department at the National University of Ireland, Galway. His acclaimed biography of George Moore was published in 2000.

J. ANTHONY GAUGHAN is a priest in the archdiocese of Dublin. A prolific author, he is the chairman of the National Library of Ireland Society.

FERGUS GILLESPIE is the chief herald in the National Library of Ireland.

ADRIAN HARDIMAN is a judge of the supreme court of Ireland.

MAURICE HARMON is professor emeritus of Anglo-Irish literature and drama at University College, Dublin. His *Selected Essays*, edited by Barbara Brown, was published in 2006.

SEAMUS HEANEY won the Nobel prize for literature in 1995.

MONICA HENCHY is a retired librarian. Her late husband, Dr Patrick Henchy, was the director of the National Library of Ireland, 1967–76.

WESLEY HUTCHINSON is professor of Irish studies at the Université de la Sorbonne Nouvelle in Paris.

FINOLA KENNEDY is an economist and the author of *Cottage to Crèche: Family Change in Ireland* (2001).

BRENDAN KENNELLY is a much loved poet. In 2004 he retired as professor of modern literature at Trinity College, Dublin.

BRIAN LALOR is a printmaker and author, and the chairman of the Graphic Studio Dublin. He edited the award-winning *The Encyclopaedia of Ireland* (2003).

FELIX M. LARKIN is the vice-chairman of the National Library of Ireland Society. A career public servant, he is now head of retail debt with the National Treasury Management Agency in Dublin.

GERARD LONG is an assistant keeper in the National Library of Ireland. He contributed the chapter on the National Library of Ireland to A. Black and P. Hoare (eds), *The Cambridge History of Libraries in Britain and Ireland*, iii: *1850–2000* (2006).

GERARD LYNE is the keeper of manuscripts in the National Library of Ireland and the author of the magisterial *The Lansdowne Estate in Kerry under W.S. Trench, 1849–72* (2001).

CIARA McDONNELL is an assistant keeper in the National Library of Ireland and the author, with James Quin and Éilís Ní Dhuibhne, of *W.B. Yeats: Works and Days* (2006), published by the National Library.

ELLEN MURPHY is an archivist with Limerick Archives, the repository for local government archives in Limerick city and county.

ÉILÍS NÍ DHUIBHNE is a writer and assistant keeper in the National Library of Ireland. Her latest books include *W.B. Yeats: Works and Days* (with James Quin and Ciara McDonnell; 2006), published by the National Library.

BRENDAN O DONOGHUE retired as the director of the National Library of Ireland in 2003. He was secretary of the department of the environment from 1990 to 1997, and is the author of *In Search of Fame and Fortune: the Leahy Family of Engineers, 1780–1888* (2006).

DENNIS O'DRISCOLL is a poet and the editor of *The Bloodaxe Book of Poetry Quotations* (2006). He works as a civil servant in Dublin.

CIARÁN Ó HÓGARTAIGH is associate professor in accounting at the Victoria University of Wellington, New Zealand. He has published widely in accounting history and financial accounting.

MARGARET Ó HÓGARTAIGH is the author of *Kathleen Lynn: Irishwoman, Patriot, Doctor* (2006). She is a research fellow at the Stout Centre, Victoria University of Wellington, New Zealand.

DIARMUID WHELAN is a lecturer in contemporary history in University College, Cork. In 2006 he published *Founded on Fear: Letterfrack, War and Exile*, the memoir of an inmate of the Letterfrack industrial school, Peter Tyrrell.

Index

Compiled by J. Anthony Gaughan